Friendship and Hospitality

SUNY series in Chinese Philosophy and Culture

Roger T. Ames, editor

Friendship and Hospitality

*The Jesuit-Confucian Encounter
in Late Ming China*

DONGFENG XU

Cover image: Chinese world map, drawn by the Jesuits, early seventeenth century. Reproduction in *Historic Maritime Maps* by Donald Wigal. Author unknown.

Published by State University of New York Press, Albany

© 2021 State University of New York

All rights reserved

Printed in the United States of America

No part of this book may be used or reproduced in any manner whatsoever without written permission. No part of this book may be stored in a retrieval system or transmitted in any form or by any means including electronic, electrostatic, magnetic tape, mechanical, photocopying, recording, or otherwise without the prior permission in writing of the publisher.

For information, contact State University of New York Press, Albany, NY
www.sunypress.edu

Library of Congress Cataloging-in-Publication Data

Name: Xu, Dongfeng, author
Title: Friendship and hospitality : the Jesuit-Confucian encounter in late Ming China
Description: Albany : State University of New York Press, [2021] | Series:
  SUNY series in Chinese philosophy and culture| Includes bibliographical references and index.
Identifiers: ISBN 9781438484952 (hardcover : alk. paper) | ISBN 9781438484945 (pbk. : alk. paper) | ISBN 9781438484969 (ebook)
Library of Congress Control Number: 2021939445
Further information is available at the Library of Congress.

10 9 8 7 6 5 4 3 2 1

Contents

Acknowledgments — vii

Introduction — 1

PART ONE
FRIENDSHIP AND THE JESUITS

1 Striving for Divine Union: The Wholly Other and the Jesuit Vocation — 17

2 Other Rhetoric: Reading Matteo Ricci's *On Friendship* — 55

PART TWO
HOSPITALITY AND THE CONFUCIANS

3 The Subject of Hospitality and Sino-centrism: Theory and Chinese Cultural Background — 97

4 Situating the Middle Kingdom: Matteo Ricci's World Map, the Wobbling Center, and the Undoing of the Host — 113

5 Reforming the Calendar: The Ming Empire's Stairway to Heaven through the Jesuits — 135

6 The Confucian Hospitality: Responding to the Jesuits — 157

Conclusion	177
Notes	181
Selected Bibliography	245
Index	267

Acknowledgments

In the course of writing this book I have incurred numerous debts to many teachers, friends, and colleagues, so many that it is impossible for me even to recall, much less mention, them all.

I must first thank my teachers, and first and foremost the late Professor Anthony C. Yu, my mentor and supervisor, under whom it was my good fortune to study and to whom I owe the deepest thanks. Throughout the years, he was always in my corner, providing guidance, encouragement, and support, and from him I learned a great deal about literature, religion, and culture. He greatly contributed to my intellectual and professional growth, and his absence has left a void in my life. I thank Professor Walter Rulph Johnson for teaching me. He is a teacher who is impressive, with his vast knowledge of literature and culture, ancient, modern, and postmodern, and at the same time extremely easygoing, with his good humor and unpretentious personality. Only I know how much appreciation I have for him for his kindness and instruction. My heartfelt thanks go to Professor Françoise Meltzer for her immense kindness to me. Forever supportive, she is always genuinely happy to know whatever little progress I make. Her sharp-mindedness and excellent scholarship have always been inspiring to me. To Professor Joshua Scodel, I owe special thanks for his support and encouragement to me through the years. His help to me continues up to this day. His support and kindness have meant a great deal to me. I wish to mention with deep gratitude these Chicago teachers who taught and helped me: Professors Edward Shaughnessy, Michael Murrin, Marshall Sahlins, Robert von Hallberg, Susan Schreiner, David Tracy, Bernard McGinn, Prasenjit Duara, Judith Zeitlin, Donald Harper, William Schweiker, Peter White, George Zhao. I thank Mr. Cai Fangpei, Dr. Yang Jun, and Dr.

Wang Youqin. I must also thank the late Professors David T. Roy, Nancy Helmbold, and Frank Reynolds, who taught and helped me.

At Chicago, I was particularly privileged to have a group of good friends, many of whom are now experienced teachers and accomplished scholars. First, I want to mention these close friends of mine. Li Sher-shiueh has helped me in many ways. Because we both work on the Jesuit mission to China, he has always been generous and helpful in sharing with me his ideas and work. It was with his help that I spent a year working as a postdoctoral fellow at the Institute of Literature and Philosophy, Academia Sinica, in Taiwan. Zhou Yiqun, my fellow student of Professor Yu, is one of the first friends I made at Chicago. The many conversations we have had have been as enjoyable as they have been inspiring to me. A good and true friend, she is always ready to give her support and help. For her unfailing support, thoughtful help, and constant encouragement, to say that I am most grateful to her is somewhat of an understatement. Richard G. Wang, also a student of Professor Yu, has been a true friend from the beginning. He always encourages me and helps me. A dedicated and learned scholar, he never fails to impress me with his broad knowledge and good understanding of Chinese culture, literature, and religion. His friendship has been the source of my strength. Lam Ling Hon and Bao Weihong have been good and inspiring friends who, with their unfailing devotion to scholarship, constantly read, think, and write. The laughter we have shared, the numerous discussions we have had, and the movies we have watched together will always be remembered. It is a pity that we now live with virtually the entire country of America between us. But every communication we have, by phone or email, brings the same immense joy and scholarly stimulation as before. Corinne Bayerl, Ichiro Yuhara, Max Bohnenkamp, and Helen Hi-sun Kim have been great friends through the years.

Good friends from the Chicago years also include Rebecca (Rivi) Handler-Spitz, Hulya Adak, James St. André, Catherine Stuer, Paize Keulemans, Eugenia Lean, Nicole Zhan'ge Ni, George Streeter, Rocco Lacorte, Magnus Fiskesjö, Chris Lehrich, Kimberley Borchard, Juan Pablo Gil, Li Yuhang, Viren Murthy, Dr. Elias Dakwa, Liu Wei, Wang Shengyu, Paulo Brito, Xu Peng, Yang Lin, Justin Howell, Peng Ke, Wang Yi, Miao Xin, and many others. Their kindness, help, encouragement, and support brought much warmth and joy to me. The ties we formed remain strong and continue to get me support and help.

My thanks also go to Dr. Zhou Yuan, and the late Dr. Tai-loi Ma, present and past curators of Regenstein Library's East Asian Collections, and the able librarians Qian Xiaowen and the late William Alspaugh, for helping me locate needed books. I am grateful to Michael Berger at the

Center for the Studies of Languages for his help and friendship through the years. He has been a good friend. To Theodore N. Foss, former vice director at the Center for East Asian Studies, I owe special thanks. I have learned tremendously from him about the Jesuit mission to late imperial China. The many books he lent to me, and the books he gave me as gifts, which include a set of the invaluable, beautiful, and useful *Fonti Ricciane*, have been crucial for my work.

After leaving Chicago, I have come to know a number of friends and fellow scholars through jobs and at conferences who have been so kind as to share ideas, provide help, and offer support. They include Ho Wan Li, Raymond Ho, Joan Qiong Le, Zhang Na, Ao Xuegang, Li Hong, Li Yu, Elena Glazov-Corrigan, Cai Rong, Julliette Stapanian-Apkarian in Atlanta, Georgia; Lin Hsi-chiang (Kid), Liao Chin-Ping, Huang Ya-hsien, Chao Tung-ming, and Hsu Yu-lung at Academia Sinica, who, so kind to me during my stay in Taiwan, have been good friends; Professors Hu Siao-chen, Chow Ta-hsing, Lin Yueh-hui, Liao Chao-heng, Yang Chen-te, Yang Chin-lung, Tsai Chang-lin, Chiang Chiu-hua, Chang Ji-lin, Chen Hsiang-yin, Liu Chiung-yun, Lin Mei-yi, and Pham Lee-moi at Academia Sinica, who offered help and displayed hospitality to me; and Professors Huang (Kevin) Kuan-yun (now at City University of Hong Kong) and Liu Cheng-hui at Tsing-hua University.

In 2012–2013, when I taught in the Department of East Asian Languages and Literatures at the University of Hawaii at Manoa, I got much help from Ming-Bao Yue (then chair of the department), David McCraw, Roger Ames, Cynthia Y. Ning, Hong Jiang, and Daniel Tschudi. I thank them all for their support and friendship. I must also thank C. S. Tang, Wenjing Yang, and the legendary Professor Chi-tang Lo, who, into his early nineties, would still go to campus every day to read in the library. All these colleagues, who remain good friends, enriched my work and my stay there.

Bringing this book project to completion, I must go back in time to thank the late Karl S. Y. Kao, my mentor at the University of Alberta. An extremely kind man and erudite scholar, he introduced me to sinology in the West. He taught me, both by example and by precept, how to apply Western critical theories in my own studies. I miss him. Also, I must thank Jennifer Jay for her help and support for many years. I owe heartfelt thanks to Garry Sherbert and Troni Grande at University of Regina. Our friendship began when we were fellow students at Alberta. Throughout the years, they gave me so much academic and emotional support that I will never forget.

Now I must mention with deep thanks my colleagues and friends at Colgate University, my home institution. First, I thank my colleagues in the department. Yukari Hirata is so kind and thoughtful all the time. Jing Wang is always ready to lend a helping hand. Gloria Bien, now in retirement, never hesitates to offer me needed advice. John Crespi, departmental chair, has done a great deal to help me, including taking time to read my paper and provide searching criticism. Scott Mehl and Nicholas Albertson have been friends who are caring and learned, so that I always learn a great deal each time I spend time with them. Nicole Catgenova, our able and kind administrative assistant, is always gracious and efficient in giving help. To go beyond my department, I must thank Elizabeth (Liz) Marlow and Alan Cooper, university professors, respectively, of Colgate's famous CORE151 course group. They and other colleagues of the group have taught me at our meetings, more by example than by precept, how to teach CORE151 productively.

I am most grateful to Dean Tracey E. Hucks for her enthusiastic support. She took time off her busy schedule to talk with me about my teaching and research and offer wise advice. David McCabe, director of the Division of the Arts and Humanities, often goes out of his way to give me help. Lesleigh Cushing, my faculty mentor upon my arrival at Colgate, has been particularly thoughtful, kind, and supportive. Georgia Frank always impresses me with her profound knowledge of the Bible and religion. David Robinson is a good friend who, with his marvelous scholarship, has been an example for me. Many other colleagues, Dai Yamamoto, Benjamin (Ben) Stahlberg, Doug Johnson, Ken Belanger, Brenton Sullivan, Spencer Kelly, Meg Worley, Graham Hodges, Jessica Graybill, Diane Beach, and Helen Payne, are colleagues and friends I know I can rely on. To complete my project, I became much indebted to Richard (Rick) Braaten and Dominika Koter, past and present directors of Colgate's Research Council, for being both thoughtful and resourceful in making available needed funds at various stages of my research.

My deep thanks to staff members of Colgate libraries, especially Mike Poulin for speedy and timely acquisition of new books I suggest and request, and Lisa King for the numerous interlibrary loan books she has got for me.

The work on this book at different stages received generous support from various institutions. The University of Chicago's Center for East Asian Studies granted me a Dissertation Fellowship, just when I began my writing. The Martin Marty Center in the Divinity School, Chicago, offered me a Martin Marty Center Fellowship. The Institute of Chinese Literature and Philosophy, Academia Sinica, offered me a postdoctoral fellowship. The

Research Council at Colgate University provided me with a Picker Fellowship to help me complete the final manuscript. To all these institutions, I owe special thanks.

I thank Mr. Mark Stephen Mir of the Ricci Institute, University of San Francisco, for his assistance and kindness during my visit in the summer of 2018.

My special thanks are due to Professor Roger Ames, who serves as series editor of Chinese Philosophy and Culture at the State University of New York Press. He constantly encourages me and helps me. And he is always swift to offer counsel and support whenever they are needed. To Mr. James Peltz, my editor at the press, I owe special thanks. He has been enthusiastically receptive from the very beginning. It is because of his matchless assistance that my manuscript could be accepted so quickly by the editorial board. I am indebted to Ms. Eileen Nizer and Ms. Jenn Bennett-Genthner, two production editors of my book at the press, for their patience and assistance. The entire manuscript has benefited enormously from the expert editorial advice of Mr. Gordon Marce, though I alone am responsible for the final version of the book.

Here, I would also like to take this opportunity to thank the two anonymous readers of my manuscript for their helpful suggestions and constructive criticism.

Last but not least, I give my deepest thanks to my family. I thank Xu Danfeng and Xie Baohui, my brother and sister-in-law, for their enduring love and ongoing support. I thank Zhao Xiangnong, my cousin, for all the love she has given me. The books she purchased for me and sent to me all the way from China through the years fill several of my bookshelves. I must thank my aunt and uncle, Dr. Yang Jiantao and Dr. Liu Chengzheng. Their support through the years has been an important part of the strength that kept me going. What they all have done for me continues to teach me the meaning of unconditional love.

It is my deepest pain that my parents are no longer living. I dedicate this book to their memory with all my love and gratitude.

Introduction

> The Jesuits' approach to their enterprise of propagating Christianity in China was so different and so promising in itself, and is so much to the point today, that our discussion of the Asian peoples' encounter with the West would be incomplete if we did not take into consideration the line which the Jesuits in China and India opened out.
>
> —Arnold Toynbee, *The World and the West*

> The fact is that the Jesuits had become certain by the end of the sixteenth century that cultural affiliation was an indispensable first step if the Christians were to win acceptance among Asian peoples of high culture. The Jesuits, as revealed in their writings, nonetheless retained conversion as their ultimate goal, and this objective should never be lost sight of in using their writings as historical sources.
>
> —Donald F. Lach, *Asia in the Making of Europe*

This book considers the concepts and practices of friendship and hospitality in the Jesuit mission to China during the late sixteenth and early seventeenth centuries. The arrival of the Jesuit missionaries in China marked not only the coming together of the West and China that has been ongoing until the present day, but also an early stage of globalization, which has shaped and continues to reshape the world. During this Jesuit-Chinese exchange four hundred years ago, both friendship and hospitality were practiced and discussed. While the Jesuits promoted the Western concept of friendship as they sought to befriend the Chinese, especially the Confucians (the elite class in China), the Confucians displayed their hospitality—responding in their own way—to these missionaries from the West. Given this fact, a study of the exchanges between the Jesuits and the Confucians, with a focus on friendship and hospitality as they were practiced, will advance primarily scholarly understanding of the Jesuit mission to China and, at the same time, general understanding of the current world.

To study in depth the cross-cultural and interreligious exchanges between the Jesuits and the Confucians, friendship and hospitality provide a unique perspective, as both of these social conventions were frequently articulated, practiced, and displayed by the Jesuits and the Confucians in their encounters. More importantly, friendship and hospitality as concepts are primarily concerned with two subjects in a relation; that is, concerning the relation and exchange between the self and the other, concepts of friendship and hospitality offer guidelines to how the self should see and deal with the other. Bearing in mind the essential use of friendship and hospitality when reviewing the Jesuit-Confucian encounter, it becomes obvious why both the Jesuits and Confucians resorted to friendship and hospitality in their exchange. In taking their mission to China, the Jesuits—and the Confucians they met as well—found themselves faced not only with people of strange customs and faith but also with a culture vastly different from their own. To help negotiate the differences, personal as well as cultural, the Jesuits and Confucians each sought guidance from their own understanding of friendship and hospitality. Through their respective use of friendship and hospitality, both sides hoped to achieve their separate goals. For the Jesuits on an evangelical mission, that goal would be to bring China into the Christian community by assimilating its fundamental cultural and religious differences, while, for the Confucians, proud of their civilization, the goal would be to assert the Middle Kingdom's cultural supremacy by rejecting the religious faith of the Jesuits. To clarify the topic of this book, friendship and hospitality being understood and used more as models for a cross-cultural relationship than for a relationship between two individuals in the Jesuit-Confucian encounter, it is necessary to look at some examples, starting with the Jesuit understanding of friendship.

Rooted in the Christian ideal of a brotherhood under God, Jesuit understanding and practice of friendship were fundamentally governed by the spirituality developed in the works of Ignatius of Loyola (1491–1556), founder and first general of the Society of Jesus. Ignatius's spirituality, as one scholar points out, "was shaped not only by his religious experience but also by the world he lived in."[1] Witnessing the unfolding of the Protestant Reformation, Ignatius lived at a time when papal authority was severely undermined, owing to the schism of the church, which became irreversible and final. Determined "to live the Christian gospel in response to questions and needs in the world of his time,"[2] Ignatius developed his spirituality "to aid souls" (*juvare animas*),[3] helping individuals become friends in God (i.e., form their divine union with God). Because Ignatius's plan was to aid not only the souls of his followers but also the souls of those people to be converted to Christianity, he offered his order to the pope as the leader of the worldwide church, vowing that Jesuits would take Christian missions to countries beyond Europe. The fact that Ignatian spirituality from the beginning closely related the conversion of hearts to the conversion to Christianity determined the nature of Jesuit friendship and its application during the Jesuit mission.[4] To show how the Jesuit missionaries to China used friendship for their evangelical goal by blending together Jesuit spirituality, Christian theology, classical literature, and the philosophy of the West, Matteo Ricci (1552–1610), an early Jesuit missionary to China, and his work on friendship should offer a telling example.

An Italian Jesuit, Ricci was one of the first to take the Catholic Church's expansion to China. From his arrival in 1582 until his death in 1610, he spent twenty-eight years in China. Ricci's mission has been regarded as "the first successful penetration into China by representatives of the modern—that is, the post-Renaissance—West."[5] Indeed, his extended stay in China marked the beginning of a new era of Chinese-European relations. And his association with many Chinese literati and Confucian officials provided him with an excellent opportunity to carry out many cultural exchanges and execute his missionary project of converting the Chinese to Catholicism.

Ricci hoped to achieve more than simply converting the Chinese. Owing to his faith and theology that the world was created and externally controlled by a divine being called God, one argument Ricci repeatedly made was that the Chinese civilization had from the very beginning been a "natural" segment of Christianity. As one scholar puts it, Ricci's work in China aimed at serving his evangelical goal: "to naturalize Christianity in the Chinese setting."[6] It was to this end that he wrote in Chinese many of his works, including *Jiaoyou lun* (交友論), or *On Friendship*.

Composed in 1595, *On Friendship* is a collection and translation into Chinese of one hundred aphorisms and anecdotes concerning friends and friendship from Plato, Aristotle, Alexander the Great, Cicero, Seneca, Saint Augustine, and other authors.[7] The work introduced to Chinese readers the Western understanding of friendship. Though the book certainly had an immediately practical need to meet—that is, to thaw or to attenuate the strong Chinese xenophobia that regarded virtually everything and everyone foreign to be hostile and dangerous to Chinese culture—the real use of the work was to help achieve the ultimate goal of Ricci's mission.

Ricci's expectation that his book on friendship should help his project of cultural and religious assimilation reveals his excellent understanding of the traditional concept of friendship and his adept application of it to his cross-cultural context. As is well known, Western thinkers in history seldom fail to see the political and religious implications that underwrite friendship. In works by such pagan philosophers as Plato, Aristotle, Cicero, and others, one finds repeated emphasis on how friendship unites humans with sameness or binds friends together by and for a common cause. In the works of the church fathers, friendship was viewed as synonymous with Christian solidarity, sharing a heart and love for God.[8] Related closely to, if not always identical with, such terms or concepts as *agapē*, *caritas*, and others, Christian friendship means it is a person's duty both to accept grace, a current of love flowing from God to oneself, and to communicate it to one's neighbors.[9] To these theologians, friendship always remained a crucial issue. There was the biblical command to love one's neighbor as one's self, which readily incorporated elements of the classical belief in "the friend as another self."[10] What is more, many have shared the assumption expressed in Aquinas's dictum, in *Summa Theologica*, "Charity [*caritas*] signifies not only love of God but also a certain friendship with God," a "familiar colloquy with God" begun in this life and culminating in the next.[11] What should become clear from this quick summary is that friendship, by no means a simple concept, must be seen as a politically conditioned metaphor and subtext of a culture.[12] In other words, encompassing a complicated set of political, religious, social, and cultural values, friendship often requires the individuals involved in a relationship to submit to certain transcendent ideals.

Another reason for Ricci to find friendship a fitting topic for his Chinese readers must be that, since antiquity, friendship has been used to describe, evaluate, and even form allies between cultures. Here the Greeks offer a good example, because they frequently applied the language of friendship to foreign relations. According to scholars, in Greek usage beginning at least as early as the sixth century BCE, *philia*, an abstract noun commonly rendered as "friendship," was the normal word for a treaty or alliance between states. Also, their word *xenoi* (*xeinoi* in epic diction) describes friends belonging to different communities.[13] The inference from such Greek understanding of friendship certainly goes beyond the confirmation that friendship is seldom a simple concept. It is often a metaphor and subtext, politically conditioned, of a culture. To reiterate, a model for the relation between any two individuals, friendship does not merely represent a highly valued relationship within a culture. It often reflects the attitude of a culture in dealing with other cultures.

Taking into consideration the political and religious aspects of friendship and its usefulness and suitability in cross-cultural relations, one can say that

Ricci's *On Friendship* exemplifies an effort, purposefully made, to negotiate the Western and Chinese cultures and to eliminate the differences between the two. For Ricci, there had to be a higher ideal or principle to regulate the relation of the two cultures, just as there was, supposedly, one to determine the relation between two friends. That is perhaps why one of the first aphorisms in *On Friendship* came from Aristotle: "My friend and I exist as two bodies. But within the two bodies, there is only one mind" (友之於我, 雖有二身, 二身之內, 其心一也). The idea of "one mind" was emphasized time and again in *On Friendship*, sometimes as "perpetual virtue" (永德). Though Ricci in this work never specified what this higher principle was, the reader would have no difficulty in identifying it with the Christian faith, given Ricci's religious faith and his overall theological agenda. To examine how this higher principle supposedly regulates the relationship between the West and China—that is, to see how *On Friendship* was designed to help his assimilation of China—it is appropriate to discuss the relationship between Confucianism and Catholicism as Ricci presented it.

Though Ricci found certain parts of Confucianism acceptable from his Christian point of view, he insisted that the true meaning, or teaching, of what he called "original Confucianism" (先教) had been lost in China. For Ricci, many Confucian notions failed to restrain people from sinfulness, because these teachings had their own innate inadequacy. As Ricci saw it, the only way to regenerate the usefulness of these teachings was to have them either substituted or enhanced by Christian morals. A good example here would be his discussion on Confucius's teaching that "a man of benevolence [*ren* 仁] loves others" in his *Tianzhu shiyi* (天主實義), or *The True Meaning of the Lord of Heaven*, a catechism propagating the Catholic faith to the Chinese.[14] Ricci believed that the idea of "benevolence" had been partially forgotten or completely misunderstood by his Chinese contemporaries, owing to many of them yielding more and more to their selfish desires. The remedy—for both the idea of benevolence and for the morality of the people—recommended by Ricci was the love of God. According to him, only the love of God could assure that people would love each other genuinely and continuously. Ricci made this point when he offered a new and clearly extended definition of Confucian benevolence:

> The definition of *jen* [*ren*] can be summed up in the following two sentences: "Love the Lord of Heaven," [and] "Regard him as superior to all as well as love others as you love yourself for the sake of the Lord of Heaven." If one carries out these two

commands, everything one does will be perfect. But these two commands are, after all, one. If one loves a person passionately one will love what that person loves. The Lord of Heaven loves people; if I genuinely love the Lord of Heaven can I fail to love the people he loves? The reason why the virtue of *jen* is so noble is precisely that it signifies love for the Sovereign on High.[15]

As is indicated clearly in the above passage, Ricci's ideal love is the love of and for God, and it is far more important than the love for any other fellow men, even one's parents. God must be loved because, in Ricci's words, God as the creator of the world is the "common father" *gongfu* (公父), or father of all:

The supreme head of a nation and I stand in relationship to each other as sovereign to subject, and the head of my household and I stand in the mutual relationship of father and son. Although human beings make distinctions between sovereign and subject, father and son, when they are seen in their relationship to the common fatherhood of the Lord of Heaven they all become brothers with an equal standing; it is essential to understand this principle.[16]

Posing God on top of the most fundamental values or morals of the Chinese, Ricci does not merely supplement Confucianism. Under his notion of a unified history in which nothing takes place without God and nothing makes sense until it is related to God, Ricci appropriates Chinese civilization as a whole and makes it a subordinate part of the Christian God.

From this hierarchical relationship that Ricci perceived between Confucianism and Christianity, and from his assurance that Confucianism could regain its legitimacy as a system of thought or a religious doctrine, what can be expected from the Western ideas of friendship so earnestly presented by Ricci and his fellow Jesuits becomes clear. Cultivating among the Chinese a friendship in which all must submit to the Christian God was certainly a way to help Ricci not only convert the Chinese but also achieve China's assimilation to the West.

By now, the close association between friendship and hospitality should become apparent. When Ricci preached Christian friendship to the Chinese, friendship was supposed to serve as a hospitable gesture, welcoming China into Christianity. From early on, hospitality has been described as a virtue in the Hebrew scriptures, to be displayed by a host to his or her guests or strangers.[17] In Christian theology, hospitality is viewed as the very nature and meaning of God's love for humans. That is why God is called a welcoming deity—because he gives his unconditional love and shows his hospitality to humans who have fallen away. Specifically, God's hospitality to people suggests both a type of knowledge that every human being must have and an effort that he or she must make. In other words, humans are created by God for communion with God and others. Such communion, as seen from the Christian perspective, means

> that we are part of a tradition in which we are dependent on others (including those not explicitly within our tradition) to demonstrate to us what we are to be. Such a politics does not depend on individualism but rather on *friendship*. It depends less on the language of rights and more on the language of *gift*. In fact, education made possible by friendship can be described as *the circulation of gift*, which is also a way to describe hospitality.[18]

Though this passage seems to limit its argument to Christians, its identification and relation of hospitality with friendship—that is, relating *agapē* and *caritas*—serves to demonstrate the very structure of Ricci's mission to China. Hoping to convince the Chinese that God's love, exemplifying his friendship and hospitality, was his ultimate gift to humans, Ricci worked to expand "the circulation of gift" under God to China.

Concerning Christian friendship and hospitality and their relation to *agapē* and *caritas*, one more point must be considered. One would be particularly naive to assume that the ideal of Christian charity is as unreserved and comprehensive as the Christian love for God.[19] Indeed, Saint Augustine answers, "Everyone" (*Omnis homo*), as many other Christian thinkers also would, to the question "Who is my neighbor?" (*Proximus quis*, meaning literally "Who is next to me?").[20] Reality, however, often poses a different picture with numerous examples of Christians dividing and distinguishing the self from the other based on religious and political beliefs. Even if one chooses to exclude the dynamic, aggressive, and continuous conflict between Jesus and Satan,[21] the Holy Scriptures still contain abundant telling examples of how humans often oppose one another. There is the story of how the ancient Israelites in captivity hang up their harps and refuse to sing their holy songs so as not to grace their captors and a foreign land (Ps 137:1–4), or another about how Jesus insists that his followers demonstrate their absolute devotion to him by hating and abandoning their family members (Lk 14:26). Even one of the best-known and most-quoted teachings of Jesus, "love your enemies" (ἀγαπᾶτε τοὺς ἐχθροὺς ὑμῶν; *diligite inimicos verstros*),²² may contain less benevolence than is often supposed. Here is why. In Koine Greek, the language used in the majority of the original texts in the New Testament, there are two commonly used terms to signify "enemy": πολέμιος (or *hostis*, in Latin), meaning a political or public enemy to be fought against collectively, and ἐχθροὺς (or *inimicus*), signifying a private or personal adversary. And the word used by Jesus in this teaching, as quoted above, is none other than ἐχθροὺς (*inimicos*) or "private enemies." According to Carl Schmitt, who discusses the importance of distinguishing friend and enemy in his *The Concept of the Political*, Jesus's selection of "private enemies" instead of "public enemies" should confirm that he is fully aware of the impossibility of befriending certain groups of people.²³ Whether Jesus's wording reduces the significance and power of Christian charity lies beyond the scope of this discussion. What is certain from Schmitt's interpretation is that, while one must stand and fight without compromise against political and public enemies, one should always have love for one's private enemies.²⁴ It is true that Schmitt in his book is more concerned with what determines the political, but his argument that the political only becomes possible with the identification of friend and enemy is readily applicable to religions, where such identification is no less crucial and decisive.²⁵

Looking back at the Society of Jesus, one sees that a similar dichotomy of friends and enemies—self and other—sustains the work and life of the Jesuits, a fact to be borne in mind in a discussion of the Jesuit mission in China. It is a fact worth noting, because the Jesuits in China, while promoting friendship and extending hospitality mainly to the Confucian class, rejected vehemently and completely other religious groups such as Chinese Buddhists and Daoists. It is true that some early Jesuits, out of their misunderstanding, dressed themselves up as Buddhist monks in the hope of attracting the attention of the Chinese. They later not only shed the monk's robes to replace them with the Confucian gowns but also would frequently engage in written and face-to-face debates with Buddhist and Daoist representatives to reject their doctrines.

Having spoken of the Jesuit distinction between friends and enemies, or their hospitality to the Confucians and lack of it to others such as the Buddhists and Daoists, I would like to look at Confucian hospitality, or their response to the Jesuits, a topic to be discussed later in this book. As there will be a short chapter outlining the deconstructive theory of hospitality and reviewing the Confucian definition and use of hospitality in history, including the late Ming period, what will be said here will be brief.

The Confucian response to the Jesuits—both friendly reception and outright rejection—is referred to here as hospitality primarily because the term hospitality, or *bin* (賓), was applied exclusively to the governmental agency in charge of international affairs in traditional China. Until a little more than one and a half centuries ago,[26] China had never in its history had a foreign affairs office in its government. The agency in charge of receiving and hosting foreign guests had been a section in the Department of Rites (禮部). This section was responsible for extending the so-called *binli* (賓禮), or rite of hospitality, to foreign delegations, and it often worked as, among other things, the instrument of the government to propagate, subtly or bluntly, the Chinese idea of Sino-centrism founded on an assumed hierarchy of cultures. The Department of Rites could serve this role simply because, like the Christian idea of hospitality that encompasses virtually all the aspects of the human-God relationship, Confucian hospitality represented all of the most important ideologies governing human relations in China.

To be sure, as uninvited guests, the Jesuit missionaries did not have to deal directly or formally with the Department of Rites. But this fact does not mean that they were free from Confucian hospitality. As a scholar points out, "Hospitality is always inseparable from power because it is an ability, capacity, or strength to receive and give shelter to a stranger, foreigner, or other."[27] Indeed, out of the Jesuit-Confucian encounter manifested an unbalanced and highly complicated power relation involving the two parties. Such a relation required first of all that the missionaries behave in a way deemed acceptable by the host, who would accordingly chose either to be receptive by displaying hospitality or to be rejective by denying it. The judgment of the Jesuits' behavior was based on the Confucian view of "a dichotomized world," in which, as Mark Mancall observes, individuals would be defined in terms of a pair of concepts, civilization or barbarism.[28] In general, as Mancall elaborates, the inhabitants of this dichotomized world "will not perceive the emblem of civilization to be the nation with its flags and titles; rather, they will perceive the emblem to be the palpable form of civilization, which is culture in the sense of manners, morals, and arts, including the foods eaten and the clothes worn."[29] Ming history carries many examples about hospitality being either given to or reserved from the Jesuits, depending on how the missionaries were perceived.[30] These examples make clear that hospitality is truly a matter of power that, displayed or denied, means to impose hegemony and homogeneity.

This discussion, however, seeks to do more. It will demonstrate that what futher complicates the Jesuit-Confucian relation is that the Confucian host was not always the one to determine when and if to give or withhold hospitality. With their arrival in China and by staying in different places in the country to carry out their evangelical activities, the Jesuits were the other with whom the Confucian host was forced to negotiate. Facing the missionaries, the Confucian host ceased to be the one to decide when and if he would relate and respond. In the exchange with the missionaries, the Confucian hospitality could no longer be reserved or controlled but became unconditional in the sense that the host had to receive the Jesuit strangers, or deal with them, as Jacques Derrida puts it, "without invitation, beyond or before the invitation."[31] In this book, the discussion on the Confucian reception of the missionaries will highlight the implications of the Confucian imperial ideology and expose the limits of the empire by revealing the dilemma facing Confucian Sino-centrism.

In the pages that follow, the book will treat friendship and hospitality as concepts, discourses, and recognition of alterity, as postulated by some deconstructive philosophers, mainly Emmanuel Levinas and Jacques Derrida. Through examples from the works of the Jesuits and the Confucian response, I will argue that difference is the absolute condition of possibility under which friendship and hospitality—the friendship and hospitality between two individuals or between two cultures—happen.

A deconstructive reading, enhanced by recent theories of cultural studies, will be particularly conducive to the present study of friendship and hospitality because of the subject's historical import, its philosophical and theological richness, and its applicability to actual human relations on both interpersonal and intercultural levels. Treating the concepts of friendship and hospitality in an intensive fashion, I hope both to reveal and critique the ideological and religious implications behind the friendship and hospitality exercised by the Jesuits and the Confucians. The analysis of how the Jesuits presented their concept of friendship in order to realize their religious agenda and how the Confucians reacted, through displaying or denying their hospitality to the missionary strangers, will shed light on the comparative study of culture and of the interaction between religion, philosophy, and literature.

The book is divided into two parts, each of which approaches from a specific perspective the issues concerned. Part 1, under the title "The Concept of Friendship and the Jesuits," contains two chapters concentrating on the missionaries and their discourse on friendship. Entitled "The Culture of Hospitality and the Confucians," part 2, with three main chapters following a brief introductory chapter, applies the deconstructive discussion on hospitality to the interpretation of the Chinese response to the Jesuits. The following is an outline of the chapters.

Chapter 1 examines Jesuit spirituality and mission strategy, both determined by and related to the Jesuit understanding of Christian friendship, that is, union with God. The discussion begins with a detailed analysis of Jesuit spirituality, which required all Jesuit members to become friends in the Lord, the Wholly Other. Following the gospel teaching to "deny the self" (Matt 16:24), the Jesuits took the erasure of the individual's self, an indication of this person's undivided devotion to God, to be an absolute condition for his union with God. Such submission to God and constant effort for union with God seemed to go well with another Jesuit commitment, the commitment to mission, which likewise aimed at a divine union, the union/reunion between God and the pagans and unbelievers to be converted through Jesuit missions. In my discussion, I point out that the seemingly closely connected and interdependent Jesuit spirituality and mission are actually paradoxical. The paradox or dilemma manifests because of the Jesuit attitude toward the otherness. For Jesuits, only one otherness is impossible to appropriate. It is the otherness of God, the Wholly Other. All other otherness including the self, which is something preventing humans from the union with God, is deemed to be the otherness to be eliminated. However, going through the Jesuit spiritual process and mission, I argue that the human otherness, exactly like the otherness of the Wholly Other, cannot be erased. Quite the contrary, both when the Jesuits cultivate their spirituality and during their missions, especially their mission to China, it is clear that the Jesuit actions confirm that the human otherness is what must be kept, even pursued, in the same way God the Wholly Other is kept, respected, and pursued.

Chapter 2 continues the investigation of the Jesuit promotion of friendship. But the focus is placed on one single work, *On Friendship*, by Matteo Ricci. It is clear that Ricci hoped to use this work on friendship to assimilate China by forming a friendly relation with the Chinese. But through a close reading of the work, the reader finds that Ricci, owing to his accommodation, failed to fully present the Jesuit or Catholic concept of friendship; that is, instead of urging the Chinese to become God's friends, Ricci presented in the main the classical or pagan view of friendship, the friendship that concerned itself more with other humans than with a divine being. The discussion will argue that Ricci's deviation showed that the deviation was inevitable, given Ricci's mission. It was his dilemma. Living in China, mingling with Chinese, and studying Chinese language and Confucian classics in order to convert the Chinese into Christians, Ricci seemed to succumb at first to the cultural transformation instilled in him by the Chinese. In other words, his mission of assimilation was designed to make China and the Chinese the same as Christian Europeans. But instead, he had the other in his self.

With the conclusion of this chapter, the book moves to part 2 of the discussion—examining through the concept of hospitality the Confucian response, hospitable or hostile, to the Jesuit strangers. Chapter 3 introduces and sets up the theoretical framework for the discussion by summarizing some of the important points about hospitality from the works of Levinas and Derrida. It then briefly reviews the Confucian rite of hospitality in traditional China, particularly during the Ming dynasty (1368–1644), showing in particular how the Confucian worldview shaped the use of hospitality.

Once the theoretical underpinning and the historical background have been elucidated, the three remaining chapters of part 2 approach the topic of Confucian hospitality from three separate but related angles—namely, how the modern science and technology introduced into China by the Jesuits put into question Confucian Sino-centrism by generating new understandings of the self and other in the country. Even the Christian teachings, as will become clear later in the book, stimulated some renewed energy to elaborate on and explore old Confucian doctrines.

Chapter 4 concentrates on the world map that Ricci made in Chinese around 1584. It will argue that this map, presenting a world entirely new to the Chinese, marks off an ideological high ground where the Confucian host and the Jesuit visitor enact some of the very essence as well as paradox of hospitality as discussed by Levinas and Derrida. In the Jesuit-Confucian encounter, the map and the Chinese reactions to it represent some vigorous and highly complicated cultural negotiations or accommodations through which both sides would, knowingly or not, cross back and forth over the boundaries that they themselves had set up. Both sides would keep blurring the demarcation between inside and outside, the distinction between the Self and the Other, and the host and the stranger. Without doubt, each side would attempt to claim authority over the other—the Confucians with their Sino-centrism and the Jesuits with the map containing new geographic information and modern cartographical presentation, plus the Catholic faith in the omnipotence of God. The chapter will concentrate on the impact the map left on the Chinese worldview. It will demonstrate how the seemingly closed Ming circle of the Same was more than penetrated and infiltrated by the missionaries; it was ripped open by the world map. What the map made manifest, first of all, were the limits of the Middle Kingdom. These imperial limitations in turn demonstrated the fact that the Middle Kingdom existed and functioned in a world where innate heterogeneity granted no stability to the roles of host, stranger, or hostage.

If Ricci's world map only worked to remove, in a symbolical fashion, the Middle Kingdom from its imagined center of the world, the Jesuits' work for the Ming court regarding the calendar reform, the topic of chapter 5, actually turned the Confucian host into a hostage. In traditional China, the calendar was central government's monopoly, because the calendar, besides serving practical agricultural needs, had crucial political and religious uses for the government. That is why the Ming, like many previous dynasties, had a ban on any private study of the calendar and astronomy. The government even made the positions at the royal agency of astronomy hereditary to prevent outsiders from acquiring this highly guarded and particularly sensitive knowledge. It is from this perspective that I argue that the Jesuits' work on the Ming calendar became significant. It shows that the Ming host, so proud of its cultural supremacy, had now to depend on the assistance of missionary strangers in order to sustain the well-being of its government and country. To further illustrate this reversed power relation, I also investigate the Confucian response that resulted in Chinese thinkers and scholars debating how to maintain the hegemony of China while continuing, without losing face, to benefit from the usefulness of foreign technology. Turning to some of the arguments emerging from these debates, I point out that the effort to rethink the China-West relation in the late Ming period should be seen as the herald of what happened in the second half of the nineteenth century, when, faced again with advanced technology from the West, some Confucians expressed concerns about how to maintain their doctrine and at the same time make use of the imported technology.

Of the three main chapters in this part, chapter 6 tackles a delicate as well as complicated problem—that is, how the Christian teaching of a deity and revealed religion seemed to stimulate, among the anti-Christian Confucians, certain new ways to think about old Confucian doctrines. In their apologetic writings, these Confucians certainly mounted a harsh rejection of the Jesuits and their religion. But it is in this clash of Confucian and Christian ideologies and theologies, the discussion will show, that the inhospitable Confucian host, afraid of being transformed by the foreigners and eager to sustain the assumed univocality of Confucianism, opened up in a curious fashion to Christian teachings and doctrines so as to find models for their attempt to rebuild Confucianism.

The conclusion will summarize the discussion in the book by reiterating how the encounter between the West and China, through a small group of men in China over four hundred years ago, actually initiated the beginning of a changed world, a world that has since then been fundamentally different. As there had never been unicity in this world, the coming together of the two continents represented by two civilizations has made this fact much more keenly felt. And it instilled in people a new understanding of the relation between the self and the other and a recognition that the other has always been a part of the self.

PART ONE
FRIENDSHIP AND THE JESUITS

No one has ever seen God; if we love one another, God abides in us and his love is perfected in us.

—1 John 4:12

1

Striving for Divine Union

The Wholly Other and the Jesuit Vocation

There is no one who does not love; but he asks what he should love. Therefore I do not exhort you not to love, but to choose what we should love.

—Saint Augustine, Sermon 34

We [Jesuits] are not monks. . . . The world is our house.

—Jerónimo Nadal, SJ

Tout autre est tout autre. (Every other is wholly other.)

—Jacques Derrida, *The Gift of Death*

Drawing examples from *Spiritual Exercises*, the *Formula of the Institute*, the *Constitutions*, and other related Jesuit documents, this chapter examines from a theological as well as a historical perspective the concept and practice of friendship in the tradition of the Society of Jesus. As is known, the importance and usefulness of friendship or companionship—with the Society being "a community of companions," or a "community of friends in the Lord"—are fully recognized by the Jesuits from the very beginning.[1] Going through the Jesuit literature, one sees that so much importance and significance are assigned to friendship (or companionship or union) that its concept and practice not only make up the very core and essence of Jesuit spirituality but also determine to a large extent the nature and goal of the Jesuit vocation.

It is known that the Society of Jesus as a religious order is, in the words of a Jesuit scholar, "simultaneous[ly] apostolic and communitarian."[2] The Society's militant nature[3]—the members' commitment to evangelization and conversion,[4] a commitment much in line with what scholars have often referred to as "the spirit of Counter-Reformation"[5]—finds its religious underpinning in the Jesuit understanding and use of friendship. This point is adequately evidenced by numerous examples in Jesuit documents, some of which will be presented in this chapter. For the moment, a brief review of the early history of the Society of Jesus should suffice.

According to Jesuit records, eight or ten devout Christians gathered in Paris in 1534, about six years before the order was formally founded,[6] and they soon decided to refer to their small band as a company of Jesus (*la compañía de Jesús*).[7] This name remained informal until most members of the group reached Rome in 1536.[8] During the time when the designation of the group evolved from the lowercase Spanish phrase to the uppercase Compañía de Jesús, and finally to the Latin Societas Iesu, the sense of companionship, a companionship with Jesus, whom the group regarded as their head, was beyond any doubt a consistent factor. Indeed, Jerónimo Nadal, an early Jesuit, in an attempt to define the Jesuit identity, once observed that being members of the "Company of Jesus" meant being "companions of Christ Jesus"—*socii Christi Iesu*.[9]

Obviously, the Society has through the centuries remained committed to this initial project of serving Christ as his army or companions. A recent example confirming this Jesuit commitment comes from decree 2 of the Society's thirty-second general congregation, held in Rome in the mid-1970s:

> It is in companionship that the Jesuit fulfils his mission. He belongs to a community of friends in the Lord who, like him, have asked to be received under the standard of Christ the King. This community is the entire body of the Society itself, no matter how widely dispersed over the face of the earth. The particular local community to which he may belong at any given moment is for him simply a concrete—if, here and now, a privileged—expression of this worldwide brotherhood.[10]

The passage quoted here presents what has been the tradition and the understanding of the Society of Jesus throughout the centuries.[11] These words from the decree demonstrate the order's double commitment—its apostolic-communitarian orientation. Jesuit companionship has two aspects: (1) the members' own spirituality (i.e., their own companionship with God); and (2) the divine or spiritual union extended through the Jesuit mission to include the entire world.

It is owing to this twofold purpose that the Society of Jesus has from early on regarded itself to be *ecclesia militans* (the church militant).[12] As such, the order and its members devote themselves to their crusade—be it spiritual enlightenment or an apostolic mission—called for by their time following the Reformation.[13] Given this fact, to understand properly the Jesuit practice of friendship or companionship, which stands as the very essence of Jesuit spirituality and vocation, this investigation must take two steps: to examine how individual Jesuits are expected and instructed to achieve their spiritual union with the divine, and how their spirituality correlates with their mission and missiology.

From the decree cited above, it can be said that both Jesuit spirituality and its mission fall under a unified concept of friendship. Friendship is referred to three times in the passage, with three different terms. First, there is *friend* in "friends in the Lord"[14] who hope "to be received under the standard of Christ the King." This refers to a spiritual union Jesuits strive to form with the divine. The second reference is to the *companionship* cultivated by and among the Jesuits themselves. Third, the decree mentions *brotherhood*, the Christian fellowship that the Jesuits hope to extend to the entire world, including all peoples and all cultures.[15]

The divine union as the ultimate goal of spirituality both shapes and guides the entirety of the Jesuit community, because a bond with God requires the service and support of the other two kinds of relationships that the Jesuits work to have with people, including, apart from the Jesuits themselves, lay Christians, pagans, unbelievers, and infidels encountered during their missions.[16] In other words, the union with the divine stands as the final form of Christian companionship, which the Jesuits aspire to cultivate and preach about both in and out of the Society. It is around this notion of the divine union, the very ideal of the Society, that the Jesuits envision their vocation—their *Constitutions*, education, missiology, and so forth. Just as the famous Jesuit dictum "everything for the greater glory of God" (*omnia ad maiorem dei gloriam*) indicates, nothing in the world stands alone or idle to a Jesuit.[17] His view is that in this created and unified world, nothing is irrelevant to the creator. Based on this, a Jesuit is expected and trained to see, or at least to presume, that all can be used for the purpose of understanding, proving, and serving God. He must see that all of God's creations are not merely related to each other but are related through the Holy One, the Creator, and the Redeemer.[18]

Here, it is necessary to point out that the Jesuit spiritual goal of friendship or union with the divine,[19] based on what has been said so far, appears to be in agreement with the doctrine of the church that Christians should seek the human-divine communion.[20] In fact, to help form that divine union has been the sole purpose of any Christian community or organization. Here, Jean-Luc Nancy offers an illustrious description:

> The community . . . is understood as communion, and communion takes place, in its principle as in its ends, at the heart of the mystical body of Christ. At the same time as it is the most ancient myth of the Western world, community might well be the altogether modern thought of humanity's partaking of divine life: the thought of a human being penetrating into pure immanence. (Christianity has had only two dimensions, antinomical to one another: that of the *deus absconditus*, in which the Western disappearance of the divine is still engulfed, and that of the god-man, *deus communis*, brother of humankind, invention of a familial immanence of humanity, then of history as the immanence of salvation.)[21]

Nancy's opposition of *deus absconditus* and *deus communis* seems to reveal his partial knowledge of the dual nature of the Christian God as the wholly other—namely, God's simultaneous transcendence and immanence—of which more will be said later in the discussion of Ignatius's theology. But for the moment, it is quite clear that the Jesuit understanding of communion and spirituality focuses more on the second of the two Christian dimensions mentioned by Nancy, though the first, as it will soon become clear, also has its place of great importance in Ignatius's understanding of God. The question to be asked here, however, is how this communion or union that supposedly includes all people—beginning with individual Jesuits and ending by embracing everyone—and God is to be achieved and practiced.

Because one of Ignatius's favorite books is the *The Imitation of Christ*, by Thomas à Kempis (1380–1471),[22] and because he urges his followers to "imitate" Christ,[23] scholars tend to see Ignatian spirituality as "inner imitation,"[24] or a specific spiritual endeavor expected to "occupy the totality of [a person's] mental territory."[25] This discussion will follow other scholars' to argue that Ignatian theology targets much more than just a member's own spiritual perfection. But for now, one can use a borrowed term to describe the nature of Ignatius's spirituality as "interiorization,"[26] meaning that the Society's members are both expected and instructed, in their pursuit of spirituality, to internalize the Christian spirit. One important way for the Jesuits to infuse in themselves that spirit to secure their union with God is to learn to give up or eliminate their individualism, their very self, including self-will. This negation of individualism and the assimilation of the self, in Ignatius's view, is not just a practice of spirituality for the Jesuits. It is the very essence of Christianity. As Paul Dudon observes in his biography of Ignatius, "To all, he [Ignatius] repeats the same refrain of the Gospel: 'deny yourself,' for love of the suffering and humiliated Christ."[27]

Ignatius founded the Jesuit order partly in reaction to the Protestant Reformation, a movement with a message that, as the scholarly consensus has it, boils down to individualism and individuality—either an individual or a nation—against the Catholic Church and papal supremacy.[28] It is, therefore, by no means accidental that the Jesuit understanding of divine union has as its condition of possibility the elimination of, or at least a drastic reduction in, individualism and individuality. Of course, such a requirement of the Society's members is not Ignatius's invention. It is part of a tradition in the Catholic Church since the early fathers. For instance, Saint Augustine sees that "horror of death rests on the love of the [mundane] world,"[29] and that "the love of this world is fornication against" God.[30] Therefore, for him to extend *caritas*, or Christian love, would mean "death to the world, and . . . life with God."[31] What this "life with God" or "being out of the world" leads to is first and foremost the destruction of the individualization and isolation of individuals.[32] It is a fact that Ignatius lived before the time of Descartes, and thus before the birth of modern philosophy on the subject. But it is certain that Ignatius was fully aware of the theological history, in which the relation or the interaction between an individual and God had been a topic frequently discussed.[33] Despite the fact that there were accusations that his *Spiritual Exercises* promoted individuality, he had a clear enough idea of what individualization could do to a religious person like a Jesuit.[34] For him, as for Saint Augustine and the church, individualization as subjectivity that reflects the concept of self is otherness to, or estrangement from, God. The self is an obstacle to the union with the divine. As Karl Rahner said in an interview about his understanding of the spiritual exercises designed and articulated by Ignatius:

> In contrast to exercises in self-awareness (so far as this is possible), and in contrast to a verbal theological indoctrination, however important this latter can be, the Exercises are concerned with something else. It is a matter here . . . of letting the Creator and the creature, as Ignatius says, deal immediately with each other. . . . It is nothing other than this experience to which Ignatius in the Exercises wants to lead a person.[35]

As Ignatius sees it, when the Jesuits strive for divine union in offering "their services to the pope," any retention of the self would certainly be counterproductive to the Society's own agenda.[36]

To illustrate the Society's effort to "unite the human instruments with God,"[37] this discussion will begin with how the Jesuits are urged and trained to become "friends in the Lord," by focusing first on Jesuit interiorization, that is, the Jesuit attempt to respond to "an inner call for intimacy with the divine."[38] Once it is clear how the Jesuits work toward spiritual perfection and—if they succeed—achieve spiritual elevation with the death of their selves, my discussion will proceed to examine the Jesuits' mission plan to unite all by "finding God in all things." Now I turn to the Jesuits' spirituality.

Of the variety of means explored by the Jesuits in their pursuit of spiritual fulfillment, the religious vows that all novices of the Society must take stand out as the most extraordinary and crucial for a Jesuit vocation. The *Formula Instituti*, a papal document regarded as the fundamental law of the Jesuit order, thus describes three of these vows:

> Whoever desires to serve as a soldier of God [*militare Deo*] beneath the banner of the cross in our Society, which we desire to be designated by the name of Jesus, and to serve the Lord alone and the Church, His spouse, under the Roman pontiff, the vicar of Christ on earth, should, after a solemn vow of perpetual chastity, poverty, and obedience, keep what follows in mind.[39]

These three so-called regular vows of poverty, chastity, and obedience, plus a special vow of obedience known as the fourth vow—a "vow of instability" or "mobility"—to be discussed later, form part of the basic "rule" for the Society.[40] Purported both to urge and assist the Jesuits to embrace the ideal and perfection of religious life, the vows with their binding power demand the members' complete submission, physical and spiritual, to God. In order to show how the three regular vows are supposed to help the Jesuit pursuit of spiritualty, one must look at some details of the vows. In the following, the discussion will focus on the vow of poverty.

It is necessary to mention that these regular vows do not originate with Ignatius or the Society.[41] In addition to the numerous biblical references showing that a Christian should live with poverty and asceticism as an indication of religious obedience, some church fathers from early on already pointed out the need to maintain certain regulations to guarantee and guard the apostolic lifestyle for Christians wanting to be spiritual.[42] Concerning how the vows in their primitive forms turned into a distinctive feature of monasticism in late antiquity, Bernard McGinn makes this observation:

> Latin monasticism of the late fourth century and early fifth formed the matrix for the origins of the earliest distinctively Western mystical theorists: Ambrose, Augustine, and John Cassian, the three founders, were all "monastic" in one sense or another. These three reflect different views about how far immediate contact with God may be present outside the monastic life (a continuing issue in the tradition), but there can be no question that they saw the religious values manifested in monasticism—communal poverty and asceticism, virginity, devotion to prayer, and biblical study—as essential for the attainment of the highest stage of the Christian life.[43]

As time went on, monastic asceticism and other religious obligations evolved into religious vows. Known as evangelical counsels (*consilia evangelica*) and regularly professed and observed in religious communities, these vows served as obligatory counsels to regulate, direct, and guarantee a virtuous life in Christian orders. As one scholar observes when accounting for religious communities making personal poverty part of the rule in the eleventh and twelfth centuries, they were doing so to join a movement "that sought to recover the life of the primitive church (*ecclesia primitiva*) and to embrace the ideal of the apostolic life (*vita apostolica*)."[44]

When the Jesuit community came into existence in the early sixteenth century, there was a need, more urgent than ever, to return to the apostolic life.[45] Though the Society was founded quite some time before the earliest sessions of the Council of Trent, the division of the church as the result of the rise of Protestantism had become final and obvious to all. This grave reality created the context in which Ignatius responded in his own way to his time's prevailing call for "unity of faith," an appeal first uttered by some medieval fathers but now made ever more pressing by what had happened in and to the church. It is at this time that Ignatius's conversion led him to the discovery of God and to his determination to become a servant of God. As a result, he, in the words of a Jesuit historian, "gave up all service to an earthly king in order to vow himself solely and passionately to the service of this unique King of kings and Lord of lords."[46] Some of Ignatius's deeds following his conversion should help clarify what the Jesuit vows expect.

Ignatius displayed his loyalty to and love of God by enduring absolute poverty. His *Autobiography* says that in his early years he tried to make his pilgrimage to the Holy Land—to go alone and without any money.[47] He refused those offering to accompany him on the trip. In his view, a companion would come to his aid in hunger, and he would expect many things from such a companion. This trust in creatures was what he wanted to place in God alone.[48] What Ignatius did influenced the early Jesuits, who followed him to live and work in a similar fashion—in extreme poverty and with no fixed stipends.[49] As a result, these first companions became known as beggars in Paris.[50]

Since the founding of the Society, the Jesuit vows of poverty, chastity, and obedience certainly represent the institutionalized code of behaviors translating the service that Ignatius had committed himself to. The vows are taken to ensure that the members of the Society will live, work, and serve "in company with Christ."[51] With respect to poverty, the following words from the *Formula Instituti* attest that the Jesuit members must remain poor:

> Our members, one and all, should vow perpetual poverty in such a manner that neither the professed, either as individual or in common, nor any house or church of theirs can acquire any civil right to any produce, fixed revenues, or possessions or to the retention of any stable goods (except those which are proper for their own use and habitation); but they should instead be content with whatever is given them out of charity for the necessities of life. (5 [p. 69])

The same section of the *Formula* also explains the importance of, as well as reasons for, Jesuit poverty:

> From experience we have learned that a life removed as far as possible from all infection of avarice and as like as possible to evangelical poverty is more gratifying, more undefiled, and more

suitable for the edification of our fellowmen. We likewise know that our Lord Jesus Christ will supply to His servants who are seeking only the kingdom of God what is necessary for food and clothing. (5 [p. 69])

Besides manifesting the deep impact left on the Society by Ignatius's one-man and penniless pilgrimage, these passages speak much about the Jesuit vocation and spirituality. The primary function of the vow of poverty, like those of chastity and obedience, is to make sure that the Jesuits direct their attention and loyalty to God. Professing this and other vows, the Jesuits pledge to place their trust and dependence, completely and squarely, in God instead of in anyone or anything else. Specifically, to make sure that they devote all of their love to God, they are requested to turn away from the material world and earthly life.[52] Here, it is necessary to consider why love for God and the world have to be in opposition.

In Christian thinking, the world and love of God are often in conflict rather than in peaceful cohabitation. As indicated in the previously quoted passages from Saint Augustine, to be spiritual for Christians requires abandonment of the world and material possession. To take the example of Teresa of Avila (1515–1582), a virtual contemporary of Ignatius, she calls on her fellow nuns, to whom she writes, to "abandon all worldly things and possessions for Him—even though these possessions may amount to no more than the nets Saint Peter possesses."[53] One can also turn to the Johannine writings for specific discussion of this determinate disdain for the world and "worldly things." While the world is certainly part of God's good creation, like humans it has become tainted and corrupted by the fall, making it impermanent in nature. What is worse, when the Word to which the world owes its existence turned flesh, the world not only failed to recognize it but also turned against it (John 1). Therefore, those who want to be with God in his kingdom, which is "not of this world" (John 18:16), must choose to abandon this world that denies its Savior.[54]

Coming back to the Society's vows, one sees that the Jesuits abandon the world out of the same Christian longing for God's kingdom. Furthermore, because many Christians accept the theological position that one function of love is hate, the Jesuits, in order to give all love to God, find hateful and thus contestable things that, as well as people who, stand as estrangements on the Jesuit path to spirituality.[55] The Jesuit vows of poverty, chastity, and obedience are, therefore, implemented not only to oblige the members to love God, but also to separate them from those real and potential enemies and alienations. If, as has been mentioned, the principle is that people can wholeheartedly devote their love to God only after they are free from all earthly feelings and mundane company, the vows are there to provide a general guideline for the members, who by following them hope to enter a safe haven where their cultivation of spirituality can proceed. The Society's *Constitutions* repeatedly addresses the question of how the vows might specifically serve the desired spiritual union. Of the many reasons given, to ward off enemies is an important function of the vows. For example, the following passage from part 10 of the *Constitutions* explains the purpose of being poor:

> Poverty is like a bulwark of religious institutes which preserves them in their existence and discipline and defends them from many enemies; and since the devil uses corresponding effort to destroy this bulwark in one way or another, it will be highly important for the preservation and development of this whole body that every appearance of avarice should be banished afar. (816 [pp. 333–34])

As seen here, poverty serves to safeguard the spiritual fulfillment of the Jesuits by helping them fend off possible enemies. According to a comment by George E. Ganss, a Jesuit historian and scholar, "In its profound sense for Ignatius, poverty is our total emptiness before God and need of him for any and all spirit proper."[56]

As this discussion has argued so far, Jesuit spirituality dictates that a member of the Society only relates as a friend to God when he submits to him in a total fashion—that is, when he has completely given up his selfhood. Just as Ignatius argues when he insists on Jesuit obedience—before God, the pontificate, and the superior of the Society—a Jesuit member "ought to allow himself to be carried and directed . . . as if he were a corpse [*prinde ac si cadaver essent*]" (*Const* 547 [p. 249]). His self and self-will must disappear before a Jesuit becomes qualified for and entitled to the alliance with God.

Speaking of human defiance and human otherness hindering spiritual progress, one must, however, make one explicit point about the Jesuit effort to rid selfhood. It is important to remember that the Jesuits do not indiscriminately take every type of otherness to be the target of spiritual purification. While it is true that they work hard for God in order to free themselves and others from all their human otherness, the Jesuits at the same time maintain that they cannot appropriate God—the absolute otherness or infinite alterity—in the relation. Quite the contrary, they acknowledge and revere God's divine or wholly otherness by devoting themselves to God, and make serving him their end and goal in life.[57] This respect for God as the absolute or wholly other, or the transcendental alterity, certainly contrasts sharply with the Jesuit disdain for and renunciation of the human otherness represented first and foremost by the corrupted and corruptible selfhood and self-will.

There is no doubt that the Jesuit distinction of human otherness and divine otherness depends on Jesuit theology and Christian thought. But the question here is whether the Jesuits can sustain for their spirituality these two opposing attitudes about the two types of otherness. One must ask whether the Jesuits can, on the one hand, open totally to God, the wholly other, while, on the other, stay closed to other otherness such as self, self-will, and all other—mundane and human—defections believed to separate Christian men—and in fact all people—from God. The remaining pages of this chapter will focus on this question to examine whether the Jesuit divine union is a relationship that has in it only one party—God—since the Jesuits may enter in relation with God only after their spiritual exercises have converted them into a group of phantoms with no substance or shadow of self. Once this question is answered, the discussion will examine the role that otherness—human otherness or wholly otherness—plays in the Christian world order, particularly in the Christian confraternity of all people under God that the Jesuits work to establish through their mission. I first focus on how God's wholly otherness determines the human-God relationship.

The idea of God's wholly otherness, or his transcendence, has from the beginning been in the religious discourse of both the West and the East.[58] But "wholly other" as a phrase gains popularity only after the publication of Rudolf Otto's *The Idea of the Holy* in 1917. In this thought-provoking book, a comparative study of religion rather than a discussion of Christianity alone, Otto defines the concept of the holy. According to him, a feature typical in all forms of religion and religious experience is creature-consciousness. Also called creature-feeling, creature-consciousness represents "the emotion of a creature, submerged and overwhelmed by its own nothingness in contrast to that which is supreme above all creatures."[59] Describing it as "something 'numinous,'"[60] with *numinous* being a term of his coinage from the Latin *numen*, Otto is convinced that this feeling results in what he calls "*mysterium tremendum*."[61] In his view, this sense of the "numinous" identifies what is fundamental to religion. As he goes on to elaborate, while the *tremendum*, from *tremor*, points to a specific type of "'numinous dread' or *awe*,"[62] *mysterium* means simply "the wholly other." He explains:

> Taken in the religious sense, that which is "mysterious" is—to give it perhaps the most striking expression—the "wholly other" (θάτερον, *anyad*, *alienum*), that which is quite beyond the sphere of the usual, the intelligible, and the familiar, which therefore falls quite outside the limits of the canny, and is contrasted with it, filling the mind with blank wonder and astonishment.[63]

He reiterates the same point later in the book:

> The truly "mysterious" object is beyond our apprehension and comprehension, not only because our knowledge has certain irremovable limits, but because in it we come upon something inherently "wholly other," whose kind and character are incommensurable with our own, and before which we therefore recoil in a wonder that strikes us chill and numb.[64]

Otto's point is clear. The one essential feature of the object in a religious experience is the deity's complete transcendence of infinity, which differentiates it clearly and completely from anything knowable or recognizable through the human senses in this world. The idea of the holy means that the deity is "wholly unlike us."[65]

One must hasten to clarify that divine transcendence does not mean that a god remains forever aloof from believers. The Christian God, for one, is understood to be as omnipresent as he is transcendent. Despite the suggestion from the Bible that "no one ever has direct or immediate contact with or experience of God," God's *agapē*, his profound love for humankind, is taken to represent God's immanence and presence in this world.[66] Though God is understood as the "undecidable mystery" wholly independent of humans, his *agapē* is the principle aligned with the Christian doctrine of grace, through which he relates to this world.[67] This duality of God, being at once transcendent and present or immanent, means that God, despite his nature as the wholly other and *mysterium tremendum*, can nevertheless be unusually close to a religious person, closer even than the person's self to humankind.[68]

To Ignatius, there is no doubt that humans can form a close relation with God and feel his nearness through divine immanence. But this immanence does not afford humans any opportunity or possibility to appropriate God. It is certainly unlike the way in which through traditional friendship people tend to appropriate their friends. Furthermore, a person's vision of

God is always more a mental or spiritual discernment than it is a sensate visualization. For Ignatius, in short, not only should there always be the *mysterium tremendum*, as described by Otto, felt by one before God, but also there should always remain some separation between humans and God, even in the relation humans have with God.[69] And what sustains this human-divine divide is nothing other than God's transcendence—wholly otherness or holy infinity—that keeps the loving Father distant, different, heterogeneous, and dissociated even in an alliance that the Divine permits humans to have with him. Needless to say, this distance, this difference and separation, determine in turn what is called Christian faith—the belief that persists in the midst of certainties and uncertainties, of possibility and impossibility.

One must clarify again, this time with some details, that Ignatius's insistence on God as infinite and transcendent, plus his own complete surrender to God, should not be regarded as his declared intention to deconstruct. Undoubtedly, infinity and transcendence point to heterogeneity and dissociation that result in the divide between God and humans, including Ignatius himself. But this, for reasons that will soon become clear, does not mean that Ignatius saw what the deconstructionists advocate today. It is true that, in his discussion of friendship, Jacques Derrida takes dissociation and separation to be the condition of one's relation to the other, a condition that he reiterates. The resultant distance for him keeps a friendly relationship healthy, because this relation would be, as he calls it, following Maurice Blanchot and Emmanuel Levinas, *rapport sans rapport*, or a "relation without relation."[70] It is only in this kind of relation, he asserts, that the other retains his or her "absolute transcendence."[71] And absolute transcendence, which in Derrida's terminology equals what he often refers to as "singularity," is what keeps a person or entity heterogeneous and beyond appropriation in the relationship.[72]

Recent years have seen such deconstructionist concepts as absolute transcendence, singularity, *aporia*, and other related notions applied frequently in the discussion of religion, particularly Christianity and the concept of God.[73] For instance, based on the deconstructive idea that friendship is a relationless relation, John D. Caputo has developed his own theory of the "impossibility" of God. In one of his recent articles, quoting Jesus's words from the Gospel of Matthew, "For human beings it is impossible, but for God all things are possible" (19:26), Caputo refers to God as "the possibility of the impossible." He insists that the impossible "is a sign of God." And thus "the love of God is our love of the impossible."[74] For Caputo, as a matter of fact, the idea of God is the same as the prototype or *aporia* of deconstruction.[75] The cogency of Caputo's theory of God and the impossible is not the concern of the discussion here.[76] But what he and other contemporary theologians and philosophers have written about God can be useful in offering a contrast to Ignatius's view of God's transcendence.

It is true that the way in which Ignatius saw God to be the wholly and absolute other may look similar to the argument by Caputo and others. But the difference is nothing less than fundamental. While the postmodern theologians and philosophers see a "God after metaphysics" or "after onto-theo-logics,"[77] Ignatius's emphasis on God being both transcendental and immanent serves as the basis of his spiritual enterprise of returning to a purer origin or an "abundant fount of grace."[78] To emphasize, the wholly otherness of God simply indicates God's unicity, which in turn affirms that God, as the Logos, Being, or the One without Being, is what humans must recognize and accept.[79] Given this view, it is never possible for humans to appropriate God by reducing the divine otherness, or overcoming the fundamental gap between God and themselves. As Ignatius sees it, human history, as a univocal and closed system with no opening, drives to a predetermined end, meaning that humans as creations by and for God must not only be submissive and open to their creator but also enter the divine system stripped completely of their selves or otherness.

Ignatius certainly knows and therefore often laments over the fact that, owing to human's pride, arrogance, and faults, the God-given and otherwise perfect and original union has been torn, so that humans fell through to the earth. But God has shown his love for people and made manifest his plan for their redemption, for which the life of Jesus, particularly his crucifixion, offers proof. As a result, what is left for one to do is, again, deprive oneself of the very self and the "I" to earn the qualification to return to God. As was mentioned, for Ignatius it is only through this theologico-economic affirmation of human submission to God that one can hope to relate again to the Christian deity. It is obvious that Ignatius sees that only a self-less or I-less person can be with God, because, as far as divine union is concerned, a person's self and the I identify with an otherness or singularity, which in turn equals his or her arrogance, defiance, and challenge before God. Therefore, as the reader often finds in various Jesuit documents and literature, it is reiterated that only selflessness—an ultimate form of human humility—leads to heaven. Unless one desires to become part of the collaborative human "instruments in the hand of God" (*Const* 813, 814 [pp. 332–33]), one is neither ready nor able to return home to God. If what has been said so far is a faithful outline of Ignatius's understanding of the human-God relation, the task now is to see how a person's selfless stance can be achieved, or more specifically, whether a Jesuit can reach spiritual perfection and actually function without selfhood and self-will. For this purpose, some basics from the *Spiritual Exercises* will help.

In the *Spiritual Exercises*, there is one example after another, given by Ignatius, to assert that the I, as a critic observes, "has no value in existence."[80] The book contains advice that the exercitants not seek to satiate their physical needs. Speaking of food and drink, for example, Ignatius states, "In regard to foods, greater and more complete abstinence ought to be practiced. For in this area just as the appetite is more prone to become disordered, so is temptation more likely to assail us" (*SpEx* 212).[81] In addition to the advice for physical restrictions much in line with the Jesuit vows already discussed, what the exercitants receive most from Ignatius's manual are instructions on how they can work directly on their spirituality by thinking right, or thinking the way that God would expect them to think. To give some examples: "I must make myself indifferent to all created things" (*SpEx* 23); "When I am arising and dressing, I will endeavor to make myself sad and sorrowful over the great sorrow and suffering of Christ our Lord" (*SpEx* 206). Because God out of his deep affection gave humans "his very self" (*SpEx* 234), an exercitant must, insists Ignatius, "consider what I on my part ought in all reason and justice to offer and give to his Divine Majesty, namely, *all my possessions*, and *myself* along with them" (*SpEx* 234; emphasis added). In short, in Ignatius's view, it is simply self-contradictory if anyone hopes to retain one's I or *ipseity* while pursuing Catholic spirituality.[82]

To assist the exercitants in engaging spiritually with God, Ignatius lays much emphasis at the beginning of the *Spiritual Exercises* on such activities as "examination of conscience, meditation, contemplation, vocal or mental prayer" (*SpEx* 1). He has various and specific suggestions about how and what to do in the examination and contemplation. For instance, speaking of an educated and intelligent exercitant involved in public affairs or pressing occupations, Ignatius suggests that this person "make a meditation for an hour each morning on the first, second, and the third sins; then for another three days at the same hour the meditation on the court-record of one's own sins; then for a further three days at the same hour the meditation on the punishment corresponding to sins" (*SpEx* 19). Later in his book, he explains how such meditations can be carried out. Concerning the meditation on the first sin, for example, he suggests the following from the perspective of the exercitant: "I will call to memory the sin of the angels: How they were created in grace and then, not wanting to better themselves by using their freedom to reverence and obey their Creator and Lord, they fell into pride, were changed from grace to malice, and were hurled from heaven to hell. Next I will . . . move myself to deeper affections by my will" (*SpEx* 50). Emphasizing the reason for the fall of anyone from God while identifying the only path to return to the Divine, Ignatius's words here point to, besides the ultimate goal of the exercises, primarily the mechanism through which one can achieve this goal. An exercitant can, by meditating on and learning from the lessons of the fallen angels and himself, identify God to be the ultimate end of his deeper and greater love. The exercitant can then return to God or reunite with God through the use and assistance of his meditation and intellect.

Such exercises and other similar ones suggesting specific meditations, contemplation, reflection, prayers, and so forth, continue through the book. Altogether they oblige the exercitants to make conscious choices to demonstrate that they are both ready and willing to give up their all to God in exactly the same fashion as Ignatius gives himself up with this prayer, known as his *suspice*, found toward the end of the *Spiritual Exercises*: "Take, Lord, and receive all my liberty, my memory, my understanding, and all my will—all that I have and possess. You, Lord, have given all that to me. I now give it back to you, O Lord. All of it is yours. Dispose of it according to your will. Give me your love and your grace, for that is enough for me" (234). Commenting on these words that express Ignatius's willingness to sacrifice his all-including self to God, Ganss asserts in his note to the *Spiritual Exercises*, "Notice the totality of this offering: The exercitant, in deep fervor from the month of spiritual experience and moved by profound gratitude to increased effective love, offers his or her whole self back to God, to be guided henceforth by his good pleasure through the rest of life."[83] Given the self-denying teachings in the Gospels,[84] one can say that what Ignatius elaborates in his theology represents the very core of Christian doctrine. Following Jesus's words from Matthew that "those who find their life will lose it, and those who lose their life for my sake will find it" (10:39),[85] it is only fitting that, when God's Son becomes man passing through death, "Christian death" becomes a new experience for believers.[86] In other words, a believer, or an exercitant, is only born again through death, the complete sacrifice of the self. To use the Christian parlance, an exercitant must die into Christ before he or she gains a new and real life, a life of friendship, companionship, or union, a life with Christ or within Christ. It is a life after death, or it is an existence deprived of all self and enclosed in the universal and at the same time well-marked system of God.

But the qualification for the divine union may not be as easily obtained as it first appears. Despite the offering of the "gift of death," to use Jacques Derrida's phrase,[87] the exercitant's meditations, contemplations, and considerations—in short, his or her commitment, obligation, or responsibility to God—represent what would likely be a prolonged procedure with no guaranteed and predestined result. It seems that Ignatius is well aware of this fact, as when he stresses that one must repeatedly offer one's choice to God so as to "beg his Divine Majesty to accept and confirm it, provided it is conducive to his greater service and praise" (*SpEx* 183).[88] The fact that the offering must be made repeatedly means, no matter how ironic it may look, that an exercitant must repeatedly die until no self or self-will is left in him or her. Otherwise, the exercitant's death may not be deemed to be final, or the exercitant, despite this death, may not be dead enough, or this offering of death, owing to some residual dosage of self still retained, may not have the merit of a "gift outright." Such an offering is understandably not good enough to be confirmed and accepted by the divine, because an offering from someone not yet completely abnegated of self would appear to God as a limited gift or a surrender with reservations and conditions. It is clear to Ignatius that a half-hearted attempt would turn what would be a perfect relationship or an ideal friendship or a divine union into an association imbued with human otherness, alienation, pride, and defiance.

There are many examples from the history of the church to show cleansing the self as otherness to be constant drudgery to Christians. Again, one should consider Saint Augustine, who talks repeatedly about how the mystery of his self puzzles him. He worries that he does not seem to have the ability to successfully control his self, which forces Augustine to beg God for help in his *Confessions*: "I beseech now, O my God, discover me unto myself, that I may confess unto my brethren who are to pray for me, what I now find myself defective in" (10.37). Obviously, Augustine hopes that, with certain divine revelation, he can begin, once learning what and where his defective self is, to search for a solution. To be sure, sometimes his problem appears to be clear. Augustine, already a pious Christian priest at the time of writing his *Confessions*, admits in his book that he still has sexual dreams.[89] Here one does not need to resort to Sigmund Freud to see why Augustine's suppressed wishes emerge in these dreams. What is significant is that these things that happen or do not happen to Augustine are by no means isolated. Ignatius and Nadal seem to experience similar problems, judging by what is implied in their letters.[90] In fact, to prevent any undesirable relationship between Jesuits, the Society makes it a rule that its members are to "sleep one to a bed," and that they are not "to show fraternal affection for each other by embracing."[91] These and other examples only help demonstrate the fact that the self is difficult to control and eliminate for spiritually hungry Christians, including Jesuits. To understand and explain why the human self proves so resilient an obstacle in Christian spirituality, one must begin by not only recognizing and acknowledging but also accepting the singularity of the self (i.e., the impossibility of eliminating the self, or selfhood, or subjectivity, just like the impossibility of eliminating otherness).

In *The Gift of Death*, Jacques Derrida focuses his discussion on religion and religious faith. Taking as his point of departure the analysis in *Heretical Essays on the Philosophy of History* by Jan Patočka (1907–1977)— who discusses such religious concepts as gift, *mysterium tremendum*, human relations with God, responsibility, and so forth—Derrida develops his view on gift, death, and gift of death (i.e., gift as death and through death). In chapter 2, "Beyond: Giving for the Taking, Teaching and Learning to Give, Death," Derrida relates death and death as a gift to the self. After presenting Patočka's theory that the first awakening of responsibility corresponds "to a conversion with respect to the experience of death" that in turn gives birth to philosophy, he observes that the *mysterium tremendum* announces another and different death. It is different because this death, or this way of apprehending death, "comes from a gift received from the other, from the one who, in absolute transcendence, sees me without my seeing, holds me in his hands while remaining inaccessible."[92] He further paraphrases Patočka, saying that this giving of the gift, in Christianity, has an aim to transform "the Good into Goodness forgetful of itself, into a love that renounces itself."[93] Obviously, by such a gift that instills Goodness in others, Patočka is suggesting grace from God.[94] However, Derrida takes this idea of gift and applies it to anyone or any self who gives such a gift. To show why this gift represents another death, he probes into what he deems to be the key of this death, the uniqueness and irreplaceable singularity of the self. In his discussion of the self's irreplaceable singularity, he makes references to Martin Heidegger's theory of death that argues that to die or to give one's life for the other is an unmistakable demonstration of individuality. It is individuality because, as Heidegger suggests in *Being and Time*, "by its very essence, death is in every case mine, insofar as it 'is' at all." He continues elaborating on his reason: "No one can die for me if 'for me' means instead of me, in my place."[95] From this perspective, death becomes a rather strange gift, because it is an impossible gift to give. To use Derrida's summary of Heidegger: "Giving one's life *for* the other, dying *for* the other . . . does not mean dying in the place of the other. On the contrary, it is only to the extent that dying—insofar as it 'is'—remains mine, that I can die for another or *give* my life to the other. There is no gift of self, it cannot be thought, except in terms of this irreplaceability."[96] Derrida elaborates on this view of the gift of death:

> I can give the other everything except immortality, except this *dying for her* to the extent of dying in place of her, so freeing her from her own death. I can die for the other in a situation where my death gives him a little longer to live; I can save someone by throwing myself in the water or fire in order to snatch him temporarily from the jaws of death; I can give her my heart in the literal or figurative sense in order to assure her of a certain longevity. But I cannot die in her place, I cannot give her my life in exchange for her death.[97]

These words make it clear that the irreplaceability of the self in the eyes of these philosophers determines the nature of the gift of death.

The above references to Derrida and other philosophers should help explain the issue at hand—why the self proves so difficult to renounce and eliminate in the eyes of Ignatius and other Jesuit fathers. Given its irreplaceability, which means "dying can never be borne, borrowed, transferred, delivered, promised, or transmitted," the self is irreducible and impossible to eliminate, despite the vigorous measures of spiritual exercises or deaths.[98] In fact, through death, or through giving up one's life or self to the other—any other, including God, the wholly other—the self remains, even grows. As Derrida asserts:

> The sameness of one's self [*le même du soi-même*], what remains irreplaceable in dying, doesn't become what it is—in the sense of a same that relates to self in the oneself—before encountering what relates it to its mortality understood as irreplaceability. . . . It is in the being-towards-death that the oneself of the *Jemeinigkeit* is constituted, comes into its own, that is, comes to realize its unsubstitutability. The sameness of the oneself is *given* by death, by the being-towards-death that *promises* me to it. It is only to the extent that this sameness of the oneself is posited as irreducibly different singularity that death for the other or the death of the other can make sense.[99]

These words clarify why the self—self of anyone including Saint Augustine and Ignatius—does not go away in spite of religious faith, devotion, and measures of spiritual purification. The self remains in spite of the effort to die, or through the gift of death.

Bearing in mind that the self is constituted through dying because of its irreplaceability, one looks back at the Jesuit attempt to reduce and eliminate the self through spiritual exercises to see that Ignatius's call for repeated offering from the exercitants, or for repeated effort by the exercitants to choose and elect, comes from no other reason than from his recognition and acknowledgment of the resilience, possibly the irreducibility, of the self. Undoubtedly, Ignatius would not be familiar with the deconstructive concept of the self's irreplaceability through the dying or death of the other. But that would not have prevented him from seeing the possibility of a self becoming more complicated in spite of all the meditation, contemplation, and consideration prescribed for the exercitants. To put it differently, out of the exercises of spirituality, the self may indeed appear to be a much enhanced Christian self more devoted to God and striving with more vigor toward God owing to its realization, with pain and sorrow, of its inadequacy before the divine.[100] But at the same time, from the exercises may come a more meditative self with a keener and sharper awareness of all the choices available, and of all the otherness active in the world. It is likely that Ignatius could see what might happen with this enhanced, split, and complicated self. That is why at the end of the second week, a couple of days after the exercitants are urged to choose between the world of Satan and that of God, he again stresses the importance of elections and talks about the possibility of the self making wrong choices.[101]

There are other indications that Ignatius realizes as well as concedes, explicitly or implicitly, the irreducibility of the self. For instance, it is known that later in his career he modifies and relaxes both his view on poverty and the Jesuit practice of poverty. Recognizing the impracticability of "actual poverty" that turned out to hinder his goal "to aid souls," Ignatius and his fellow Jesuits modified their rule of poverty. Rather than insisting strictly that the members should be in want, they relented by asking that no one in the Society should have anything to call one's own.[102] Such relaxation concerning poverty shows the acknowledgment as well as acceptance of the fact that the self, in Ignatius's view the otherness to God and spirituality, could not be reduced to none.[103] In the following, a better example to illustrate the Jesuit concession of the irreducible self comes from the required obedience in the Society.

Of the three basic Jesuit vows mentioned and discussed earlier, obedience bears special importance to the Jesuit order because it determines the very nature of the Society.[104] The need for obedience is made most clear in the *Formula Instituti*: "Assuredly, too, because of the great utility to the order and for the sake of the constant practice of humility which has never been sufficiently praised, the individual subjects should not only be obliged to obey the general in all matters pertaining to the Society's Institute but also to recognize and properly venerate Christ as present in him" (4 [p. 69]). This call for obedience certainly serves to make the Society an order with a strict and unquestioning discipline. To demonstrate his view of authority and hierarchy, it is necessary here to quote Ignatius's famous letter written on March 26, 1553, to some fellow Jesuits in Portugal. In this letter, often hailed as "the most celebrated, the best known, and most widely read of all letters of St. Ignatius,"[105] he asserts that obedience is what makes the Society of Jesus a special and unique order:

> We may allow ourselves to be surpassed by other religious orders in fasts, watchings, and other austerities, which each one following its institute holily observes. But in the purity and perfection of obedience together with the true resignation of our wills and the abnegation of our judgment, I am very desirous, my dear brothers, that they who serve God in this Society should be conspicuous, so that by this virtue its true sons may be recognized as men who regard not the person whom they obey, but in him Christ our Lord, for whose sake they obey. For the superior is to be obeyed not because he is prudent, or good, or qualified by any other gift of God, but because he holds the place and the authority of God, as Eternal Truth has said: "He that heareth you, heareth me; and he that despiseth you, despiseth me."[106]

The resignation and abnegation of the self-will and self are perhaps best summarized by John W. O'Malley, who, in his discussion of early Jesuit history, succinctly relates the self and the difference between the Society and other religious orders: "Others might practice Christian self-denial in their great austerities or long periods of prayer, but Jesuits did so through the abnegation implied in obedience to their superiors."[107] Based on Ignatius's words and those of O'Malley, obedience—one of the first obligations that, according to Genesis, humans failed to perform before God—targets human pride, ultimately the human self, by demanding total submission from Jesuit members. Specifically, obedience means the commitment and responsibility of the members who do not sustain, much less display, their self before the order from their superior—the general of the Society or the pope. Clearly, what Jesuit obedience expects from the members is the same commitment and responsibility expected through the spiritual exercises: emptying the self completely.

Despite the best intentions of Ignatius and other Jesuits, it is exactly out of their insistence on obedience that the self again emerges as irreducible. As has been mentioned, Jesuit obedience is certainly imposed to assure total commitment and complete responsibility to the Society, the church, and ultimately God. Given the aporetic nature of responsibility discussed by Derrida, however, Jesuit obedience, along with its needed commitment and responsibility, predetermines as its own condition of possibility certain irresponsibility on the part of the Jesuit. And it is in this aporia, or undecidability of responsibility and irresponsibility, that the self as otherness manifests most convincingly. I will explain. Obedience, which means following an order as an election or action prescribed, certainly makes it unnecessary for any other personal engagement on the part of the Jesuit self. Taking and executing orders "with blind obedience," the Jesuit is not required or expected to think on his own, or express his own opinion or make his own decisions. Though such nonthinking as "a lifeless body" may help conduce what Ignatius and O'Malley have called abnegation of the self,[108] following a dictated path and acting on a prescribed "decision" speak exactly of irresponsibility. The self has nothing other to do than execute what is ordered. What is more, this irresponsibility does not actually reduce or abnegate the self. On the contrary, it confirms the irreducibility of the self. What the vow of obedience means to make clear first and foremost is that it chooses to ignore or disregard the existence of the self. In other words, obedience represents not only the concession to acknowledge but also the willingness to accept that the self is irreducible. Manifesting the tension between the institutional obligation, religious commitment, personal intuition, and individual election, the call to obedience thus takes the irreducible self to be a fact by obliging it to obey orders. Here, agreeing with Derrida that the condition of the possibility of responsibility "is a certain *experience and experiment of the possibility of the impossible*,"[109] one can certainly say that the Jesuit self that remains, or the self impossible to eliminate, makes it possible and at the same time necessary for the Society to implement its rule of obedience.

However, in speaking of the self's irreducibility, irreplaceability, and singularity as they manifest through death and obedience, one has not covered all the inconveniences (i.e., the self as the other to the divine system of God challenging the Jesuits on their way to spirituality). In addition to what has been discussed so far, one should mention that what also makes the self a lingering problem is the necessity compelling the self to remain constantly open to the other. When a Jesuit opens to God and devotes himself to God, he also splits his self in this pursuit of spirituality. Just as Emmanuel Levinas argues, a being "can take itself for a totality only if it is unthinking."[110] But that totality ruptures, or exteriority comes in, as soon as the being's thinking begins.[111] Trained to devote himself to God alone, the Jesuit's love for God—supposedly exclusive and wholehearted—means that, as Levinas says, "the *I* [is] satisfied by the *thou*, grasping in the other the justification of its being."[112] Cultivated through meticulously carried out spiritual exercises, the Jesuit's love of and death for God confirm both the singularity of the self—as this self is repeatedly disdained to be the other to God—and at the same time the split of this very self. To reveal how the self is split, one must return to the discussion of Derrida.

The discussion that confirms further the irreducibility of the self is found, again, in *The Gift of Death*. In the last chapter of this book, Derrida advances a new argument or "formula" thematized as well as summarized in a single sentence, which he also uses to name this chapter, *tout autre est tout autre*, "every other (one) is every (bit) other" or, simply, "every other is wholly other."[113] As he explains, what the homonyms in this sentence present is by no means a seeming and simple case of tautology but "a radical heterology," "the very proposition of the most irreducible heterology."[114] Earlier in his book, when concluding his discussion of the human-divine relation, including a human's responsibility and response to God through the Genesis story of Abraham's willingness to slaughter his son Isaac for sacrifice (22:1–24), Derrida introduces his formula:

> If God is completely other, the figure or name of the wholly other, then every other (one) is every (bit) other. . . . It implies that God, as the wholly other, is to be found everywhere there is something of the wholly other. And since each of us, every one else, each other is infinitely other in its absolute singularity, inaccessible, solitary, transcendent, nonmanifest, originarily nonpresent to my *ego* . . . , then what can be said about Abraham's relation to God can be said about my relation without relation to *every other (one) as every (bit) other* [*tout autre comme tout autre*], in particular my relation to my neighbor or my loved

> ones who are as inaccessible to me, as secret, and transcendent as Jahweh. Every other (in the sense of each other) is wholly other (absolute other).[115]

Derrida arrives at this formula out of his dissatisfaction with Levinas's critique of Kierkegaard's attempt at "reserving the quality of the wholly other, in other words the *infinite other*, for God alone, or in any case for a single other."[116] He points out that, despite his criticism, "Levinas' thinking stays within the game—the play of difference and analogy—between the face of God and the face of my neighbor."[117] In Derrida's view, "If every human is wholly other, if everyone else, or every other one, is every bit other, then one can no longer distinguish between a claimed generality of ethics that would need to be sacrificed in sacrifice, and the faith that turns towards God alone, as wholly other, turning away from human duties."[118] Here, Derrida's hope is to link "alterity to singularity or to what one could call the universal exception, or the rule of the exception." What he wants to signify with his *tout autre est tout autre* is "that every other is singular, that 'every' is a singularity, which also means that every is each one, a proposition that seals the contract between universality and the exception of singularity, that of 'no matter who.'"[119]

Clearly, what Derrida means to present in his formula is a new understanding of the individual. Here is how, according to him, the dictum "every other (one) is every (bit) of other" can be reproduced:

> It can do so to the extent of replacing one of the "every other's" by God: "Every other (one) is God," or "God is every (bit) other." Such a substitution in no way alters the "extent" of the original formulation, whatever grammatical function be assigned to the various words. In one case God is defined as infinitely other, as the wholly other. In the other case it is declared that every other one, each of the others, is God inasmuch as he or she is, *like* God, wholly other.[120]

Taking the wholly other as "every other one," these words alter drastically the human-God relation—the relation between the self and the wholly other. Open to and split by the other whose singularity instills wholly otherness in every one, every one is now wholly other like God, irreducible and singular.[121] Equipped thus to resist any attempt of appropriation and elimination, every other one now simply has wholly otherness or divinity within his or her or its self. Just as Derrida puts it, "God is in me, he is the absolute 'me' or 'self,' he is that structure of invisible interiority that is called . . . subjectivity."[122] What he means is not that one no longer needs to look out for God. It is rather that one can find God-like wholly otherness everywhere. And in every other one, including the self or subjectivity, there is this wholly otherness that makes every other as irreducible and singular as God. Here, Caputo offers a good interpretation of Derrida's formula:

> The wholly other is any singularity whatever, whoever, whose this-ness we cannot lift up, cannot generalize, cannot universalize, cannot formalize, any singularity which fixes us in this place so that we cannot look away, cannot look up to the *eidos* of which it would be 'but an example,' which would allow us to get on top of it, dominate it, enable us to envisage it instead of finding ourselves fixed by its gaze. Derrida here takes up a uniquely biblical sense of singularity, as opposed to a Greek sense of subsuming the less real particular under the truer universal. *Tout autre*—it does not matter what or who—*est tout autre*.[123]

Following the "biblical sense of singularity" mentioned in Caputo's passage above, one should consider specifically the Genesis tale of creation implied in Derrida's "God is in me." In the Holy Scriptures, there are numerous passages asserting the view that "there is . . . one God and Father of all, who is above all and through all and in all" (Eph 4:4–6).[124] Of all God's creatures, it is important to emphasize, man is particularly favored for being given the likeness of the Divine. In return, this divine likeness, or *imago dei*, according to Mark C. Taylor, "confers upon man an identity, appearance, or shadow of divinity."[125] One must, however, remember that the human subjectivity thus determined carries within itself, besides its irreducibility and irreplaceability, a breach or, at least, a tension signaling on the one hand a surplus in man—given his image of God—while, on the other, a lack in him owing to the fall. Furthermore, this state of being ruptured and split in turn generates much instability in the human-God relation. In other words, while Taylor is correct to say that man's *imago dei* points to a certain "God-self relation [that] forges an inseparable bond between the name of God and the name of man,"[126] this bond is at the same time severed and uncertain. The instability and mutability in this both inseparable and torn God-self bond leave man in a constant need to open up the self. In fact, this need impassions man to be in a perennial search for meaning or purpose that is always in the making. Such need and the search that it entails, in the case of the Jesuits, compel the self to open and extend its irreducible being repeatedly toward the wholly other, be it God or "every other one."

It should be a safe conjecture that Ignatius and the early Jesuits, had they known of it, would not have cared much for what Derrida has to say about humans and God. But there is no doubt about their familiarity with and faith in creation. And their belief that God created everything is found throughout many Jesuit doctrines, particularly in the aforementioned Ignatian commandment "finding God in all things." This commandment, like the Society's motto "everything for the greater glory of God," represents a most ambitious plan that Ignatius has for Jesuit spirituality. It serves as an instruction as well as a reminder to his disciples that they must remain spiritually alert and dedicated at all times and in doing all things. They must seek, contemplate, and comprehend the presence and will of God no matter where they are and what they are doing. The thoroughness and comprehensiveness of Jesuit spirituality revealed through this formula is exemplified in the following from a letter by Ignatius: "When men go outside themselves, and enter wholly into their Creator and Lord, they have a continual awareness, attention, and consolation; and they perceive with relish how our eternal and highest Good dwells in all created things, giving existence and conservation to all of them by his own infinite being and presence."[127]

So far, it is clear that "finding God in all things" confirms Jesuit spirituality to be unlimited by interiorization. In fact, the formula "finding God in all things" marks where the spiritual interiorization of the Jesuits converges with what can be seen as the order's exteriorization—its commitment to and execution of proselytical missions—an integral as well as crucial part of Jesuit vocation. Imposing one encompassing homogeneity on all—the entire earth plus its people—"finding God in all things" reveals most fully the "crusade spirituality" of the Society. At the same time, it is exactly this crusade spirituality—a totalizing spirituality aimed at making all others open to God just like the Jesuits themselves—that further deconstructs the Ignatian theology. This is so because, in their mission, the Jesuits find themselves compelled constantly not only to acknowledge the otherness of peoples and cultures encountered but also to open themselves up to such otherness in the same fashion as they open to God, the wholly other. To argue for this point by revealing the very essence of the Society's crusade or mission spirituality, one must look into the fourth vow of the Jesuits.

Designated as an "army of Christ" and *ecclesia militans*, the Society, in addition to the three regular vows already mentioned and discussed, has its members take a fourth vow of obedience. This vow, also known to be the special vow, receives the following definition in the *Formula Instituti*:

> In addition to that ordinary bond of the three vows, we are to be obliged by a special vow to carry out whatever the present and future Roman pontiffs may order which pertains to the progress of souls and the propagation of the faith; and to go without subterfuge or excuse, as far as in us lies, to whatsoever provinces they may choose to send us—whether they are pleased to send us among the Turks or any other infidels, even those who live in the region called the Indies, or among any heretics whatever or schismatics, or any of the faithful. (4 [p. 68])

The vow points to the missionary spirituality of the Jesuit order. It means that, according to Ignatius's vision, the Jesuits are not a group of religious men devoted to the salvation and perfection of their own souls alone. They are also expected to "labor strenuously in giving aid toward the salvation and perfection of the souls of their fellow men" (*Const* 3.2 [p. 67]). Besides cultivating their own spirituality, members join the Society in response to Jesus's commission in Matthew 28:19–20—to spread Christianity to all others. To this end, the Jesuits stand willing and ready to work with all, either infidels to be converted or heretics to be challenged and rectified, by taking their evangelical missions to all regions and places around the world, wherever the pope chooses to send them. The Jesuits express without disguise their view of the conflicted relations they think they have with their neighbors and other human beings and their obligation to God. Concerning this special vow, two points are worth making. The first has to do with the Society's self-assigned role during the Reformation and Counter-Reformation. The second addresses the fact that this vow signals what breaches further Jesuit spirituality: the Society and its missionaries have to remain open to earthly or human otherness despite their intention to be open only to God. What follows immediately is an elucidation of the first point.

Because this special vow leaves the distribution of the Jesuit missionaries solely to the pope, many take it to be unmistakable proof of the Society's unwavering and aggressive participation in the Counter-Reformation. As is well known, one key point raised by Martin Luther (1483–1546) in his ninety-five theses on October 31, 1517, and during the Reformation is none other than the choice between the Holy Scriptures and the pope. Luther questions papal supremacy and rejects the claim that the pope represents Christ by divine right. He insists that the only and "ultimate criterion for Christianity is the message of the gospel."[128] While Luther is found to be a heretic for his disobedience to the church and criticism of the pope,[129] for Catholics, "the pope is the highest authority and foundation of the universal church."[130] For instance, in the eyes of the Dominican Sylvester Mazzolini of Prierio (1456–1527), a papal court theologian and later the judge at Luther's trial, the pope represents "the infallible rule of faith, from which the Holy Scriptures too draw their strength and authority."[131] As indicated in the special vow, papal infallibility is exactly what the Society as a Catholic organization endorses. Subjecting themselves to the authority of the pope, the Jesuits do not want to have anything to do with individualism, the backbone of Luther's Protestantism. In fact, "of all Catholic institutions, the Jesuits identified themselves *most closely* with the papacy."[132]

Given such a historical and doctrinal context, and despite their vow and willingness to take their mission to all people, it becomes virtually impossible for the Jesuits to work among certain groups, especially schismatics like Luther and other Reformers. Undoubtedly, they contest the Reformers and reject them. However, realizing and accepting that the separation of the church is irreversible, the Jesuits turn much of their attention to peoples in regions and places beyond Europe. This change of direction may mean, ironically, that the Jesuit formula of "finding God in all things" is now practically limited to finding God in only some things. Nevertheless, the Jesuit determination to go out for God never wanes. And the special vow, with which they profess to be dedicated missionaries for "a crusade that gave battle in the remotest regions of the earth,"[133] is often referred to as, as was mentioned, a "vow of instability" or "vow of mobility." Speaking of Jesuit mobility, however, leads the discussion to the second point to be made here—that is, how Jesuit spirituality appears to be ruptured owing to the Society's commitment to missions.

Placing the Jesuit vow of obedience in the monastic tradition of the church, Knowles points out that "the teaching of St. Ignatius differs widely in spirit from that of the predecessors from whom he borrows his expressions."[134] One factor that makes Ignatius different, according to Knowles, is this: "Whereas they are concerned with individual actions within the ambit of a life regulated by a rule, he is considering, or at least including, activities of all kinds carried out, anywhere in Christendom or among the heathen."[135] To see how the Jesuit commitment to evangelical mission or mobility differs from the monastic tradition, one can look at *The Imitation of Christ* by Thomas à Kempis for a quick comparison.

As has been mentioned, Thomas remained one of Ignatius's favorite authors. Ignatius would not only read *The Imitation of Christ* again and again but also recommend the book to all his followers and friends.[136] In fact, it is because of him that this book became an important guide in Jesuit spirituality. Just as O'Malley rightly points out, "The privileged place that the *Imitation* enjoyed in the *Exercises* as the only work besides the New Testament and the life of Christ recommended for reading during their course very much inclined them to the book."[137]

Clearly, Thomas has much to offer Ignatius in his needs for Jesuit spirituality. For example, in the book, Thomas calls for such Christian characteristics as humility, obedience, self-surrendering, self-abnegation, and world-negation, which he believes can help an individual attain the deep interiority in which this individual will be able to cultivate love of Jesus.[138] For him, only those who submit to God, as "those to whom the Eternal Word speaks[,] are delivered from uncertainty."[139] As he advises his readers, they should "above all things and in all things rest always in the Lord" (120). To this end of giving oneself to God, he suggests a similar method of abnegation also seen in Jesuit spirituality. He urges his readers to give up the self and self-love altogether, just as is found in what Christ might have to say to humans: "I desire to have you wholly divested of self: otherwise, unless you are wholly stripped of self-will, how can you be Mine, or I yours? The sooner you do this, the better it will be with you, and the more completely and sincerely you do it, the better you will please Me, and the greater you will be your gain" (143). The individual's progress in the process of holiness, the amount of peace, tranquility, certainty, and freedom in his or her heart, and the size of his or her reward, all depend on to what extent the individual can detach him- or herself from the self and other worldly attachments. Obviously, as long as abnegation for interiorization of spirituality is considered, both Thomas and Ignatius would agree with each other, as both are Christian spiritual writers concerned with how a Christian can establish or reestablish a communion with God through various forms of meditation, prayer, and mental activity. At the same time, as Knowles has remarked, the two entertain fundamentally different, virtually opposite, attitudes toward action and human relation.

Owing equally to his monastic background and his association with the order of Devotio Moderna as well as his theological agenda, Thomas lays his emphasis on a life of isolation and retreat. He suggests that those devoted to Christian spirituality and Christ shun human association and even human language. In his view, human company, relationships, and even friendship, all pose certain dangers of bogging down the persons involved. "A wise man once said," he writes, "as often as I have been among men, I have returned home a lesser man" (50). Thomas also points out the positive effects of silence and solitude on an individual: "No one is worthy of heavenly comfort, unless they have diligently exercised themselves in holy contrition. If you desire heartfelt contrition, enter into your room, and shut out the clamor of the world, as it is written, 'Commune with your own heart, and in your chamber, and be still'" (51). At the beginning of book 2 of *The Imitation*, he urges his readers thus: "'The Kingdom of God is within you,' says Our Lord. Turn to the Lord with all your heart, forsake this sorry world, and your soul shall find rest. Learn to turn from worldly things, and give yourself to spiritual things, and you will see the Kingdom of God come within you" (67). In short, the fact that the book is commonly referred to as the *Contemptus mundi* in Spain indicates that Thomas sees the abandonment of the material world as the sine qua non of virtue for Christian spirituality.[140] Owing to his determination to shun the entire world, Thomas has been called the anti-intellectualist.

In comparison, the difference between Thomas's views and the Jesuit view regarding action and human relation is apparent. It is true that the Jesuits cultivate their own spirituality by turning away from terrestrial attachments. At the same time, they commit themselves to ministry, a commitment that sets them apart from Thomas and what Thomas advises his readers to do. Instead of keeping its members within the walls of a monastery for meditations on spirituality, the Society vows to follow the papal directive to send them to the remotest corners of the world for God. To make clear to the Jesuits that they must be prepared to go anywhere in the world, the *Constitutions* has the following:

> The intention of the fourth vow pertaining to the pope was not to designate a particular place but to have the members distributed throughout the various parts of the world. For those who first united to form the Society were from different provinces and realms and did not know into which regions they were to go, whether among the faithful or the unbelievers; and therefore, to avoid erring in the path of the Lord, they made that promise or vow in order that His Holiness might distribute them for greater glory to God. They did this in conformity with their intention

to travel throughout the world and, when they could not find the desired spiritual fruit in one region, to pass on to another and another, ever intent on seeking the greater glory of God our Lord and the greater aid of souls. (605 [p. 268])

Besides reiterating the Jesuit determination to go anywhere and work with any people, the passage declares peremptorily the ultimate goal of the Jesuit mission: seeking the greater glory of God through helping souls. That is, what animates the Jesuits to model their lives on Jesus and the apostle Paul is to serve God. Their work "to aid souls" by spreading the gospel is then a simple means to the end or *telos*—magnifying the glory of God and finding God in all things.

The goal of the Jesuits obviously determines the nature of the Jesuit mission. The Jesuit mission, like virtually all Christian missions, is fundamentally different from an ordinary journey by missing some essential features defining an ordinary journey. A journey may be, and often is, adventurous as well as educational for a traveler with "an innovative mind that explores new ways of looking at things or which opens up new horizons."[141] But a Christian mission, a Jesuit one in particular, offers, in theory if not in practice, nothing fundamentally new, no surprises, to the missionary in the sense that one knows already that those with whom one comes to work are unbelievers and infidels to be confronted and converted. In fact, to propagate and implement one's own or the church's doctrines to and among the people to be converted, the mission can be called rather narcissistic in nature, because the missionary has the sole agenda set up long before setting out.

Furthermore, a journey by definition represents an action confined within certain limits—a circle of the home, *oikos* or *domus*, already clearly identified by the traveler to be his or her fixed point of reference.[142] But a Jesuit mission, given the Society's formulae of "everything for the greater glory of God" and "finding God in all things," is taken to be limitless and boundless. To help reflect on a mission's specificities, one can quickly examine the early Christian ministry. In his discussion of Paul, John Ziesler insists that it is misleading to see Paul's work as consisting of "three missionary journeys." Paul, Ziesler explains, "did not set out on missionary expeditions and return periodically for home leave, and there is no evidence that he saw any particular place as his headquarters or his journeyings as having beginning and endings."[143] The Jesuits, like Paul, make it their policy that their missionaries should remain constantly on the move. For instance, those sent to China are not supposed to return to Europe but to do their ministry around that country for the rest of their lives.[144] In short, the missionaries are required to be mobile, not just because of their totalizing plan of converting everyone by finding God everywhere but also because of their understanding of the entire world to be already a giant house in which everyone and everything is from the beginning from God and must go back to God. The members are therefore instructed to see the missions, as described by Nadal, to be their "principal and most characteristic 'dwelling.'"[145] Here, the following passage from Nadal's second *Dialogue* describes well the Jesuit view concerning the mission:

> That is altogether the most ample place and reaches as far as the globe itself. For wherever they can be sent in ministry to bring help to souls, that is the most glorious and longed-for "house" for these theologians. For they know the goal set before them: to procure the salvation and perfection of *all* men and women. They understand that they are to that end bound by that Fourth Vow to the supreme pontiff: that they might go on these universal missions for the good of souls by his command, which by divine decree extends throughout the whole church. They realize that they cannot build or acquire enough houses to be able from nearby to run out to the combat. Since this is the case, they consider that they are in their most peaceful and pleasant house when they are constantly on the move, when they travel throughout the earth, when they have no place to call their own, when they are always in need, always in want—only let them strive in some small way to imitate Christ Jesus, who had nowhere on which to lay his head and who spent all his years of preaching in journey.[146]

For all its extravagance, the rhetoric of Nadal's passage, besides asserting again the Jesuit mobility and thus the "world-affirming" nature of the Jesuit spirituality,[147] reiterates both the Jesuit faith and worldview outlined in the order's motto and commandment: "everything for the greater glory of God" and "finding God in all things." Indeed, Nadal here is talking about the need for Jesuits to go out to the whole world. At the same time, he makes clear that the entire world, which the Jesuits can take to be their mission house, is a Christian house from the beginning, created and controlled by God. Though the house is rather disorderly for the moment, with many in the human race—as early modern explorations and expeditions have discovered—not yet aware of this fact, the Jesuits, following the examples of early missionaries, including Jesus himself, are on the move to enlighten the infidels about the Christian truth. To put it in other words, Jesuits are determined to accord a Christian welcome and hospitality, to invite and receive infidels into the home that these infidels already occupy.[148] Furthermore, it is when converting the infidels to Christianity that the missionaries find and confirm the God already in these estranged people and in their corner of the house. Once the Jesuit missionaries finish perfecting everyone on the surface of earth, that is, once everyone accepts the divine hospitality and invitation by returning to and reuniting with God for a new brotherhood and neighborhood, there will be no otherness—except the Wholly Otherness of God—in this world.

The Jesuits prepare themselves for their mission with burning dedication and unyielding determination. But their conviction that they can make the entire world a single and closed house of Christianity, which will contain everyone stripped of any otherness, seems to base itself on the same belief that the Jesuit self and self-will can disappear through spiritual exercises. As has been argued, the Jesuits' work on their own spirituality simply proves the irreducibility of the self and self-will—both human otherness and defiance to God. Examining what happens in the mission, one sees that the Jesuits are likewise unsuccessful in their attempt to assimilate people of different cultural beliefs by removing their otherness and replacing it with a divine union.

To see what impedes the Jesuit project of totality, that of "finding God in all things" and of "everything for the greater glory of God," one must bear in mind that the Jesuit home at the time was in a post-Reformation Europe, which was rapidly, immensely, and irreversibly diversified with people upholding new and different—in fact, defiant—views of Christianity. What further complicated and intensified such uncertainty on the European continent was an outside world with new peoples, cultures, and faiths discovered through maritime explorations and expeditions.[149] Expressing their loyalty to the pope and following the spirit of the Catholic Church, the Jesuits hoped to help turn the tide of religion, ideology, and history with their proselytical missions. It was exactly against this historical, cross-cultural, and interreligious background that the Jesuits became convinced of the necessity of their mission.

However, to go out into a new world, one that was strange and had people with different cultures, politics, religions, and so on, took more than just religious fervor and dedication. It is true that, like their self-emptying *kenosis*, the Jesuits planned to erase through their mission all otherness of all people so that the entire world could become a unified one under God. But during their mission the missionaries found it necessary and even compulsory to open themselves up from time to time to these strange people and customs. This fact, of course, contradicted Jesuit theology, spirituality, and missiology, all of which, as has been argued so far, dictate that the members open and relate only to God. In other words, it is in the mission that Jesuit responsibility to God became apparently incoherent. Though Jesuit responsibility aimed at assimilating the otherness of the other people, infidels and unbelievers included, for an extended Christian community with a new and all-encompassing brotherhood, or neighborhood, the irreducibility and undecidability of differences to be encountered often turned the Jesuit mission into an experience of the impossible. Just as their self could not be emptied thoroughly or removed completely through their spiritual exercises, the Jesuits found that they were often compelled to open up to, or accommodate, the infidels or unbelievers and their otherness. They often had to deviate from their responsibility to God by bearing certain responsibilities to the infidels.

A discussion of how Jesuit accommodation ruptured the missionary responsibility to God begins with Ignatius's writings. In September 1541, Ignatius wrote in a letter what is called his "Further Instruction to the Same Legates," in which he shared some of his tactics in dealing with people to be won for the church:

> In conversing with those in authority and superiors, and to win their countenance for the greater service of God our lord, consider first of what temperament they are, and conform yourselves to it; for example, if one be passionate and speak quickly with life, adopt to some extent his manner in ways that may be good and reverent, and do not show yourselves to be grave, phlegmatic, or melancholic. With those who by nature are retiring, slow in speaking, grave and mature in their conversation, assume their manner with them, for that is what suits them best: *omnia omnibus factus sum*.[150]

In quoting the Pauline phrase *omnia omnibus factus sum* ("I have become all things to all people") from 1 Corinthians,[151] Ignatius meant to tell the Jesuits on missions that they should, following the example of Paul, convert the infidels through accommodation.

Indeed, Christian accommodation goes back before Paul, one of the first apostles, to God at the very beginning. In his interpretation of a fragment in Deuteronomy 1:31, Origen advances his understanding of God's accommodation to humans: "He was accommodated and condescended to us, identifying himself with our weakness, like a teacher babbling with the children, like a father fostering his own children, putting on their ways and leading them in a manner suitable to their smallness to the more perfect and higher things."[152] Whoever the innovator is, accommodation has the clear purpose of converting or, as Origen indicates, "perfecting" the masses. Here, one can also quote Clement of Alexandria on Paul's accommodation: "Not only is it reasonable to become a Jew for the sake of Hebrews and those under the law (acceding to the apostle), but also for the sake of the Greeks to become a Greek, so that we might *gain all*."[153] To "gain all" for God was exactly what Ignatius and the Jesuits had in mind for their mission. Whether they took the Pauline accommodation to be their model, or they chose to follow directly the example of God, the Jesuits accommodated, or condescended in their mission, for the purpose of winning all infidels or unbelievers for the church.

To be sure, from the Jesuit perspective, adopting accommodation to be their missionary policy was meant to ensure the success of their mission. From a different perspective, their decision to accommodate can also be seen as an obligation, imposed on them by the unbelievers to be converted, to prepare the Jesuits' Christian self before the alien other. The decision was dictated to the Jesuits by the reality of countless doctrinal or religious incongruities found during the mission and the considerable cultural otherness that they encountered. In the remaining part of the chapter, the discussion will outline what took place from a deconstructive perspective when missionaries accommodated infidels or their otherness.

It is true that accommodation, by the Jesuits' design, aimed at disseminating Christianity in a humane, sensitive, and thus acceptable fashion to the unbelievers. But in missions, accommodation to indigenous peoples and cultures often appeared to be a tactic, forced upon the missionaries, that acknowledged the other. In the China mission, the Jesuit accommodation was certainly the missionaries' recognition and acknowledgment of the advent or incoming of the Chinese other, an advent that should be discussed by following Derrida's discussion of *l'invention d'autre*, or the "invention of the other."[154] Drawing lessons from their unfruitful and thus disappointing mission in Japan, because of the missionaries' lack of knowledge of Japanese culture and religion, the Jesuit missionaries to China identified accommodation to be their missionary policy from the beginning. Alessandro Valignano (1539–1606), once the Visitor of the Indies known to the Chinese as Fan

Li'an (范禮安), "insisted in the first place on knowledge of the Chinese language."[155] As time went on, the Jesuits' accommodating measures grew into virtual full-fledged sanitization, including dressing in Confucian robes, befriending Chinese officials, studying the classics, rewriting catechism with increased references to Confucian classics, and so forth.[156] All these measures taken by the Jesuits were certainly part of the missionary effort to implement the teaching of Ignatius or Paul or Jesus to "become all things to all people." In short, in answer to their calling *omnia omnibus*, the early Jesuit missionaries to China felt that they had, as one of them claimed, "become Chinese to win China for Christ."[157]

Aiming to help christen the Chinese, the Jesuit work to become Chinese—the missionary accommodation to the Chinese culture—proved to be a task both endless and disruptive. It was endless and disruptive because, for the Jesuits, as Willard J. Peterson has pointed out, "learning to speak Chinese led to reading, which led to writing. Writing Chinese entailed using Chinese vocabulary to express non-Chinese concepts, and losing important distinctions in the translation."[158] Indeed, in the midst of accommodating to the Chinese and adapting to the Chinese culture for the sake of God, the early Jesuits exercised more than doctrinal laxity. Their accommodation appeared to be distorting, reducing, and even hereticating some crucial issues of Christian theology. For example, their attempt to avoid offending the patriarchal Chinese society led them to postpone the introduction of the Trinity in their writings on Christian teachings and theology for Chinese readers. Further, their use of ready phrases in Chinese for the translation of the term and concept of *Deus*, or God, later became one of the main reasons for the pope to disband the Society in 1773 for heresy. Indeed, some missionaries even opened themselves up to and tolerated the official—arguably religious—rituals routinely performed by the Confucians.[159]

Here, to understand the problem posed to Catholic theology through Jesuit accommodation, one must take the endless need for the Jesuits to accommodate to be an important cause for the continual disruption to the Jesuit self and evangelization in China. To offer a quick argument for this point, one can say that the Jesuit becoming "all things to all," rather than helping to put an end to China's otherness, confirmed and perpetuated this otherness—that is, China's difference from the West and Christianity. The Jesuit attempt to become Chinese, in fact their overall accommodation, put the missionaries on constant alert, forever anticipating and waiting for the coming of the Chinese other in the same fashion as they waited for God the wholly other. To be sure, the Jesuits took their mission, including their accommodation, to be their turn to invent or find,[160] instead of difference or otherness, the Same, as commanded by the formula "finding God in all things." This Jesuit effort and desire to invent or find God in all things can certainly be called the Christian politics of invention, or what Derrida has called "the invention of the Same."[161] Following the Jesuit expectation, what comes through such invention or finding, as in Ignatian "finding God in all things," should be nothing other than the revelation of God the Same. Indeed, unlike *creatio ex nihilo*, invention or finding only meant to find or unveil what is already there so as to prove and establish a Christian "order of totality," pregiven and predetermined by God. To paraphrase Derrida's point, one can say that, for the missionaries, the others in the world were innate and integral parts of God's creation. Those others might be people, religions, or civilizations, and they might also be, at least in that moment, the alienated and defiant. But to the missionaries, they were also waiting to be invented and returned to the Christian order.[162] The problem was that what actually happened during the mission never seemed to be as neat and tidy as expected and planned by the missionaries. The Jesuits in China were often in situations where either the Chinese other proved to lie outside the God-given totality or, instead of converting the other, the missionaries' own self was invented or reshaped through accommodation by the otherness of China. Specifically, the following are some of the things that upset the Christian cultural and religious totality that the Jesuits hoped to establish.

As the Jesuits learned more about Chinese culture and religions, countless and unanticipated differences of culture and religion were invented. One example is the identification of Confucianism as a true religion, though not the same as—and certainly not part of—the definitely true religion of Christianity. This rose up to surprise and disturb the monovalent and monotheistic faith of the missionaries.[163] The invention of Confucianism with its legitimate standing as a true religion, while at the same time seen as an other still beyond appropriation and outside the all-encompassing Christian religion, poked holes in the universal order of the Same, in which all are taken to be determined and created by the divine. No matter what accommodation and acculturation the missionaries applied, Confucianism as other, as wholly other to be exact, remained structurally and ritually out of place as far as Christian theology is concerned. The fact that it was beyond control and impossible pointed to the incompleteness or inadequacy of the order under God.

If, like many other Chinese cultural and religious phenomena, Confucianism rose, once invented by the missionaries, as the wholly other to pose questions to the coherence and plausibility of Christian doctrines, the Jesuit accommodation to "become Chinese" or, specifically, to become Confucians by wearing scholarly gowns, reading the classics, and so forth, can be seen as an act attending this wholly otherness. When the Chinese otherness represented by Confucianism breached the totality of Christianity, the Jesuit self seemed to yield. Incapable of forming or expanding a Christian enclosure to include China, the Jesuit *omnia omnibus*—the missionary response to the otherness of China—put them into a tedious and daunting, not to mention perpetual, process of becoming all others to all others, or becoming every Chinese to every Chinese. Such Jesuit dedication to the other—transforming and sacrificing the self for the other—has been seen only in their spirituality or their striving for divine union. It is, therefore, not an exaggeration to say that the incessant turns the Jesuits took and the unceasing effort they made for the other of China only meant that they regarded the Chinese other as the wholly other. Following Ignatius's formula "finding God in all things," the missionaries arrived in China with the hope of inventing God the wholly other there. Instead, they found China the wholly other for the simple reason that "the other is not the possible."[164] When the other to be invented must be the impossible, "the only possible invention," according to Derrida, "is the invention of the impossible. . . . An invention has to declare itself to be the invention of that which did not appear to be possible; otherwise it only makes explicit a program of possibilities within the economy of the same."[165]

To conclude, it has become clear that if, in the Jesuit spirituality discussed earlier, we have seen how the members seek the impossible God, the wholly other, then the Christian *omnia omnibus* or accommodation exercised in China can be taken as the missionaries' unintended declaration of China to be the impossible and wholly otherness found in the mission.

With this much said, the discussion now turns to more examples of the Jesuit-China relations and interactions.

2

Other Rhetoric

Reading Matteo Ricci's *On Friendship*

Est enim amicitia nihil aliud nisi omnium divinarum humanarumque rerum cum benevolentia et caritate consensio, qua quidem haud scio an excepta sapientia nil quicquam melius homini sit a dis immortalibus datum. (For friendship is nothing else than an accord in all things, human and divine, conjoined with mutual goodwill and affection, and I am inclined to think that, with the exception of wisdom, no better thing has been given to man by the immortal gods.)

—Cicero, *De amicitia*

Affirmed, negated or neutralized, these "communitarian" or communal values always risk bringing a brother back [to haunt us]. Perhaps this risk must be assumed in order to keep the question of the "who" from being politically deframed by the schema of being-common or being-in-common even when it is neutralized, in a question of identity (individual, subjective, ethnic, national, state, etc.).

—Jacques Derrida, *Politics of Friendship*

This chapter continues to tackle the irreducibility of otherness challenging the Jesuit idea of union or friendship but with the friendship—its concept as well as its practice—placed in a cross-cultural context where the Jesuits encountered late Ming China. The discussion will take as its focal point Matteo Ricci's *On Friendship*, which was, as has been mentioned, a work written in classical Chinese to introduce to the Chinese the Western concept of friendship. Through a close reading of the ideologies elaborated upon and the rhetoric employed in this work, this chapter will examine this writing by Ricci and his mission from their intercultural and interreligious (i.e., social and historical) setting. The discussion will question further the Jesuit understanding and interpretation of friendship that, as part of the Christian theology of human-God relation, aimed at not only erasing differences between friends but also assimilating China according to what can be called the Western metaphysics of identity and the Christian nostalgia for a restored alliance between God and humans. My discussion will treat friendship as a concept concerning alterity in a Derridean fashion. Examining closely examples from *On Friendship*, it will argue that the other is the absolute condition of possibility under which friendship happens.

Friendship as a sophisticated question concerning the self and other has recently received repeated theological, scholarly, and philosophical treatment, among which one sustained effort to rethink the traditional view of friendship has been made by Derrida. Discussing the concept of friendship in a series of his works,[1] Derrida points out that the importance of friendship comes from its relevance to issues crucial not only to contemporary politics and life, but also to the understanding of philosophy, culture, and religion in human history. Through his reading of authors such as Plato, Aristotle, Cicero, Montaigne, Nietzsche, Carl Schmitt, Maurice Blanchot, and others, Derrida argues that language pushes friendship into an ongoing process where friendship remains open—at once as a commitment from the past and a promise for the future—to difference or the Other.

To show how the traditional concept of friendship prefers the Same to the Other, one can take the example of Cicero. One of the first authors discussed in Derrida's *Politics of Friendship*, Cicero declares from the beginning of his *De amicitia* or *On Friendship* that he is "not now speaking of the ordinary and commonplace friendship [*de vulgari aut de mediocri*]—delightful and profitable as it is—but of that pure and faultless kind [*sed de vera et perfacta loquor*], such as was that of the few whose friendships are known to fame [*qualis eonum, qui pauci nominantur, fuit*]" (6.22).[2] From the phrase *pauci nomnantur* and how Cicero speaks of the kind of friendship possessed by "the few," Derrida sees an expressed narcissism and nostalgia for a model of true and perfect friendship.[3] Indeed, Cicero adds almost immediately that "he who looks upon a true friend, looks, as it were, upon a sort of image of himself [*verum . . . amicum qui intuetur, tamquam exemplar aliquod intuetur sui*]" (7.23). Here, because the Ciceronian friendship takes on the value of exemplary heritage, which equals "[a] narcissistic projection of the ideal image, of its own ideal image (*exemplar*), [which] already inscribes the legend,"[4] Derrida asserts that, of the choice to treat the friend as the same or as the other, "Cicero prefers the same."[5] Cicero's word *exemplar*, Derrida points out, "means portrait but also, as the *exemplum*, the duplicate, the reproduction, the copy as well as the original, the type, the model."[6] He goes on to argue that, to Cicero, "his *exemplar* is projected or recognized in the true friend, it is his ideal double, his other self, the same as self but improved."[7]

To ensure that friends are the same or duplicates, the traditional concept of friendship often imposes on the involved individuals a set of political ideologies that underwrites the relation. As Derrida observes, "As one knows, from Plato to Montaigne, from Aristotle to Kant, from Cicero to Hegel, the *great philosophical and canonical discourses* on friendship . . . will have linked friendship explicitly to virtue and to justice, to moral reason and to political reason. These discourses will have even set the moral and political conditions for an authentic friendship—and vice-versa."[8] He analyzes how political ideologies serve to determine friendship and friends:

> The concept of politics rarely announced itself without some sort of adherence of the State to the family, without what we will call a *schematic* of filiation: stock, genus or species, sex (*Geschlecht*), blood, birth, nature, nation—autochthonal or not, tellurian or not. This is once again the abyssal question of the *phúsis*, the question of being, the question of what appears in birth, in opening up, in nurturing or growing, in producing by being produced.[9]

For Derrida, "the figure of the friend, so regularly coming back on stage with the features of the *brother* . . . seems spontaneously to belong to a *familial, fraternalist* and thus *androcentric* configuration of politics."[10] He finds such politicization, which is at the same time naturalization, of friendship to be problematic. "Why would the friend be *like* a brother?" he asks.[11] In his work, he mounts persistent resistance to the attempt at naturalization in traditional friendship, because such naturalization, or what he calls "the natural bond between *nómos* and *phúsis*,"[12] tends to appropriate the other in the relationship. More details from Derrida's deconstructive reading of friendship will be referenced and applied in this chapter's discussion. For the moment it is significant to mention another important aspect of the naturalizing tendency in the traditional discourse of friendship—the application of the concept of friendship in interracial, interreligious, cross-cultural relations.

At least since ancient Greece, the traditional concept of friendship, assumed to represent, or identify with, brotherhood, has been applied in relationships between races, religions, cultures, and nations. For the Greeks, to give an example, there is a distinction between *polémios* or public or political enemy and *ekhthrós* or private or personal enemy.[13] Following such a distinction or dichotomy, Plato in his *Republic* (470), as Derrida notes following the discussion of Carl Schmitt, "opposes war strictly speaking (*pólemos*) to civil war, to rebellion or to uprising (*stásis*)."[14] It is exactly this opposition that has led to Schmitt's understanding of the Platonic idea of friend and enemy: "Real war for Plato is a war between Hellenes and Barbarians only (those who are 'by nature enemies'), whereas conflicts among Hellenes are for him discords. . . . The thought expressed here is that a people cannot wage war against itself and a civil war is only a self-laceration and it does not signify that perhaps a new state or even a new people is being created."[15]

Derrida does not see the Platonic dichotomy in the *Republic* to be as rigid and uncompromising as Schmitt takes it.[16] But he shares in the main Schmitt's interpretation that for Plato and his fellow Greeks the distinction between a friend and enemy was based on blood, birth, and nationality. Derrida identifies as follows the basis for the Platonic thinking of friend and enemy developed in book 5 of the *Republic*:

> The Greek *génos* (lineage, race, family, people, etc.) is united by kinship and by the original community (*oikeion kai suggenés*). On these two counts it is foreign to the barbarian *génos* (*tô de barbarikô othneión te kai allótrion*) (470c). As in every racism, every ethnocentrism—more precisely, in every one of the nationalisms throughout history—a *discourse* on birth and on nature, a *phúsis* of genealogy (more precisely a discourse and a phantasm on the genealogical *phúsis*) regulates, in the final analysis, the movement of each opposition: repulsion and attraction, disagreement and accord, war and peace, hatred and friendship. From within and without. This *phúsis* comprises everything—language, law, politics, etc. Although it defines the alterity of the foreigner or the barbarian, it has no other. "We shall then say that Greeks fight and wage war with barbarians, and barbarians with Greeks, and are enemies *by nature* (*polemíous phúsei einai*) and that war is the fit name for this enmity and hatred (*kai pólemon tēn ékhthran taútēn klētéon*)."[17]

What can be said in general here is that, owing to its political and ideological implications, friendship, rather than a simple concept concerning interpersonal relationships, functions as a metaphor or a subtext reflecting political values and religious beliefs as well as ideological implications of a culture. As a model for the relation between any two subjects, friendship not only represents a highly valued relationship within a culture but also—as manifested by the example of Plato and the Greeks—reflects the ideology and attitude of that culture in dealing with other cultures.[18]

With little surprise, the lapse of over twenty centuries between ancient Greece and the contemporary world has not dimmed the charm of the *pólemos*-versus-*stásis* opposition. Some still find themselves much attracted to as well as convinced by the idea that friendly and adversarial civilizations are determined and predetermined by more or less the same method employed in Plato's time. In *Clash of Civilizations and the Remaking of World Order* by Samuel Huntington, for instance, one sees similar Platonic thinking. Claiming to be interpreting "the evolution of global politics after the Cold War," or picturing such politics that have in the post–Cold War world "become multipolar *and* multicivilizational,"[19] Huntington nevertheless resorts to the convenient model of dichotomy from the ancient Greeks to theorize his new world order. He quotes the following words from Herodotus's *The Persian Wars* as his ancient exemplar for the friendship or enmity between civilizations:

> For there are many and powerful considerations that forbid us to do so, even if we were inclined. First and chief, the images and dwellings of the gods, burnt and laid ruins: this we must needs avenge to the utmost of our power, rather than make terms with the man who has perpetrated such deeds. Secondly, the Grecian race being of the same blood and the same language, and the temples of the gods and sacrifices in common; and our similar customs; for the Athenians to become betrayers of these would not be well.[20]

"Blood, language, religion, way of life," Huntington's comment on the passage reads, "were what the Greeks had in common and what distinguished them from the Persians and other non-Greeks." For the unification and division of civilizations of the present time, he goes on to assert, "the most important [element] usually is religion."[21] This is so because, in his words, "people of the same race can be deeply divided by civilization; people of different races may be united by civilization. In particular, the great missionary religions, Christianity and Islam, encompass societies from a variety of races. The crucial distinctions among human groups concern their values, beliefs, institutions, and social structures, not their physical size, head shapes, and skin colors."[22] Despite his emphasis on religion's importance in defining and identifying the self and other, Huntington's definition of civilization does not seem to differentiate much from the ancients. Besides religion, he would still take race and blood, both of which the Greeks have called the *oikeios* or familiar,[23] to be important factors in the distinction of civilizations. That is why he calls for Western people in "accepting their civilization as unique not universal and uniting to renew and preserve it against challenges from non-Western societies."[24]

Needless to say, Huntington's theory of radical inclusion and exclusion represents only one among the current theories on international relations. An equally famous—though less popular—and seemingly vastly different argument comes from Francis Fukuyama. Fukuyama's theory appears to be the exact opposite of that of Huntington because, while Huntington argues that democracy is a unique and distinctive value of the West but not a general one of every society, Fukuyama holds that democracy will eventually win the entire world. Basing his optimism on the fact that more and more powerful Muslims are attracted to liberalism,[25] Fukuyama regards democratization to be the teleology of human history. From his reading of Kant, Hegel, and Nietzsche, he forms his vision of "a meaningful pattern in the overall development of human societies generally."[26] Specifically, the political changes taking place in Eastern European countries in the late 1980s to put an end to the Cold War fostered in him much hope for a fundamentally Hegelian and holistic view of world history whose *oikeios* or familiar means that the population of the world in its entirety is moving down the same road of liberalism towards the same end of democracy.[27] To be sure, many, including Huntington, find laughable such a naively optimistic view of the world.[28] But given the *oikeios* that has its equivalents in liberalism, democracy, and other political arenas, and that is expected to unite all at the end, Fukuyama's theory does not differ in any fundamental fashion from those of Huntington and some other scholars. Quite the contrary, he likewise shares the belief that there is a model or exemplar regulating and uniting the relations between nations and peoples. His exemplar, rather than that of blood and brotherhood, happens to be such political ideologies as democracy and liberalism. In short, whether it is the exclusionism of Huntington or the endism of Fukuyama, these theorists have founded their arguments on what Derrida would call homogeneity or, simply, "homophilia."[29]

Here, one should quickly clarify the difference between Derrida and the traditional authors on friendship and contemporary theorists on international relations. Following in part Blanchot and Levinas, who treat friendship as a "relation without relation," a theory already mentioned in the last chapter, Derrida argues for "a friendship without hearth, of a *philia* without *oikeiótēs*. Ultimately a friendship without presence, without resemblance, without affinity, without analogy."[30] For him, the friend is to be thought of not as the same but as the *other*, not the other to be subsumed under the name of the Same or that of God, but the other as an irreducible singularity that both sustains a friendly relation and keeps it open. He puts it thus:

> The other appears *as such*—this is to say, the other appears as a being whose appearance appears without appearing, without being submitted to the phenomenological law of the originary and intuitive given that governs all other appearances, all other phenomenality *as such*. The altogether other, and *every other (one) is every (bit) other* [*tout autre est tout autre*], come here to upset the order of phenomenology.[31]

Without the familiar or *oikeios*, a friend as the wholly other upsets the order of phenomenology with its singularity in the sense that this singularity remains unknown and is thus impossible to reduce or subdue. As summarized by Caputo, this other—one's friend—arrives "in a night of un-knowing, to be described in the deeply unphenomenological discourse of appearing *without appearing*."[32] Derrida argues that this dissymmetry or unbalance resulting from this unknown otherness means that a friendly relation can hardly be a fusion established on a homophilic foundation as seen in the traditional discourse of friendship.

Judged against the authors of friendship discussed so far, Ricci with his *On Friendship*, a homophilic discourse in its own way, would fit well in the category of those with a traditional concept of friendship, including contemporary theories on international relations. A Jesuit priest and missionary, Ricci was in China to convert the Chinese using the one and only model and exemplar of the Christian love of God.[33] This love of God or *amor dei*—a double genitive signifying both the love from God to humans and, at the same time, humans' love for and of God (in short, both *agapē* and *caritas*)—is true to the very core of Christianity. Ricci hoped to instill in the Chinese, on the one hand, the knowledge of and gratitude for God's love of humans and, on the other, the fundamental Christian virtue, *caritas*, that would in turn motivate the Chinese to love God by loving all people, including, in particular, the missionaries.

To situate and examine Ricci's *On Friendship* in its historical context, the discussion that follows is twofold. First, it will expose the fashion in which *On Friendship* elaborated the Western and Christian concept of friendship in order to effectuate a parallel or analogy between China and the West. This chapter will contend that the Western and Christian logocentric view of friends and friendship, as presented in Ricci's text, not only constituted in general the author's understanding of friendship but also represented in particular his attempt to assimilate the Chinese. Second, it will be argued that, despite Ricci's best efforts, *On Friendship* demonstrates through its own rhetoric that the difference between friends could not be eliminated. The difference remained for the simple reason that Ricci's language and his very act of talking to his Chinese friends affirmed that the difference of the Other—the disparity between China and the West—was, and still is, irreducible.

Written in 1595, Ricci's *On Friendship* was a collection and translation of one hundred aphorisms about friends and friendship by famous Western thinkers, philosophers, and figures, like Plato, Aristotle, Alexander the Great, Ovid, Cicero, Plutarch, Martial, Seneca, Quintilian, Saint Augustine, and so on.[34] In the preface, Ricci first introduced himself and stated his interest in and admiration for Chinese culture and civilization: "I, [Ma]dou [Matteo], navigated to the Middle Kingdom by sea from the Far West because of my reverence for the good government of the Son of Heaven of the Great Ming Dynasty and the teachings of ancient Chinese rulers."[35] Later in the preface, Ricci also said that *On Friendship* was written at the request of a Chinese prince to introduce to the Chinese the Western concept of friendship. According to Ricci, he visited the prince in the city of Nanchang (南昌), Jiangxi (江西) Province:

> It was my good fortune that the Prince, instead of disdaining me, received me with the appropriate guest ritual, permitting me to greet him with a deep bow. He offered rice wine, over which we chatted happily. In the midst of our conversation, the Prince left his seat and came to me. Holding my hands, he said to me: "I never fail to befriend, and show my hospitality to, gentlemen of virtue and merits whenever they honor my fief with their

visits. Since the West is a place of righteousness and morality, I would like to know how people there think of friendship." On my return, I wrote down what I had learned in the past and my writing forms the volume of *On Friendship* that follows.[36]

Ricci's remarks make it clear that *On Friendship* served as a response to a friend as well as a return for the hospitality of this friend. This act of response and that of reciprocity are exercised to present the Self to the Other. And this presentation, responding or pointing to the prince representing the Other and the Otherness of another culture, indicates Ricci's awareness of the difference between himself and the Chinese.

As soon as the text of *On Friendship* begins, however, Ricci displays a different attitude toward the other. To show this difference in attitude toward friends, the first aphorism that opens *On Friendship* provides a good example. Taken from Saint Augustine's *Confessions* 4.6, it reads: "My friend is no other but half of my very self. That is, a friend is the second me. One should therefore regard a friend as oneself."[37] A friend is "no other" but a "second me"? Different from the awareness of the friend as other than the self just displayed in the preface, these words of identifying one's friend as being part of the self sound like a retreat from the recognition of the otherness of a friend. To be sure, in the context from which this statement is taken, Augustine, who adopted Aristotle's apt definition of friends as "one soul in bodies twain,"[38] was talking about his memory of a dead friend. But by reducing this friend to a "no other" or "second me," Augustine seems to be expressing a certain twinship that is by nature congeneric or consanguineous. One sees from the metaphor of comparing one's friend to a second self a desire to reconcile oppositions and differences through a movement of thought that would finally reduce them to aspects of a single, comprehensive vision.[39]

Limited by the aphoristic format of *On Friendship* and for other reasons to be discussed soon, Ricci did not elaborate on Augustine's idea of friendship and love in spite of the fact that what Augustine had to say would suit well Ricci's purpose in China.[40] It should be pointed out that *On Friendship* does not present Christianity as its most dominant and manifest theme, though Christian understanding of love and friendship is certainly embedded in the book. However, judging by its overall content and given what Ricci said in his preface, it seems that throughout *On Friendship* he was eager to formulate without much diversion a more classical exemplum of friendship for his readers to follow. That is, he was writing to present a moral imperative that he hoped would motivate his readers to befriend each other. It might be owing to this intention on Ricci's part that the scriptural commands of friendship and love do not have centrality in the formulation of the moral imperative. Instead, the book for the most part reads like an ardent hope expressed by the author for humanity or for friendly relationships between humans regulated by some golden standards of ethics from the past. To be sure, given the fact that Ricci actually composed this treatise during his second stay in Nanchang after he was forced to leave the city of Nanjing (南京),[41] it would not be difficult to discern that Ricci through this book also hoped for and proposed friendly relations between the Chinese and visitors from the West. While it is understandable that Ricci, in order to stay in China, wanted to have a friendly relationship with the Chinese, he expected friendship, it must be emphasized, also because of his mission.

As has been mentioned, Ricci's mission to China was to naturalize Christianity among the Chinese. To convince the Chinese of the omnipotence of his God, first Ricci himself had to win their trust and establish a good enough relationship with the Chinese. But the trust from the Chinese was difficult to earn. The sense of Chinese cultural ethnocentrism in the Ming dynasty was particularly heightened, with all its scorn of people and things from the outside. Besides continuing to uphold the inherited prejudice that barbarians, by definition, were those who did not participate in Chinese culture, the Ming empire launched several maritime expeditions with armed soldiers to "visit" some Southeast Asian countries to collect tributes. In Ricci's time, the typical and strong distrust of foreigners, who the Chinese thought could only disturb the Chinese order, was further intensified with the decline of the empire and the increased challenges from the outside world.[42] In this situation, Ricci found to his own dismay that, despite all his familiarity with Chinese culture, the task of conversion progressed slowly. Even after he had won the favor of the Ming court and that of Emperor Wanli, Ricci was still largely viewed, ironically, by the Chinese as an outsider who had submitted to the Middle Kingdom out of his admiration for Chinese civilization. To expose the Chinese tendency to subordinate the Other, it is worth giving the example of Li Zhi (李贽; 1526–1603), a prominent Chinese scholar and thinker of his time. After meeting Ricci in 1599 in Nanjing, Li Zhi, as he admitted in a letter to a friend, was much impressed by Ricci's familiarity with the Chinese classical tradition, his good command of Chinese language, and his behavior observing the Confucian mores.[43] Li's respect for Ricci, however, did not remove his sense of cultural superiority, because in the very same letter, Li confessed that it remained unclear to him why Ricci should have come all the way to China. As he put it, "Ricci would be all too foolish if he thought that he and Western culture might have something to offer China that it had not already possessed in Confucianism."[44]

Such suspicion, xenophobia, and disdain from the Chinese undoubtedly frustrated Ricci. He and his fellow Jesuits exerted great effort to get themselves accepted into Chinese society. For instance, in exchange for an official permission to stay in China, Michel Ruggieri and a fellow Jesuit offered "to become 'vassals' of the Chinese emperor."[45] In general, to quickly repeat this point, the Jesuits, following their accommodation policy, devoted themselves to studying the Chinese language, reading Confucian classics, and dressing up like Chinese scholars.[46] They even selected Chinese names for themselves. Of all the Jesuits in China, Ricci was certainly one of the first and the most dedicated in executing the Jesuit accommodation, including his promise and promotion of friendly relations with the Chinese. However, with all his and others' efforts, Ricci felt that there was always a wall between the Jesuits, as strangers, and real Chinese society. In a letter to a friend in Rome, Ricci expressed his bafflement:

> It remains hard for us to believe how such a huge kingdom with so many soldiers could live in continual fear of other states that are so much smaller, so that they fear some great disaster every year and spare no pains to protect themselves from their neighbors either with troops or with deceit and feigned friendship: the Chinese place absolutely no trust in any foreign country, and thus they allow no one at all to enter and reside here unless they undertake never again to return home, as is the case with us.[47]

Ricci's words tell of his frustration and also indicate clearly to the reader the reason and purpose for which he wrote *On Friendship*. Obviously he did not enjoy being treated as a person unworthy of trust. He wanted the wall to tumble down and to see the relationship between the Chinese and himself—Christianity and European civilization at large—to be naturalized. He wanted to use his writing on friendship to generate a true friendship—"the most perfect of their [friendships'] kind," for example, a unity with the Chinese under God. Such unity based on similarity would replace the difference that not only separated him and the Chinese but also kept the Chinese away from accepting his belief—the Christian faith in God that he wished to share with them.

How Ricci attempted to naturalize a unity between the Chinese and the West can be illustrated by another example from *On Friendship*, this time a quotation from Aristotle. Placed as the second saying in the book, Aristotle's maxim seems to be reiterating more or less the same idea of reducing difference: "A friend and I exist as two bodies. But within the two bodies, there is only one soul."[48] Translated back from the Chinese, Aristotle's statement appears somewhat verbose, different from its (also translated) version in English, "One soul in bodies twain."[49] But the meaning remains clear. Aristotle, like Saint Augustine, does not think that there is much room for difference between friends except for the fact that two friends were born as two different persons. Both Aristotle and Saint Augustine echo a basic idea in the Western concept of friendship: similarity fosters friendship. But Aristotle's phrase "one soul" implies much more than may first appear. It states that even if friends remain as separate persons, their thoughts, interests, and beliefs must be the same. They must have the same soul. This is to say, to Aristotle as well as to Ricci, friends must not only throw away disparities but also share a similar and moral principle. This moral principle governs the ideal form of friendship that determines and identifies all actual cases of friendship. As a matter of fact, this quotation from Aristotle, for long a seemingly infallible law of friendship, contains all the ideological implications concerning the nature of relations between friends in the traditional Western discourse of friendship. Since this quotation from Aristotle also served as one of the central theses suggesting the ultimate purpose in *On Friendship*, some details from Aristotle's theory of friendship must be examined.

In his *Nicomachean Ethics*, Aristotle defines three types of friendship. The first is the ideal friendship, in which friends "bear good will and good wishes for one another, not without recognition, for the sake of one of the objects discussed" (1156a3–5).[50] The other two types Aristotle designates as friendship for utility and pleasure. About them, Aristotle says:

> Those [friends] who love each other for their utility do not love each other for themselves but in virtue of some good which they get from each other. So too with those who love for the sake of pleasure; it is not for their character that men love ready-witted people, but because they find them pleasant. Therefore those who love for the sake of utility love for the sake of what is good for *themselves*, and those who love for the sake of pleasure do so for the sake of what is pleasant to *themselves*, and not in so far

as the other is the person loved but in so far as he is useful or pleasant. (1156a10–17)

In his works, Aristotle theorizes the relation between three kinds of friendship in the same way that he theorizes the relation between the concepts of essential Being and accidental being. Of these three kinds of friendship, Aristotle calls the first the "essential" or "primary," therefore ideal, friendship, whereas the second and third types of friendship he refers to as "accidental."[51] Aristotle states in the *Eudemian Ethics*:

There must, then, be three kinds of friendship, not all being so named for one thing or as species of one genus, nor yet having the same name quite by mere accident. For all three senses are related to one which is the primary. . . . The primary is that of which the definition is contained in the definition of all. (1236a16–18)[52]

The complexity of Aristotle's philosophy of friendship exceeds the scope of this discussion.[53] Here, two premises can be discerned from Aristotle's assertion. First, according to Aristotle, as the highest and most real form of human relations, the first type of friendship represents a pure, ideal, and naturalized relation between friends. In comparison, the second and third types of friendship, egoistic and utilitarian by nature, are only bad and accidental relations. Second, emerging from the above hierarchization of different types of friendship, the ideal type becomes the beginning, origin, and center of all relationships. It serves as the guiding code against which friendship can and should be judged and evaluated. These two Aristotelian formations concerning different forms of friendship, as I will argue, are what constitute Ricci's central argument and his naturalization of his relationship with the Chinese in *On Friendship*.

In this work, Ricci privileged the ideal friendship over other, supposedly lower, types of friendship. He cited widely to assert that ideal friendship was the only legitimate type of relationship friends should have. Ricci's presentation could be called a binary opposition. He opposed what was the ideal form of friendship to what was not. Following Ricci back and forth, the reader in turn sees quotations such as Diogenes's "To friends, one should remain the same no matter where or when one is"[54] standing in opposition to an anonymous saying stating, "The friends tested only during my good and fortunate days are not to be depended upon";[55] then he juxtaposes

Cicero's "If one is a true friend, he will love me for the friendship but not for anything else" with, also Cicero's, "He who befriends others for his own benefit but not for that of the others is a businessman"[56] and "It is trading at the marketplace if one gives a gift to his friend in the hope of some return."[57] Sometimes the sayings contain opposition within themselves. For instance, an anonymous saying states, "When vulgar friends get together, they have more diversion than joy. After parting, they have worries. Moral friends, when together, have more joy than diversion and they have no remorse after parting" (309).

The different forms of friendship discussed by Ricci may be the common understanding of friendship shared by many. The problem, however, is that Ricci's presentation of the ideal form of friendship expresses a totalizing desire, showing that ideal friendship should be pursued and practiced, whereas friendship for utility and pleasure should be denounced and disdained. By treating ideal friendship as the only worthy form of relationship, Ricci made ideal friendship an intolerant form of relation that rendered illegitimate other forms of friendship. In other words, Ricci took ideal friendship to be a totalizing metaphor suppressing the other two forms of friendship. According to him, for the sake of ideal friendship, lower forms of friendship should not be considered. With the sayings in *On Friendship* quoted above, he showed that lower forms of friendship such as useful and pleasurable friendships were irregularities that, by debasing human relations, disturb identity, system, order, and ideal.

Along with the subordination of the lower forms of friendship, there was another kind of appropriation—the appropriation of Ricci's Chinese friends—only this appropriation was not as declared, not an opposition between ideal and inferior forms of friendship. This appropriation was accomplished through the juxtaposition of similar ideas about friendship in China and the West; this juxtaposition was made possible because *On Friendship* was written in classical Chinese. All Western maxims of friendship presented were already translated words. With such Confucian ideas or concepts as "virtue" (德), "loyalty," and "a businessman-like friend" representing a Western discourse of friendship, the Western ideas and concepts, now retold in Chinese, assumed an appearance of China-West affinity. As a result, the cultural differences, the differences between the Self and the Other, tended to disappear. Ricci's presentation silently and powerfully served as a process in which logocentrism and its correlative ideology were naturalized and the Western idea of friends as "one soul in bodies twain" was extended to read "one soul in *cultures* twain."

In *On Friendship*, the reader easily sees Ricci's hope to prove that "one soul in cultures twain" actually works on a metaphysical level. He tried to show in an Aristotelian fashion that the first type of friendship, with its perfect form and nature, is an ideal or transcendental signifier that evaluates and identifies the nature of all actual cases of friendship; moral standards like "righteousness" and "virtue" serve as guidelines to define friendship and guard friends. To direct friends on how to subject their relationship to this higher principle, Ricci quoted, for example, "The duty of a friend is to do what is ordained by righteousness";[58] "It is only by the same virtue and the same resolution that friendship can be maintained";[59] "Everlasting virtue is an excellent enticement to everlasting friendship";[60] and "The friends who share more diversion than they do virtue in their relationship will not be friends for long."[61] According to Ricci, friendship is an intrinsically ethical phenomenon. But this phenomenon or relationship must both follow and illuminate an ideal structure of morality in general as well as serve as a test of adequacy for its theory. The phenomenon of ideal relationship is not that of friends desiring each other's well-being as the end in itself. Rather, it must meet a principle, a principle still higher up, the very idea of an ideal friendship. A shared vision between friends, the spark of friendship, means more than a suppression of difference or an emphasis on similarity. It is not enough to say that this similarity includes similar thought, interest, and will between friends. It must be said that this similarity is, as one can discern from *On Friendship*, a principle or an ideal higher than all forms as well as practices of any friendly relationship. In short, all good will between friends must constantly be measured against the omnipresent ideal called ideal friendship. Not guided by this ideal, friendship can never be realized or practiced in its ideal manner. Without this ideal, no true friendship can come into being at all.

Indeed, Ricci's emphasis on the similarity of ideal governing friendship purports to make the idea of "one soul in cultures twain" an analogy and model of the relation between China and the West. But going through the aphorisms in *On Friendship*, the reader sees that the "soul" itself may pose a problem. Before there can be a "one-soul" for two cultures, the reader realizes that, like friends who always exist in more bodies than one, there appear to be more souls, not just a single one, in the sense that there are different ideals or guidelines defining different types or understandings of friendship. What makes the matter complicated and more inconvenient is that, even in the West alone, more souls or ideals exist as definitions and ends of friendship. On the one hand is the Christian friendship defined by faith in the union with God discussed in the previous chapter, and on the other is the classical friendship based on and guided by the Aristotelian ideal of friendship discussed above. The reader finds that both "souls" are present in *On Friendship* and their copresence leads to uncertainty, deviation, and even doubleness in Ricci's text, as well as Ricci's very self as a missionary. The following explains why.

Both to affirm and to unite the defining "souls" of friendship manifest in *On Friendship*, Ricci brought into his discussion the name and concept of God. Citing Cicero, he states the following: "An individual is unable to do everything to perfection, therefore the Lord-on-High or God decreed that people should make friends in order to help each other. If this world is deprived of friendship, mankind will undoubtedly fall into the abyss."[62] As if he found it inadequate just to tell his Chinese reader that forming friendly relations between humans was a command from a supernatural being called God, Ricci went on to add more weight to his argument. A little later in his book, God is mentioned again: "Lord-on-High or God gave man two eyes, two ears, two hands and two feet, meaning that only when two friends get one another's help can they succeed in their pursuit."[63] With this maxim, identified to be a combination of sayings from both Cassiodorus (c. 490–583) and Plutarch (c. 49–120),[64] Ricci simply naturalizes friendship by attributing the very being of friendship, not just its necessity and legitimacy, to the divine. His point here is that God created not only the human body but also predisposed genetically the form of human life particularly for human relationships. The simple syllogism he created through this maxim is obvious: because God made every human being by equipping each with two eyes, ears, hands, and feet, so it must also be the biological design by the holy that humans live in pairs of friends as well. It is certainly reasonable for Ricci to take friendship to be a very important and basic relation in human existence. Nonetheless, it is both striking and ironic that, in order to assert friendship as what he believed to be a most natural and fundamental relation of humans, he had to resort to a particularly unnatural method to make his point. He had to employ, by both inserting and combining, a particularly artificial and thus unnatural technique of grafting. To identify such grafts, those both intended and unintended by Ricci, one must look into the classical and textual backgrounds of the two maxims quoted here.

It is obvious that, when quoting the two maxims in *On Friendship*, one Ciceronian and the other a mixture of sayings by Cassiodorus and Plutarch, Ricci realized that none of them alone and as such would fit completely his proselytizing agenda. He therefore altered these authors' remarks so as to make them meet his need. To show what the two classical authors actually said and what Ricci did to their words, some comparisons are necessary. First, here is, as Pasquale M. d'Elia has identified,⁶⁵ Cicero's original statement in *Pro Sexto Roscio Amerino* that forms the basis of the concerned maxim in *On Friendship*: "Non enim possumus omnia per nos agere: alius in alia est re magis utilis. Idcirco amicitae comparantur ut commune commodum mutuis officiis gubernetue" (38). Rendered into modern English, the statement reads: "For we cannot do everything by ourselves; different people have different abilities. That is why friendships are formed—that the common interest may be furthered by mutual services."⁶⁶ As no deity is mentioned in Cicero's original, the name Shangdi (上帝) or Lord-on-High appearing in the maxim in *On Friendship* is Ricci's insertion and addition.

As regards the second of the two maxims from *On Friendship*, discussed here, the reader finds similar grafting and inserting. Indeed, Ricci found in Cassiodorus's *Variae epistolae* the words, "God has bestowed on man two hands, two ears, two eyes, that each one of these members should assist the other" (10.3).⁶⁷ It must be useful to Ricci that Cassiodorus, a Christian author and politician,⁶⁸ should look at humans' paired body parts like hands, ears, and eyes, from the perspective of creation. But Cassiodorus in this part of his work did not take a further step to use these facts of the human body to argue for the need for human relationships. So Ricci supplied the missing argument he needed by quoting these remarks from Plutarch's *On Brotherly Love* (*De fraterno amore*): "And yet the illustration of such common use of brothers Nature has placed at no great distance from us; on the contrary, in the body itself, she has contrived to make most of the necessary parts double and brothers and twins: hands, feet, eyes, ears, nostrils; and she has thus taught us that she has divided them in this fashion for mutual preservation and assistance, not for variance and strife" (477d).⁶⁹ It is true that Plutarch in some of his writings dealt with the topic of friendship. In this passage, however, he was not concerned with friendship or with any gods, including the Christian God. His point here is simple: just as she has given each person several body parts in pairs, nature or *natura*—φύσις (*physis*) in Plutarch's original Greek—has ordained that brothers love one another. Needless to say, Ricci chose to ignore the irrelevant thesis of Plutarch's passage. He simply put this passage together with that by Cassiodorus to form his own saying in *On Friendship* and to present his view of friendship as naturalistic because it was not just ordered by God but also altogether created by him.

Despite the fact that from the perspective of *caritas*, Christians would not sharply distinguish terms such as friends, brethren, and neighbors, some readers may still find Ricci's quoting of Cicero and Plutarch in such an unfaithful as well as utilitarian fashion a deviation from, and even a violation of, the very Aristotelian ideal of friendship of which Ricci has just sung praises. In fact, some may be tempted to accuse him of Machiavellianism, a moral problem often referred to as casuistry and probabilism in criticism of the Jesuit ministry and missiology.[70] But to demonstrate why friendship is not as natural a relation as Ricci presents it to be—and it is not even natural in *On Friendship*, because at least two different discourses are engrafted and combined into one—one must investigate his *On Frienship* further. More specifically, one must ask why and how Ricci altered the words and ideas of Cicero and Plutarch, which might reveal the significance and implication of him having to doctor some of these classical sources that he used to introduce the Western concept of friendship to his Chinese friends.

In the above examples, Ricci certainly made inaccurate and pragmatic quotations that he attributed to Cicero and Plutarch. But one must admit that Ricci had good reason for what he did, because he was not only trained but also instructed and expected to use Cicero, Plutarch, and other classical authors to serve his mission. To understand Ricci's responsibility, one needs only to reflect on the method and goal of Jesuit education.

As is known, soon after its founding, the Society of Jesus formed its educational plan and became "the first teaching order within the Catholic Church."[71] Historically speaking, Jesuit education, as one scholar points out, was "a response to the real needs of the Church to have its clergy trained in a systematic and efficacious way, which had not occurred before and was felt as an urgent desideratum because of the challenge presented by the Reformation."[72] To be specific, the Society held firmly the "conviction in the *reductio atrium ad Sacram Scripturam* (or *ad theologiam*, which was the same)."[73] Receiving influence from Renaissance humanism, which promoted *studia humanitatis*, including, grammar, rhetoric, poetry, and so forth, and inheriting the Thomistic reconciliation of Aristotle and the Bible, which affirmed Christian truth while recognizing the inadequacy and errors of philosophy,[74] the Society of Jesus became "committed to placing humanistic studies at the beginning of an extended education."[75] As a result, the Jesuits required in their colleges and universities that their members read human letters by authors such as Erasmus, Horace, Aesop, Aristophanes, Martial, Valla, Cicero, Livy, Homer, Isocrates, Plautus, and Lucian.[76]

Doubtlessly, Jesuit education, which taught members what were called *litteras humaniares* or *letras de humanidad*, as Ignatius put it in Spanish,[77] was not an education offered as "a kind of liberal education, that is for a literary education worthy of a gentleman," or as part of "the professional ideals, intellectual interests, and literary production of the humanists."[78] Taking the pagan authors and their works from the classical period to be "the spoils of Egypt"—an old metaphor from the Bible—the Jesuits never pretended that their education aimed at training the Society's members to be mere people of letters.[79] Instead, they had their own plan and goal for the use of the ancient literature of the pagans. As stated in the Jesuit *Constitutions*, "In the books of humane letters by pagan authors, nothing immoral should be lectured on, and what remains can be used by the Society like the spoils of Egypt" (359 [p. 189]). In other words, what the Society hoped to produce through its education were capable priests and missionaries, because, the same document makes clear, "the end of the learning which is acquired in the Society is with God's favor to help the souls of its own members and those of their fellow men" (351 [p. 187]). To make absolutely clear that their understanding of the relations between the subjects taught in their colleges—the *studia humanitatis*, natural sciences, and religion—was one of utilitarianism and hierarchy, the Jesuits put in the *Constitutions* the following remarks: "Since the end of the Society and of its studies is to aid our fellow men to the knowledge and love of God and to the salvation of their souls; and since the branch of theology is the means most suitable for this end, in the universities of the Society the principal emphasis ought to be put on it" (446 [p. 213]). In short, the Jesuits hoped to establish an educational system in their colleges that "entailed the pursuit of all the liberal arts, with a thorough grounding in Latin grammar and classical rhetoric, with scholastic dialectic as a logical link with the ultimate goal of a Christian humanism, that is, orthodox theology."[80]

Given "the comprehensive importance of theology within the Ignatian provisions for Jesuit universities,"[81] the two examples of Cicero and Plutarch mentioned earlier—Ricci's inaccurate quotations of the two authors in *On Friendship*—should become understandable. No matter how disagreeable and unreasonable many may find it to be, Ricci's Christianizing of Cicero and Plutarch through such Christian ideas as the name and concept of God is simply what he as a Jesuit priest was trained to do. He used the pagan authors and their works for the purpose of his own religion. It is therefore only natural and logical for him to insert and add the name and idea of God in what Cicero and Plutarch had to say, so that their words, made in utterly different cultural, literary, and religious contexts and for completely different purposes, would appear to be part of the Christian discourse. Here, the name of God imposed on the two authors provides a quick and telling example to show both Ricci's tactic of appropriation and how he took for granted that Cicero and Plutarch—the former having lived before the formation of Christendom, while the latter never mentioned Christianity in his works—should appear to be speaking of the greatness of Ricci's God.

In *On Friendship*, as has been mentioned, the Chinese term for God that Ricci used was Shangdi or Lord-on-High, which should be discussed here briefly. Though Lord-on-High in its original sense represented an indigenous deity in ancient China, Ricci nevertheless used it, as one scholar points out, to mean the Christian God.[82] Even Ricci himself made this clear. Within a 1601 edition of *On Friendship* that he sent back to Rome for record-keeping at the Jesuit archive, Ricci enclosed his own partial Italian translation of this work. In his translation, Ricci used the Italian word Iddio, God of the Christians, to render Lord-on-High in his respective quotations of Cicero and Plutarch.[83] Replacing the original term and idea "nature" in both Cicero's and Plutarch's writings with "Lord-on-High" and Iddio, Ricci had a clear message—that is, regardless of their different understandings of friendship and their diverse historical, cultural, and religious backgrounds, pagans like Cicero, Plutarch, and many others all wrote for the *grand récit* of Christian friendship.

Clearly, Ricci's appropriation—his Christian domestication—of Cicero and Plutarch shows that his "one soul in bodies twain" begins at "home"—in the continent of Europe. His use of God or Iddio to replace the term and idea of "nature" in the Ciceronian and Plutarchian originals shows his attempt to relocate not only the pagan authors but also the pagan understanding of friendship in what he believed to be a state and form most natural and familiar in Christian theology, that is, God's love and divine union. From a Christian perspective, it is a fact that God governs all aspects of human life, and that friendly relation, first of all, solves problems like the orgiastic cults and false gods believed in by Cicero, Plutarch, and many other pagans by issuing to all in the history of the West an identity of the Christian *Same*. What Ricci did want to claim is that the formation of the European culture, including its philosophical and religious tradition, was the result of Christianity. Quoting Caputo's paraphrase of Derrida, one can say that, for Ricci, as it is for other Christian theologians, "Europe will become itself only if it becomes Christian and is no longer pagan, no longer either Greek or Roman."[84]

To Ricci, a man with firsthand experience of the post-Reformation era—a disjointed time—and living virtually alone in a strange country called China when writing *On Friendship*, what could be more assuring and heartening than to be able to say "we" Europe or "we" the West in claiming, even just rhetorically, the ancient Greeks and Romans as Christians? No matter how such rhetorical domestication, with its totalizing and violent nature, had rendered him a useful friend—a direct and outright violation, not to mention a sheer mockery, of the very ideal of Aristotelian friendship he was propagating—Ricci did it without apology. Nothing seemed to trouble him because he was, like other Jesuits, merely following the Society's motto "everything for the greater glory of God" and, again, the Ignatian formula "finding God in all things." To carry out these instructions, what the Society's members must do first is assume that Greece, Rome, and the entirety of Europe share and hold the one and only truth, a univocal message, from the Christian God.

The question one must ask, however, is whether Ricci's domestication in *On Friendship* was successful in representing the Greeks and Romans as Christians—that is, whether his attempt to appropriate them succeeded in reconstructing the Greek and Roman soul to be part of the "one soul," which for Ricci was Christian. To answer this question and reveal not only an inevitable split in Ricci's book but also a similar split in Ricci's missionary self and identity, one must examine further the Jesuit view and use of Cicero in education and missiology.

At the time of the founding of the Society, part of the literary trend in Europe is described in these words: "The ancient writer who earned their [the humanists] highest admiration was Cicero. Renaissance humanism was an age of Ciceronianism in which the study and imitation of Cicero was a widespread concern, although the exaggeration of this tendency also found its critics."[85] In the Jesuit curriculum, Cicero was likewise taken to be an important author for various reasons, one of which was that the Jesuits found in his works moral truth somewhat compatible with some of the Ignatian teachings. For instance, after quoting from *De officiis* 1.7.22, the famous passage that "every Jesuit was familiar with and that many of them taught year after year,"[86] O'Malley asserts that to many Jesuits these Ciceronian words can be easily correlated "with the section opening the *Spiritual Exercises* entitled 'Principle and Foundation' which affirms that we were created for the praise, reverence, and service of God."[87] After showering praises on Cicero's high moral standard, O'Malley goes on to say, "These 'pagan' texts were taught not simply as models of style but as sources of ethical inspiration. If Erasmus could invoke 'St. Socrates,' I think some Jesuits, if they let themselves go, could have invoked 'St. Cicero.' "[88]

Whether O'Malley's thinking here resembles Ricci's attempt in *On Friendship* to appropriate Cicero is not a matter to be addressed in the present discussion. What is relevant is that his call for sainthood for Cicero has an immediate and positive response. Robert Aleksander Maryks, a historian of early modern European history clearly specializing in early Jesuit history, named his recent monograph on Jesuit probabilism, a book he dedicated to O'Malley and another person, *Saint Cicero and the Jesuits*. In his book, Maryks offers his apologetic interpretation on the ethics of probabilism that, first developed in the sixteenth century by the Dominicans, was adopted and adapted by the Jesuits.[89] Maryks rejects the theory that the Jesuit use of probabilism, a shift from the early Jesuits' tutiorism, was a part of "the transition [in the late sixteenth and early seventeenth centuries] from the search for *veritas* to the triumph of the opinion." Instead, he argues that the probabilistic Jesuits, by insisting that discussion on morals must be based on probable arguments, were actually trying to get close to truth.[90] Most related to the present discussion is that Maryks's book aims at highlighting "the crucial link between early modern casuistry and ancient rhetoric (especially Ciceronian)."[91] And one important ancient rhetorical principle that the Jesuits took from Cicero for their probabilism is, according to Maryks, none other than accommodation.[92]

The previous chapter briefly discussed accommodation or condescension—syncatabasis or *synkatabasis* in Greek meaning "going down together with"—as an important part of Christian evangelization, begun with God and his accommodation in rendering his message understandable to humans. Inspired by this divine condescension, found especially in Christology, the early apostles and later church fathers adopted accommodation, and the Jesuits since Ignatius have also taken accommodation to be their missionizing policy. Of the classical authors who employed syncatabasis, or accommodation, for their adaptation to the level suitable for the audience to be addressed, Cicero's skillful use of this rhetorical trope both impressed and stimulated, directly and indirectly, Christian theologians, including the Jesuits in their effort to develop their doctrines and missiology.[93] Here are a few examples of Cicero's idea of rhetorical accommodation.

In his *De oratore*, Cicero says, "In fact I take him [the orator] to be a man who can use language agreeable to the ear, and arguments suited to convince [*sententiis ad probandum accommodates*], in law-court disputes and in debates of public business" (1.213).[94] A little later in the same book, he asserts again: "For this orator of ours must be adapted [*accommodanda*] to the ears of the multitude, for charming or urging their minds to approve of proposals, which are weighed in no goldsmith's balance, but in what I may call common scales" (2.159).[95] In his dialogue with his son recorded in *De partitione oratoria*, he remarks, "I adapt [*accommodo*] the whole method of arrangement to the purpose of the inquiry; for the purpose of the statement is to convince, and that of the case is both to convince and to excite emotion. Consequently when I have dealt with the case, which contains the statement, I shall have spoken of them both. . . . I say that it [how Cicero would present his case] varies according to the class of the audience. For a member of the audience is either merely a hearer or an arbitrator, i.e. an estimator of fact and opinion; consequently it must aim either at giving pleasure to the hearer or at causing him to make some decision" (3.9–10).[96]

Cicero certainly demonstrates his good understanding of the rhetorical function of accommodation by insisting on the necessity of the orator's preknowledge of his audience and his willingness to speak at the audience's level as the condition for the success of his oration. At the same time, what Cicero says also indicates that he regards accommodation to be more than a rhetorical trope. For him, as it is for some other thinkers, accommodation is also a presupposition of the difference of the audience or the otherness of the addressee. Because this presupposition tends to lead to the effort to adapt to the audience, accommodation can be seen to base itself not only on the acknowledgment of difference but also the attentiveness or opening to, even acceptance of, difference. Indeed, there is no doubt or denial that accommodation is initially a tactic, rhetorical or religious, which means that accommodation's embedded acceptance of difference is primarily for the orator's or speaker's advantage and self-interest. But the rhetorical as well as religious need to open to and accept difference may often come at a price. It may result, as accommodation often does, in certain semantic and rhetorical instability neither designed nor desired by the orator or author. And such uncertainty is exactly what happens to *On Friendship*, because through Ricci's accommodation—his recourse to the classical authors in his book—the Christian ideas of friendship such as *agapē* and *caritas* appear to give way to the classical or pagan view of what and how friends must be.

Undoubtedly, *On Friendship* has been praised as a Jesuit example of accommodation.[97] One indication of Ricci's accommodation is that most maxims in the book come from pagan authors and works such as Cicero, Seneca, Plutarch, Terence, and others. Among these pagans, Cicero certainly stands out, having to his credit fourteen out of the book's one hundred aphorisms. Needless to say, Ricci never forgot or ignored his missionary duty. He made sure that Christians had their presence in the book. Besides the insertion of the name of God into the pagan sayings discussed earlier, he included Christian authors. As a result, the reader of the book sees side-by-side with the pagan sayings the words of Ambrose, Augustine, Cyprian,

Cassiodorus, Gregory the Great (Pope Gregory I), and Erasmus. In short, it is by no means accidental that, in *On Friendship*, Ricci had at least nine maxims quoted from Augustine and thus made him the second most quoted author after Cicero. Given Ricci's sustained missionary effort and the accepted role of Cicero in the Jesuit tradition, Cicero, together with his works and thought in general, should not pose any problems to a missionary book like *On Friendship*. But as far as the idea of Cicero's friendship is concerned, there is indeed a problem. I elaborate in what follows.

Despite the fact that Christian theologians from early on used Cicero's works, including those on friendship,[98] it is known that Cicero in his discussions of friendship emphasized that only a few virtuous men can be friends. As has been mentioned at the beginning of this chapter, for Cicero, as for Aristotle,[99] true friendship "was limited to a very few."[100] To clarify the Ciceronian idea, one can borrow from Julian Haseldine's remarks that, by Cicero's view, "only a few could ever be sufficiently endowed with natural virtue to partake in friendship, and to benefit the public good as a whole thereby." For Cicero, as Haseldine goes on to quote from *De amicitia*, "friendship cannot exist except among good men" (5.18).[101] Compared with the Christian idea of friendship, Cicero's friendship certainly appears to be highly selective and restricted, because in Christianity, friendship is for the good of the entire human race. In Haseldine's words, again, "Divine love is universal, and Christians were rejoined to love all equally, as Christ had said: 'But I say to you, love your enemies, do good to them that hate you.' "[102]

To highlight further the difference between Ciceronian—classical or pagan—friendship and Christian friendship, Augustine serves as a good example, because his discussion of friendship represents the very fundamental understanding of Christian friendship or love. It is true that Augustine received as much influence from Cicero as he did from the Platonists.[103] But his idea of friendship cannot be further away from the Ciceronian *amicitia*. In his view, human friendship is only true when it has in it the Holy Spirit, a point made most clear in his discussion of his dead friend in the *Confessions*. According to him, their friendship, though long-standing and sweet, was missing something. In their childhood, they could not make their relationship a true one because, in his words, "friendship cannot be true unless you solder it together among those who cleave to one another by the love [*caritate*] that is shed forth in our hearts by the Holy Spirit, which is given unto us" (4.4).[104] What is more important is that Augustine's idea of the Holy Spirit being the ultimate defining force of friendship leads to his "Christian infinitization of friendship or of spiritual fraternity."[105]

Christian friendship, as he sees it, is not a relation among a small number of people, nor is it a relation between a few people and the Holy Spirit or God. Taking the ideas of *agapē* and *caritas* given by God to be the keys for Christian union, he sees Christian friendship or love to be what is required from most people. God's love and faith in God unite people to form a Christian community. Commenting on Augustine's statement "We have not seen and yet we are fellows because we hold the faith in common," from his *Homilies on the First Epistle of John 1*, Hannah Arendt rightly observes, "True fellowship rests on the fact of the common faith."[106]

Indeed, faith is the most important element separating Christian friendship and a pagan one. For instance, Saint Aelred of Rievaulx (1110–1167) decided to write his book on friendship for the exact reason that he found Cicero's writings on friendship "lacked the 'sweet honey' of Jesus's name and the 'salt' of the Holy Scripture."[107] And it would not be a surprise that, in book 3 of his *Spiritual Friendship*, he claims the foundation of all spiritual love to be the love of God.[108] To quote a contemporary Christian scholar, the love of God is treated as the unifying and centripetal power of Christians and Christian community:

> When Christians conform their friendship love to the Spirit of love, boundaries are broken, fears disappear, magnanimity reigns. In short, their friendship is preferential but not exclusive, for they welcome others to the way of life through which they will find their fullness in God. Through the preferential love of their friendship on earth, rooted as it is in Christ, they learn to prefer what God does, *the perfect community of all being one in God*.[109]

Such is the view of the universal community founded with and on Christian fraternity, ensured through the mediation of as well as meditation on the divine. Furthermore, following Augustine's conviction that friendship is God's gift given when he gave himself to humans,[110] Christian friendship does not request people's effort.[111] Owing to his idea of friendship as a "divine gift" that "is the heart of Augustine's conception of friendship and his great innovation," for Augustine, as a critic argues, "it is God alone who can join two persons to each other. In other words, friendship is beyond the scope of human control. One can desire to be the friend of another who is striving for perfection, but only God can effect the union."[112]

Having made clear the difference between the pagan form and the Christian form of friendship, one returns to Ricci's *On Friendship* only to find an Augustine different from other theologians for whom the Christian *agapē* and *caritas* suggest much more broadness than the Aristotelian *philia* and Ciceronian *amicitia*, both limited by "a kind of contented exclusivity."[113] What is missing from the Augustine presented by Ricci in *On Friendship* seems to be his view of friendship as God's gift, or true friendship being possible only through God. Undoubtedly, Ricci did include in his book the saying in which Augustine compares friends to brothers, a typical Christianization and naturalization of human relationship, making friendship a consanguine affinity.[114] But this rather isolated maxim, given without any elaboration and explanation of the Christian background, owing to the textual or aphoristic format of Ricci's book, would not convey the message of this Augustinian fraternization to the Chinese audience. In short, most Augustinian sayings in *On Friendship* taken out of their specific and theological context, appear to resemble any neutral and well-balanced discussion on general—in that sense, pagan—friendship with no clear implication of any specific type of religious undertone. To give a couple of examples, Augustine is quoted as saying, "Friendship and enmity are like music and discord. To distinguish one from the other, one only listens for harmony. Harmony is essential to friendship. With harmony, a small enterprise grows into a great one. With discord, a great enterprise tends to fall to decay."[115] A little later, he is quoted with advice to the reader: "Don't believe completely the compliments from friends or insults from enemies."[116] Both cautioning the reader on how to distinguish friends from adversaries and to be careful to maintain a friendship of harmony, these Augustinian maxims in Ricci's presentation do not seem to stimulate easily in the reader the idea that friendship depends solely on God.

In Ricci's book, Augustine is certainly not the only one without much of his characteristic argument that attachment to a friend must be transformed into love of God, or a "friend is to be loved in God."[117] For the rest of the Christian authors quoted in Ricci's book, the situation seems to be similar. They likewise talk about friendship from a general perspective rather than a religious one. Here are a few examples from the altogether six or so aphorisms by these other Christian authors quoted in *On Friendship*. While Saint Ambrose (c. 340–397) insists that "to give a gift to a friend in the hope of some return from that friend is no giving but trading at the marketplace,"[118] Saint Cyprian (c. 200–258) remarks that "if two who are friends in ordinary times become enemies for some small gains and losses, this is because their friendship is not based on virtue. In a good friendship, friends share profits and endure losses together."[119] Ambrose also says that "a gift from an enemy is not as valuable as the whip from a friend,"[120] and Erasmus is quoted to hold that "friends' excessive praise will cause much more damage than [will] enemies' censure."[121] Given what they say here, regardless of whether any of these Christian authors share Augustine's belief about friendship being predetermined by God and thus innate or natural, they certainly fail to make it clear in Ricci's book. Instead, they all seem to take friendship's formation and well-being as dependent on the good deeds and sound judgment of friends.

Up to this point, it should be evident that friendship as presented in *On Friendship* retains a strong and obvious pagan overtone. This fact must first of all be attributed to Ricci's accommodation and arrangement through which the Christian authors—such as Augustine, Ambrose, Pope Gregory I and Erasmus—are portrayed, as harboring a view of friendship not drastically or not fundamentally different from that of the pagan authors like Cicero, Plutarch, and Seneca. In his attempt to accommodate his introduction of Western friendship to his Chinese audience, Ricci virtually reduced the Christian understanding of friendship to the minimum, as if the divine union between God and humans often referred to in theology as Christian friendship did not exist, or was not a sufficiently significant part of the Western tradition. To sum it up, *On Friendship* fares rather badly as far as Ricci's mission of conversion is concerned.

However, to understand properly as well as interpret adequately the significance of Ricci's presentation of friendship—specifically his book's becoming largely a pagan work—one must do more than simply say, rather routinely and perfunctorily, that Ricci was following a tactic of "indirect propagation of the faith."[122] One must go further to see what happened or what it actually meant when Ricci and his fellow Jesuits in their mission, as Ruggieri admitted, had to "proceed cautiously . . . and not to behave with indiscreet zeal."[123]

What makes *On Friendship* fundamentally a book of pagan friendship rather than Christian friendship is that the authors included in the book share primarily the idea that friendship is an exclusively human affair.[124] To take the concept of friendship as being about humans alone is certainly different from the Christian view about friendly relations being a union between God and humankind. Of course, this difference does not mean that the classical or pagan friendship harbors no recognizable logocentric or metaphysical sentiment of its own. On the contrary, pagan friendship is not without its own intrinsic aporia, part of which has been discussed earlier. But in comparison with the Christian friendship that regards friendly relations to be a godsend, the classical concept of friendship presented in *On*

Friendship tends to see a certain secrecy in friendship. Rather than claiming, as many Christian theologians would often do, the entirety of the human race as a collective partner included in the body of God, the pagan authors in *On Friendship* seem to acknowledge the paradox between the finitude of friendship and the infinite otherness of the friend. Different from the spiritual friendship linking the finite to the infinite—that is, humans to God—classical friendship, as it is presented through Ricci's book, hopes to link the finite self to the infinite other, who could be God but is most likely another individual of the human race. In other words, Ricci's quoted authors offer their own examples of the Derridean *tout autre est tout autre* already discussed in the previous chapter. In their examples, the infinitude or the complete otherness expands by exceeding the supposedly exclusive divinity of the Christian God to apply to anyone involved in a friendly relationship. This infinite otherness not only keeps the other in friendship ungraspable and beyond reach but also fills the subject or self with the anxiety to bridge the gap with the other.

Some may find the anxiety generated in pagan friendship to resemble the previously discussed "something 'numinous' " humans would often feel about the *mysterium tremendum* or God. But one drastic difference between the two is that the anxiety in pagan friendship does not at all instill in the subject the Christian idea that friendship is fulfilled by divine grace. Instead, suggesting alterity and proximity in friendship and friends, pagan friendship is never readily present but always in the making or in play. For the classical authors, the constant need of human care and effort means that friendship is not a natural and innate relationship mandated by the divine. At least, this seems to be the view through which the authors, including the Christian ones in *On Friendship*, look at friendship. They seem to be more eager to share the Derridean idea of "a friendship without hearth, of a *philein* without *oikeios*. Ultimately, a friendship without presence, without resemblance, without affinity, without analogy. Along with presence, truth would start to tremble."[125] And their friendship free from *oikeios*, resemblance, affinity, and other features indicates that these authors regard the future of friendship, like the future of anything else, not to be programmable. Their persistent call for human care and effort to foster and sustain friendship suggests that, to quote Derrida again, "friendship is never a presence given[;] it belongs to the experience of expectation, promise, or engagement. Its discourse is that of prayer, it inaugurates but reports nothing, it is not satisfied with what is, it moves out to this place where a responsibility opens up a future."[126] Taking friendship to be without affinity, without knowledge and certainty of the future of friendship, and not knowing the friend, these authors seem to see friendship to be an asymmetrical and nonreciprocal relation in which the other, deemed to be beyond the subject's immediate and secured knowledge, remains infinite and singular.

The asymmetry of friendship dislodging the identity of territory for friends is exactly what makes pagan friends differ further from the Christian friendship or union. Specifically, if Christian friendship takes God to be the last dwelling place in which the entire human race will gather and settle, as if all eventually return home and go back for a family reunion, in classical friendship the friend appears rather to be placeless or without habitat, in the sense that the body of the other will not become part of the self. The other will remain separated because, unlimited and heterogeneous, the other must be thought of as the other, and as the other may visit the self as a visitor or a guest but cannot at any time be appropriated into the self. To return to and at the same time go beyond the Aristotelian aphorism "one soul in bodies twain," one must say that the asymmetry—that is, the heterogeneity preventing homogeneity from happening in friendship—keeps the body of the other or friend separate in the same fashion in which the friend retains his or her own soul. As Derrida points out, "Friendship should be outside all places or placeless, without family or familiarity, outside of self, expatriate, extraordinary, extravagant, absurd or mad, weird, unsuitable, strange."[127] In the case of *On Friendship*, supposing certain placelessness of friends, the pagan friendship puts friends outside the immediate or familial kinship often assumed in friendly relationship or fraternity. That is, it safeguards the otherness or alterity of friends by moving friendship both outside and beyond the affinity or affiliation of the Same.

It is clear by now that the friendship seen in *On Friendship* deviates sharply from the Ignatian spirituality to be followed in the Jesuit order. What Ricci presented in his book is not what he was trained and expected to do—to apply the Jesuit divine union so as to concert the Chinese to be friends in the Lord. One can certainly consider this fact to be the result of Ricci's accommodation, which includes the caution of the early missionaries to avoid straightforward preaching and religious discussions in public in China. But there is more to the cultural, philosophical and political phenomena of late Ming China that stimulated and compelled Ricci to adopt pagan friendship at the expense of the Jesuit idea of friends in the Lord.

To speak of what compels Ricci in adopting pagan friendship, it is necessary to go back to his stay in Nanchang, where he wrote *On Friendship*. It was in this city that Ricci became acquainted with some Confucian scholars, including Zhang Huang (章潢; 1527–1608),[128] the headmaster of Bailudong Academy (白鹿洞書院), a well-known neo-Confucian institution of education where such prominent Confucians as Zhu Xi (朱熹; 1130–1200) and Wang Yangming (王陽明; 1472–1528) had taught. Visiting the academy and, at Zhang's invitation, delivering a lecture there,[129] Ricci befriended the teachers and students at the institute. It is likely that through his mingling with these and other scholars he learned more about the neo-Confucian teachings at the time, including their renewed interest in and discussion of friendship. The fact is that there was among Confucians in China a noticeable emphasis on friendship, part of which can be traced back to at least the early sixteenth century when Wang Yangming began to attract a large number of students with his "New Learning of the Mind-and-Heart" (心學), for the time a supposedly revolutionary development of the neo-Confucian thought since the Song (960–1279).[130] Among Wang's students and followers, especially those attending the so-called *jianghui* (講會) or "learning and discussing meetings," friendship became not only a much discussed topic but also an earnestly pursued virtue.[131] Given the nature and function of "learning and discussing meetings," regular gatherings of scholars and students for lecturing, debating, and elaborating on Confucian teachings and mores, friendship, particularly exchanges between like-minded friends, was understandably much praised and encouraged. It is worth noting that the friendship practiced among the attendants at these gatherings was often regarded to be the most important relation in society as a whole.

In traditional China, as one of the so-called Five Relationships (五倫), friendship comes last on the list—after the relationships between ruler and subject, father and son, husband and wife, and elder brother and younger brother.[132] Out of these five relations, friendship is the only one that is not naturally formed. Yet the scholars and students at the Yangming gatherings tend to rank friendly relationship to be more important than the familial relationships, even to the extent that they see friendship as a replacement of those relationships between family members, because friendship and its like-mindedness provide an opportunity for moral cultivation among friends.[133] For instance, Wang Ji (王畿; 1498–1583), a prominent and important Yangming scholar, argues thus:

> Our ancients regarded moral exhortation not to be a responsibility between fathers and sons or between brothers, but one between friends. The reason was that the ancients took shared will or resolve [to devote to sagely learning] as the condition of

any moral exhortations. Take the two examples of King Wen and Duke of Zhou, and the two examples of Mingdao and Yichuan. The former two were father and son, and the latter two, elder and younger brothers. But they were at the same time mentors and moral friends to one another. Living together day by day, there was no possibility for any of them to hide or pretend his true character. Holding the same will and resolve, people separated by a thousand years can respond and react to each other. If the will and resolve are different, even between contemporaries, like Yao and Shun, or Shun and [Yao's nefarious son Dan] Zhu, nothing will happen.[134]

Wang's argument and similar arguments by the Wang Yangming scholars and others who value the formed relationship between friends more highly than the natural and family relationships appear to be rather unorthodox. They give unprecedented importance to friendship, likely because their wakening consciousness of individuality and self has led to their reaction to, as well as dissatisfaction with, the Ming official view that often lays more emphasis on the other four of the five cardinal relationships.[135] For instance, the *Wulun shu* (五倫書) or *The Book on Five Relationships*, a magnum opus and moral guidebook supposedly authored by Emperor Xuande (宣德; r. 1426–1435) himself, devotes only two of its total sixty-two chapters to friendship.[136] Such inessential treatment of friendship in this book is certainly consistent with the general understanding of friendship in traditional China, because, coming from outside the family, friends are often regarded as an interrupting force to the relations in the family. In addition, the importance of friendship was often downplayed in the past because, in the political discourse, "personal friendship was often considered a major element of factionalism (*pengdang* 朋黨) within the imperial bureaucracy."[137] It seems that the neo-Confucian discussion of friendship since the mid-Ming period marks an effort to wrestle with these two discriminating views against friendly relation. What is beyond doubt is that if the Confucians of the Wang Yangming school concentrated on elevating friendship for its function in character-building and virtue-acquiring, the late Ming Confucians, many of them Ricci's contemporaries and friends, promoted as well as practiced friendship mainly for political purposes. With the empire facing multiple domestic problems and foreign threats in the late sixteenth and early seventeenth centuries, friendship became particularly important for these Confucian officials and scholars in their effort and attempt to form their *camaraderie* before the different powers and authorities of their times.[138]

Given the late Ming background so far discussed, one can say that the discussions of friendship by the Wang Yangming scholars and others had actually prepared the way, by creating a convenient and favorable environment, for Ricci to present his concept of friendship. At the same time, these Confucian discussions, and Ricci's obvious knowledge of them, had put certain limits on how he could present his friendship. For Ricci, his concept of friendship certainly offered him a handy and familiar tool that he could use to challenge, preferably to replace, the other four relationships that with their dominant and authoritative status had determined the human relations in traditional China. But his understanding of how the Confucians understood friendship—that is, friendship as a purely human affiliation,[139] not a God-human union—predetermined the form of the Western friendship that he could introduce to his Chinese audience who at the time knew nothing about the Christian divine union, fallen man, and so forth. It is out of his understanding of the reality in China that, despite his total rejection of most of the ethical theories and fundamental doctrines of neo-Confucianism, including those of the Wang Yangming school, Ricci went out of his way, even further than he had ever done before, with his accommodation. That is why, around the time of writing *On Friendship*, he also did the following few things. He decided to begin dressing up like a Confucian scholar by tossing away the Buddhist robe that he had been wearing since his early days in China;[140] he familiarized himself with Confucian etiquette so as to befriend many officials and scholars in the city of Nanchang, a majority of them neo-Confucians;[141] and, to his fellow Jesuits in Europe, he reiterated in assertive rhetoric his understanding of missionary accommodation that would avoid declaring openly and preaching readily Catholicism to the Chinese.[142]

Undoubtedly, while doing all these things, he did not for a moment ignore, much less forget, his commitment, and his mission. For instance, he overcame many difficulties to purchase a house in Nanchang to create a second foothold in China after Guangdong. Also in Nanchang, he finished his manuscript *The True Meaning of the Lord of Heaven*. But even in these activities relating more directly to evangelization, his accommodation got in the way—that is, he did not plan to use his new residence as a chapel, at least not immediately,[143] and he did not mention in his catechism some of the most fundamental concepts of the Christian faith.[144] Also, what is more important to the present discussion is that, to say it again, he made *On Friendship* a discussion of classical or pagan friendship instead of the spiritual friendship or divine alliance anticipated and urged in the *Spiritual Exercises*.

Ricci's tactic of accommodation seems to work to his advantage. To illustrate, *On Friendship* offers a good example. Once published, this small book helped attract to him much attention and friendship from the Confucian scholars and officials, the group he sought to befriend. In a letter to the general of the Society of Jesus dated October 28, 1595, he reported with pride the fame brought to him by his book:

> The *Amicitia* [*On Friendship*] has won more credit for me and for Europe than anything else we have done; because the other things give us the reputation of possessing ingenuity in the construction of mechanical artifacts and instruments; but this treatise has established our reputation as scholars of talent and virtue; and thus it is read and received with great applause and already has been published in two different places.¹⁴⁵

Concerning the popularity of the book, Ricci was certainly not exaggerating. *On Friendship* was much read and well liked among the Confucians, who would sometimes quote its aphorisms in conversations and in their own works.¹⁴⁶ Here, what Feng Yingjing (馮應京; 1555–1606) wrote in his preface to the 1601 edition of *On Friendship* should be representative to account for the book's popularity in China: "Having traveled all of the eighty thousand *li* to the east, the gentleman Xitai [Far-West—Ricci's studio name] came to China for the purpose of making friends. His understanding of the Way is so profound, his longing for friends, therefore, so eager, and his friendship, sincere and earnest. Most of all, his discussion on friendship is particularly comprehensive.... Having learned from his discussion on friendship, I am now more convinced than ever that 'in the Eastern Sea and the Western Sea, people's minds are the same and Principle is the same.'"¹⁴⁷ Clearly, for the Confucians, reading *On Friendship* was a comforting and reassuring experience, because the Western idea of friendship seemingly resembled the Confucian idea of friendship.¹⁴⁸

But this resemblance, as a matter of fact, shows exactly that in Ricci's mind China and the West or, to be exact, Confucianism and Catholicism, could not be farther apart. Furthermore, to a reader familiar with not only the motive and goal for Jesuit mission but also with the Ignatian view of Jesuit or Christian friendship, Ricci was not in China to make friends, as Feng assumed in his preface. Nor was Ricci in China to establish, as a Jesuit scholar once claimed, "a link between European humanist tradition and the Confucian humanist tradition."¹⁴⁹ In Ricci's view, Confucianism and the church would remain drastically different and far apart until the day when China became a Christian nation and all Chinese, instead of cultivating human relations of different kinds, began to desire and strive for a relation with the Christian God.

Only when the reader takes into consideration Ricci's missionary plan and this goal toward which he strove, including his own understanding of friendship defined and determined by the "soul" or principle put forth by none other than that of the Ignatian spirituality, can he or she begin to see how serious a problem exists in *On Friendship*. To be sure, this problem should not be taken to mean that any change in Ricci's faith and his determination to convert China to Catholicism could have occurred. Conversion was precisely the task assigned to him by his church and order, not to mention predetermined by his faith and theology. But the problem does indicate his failure in presenting to, much less instilling in, the Chinese the true Jesuit or Christian spirituality, as he was trained to do. And the problem becomes all the more serious when, in his writing on friendship, in order to accommodate the Confucian view and tradition, he had to suppress, or reduce to a minimum, the Christian human-and-God friendship exemplified primarily by Jesus and articulated by countless theologians, to give way to the human-and-human friendship of the pagan culture. In other words, he had to reverse the hierarchy between the Christian friendship and the classical friendship to earn appreciation and friendship from the Confucians. If the letters IHS on the Christogram, the official emblem of the Society of Jesus, read, as it was usually read by the Christian church, *in hoc signo* (*vinces*) or "under this sign (you will conquer),"[150] Ricci, judging by what has been said about *On Friendship*, was attempting to conquer under the sign of the other.

It is true that some would find justification for the pagan view of friendship in *On Friendship* by pointing out, again, Ricci's method of indirect evangelization prescribed in the Jesuit motto "*everything* for the greater glory of God." From a deconstructive perspective, however, the fact that Ricci had to make his proselytization indirect and oblique to the extent that he ended up presenting and promoting the pagan view or virtue of friendship as compatible, or at least similar and thus acceptable, to that of the Confucians and neo-Confucians would look different. What happened to Ricci and his work on friendship, it can be argued, serves as what Levinas and Derrida have called *la décision passive* and *la décision inconsciente*, the passive and unconscious decision.[151] Referring to decisions of this kind as "the other's decision in me," Simon Critchley points out, "The decision is not something taken by a subject, but rather the subject (insofar as one can still employ this word postdeconstructively) is *taken by the decision* that is made without its volition. In this sense, the moment of the decision is the subject's relation to an alterity within itself."[152] In his works, Derrida would take the matter further. In his *Adieu to Emmanuel Levinas*, he argues that decision, like responsibility, is always of the other. This is so because, as he asks, don't decision and responsibility "always come back or come down to the other, from the other, even if it is the other in me? For, in the end, would an initiative that remained purely and simply 'mine' still be a decision, in accordance with the most powerful tradition of ethics and philosophy, which requires that the decision always be 'my' decision, the decision of one who can freely say 'as for myself, I,' *ipse, egomet ipse?*"[153] He reiterates this point in his *Politics of Friendship*: "The passive decision, condition of the event, is always in me, structurally, another event, a rending decision as the decision of the other. Of the absolute other [*l'autre absolu*] in me, the other as the absolute [*l'autre comme absolu*] that decides on me in me."[154]

Undoubtedly, Ricci would never regard the Confucians to be the absolute or wholly other like his God. But this does not change the fact that his accommodation, seen in his work on friendship and many of his other activities in China, evangelical or not, developed in a fashion determined and overdetermined by his view of the Confucian other. It was indeed out of his knowledge and understanding of the Confucian otherness that he began to desire for and do the impossible. He did much more than follow the humanist spirit of the pagan friendship to befriend the Confucians, his fellow human beings. He went so far as to befriend their religion or their religious rituals and practices. The following are a couple of quick examples.

In his preface to *On Friendship*, Qu Rukui (瞿汝夔; 1549–1612), studio name Taisu (太素),[155] who became a friend of Ricci in Guangdong in the late 1580s, assured the reader that it was out of his true admiration for the civilization of the Great Ming that Ricci came all the way to China to become its subject. Ever since his arrival in China, according to Qu, "the respected Master Li [Ricci] . . . has chanted praises of the texts of the Sages, observed the laws of the kingdom, and worn a scholar's cap and belt. He has participated in the offering of *the spring and autumn sacrifices*, has been chaste in his acts so as to achieve true cultivation of his character, and has displayed his respect to the commands of Heaven so as to promote the orthodox teachings."[156] Knowing what a sacrilegious undertaking it would be for a Jesuit priest like Ricci to participate in the religious ceremonies of offering sacrifices, Paul Rule expresses strong doubt about the truthfulness of what Qu said.¹⁵⁷ It is impossible to verify which among the spring and autumn sacrifices Ricci took part in and when, if he did so at all. But Ricci was by no means a stranger to the Ming court religious rites and ceremonies. *China in the Sixteenth Century* has a passage in which he recorded his experience in Nanjing to attend a music rehearsal for the sacrificial ceremony to honor Confucius. Because what Ricci said in defense of his attendance to this rehearsal of sacrifice will help conclude this chapter on his missionary identity troubled by the Confucian otherness, it is worth quoting his words at length:

> Let us here insert a word about Chinese music, an art that is of considerable interest to Europeans. The leaders of the literary class observe a solemn day of sacrifice in honor of Confucius, if sacrifice is the proper word. The Chinese honor the great philosopher as a Master, and not as a deity, and they are accustomed to use the word sacrifice in a broad and indefinite sense. This particular celebration is attended with music, and on the previous day they invite the Chief of Magistrates to attend a rehearsal of the orchestra, to decide whether or not the music will be appropriate for the occasion. Father Ricci was invited to this rehearsal and as there was no question of attending a sacrifice, he accepted the invitation. This orchestral rehearsal was arranged by the priest of the literary class, called Tansu, and it was held in a hall or rather in the Royal Temple, built to honor the Lord of Heaven. Father Matthew was accompanied by the children of the High Magistrate. The priests who composed the orchestra were vested in sumptuous garments, as if they were to attend a sacrifice.¹⁵⁸

In this paragraph, before he went on to describe the music played and the various instruments used by the orchestra, Ricci repeatedly attempted to justify his attendance at this rehearsal for the sacrifice to Confucius. He pointed out the ambiguous and thus inaccurate use of the term "sacrifice" for this occasion, and insisted on Confucius's being a philosopher, not a deity.¹⁵⁹ But whatever reasons he produced as justification for his presence at the sacrifice, there is no denial of the ritual he attended to be an event completely and thoroughly religious. To demonstrate the religious expression articulated and religious consciousness awakened at the occasion and what they did to Ricci's friendship, one needs to look at two things, both mentioned by Ricci in the quotation earlier: first, the site and performers of the sacrifice; second, the significance of the music played.

With respect to the site, Ricci told the reader that the sacrificial ritual took place in the Royal Temple that was, to use the original term from Ricci's memoirs, "*tempio de Cielo*" or Temple of Heaven.[160] Built in 1377, Temple of Heaven was the site for state sacrifices to Heaven and earth, the most sacred and religious rituals of the empire.[161] A grand construction, the temple had numerous columns inside its main hall, three wide avenues leading to its gate, and many pine and cypress trees behind its altar.[162] A sacred place, the temple marked its sacredness by differentiating itself from the places around it.[163] In the late Ming, when Ricci was in China, the temple was used exclusively for offering sacrifices to Confucius.[164] Still, there was never any doubt about its distinctiveness as a sacred space and its function in the religious system of the Confucians. As mentioned above, Ricci insisted that Confucius was not recognized as "a divinity" and the sacrifice to him, for its lack of supplication, could not be called "a true sacrifice." But Ricci with his argument did not take into consideration the fact that, from a theological perspective, a sacrifice had, in addition to supplication, three other intentions, prayer (homage), thanksgiving, and expiation.[165] Nevertheless, when he attended the ritual, that is, when he entered the temple with some Confucian officials and the priests or sacrificers, he was standing on sacred ground where the mundane world was bound to the supernatural one.[166] If sacrifice as a term denotes a religious act in the highest and fullest sense, to be part of the sacrifice at Temple of Heaven then means that Ricci took part in this religious act of and for the Confucians. Furthermore, the priests carrying out the sacrifice would further complicate Ricci's deed of befriending Confucian ritual.

Referred to as Tansu or Tausu, these priests responsible for the sacrificial ritual of the Confucians were *daoshi* (道士; i.e., Daoist priests).[167] It may strike one as strange that offering sacrifice to Confucius, the Confucian sage, should be executed by Daoist priests. But during the Ming, starting in the year of 1379 with the founding of the Imperial Music Office (*Shenyue guan* 神樂觀), Daoist priests who staffed this office served as ritual specialists, musicians, and dancers for most of the religious ceremonies of the imperial court.[168] As more and more Daoist priests were recruited into the Imperial Music Office to do rituals for the state, Daoist priests as consecrated functionaries eventually assumed responsibility for virtually all the state rituals and ceremonies, including sacrifices to Confucius, during the Ming.[169] This fact, that the Ming sacrificial rituals for Confucius were exclusively reserved for and performed by Daoist priests, means that it was no accident that the priests Ricci saw at the ritual he went to were Daoists.

Scholars often hold the view that the early Jesuit missionaries to China had an imperfect understanding of Daoism.[170] In the case of Ricci, one scholar points out that his unfamiliarity with the philosophical tradition of Daoism from Laozi resulted in his identifying Daoism "totally with the priests and practices associated with the more obviously religious form of Taoism."[171] His limited knowledge of Daoism did not seem to stop him from agreeing with some of his fellow Jesuits who found offensive the "disorderly ravings" of Daoism, " 'a low and dishonest class' of enthusiasts who believed in saints, miracles, 'a trinity of gods,' and other such follies."[172] At one place in *The True Meaning of the Lord of Heaven*, Ricci lined Daoism up with Buddhism and gave a brief but harsh criticism of both: "The devil wishes to deceive people so that they will follow him. He therefore attaches himself to the bodies of humans and animals, causing them to say that they are the sons of certain families and to give accounts of events in those families in order to prove his lies. Those who take and spread these lies must be the disciples of the Buddha and Laozi."[173] In his writings, Ricci did not have much to say about Daoism. However, there is no doubt at all about his completely negative attitude toward Daoist thinking and practitioners. Given this fact, the question one must ask is what Ricci's attendance at a Confucian sacrifice performed by Daoist priests does to his theory and practice of friendship.

Because of his view that Confucianism was in general secular and Confucians' regular sacrifice to Confucius was not religious, Ricci did not find it a problem for him to go to the Confucian sacrifice.[174] But his attendance at the sacrifice does begin to look problematic when one takes into consideration the participation of the Daoist priests who served as the consecrated ministers for the ceremony. When Ricci was at the ritual in the Temple of Heaven, witnessing the connection of Confucians and Confucius, or experiencing with the Confucians their communion with their sage, this communion had as its part the Daoist priests who as cultic functionaries made possible the link between the human and transcendental worlds. To be sure, it is difficult for today's reader to say with certainty what Ricci thought or how he felt, when he sat through the ceremony, watching the Daoist priests perform every ritual detail, such as offering sacrifice and playing religious music. Even if he found himself not completely prepared for the dominant presence of the Daoist priests at the ceremony, a class of religious practitioners he deemed to be threatening and hostile to his faith, he must have comforted himself that he was there for his mission. It was for his mission that he was there to befriend the Confucians and their culture, even their sacrificial ritual. That was his way to get to know these people and eventually win their hearts by converting them to Christianity. The discussion here is not concerned with the possible tension or irony that the Daoist penetration might have generated for the sacrificial ritual of the Confucians. What must be made clear now is that Ricci's being at the sacrifice exclusively managed by Daoist priests demonstrates further how he and his friendship opened to the other. If his attendance at the sacrifice to Confucius can be seen as his friendliness toward the Confucians, it can also be seen as his friendliness toward the Daoist priests, whose religion he denounced elsewhere. Or, following Jacques Derrida, one can take Ricci's friendliness toward the Daoists, or his acknowledgment or reception of them at the sacrifice, to be a display of what can be called his "hospitality to the worst." In short, one can see it to be Ricci's "*yes* of the other and *yes* to the other." It was his way of "letting the other come."[175]

Now a few words about music. The fact that the sacrifice was, in Ricci's words, "attended with music" should make it impossible to deny the religious implication of the music, as this is what the music for such occasions was all about.[176] Earlier in this discussion, it is mentioned that Ricci used in *On Friendship* an Augustinian maxim that compares good friendship to music, because both produce harmony. This saying from Augustine can be readily related with the Confucian view of music and friendship. In her recent book, Michael Nylan observes, "Music and friendship help temper sharp distinction between people, including a greater sense of community and common purpose among otherwise disparate groups, 'from the Son of Heaven on down to the common people.'"[177] Many ancient texts expatiate upon the Confucian expectation and use of music—to conduce harmony and generate agreement. To give an example of the Confucian view and use of music, here are the remarks from "On Music" (樂論) by Xunzi (荀子; 313–238 BCE), one of the earliest Confucian philosophers:

> When music is performed in the ancestral temple and the ruler and ministers, superiors and inferiors, listen to it together, none would fail to become harmoniously respectful. When it is performed within the home and father and sons, elder and younger brothers listen to it together, none would fail to become harmoniously affectionate. And when it is performed in the community, and old and young people listen to it together, none

> would fail to become harmoniously cooperative. Thus, music observes a single standard in order to fix its harmony, it brings together different instruments in order to ornament its rhythm, and it combines their playing in order to achieve a beautiful pattern. It is sufficient to lead people in a single, unified Way, and is sufficient to bring order to the myriad changes [足以率一道, 足以治萬變]. This is the method by which the former kings created music.[178]

Leading men "in a single, unified Way," sound and music, Xunzi continues, "enter into people deeply and transform people quickly." Once this transformation is in place, "the people will be uniformly ordered and not cause chaos." And when people are harmonious and well behaved, even the enemy states will not dare to launch an attack.[179] Relating music and rites for their unifying and transforming power, Xunzi gives his assertion: "When music is played, people's intentions gain purity. When rites are followed, conduct turns out perfectly. They make ears acute and eyes sharp; they give blood and temper balance and harmony; they reform customs and alter habits."[180]

To conclude this discussion of the example of musical celebration and the discussion of Jesuit friendship, one must admit that it would certainly be untrue to assume that Ricci's attending the music rehearsal for a Confucian sacrifice effected any actual transformation, turning Ricci's Christian faith into Confucian belief. But does his presence at this ceremony, together with his many other deeds—including dressing up like a Confucian, taking a Chinese name, and, last but not least, presenting Western friendship the way he did in *On Friendship*—indicate to the reader beyond any doubt that Ricci, while remaining a good Jesuit, had to keep going out of his way and was simply compelled to do so because of the otherness of Confucianism? The many acts of bravery and many deeds of endangering his Jesuit identity, it seems, speak of a true faith in friendship, a faith that takes one to do the impossible for the friend who is none other than the wholly other.

PART TWO

HOSPITALITY AND THE CONFUCIANS

Not only is there a culture of hospitality, but there is no culture that is not also a culture of hospitality. All cultures compete in this regard and present themselves as more hospitable than the others. Hospitality—this is culture itself.

—Jacques Derrida, "Hostipitality"

Hospitality is the deconstruction of the at-home; deconstruction is hospitality to the other, to the other than oneself, the other than "its other," to an other who is beyond any "its other."

—Jacques Derrida, "Hostipitality"

3

The Subject of Hospitality and Sino-centrism

Theory and Chinese Cultural Background

> A stranger to itself, obsessed by others, dis-quiet, the ego is a hostage [*le Moi est otage*], a hostage in its very recurrence as an ego ceaselessly missing itself. For it is thus always closer to the other, more obliged, aggravating its own insolvency.
>
> —Emmanuel Levinas, "No Identity"

> I have heard of Chinese converting barbarians to their ways, but not of their being converted to barbarian ways (吾聞用夏變夷者，未聞變於夷者也).
>
> —*Mencius*, trans. D. C. Lau

My discussion up to this point has focused on critiquing the Jesuit attempt at cultural assimilation that was behind the China-West friendship promised and promoted mainly in Ricci's work. I will now turn my attention to the Chinese side of this cross-cultural encounter. I will examine how the Chinese empire at the time perceived and received its relationship with the Christian missionaries. Analyzing the Confucian reception of the missionaries, that is, the Ming hospitality displayed to these religious Europeans, I will in this second part of the book discuss the implication of the Chinese imperial ideology and expose the limits of the empire by revealing the dilemma or paradox facing the Confucian Sino-centrism.

I must say again here that the Ming reception of the Jesuits to be discussed in the remaining pages of this book largely means the Confucian reception.[1] Besides what will soon become clear through this introductory chapter, it suffices to say that the Confucians represented the group most active in the interchanges with the Jesuits and were, to emphasize again, the group that the Jesuits sought to influence and befriend. There is no doubt that the Confucians had varied reactions to the missionaries. Some Confucian officials and scholars received baptism; some formed amicable relationships with the Jesuits;[2] some expressed interest in the imported science and technology but were resistant to the Christian religion; and some remained hostile to everything and everyone foreign, be it Christianity, modern science, or the Jesuits. Whether the Confucians welcomed the Jesuits as guests or rejected them as enemies,[3] one can nevertheless argue that all of them displayed in their own way a certain hospitality to the strangers, if one takes "hospitality" to be, as many critics do today, a philosophical term describing the Self's opening to and desire for the Other. What is relevant and important to this discussion is that the Confucian hospitality thus perceived provides a perspective from which one can demonstrate how the Ming imperial host—that is, the Confucian Self or Subject—was subjected to interruption before the Jesuit Other.

The thesis of this part of the discussion—that a split and marginalized Confucian Self was revealed through its hospitality to the Jesuits—finds its theoretical apparatus mainly in the works of Levinas and Derrida. Both philosophers treat hospitality, an ancient virtue apparent in biblical and Greek literature, as a condition of openness.[4] The arguments concerning hospitality advanced by the two thinkers—specifically Levinas's ethics of being face to face with the infinite other and Derrida's unconditionality and paradox of hospitality—will be applied in the upcoming discussion to help unsettle the normative values ascribed in the chauvinistic self of Confucianism, which is identical to Ming Sino-centrism. Before going into some Confucian understanding and the practice of hospitality in traditional China later in this chapter, I will first summarize the basics of the discussion on hospitality by Levinas and Derrida, focusing on the elements most relevant to my discussion in the next three chapters.

As part of his theory of ethics, Levinas argues for a kind of hospitality radically different. While the conventional view sees hospitality as simply a politics of power that places the host over the guest or vice versa, Levinas in his *Otherwise than Being* treats hospitality as what he calls "the one-for-the-other in the ego." He sees hospitality as "an incessant alienation of the ego . . . by the guest entrusted to it . . . torn from oneself further in giving to the other the bread from one's mouth."[5] It is in his *Totality and Infinity* where Levinas intensively examines hospitality through a concentrated discussion of both the idea and the act of the welcome of the face of the other. Guided by his "idea of Infinity in us," Levinas's hospitality represents "an irreducible relation" in which the subject never stops opening to the other.[6] As he sees it, this irreducible relation can be developed into an ethics of relation, a relation by obligation rather than by identification, distinction, and alienation. In his attempt to redefine this intentional subjectivity, he argues for an anarchic responsibility to the other—anarchic because, in his words, "to approach the Other is to welcome his expression. . . . It is therefore to receive from the Other beyond the capacity of the I, which means exactly: to have the idea of infinity."[7] By thus "submitting subjection to the infinity in the finite [the Self],"[8] Levinas perceives his ethical relation to affirm a responsibility both absolute and inviolable to the Other. According to him, subjectivity is only formed in a radically passive relation of hospitality toward the Other.[9] As he observes, "The subjectivity of an approaching subject is . . . preliminary, anarchic, prior to consciousness, an implication, a being caught in fraternity."[10] In short, Levinas sees his "infinition" of hospitality as an absolute opening, or a welcoming accorded to and at the same time received from the Other in whose traces the Self is found. The next example should demonstrate how his infinition of hospitality makes impossible any attempt to separate the Self and the Other.

In *Totality and Infinity*, Levinas approaches ethics in different ways, one of which turns out to be the idea and fact of human dwelling. To him, dwelling or home "occupies a privileged place" that gives primarily an "egoistic" impression in the sense that home is most "hospitable to the proprietor."[11] A walled and protected place, home is generally believed to secure for the subject a refuge and isolation—that is, "to shelter him from the inclemency of the weather, to hide him from enemies and the importunate."[12] According to this general view, home signifies a site reserved for as well as a space possessed by the subject to ward off the other together with anything and anyone foreign. Such assumption to Levinas, however, represents no more than an egoistic fantasy.

As Levinas continues, the sense of isolation generated from the subject's possession of a walled-up space materializes in no separation of the self from the other. Separation is rendered impossible because, despite the appearance that "possession [home included] masters, suspends, postpones" the independence of the thing possessed, "as property, merchandise, bought and sold, a thing is revealed in the market as susceptible of belonging, being exchanged, and accordingly as convertible into money."[13] For Levinas, the very fact of possessing something as one's property, while securing certain independence, like a dwelling giving the host some sense of identity, points ultimately to the economical nature of the thing. To use his words, "a thing does not resist acquisition, the other possessors—those whom one cannot possess—contest and therefore can sanction possession itself."[14] It is from this perspective that the subject's home itself, its isolation supposedly protected as well as maintained by the walls, becomes questionable. There is therefore always the need for, not to mention the act of, the welcome of the face of the Other. And with the dissolved isolation, the question of hospitality shows itself to have always arisen, because what is at issue now is not primarily about the home being "hospitable to" the host, but about how the Other calls the host into question. To put the matter in Levinas's words, "the Other paralyzes possession."[15] It is rather the welcome that the home represents and establishes, the Self's knowing how to give what the I possesses and, as a result, to "welcome the Other who presents himself in my home by opening my home to him."[16] In sum, Levinas emphasizes, "The possibility of the home to open to the Other is as essential to the essence of the home as closed doors and windows."[17]

If hospitality for Levinas confirms an irreducible relation that the Other keeps with the Self, hospitality for Derrida represents a notion as well as practice with increasing importance in the understanding of and guarantee for friendship, interreligious relationships, political justice, and democracy in the current world. During the last few years of his life, out of his growing concerns with such political and religious issues as immigration, refugees, nation-states, and international relations, Derrida developed his discourse on the nature, significance, and practice of hospitality. He even saw deconstruction to be a form of hospitality. Or he simply stated that deconstruction is hospitality itself—the welcoming of the other.[18] He showed more interest in finding a way to link the notions of gift, friendship, community, religion, justice, democracy to come, and so forth, with hospitality. And these notions indeed came together in a series of his later works, particularly in *Adieu to Emmanuel Levinas*.

In *Adieu*, Derrida pays his tribute to Levinas by carrying out a detailed analysis of the Levinasian thinking of the welcome of the other developed in *Totality and Infinity*.[19] He discusses intensively and approvingly Levinas's ethics in terms of hospitality. At the same time, he sees certain insufficiencies in Levinas's theory. For instance, he finds it problematic that hospitality through Levinas's ethics becomes a law in which a self has his or her "responsibility for the other in a sort of *oath before the letter*, an unconditional respect or fidelity."[20] Furthermore, despite his unfailing admiration for and repeated praise of Levinas's efforts to disconnect hospitality and the ownership of property, he sees it as unsatisfactory that Levinas should lay down ownership as a condition for hospitality. As has been mentioned, Levinas points out correctly that dwelling by no means separates the Self from the Other. But he insists at the same time that dwelling or home remains a necessary condition for hospitality. To welcome the Other, one has to begin with some kind of commerce, because it is impossible to welcome the guest when the host has no base and is empty-handed. For Derrida, he first of all insists on the paradoxical nature of a home, which means hospitality requires a home and at the same time risks it. Second, he sees that treating hospitality as law and as commerce suggests a similar pattern of thinking: to regard the nature of hospitality as reciprocal or economical. Such a view of hospitality, according to Derrida, amounts exactly to conditional hospitality, a type of hospitality based on economy and exchange within a realm where the Other is appropriated by the Same.

As his point of departure, Derrida takes the example of Kant's essay "Perpetual Peace: A Philosophical Sketch." In the third part of this essay, entitled "Cosmopolitan Right Shall Be Limited to Conditions of Universal Hospitality," Kant argues that the conditions under which perpetual peace can be achieved and maintained must include the perfect constitution that humanity both strives for and abides by. What is more important, such a constitution would have to accommodate the conditions of a universal hospitality, because Kant regards hospitality as "the right of a stranger not to be treated as an enemy when he arrives on someone else's territory."[21] Kant sees the right to hospitality entitled to a stranger not as a right granted by any specific legal system, but rather as one determined by an ideal, probably transcendental, legal system, for the simple reason and the very fact that human beings share this earth. So far, Kant's remarks seem to be a call for a universal hospitality owed to all people. In his argument, hospitality is much more than a state institution or a rite or a social custom. It is a universal right to which all are entitled. Anything less than that, or any limited hospitality, as one can infer from Kant, is no hospitality at all.

On Derrida's reading, however, Kant's hospitality—hospitality as a right without conditions—is not universal. It is not universal because Kant sees the state of war to be the natural state of humans, and the state of peace among people living side by side to be an unnatural phenomenon.[22] Following this conviction, Kant "thinks peace in a purely political fashion and always on the basis of the State."[23] He takes peace to be the result of various governmental measures, among which hospitality as a right granted by the state to foreigners stands out as the first and foremost means to help obtain and protect eternal peace. Based on such understanding, Kant's universal hospitality appears to be what Derrida has called "juridico-cosmopolitanism."[24] From Kant's own words of clarification, his notion of hospitality amounts at most to a territorial right that a stranger receives to enter any foreign state. In other words, unlike the right of a guest to be received and hosted in a friend's home, Kant's universal hospitality does not entitle the stranger to any friendliness, not even helpfulness. Instead, it is merely a right for the stranger to visit without being treated with hostility, or, as Derrida reminds the reader, "it grants only the right of temporary sojourn and not the right of residence."[25] What is more, Kant makes it clear that even this already limited right is conditioned on the stranger acting properly to the host state. As a result, Derrida calls Kant's idea of universal hospitality "a hypocritical promise of a hospitality without restriction" for the simple reason that "the law and cosmopolitics of hospitality that he proposes . . . is a set of rules and contracts, an interstate conditionality."[26] For Derrida, Kant's hospitality with all its rules and conditions not only reduces itself to conditional and limited hospitality but also implies a tendency toward and danger of nationalism and ethnicity.[27] As Derrida argues, such conditional hospitality has a colonial nature: "The Other is welcome to the extent that he adjusts to the *chez soi*, to the home, that he speaks the language or that he learns the language, that he respects the order of the house, the order of the nation state and so on and so forth."[28] Describing faithfully the nature and essence of conditional hospitality in general, Derrida's observation here, as will soon be clear, also depicts accurately the chauvinistic worldview behind the Ming hospitality to the missionaries.

Challenging conditional hospitality and purporting to divest the subject of the drive to appropriate the other, Derrida proposes a hospitality that is unconditional and without demands. Insisting on a morality of hospitality that goes well beyond any morality, and certainly beyond any law and politics,[29] he argues that a truly universal hospitality must give up all the conditions upheld by traditional views of hospitality. According to him, universal or absolute or radical hospitality is the hospitality with a readiness as its testimony to be given not only to the guest expected but also to the guest unexpected.[30] Just as his theory of the true gift means to give a gift that one does not have to someone who does not want it, and true forgiveness, to forgive the unforgivable, Derrida points out that if a person does only what he or she can, that person is doing virtually nothing.[31] He argues for a genuine ethics of hospitality strangely heterogeneous

THE SUBJECT OF HOSPITALITY AND SINO-CENTRISM / 103

to the politics of traditional hospitality.³² If hospitality must be a law, it should be a "law without imperative, without order and without duty."³³ Under this law, the host displaying hospitality must be brave enough to run all risks, from losing his or her status as host to losing the home or even life to the stranger. In short, as Derrida emphasizes with the following remarks, "pure, unconditional or infinite hospitality cannot and must not be anything else but an acceptance of risk. If I am sure that the newcomer that I welcome is perfectly harmless, that he or she will be beneficial to me . . . it is not hospitality. When I open my door, I must be ready to take the greatest of risks."³⁴

Regardless of whether the absolute hospitality thus proposed strikes the readers as feasible,³⁵ this new concept of hospitality for Derrida means primarily to contradict the economy of and oppression in the traditional understanding and practice of hospitality by affirming the singularity of the Other.³⁶ Exactly like Derrida's friendship based on infinite disproportion, in which, in Caputo's words, "the friend is my equal *and beyond, au-delà, hyperbole*,"³⁷ his hospitality argues for the host's nonknowing of the Other, or simply the secret of the Other. Placing the Other beyond the knowledge of the host and thus outside the appropriation or control of the host, absolute hospitality tends to dislodge the fundamental link between hospitality and ipseity, a self as the host striving to sustain his or her own subjectivity by staying as the master both of the house and over the guest.³⁸ The Other with his or her structural secrecy makes it impossible for the host to prepare for the Other's arrival. With no preknowledge of, and therefore being unprepared for, the arrival of the guest, the host is unable to control his or her home but must face the Other or foreigner as he or she is. In other words, with absolute hospitality, the guest, or foreigner, ceases to be passive or someone dependent on the mercy of the host to gain entry into a home. The guest or foreigner rather becomes a challenge, or a question to the host. Just as Derrida observes, the "question of the foreigner [*l'etranger*]," the primary concern of hospitality, must truly be seen as the question "coming from the foreigner, from abroad."³⁹ What follows this understanding is that it is in response to the "foreigner's question" that the host or the Self receives his or her mode of being on earth, a mode of being or subjectivity that is, as Derrida argues, constantly challenged and tormented.⁴⁰

Undoubtedly, the challenge to the host does not come solely from the foreigner outside. The host experiences problems from within as well. In his attempt to unsettle the traditionally distinct roles of host and guest, Levinas mentions more than once the linguistic fact that in French the term *hôte* means both the host and the guest. And with this semantic, he goes on to point out the possibility of a host turning out to be the hostage (*ostage*) through hospitality.[41] For Derrida, who makes frequent references to this Levinasian point, such linguistic undecidability points to the paradoxical or aporetic nature of the host that he believes should lead to the understanding of what he calls "originary dispossession" through hospitality:

> We must be reminded of this implacable law of hospitality: the *hôte* who receives (the host), the one who welcomes the invited or received *hôte* (the guest), the welcoming *hôte* who considers himself the owner of the place, is in truth a *hôte* received in his own home. He receives the hospitality that he offers *in* his own home; he receives it *from* his own home—which, in the end, does not belong to him. The *hôte* as host is a guest. The dwelling opens itself to itself, to its "essence" without essence, as "a land of asylum or refuge." The one who welcomes is first welcomed in his own home. The one who invites is invited by the one whom he invites.[42]

The paradox discussed in the passage does not merely reveal a perennial interruption of the status and authority of the host. The paradox ultimately reorients thinking and actions in today's international and interreligious politics. Derrida does not simply highlight the absence of homogeneity between the home and the host. He means to take away the fundamentals of the host: his or her home, community, city, and even state. Just as he points out, "Nowadays, a reflection on hospitality presupposes, among other things, the possibility of a rigorous delimitation of thresholds or frontiers: between the familial and the non-familial, between the foreign and the non-foreign, the citizen and the non-citizen, but first of all between the private and the public, private and public law, etc."[43] Pushing the host/hostage paradox to its very limits, Derrida shows that a traditional home of the Same—a city of brotherly love or, in the broadest sense of the phrase, a community of friends that with fortified walls forms a circle (*com*) and excludes (*munire*) the stranger or foreigner—is actually porous and open-ended.[44]

With their theories of hospitality that insist on the host's—likewise his or her home's and community's—opening to the other as outlined so far, Levinas and Derrida mount clear as well as powerful challenges to the traditional understanding of hospitality. Their challenges strike one as important because hospitality from ancient times in both the West and China has been not only understood but also practiced to consolidate a hierarchical relation between the host and guest by sustaining the former's superiority or subjectivity. As Derrida has observed, "No hospitality, in the classical sense, without sovereignty of oneself over one's home, but since there is also no hospitality without finitude, sovereignty can only be exercised by filtering, choosing, and thus by excluding and doing violence."[45] In the following pages of the present chapter, both to provide an example of the excluding nature of the traditional hospitality that the two philosophers contest and to prepare for the next three chapters' discussion of the unsettling normative values ascribed to the imperial self behind the Confucian Sino-centrism before the Jesuit guests, it is necessary to look briefly at how hospitality was expected to function in traditional China.

In ancient China, hospitality was practiced as a rite or law that, performed before a guest from near or afar, should do more than confirm the host's authority or master status in one's own home. The performance of hospitality in traditional China was often carried out both to generate and to maintain hierarchization between the host and the guest.[46] Because such hierarchization leads eventually to Sino-centrism, one should begin with a review of the goal and use of the so-called guest ritual or rite of hospitality (*binli* 賓禮), one of the five rites (五禮) followed by the imperial court of virtually every dynasty in Chinese history, including the Ming and Qing (清; 1644–1910).[47]

Like the rest of the five rites, the rite of hospitality in antiquity was originally formulated and performed to serve the need of the sovereign or the king, the ultimate host and owner of a country. Specifically, this rite was to help the king form good working relations with the feudal princes, or lineal lords, in charge of different states within his kingdom, while at the same time keeping in place the king's authoritative and dominant role. The following passage from the *Zhou li* or *Rites of Zhou* describes well the function and purpose of the rite of hospitality:

> The duty of the Grand Superior of the Sacred Ceremonies is to institute state rites concerning these three orders: heavenly gods, dead souls, and earthly images, so as to grant assistance to the king's cause of establishing and defending the kingdom and its principalities. He will see that . . . the rite of hospitality is performed [on behalf of the king] to establish good relations with [the feudal princes from] the principalities. The [feudal princes'] meeting with the king in the spring is called *chao*, the meeting

in the summer is called *zong*, that in the fall is called *jin*, and, in the winter, *yu*. A visit of occasion or *ad hoc* meeting is called a union; a gathering of a large number of participants is called an assembly; a visit for investigation is called consulting; and a meeting with all the princes is called an inspection.[48]

The description in the passage, like many other similar descriptions in the same book, indicates that the rite of hospitality is a ritual performed by the king, or on his behalf, to the princes traveling regularly to the capital for audiences with the king. In other words, it is a rite used virtually exclusively between the king and his feudal princes (王、侯之禮),[49] and used as the king's welcome to and reception of the latter. Besides the self-evident political agenda to be focused on at the meetings, what needs clarification is the nature of the good relations between the king and the princes supposedly formed and sustained by the hospitality ritual. It is true that the passage assures the reader about the good nature of the king-prince relation with the sentence "the rite of hospitality is performed [on behalf of the king] to establish good relations with [the feudal princes from] the principalities." But this relationship is not meant to be an amicable one. Quite the contrary, the relation thus established is expected to confirm and enhance a rigid distinction and hierarchy between the ruler and his subjects. Here, a detail from the *Rites of Zhou* will illustrate this point.

From the very verb used in the sentence, one can see the kin's intention to use the rite of hospitality to assert the king-prince hierarchy. In the original text, the verb of the sentence is *qin* (親), a word that, usually understood as "to love" or "loving," appears frequently in Confucian classics. But given the concern of the *Rites of Zhou* passage and the historical context in which the rites were performed, the term *qin*, rather than indicating the king's love for his princes or some mutual love between the two parties, points to the king's use of hospitality as his strategy to inspire or instill in the princes affection for himself. The rite of hospitality extended to the princes is a way to secure the princes' loyalty and devotion to the king. Having them come to the capital four times a year and extending to them the appropriate welcome, the king actually keeps the princes under his control. He shows the princes, through the rite of hospitality, what is expected from them. Such use of the rite has been an undisputed fact even among Confucian scholars. For example, in his *Wuli tongkao* (五禮通考), Qin Huitian (秦蕙田; 1702–1764), a specialist on Confucian classics on rites, has the following comments on the use of *qin* in this very sentence:

"This term means to make the princes affectionate [to the king]."⁵⁰ What Qin points out is that the term *qin* in this sentence was used as a causative verb.⁵¹ Like the English words *make, let, get, have*, and so on, which can be used to mean a subject causes another subject to do something, the term *qin* was used to say that the king's hospitality rite could get the princes to become affectionate to the king. Here, *qin* used as a causative verb was meant to remind the reader of the ultimate goal of the imperial Rite of Hospitality: to transform the princes into dutiful subjects serving the king with love. This goal of hospitality is perhaps best summarized in the following statement from the "Jiyi" (祭義) chapter in *The Book of Rites*: "Their [the princes'] appearance in the imperial court in spring and autumn served to inculcate in them their duty as subjects and ministers."⁵² To reiterate, it is clear that the term *qin* reveals that the rite of hospitality functions to establish a bond of the king and princes, a bond based on a hierarchical distinction between the ruler and subjects. What can be added here is that this bond, a certain oneness, assured by the rite of hospitality, requires as its condition of possibility domination and submission, through which the king controls his subjects and country.

From the examples of how the rite of hospitality, through distinction and hierarchization, rally the princes under the king, one can see what Derrida has called the possible violence in hospitality. Derrida sees a host as "both the one who gives, *donne*, and the one who receives, *reçoit*, hospitality."⁵³ When the host welcomes a guest into home, the very act of welcoming, as he argues,

> would seek its passage through the violence of the host, who always keeps watch over the rite. For the risk is great. To dare to say welcome is perhaps to insinuate that one is at home here, that one knows what it means to be at home, and that at home one receives, invites, or offers hospitality, thus appropriating for oneself a place to *welcome* [*accueillir*] the other, or, worse, *welcoming* the other in order to appropriate for oneself a place.⁵⁴

Judged against Derrida's remarks, the ancient rite of hospitality was performed exactly to appropriate the visiting princes for the king and his authority.

In Chinese history, the rite of hospitality always had an important role to play in Chinese foreign relations,⁵⁵ just as it did in the king-princes relation. But it was in the Han when, with the waning of the feudal system and the expansion of the international arena, the rite of hospitality became more and more important in the dynasty's diplomacy.⁵⁶ Besides regulating and governing ordinary people's daily activities, their meetings and gatherings, the rite of hospitality shifted its focus to, and eventually concentrated on, foreign relations between the Han and the surrounding tribes and countries. In this shift of focus, what remained unaltered was the desire and intention by the ruler to dominate his subjects or the Other, a desire and intention justified and theorized on by the Han Confucians.

In his *Spring and Autumn Annals* (春秋), Confucius first advanced the idea of the Middle Kingdom being internal, while the barbarians' regions and countries was external. Through the Han Confucians' commentaries and interpretations, this internal-external dichotomy, the very core of Sinocentrism, became a fixed Chinese worldview of totality and no-otherness.⁵⁷ Succinctly summed up in the dictum *wangzhe wuwai* (王者無外), or "the king leaves nothing and nobody outside his realm,"⁵⁸ this Confucian view of world order became both the guiding principle and the ultimate goal of Chinese foreign policy, of which the rite of hospitality formed an integral part. One can illustrate the expected effect that the rite of hospitality would have on Chinese international relations and the Confucian world order by quoting the example of the *Zhongyong* (中庸), or *The Doctrine of the Mean*. One of the Four Books since the Southern Song (1127–1279) but formerly a chapter in *The Book of Rites*, *The Doctrine of the Mean* in its discussion of rulership suggests nine standard rules (九經), with which a ruler should seek control of the world. One of the nine rules states that the ruler should "treat with indulgence men from afar" (柔遠人),⁵⁹ because, as the classic assures, "by indulgent treatment of men from a distance, they are brought to resort to him [the king] from all quarters" (四方歸之).⁶⁰ And, "once the Chinese nobility has been bestowed upon the barbarians," says the annotation in the *Gongyang zhuan*, "the time will have arrived when all countries under heaven—far or near, big or small—come to be one with no otherness."⁶¹

Such Self-enclosure, or what can be properly called state individuation, or state subjectivity, supported by the Confucian ideological as well as cultural premise, demonstrates that hospitality in traditional China anticipates one of the following two results: to keep the other as the other, or to appropriate the other into the self. Undoubtedly, the two results form two sides of the same coin, reflecting the very Chinese understanding and handling of human relations—be it the relation between the ruler and his subjects, or that between China and other countries. Virtually every imperial dynasty in China practiced hospitality by following the same Confucian principle and ideal. But it is the Ming that stands out as a time when the significance and power of Confucian hospitality were both fully understood and most exploited.

The Ming realized early the importance of Confucian rites, including hospitality. Zhu Yuanzhang (朱元璋; 1328–1398), the first emperor of the Ming, perceived the transforming power of rites and music (禮樂教化) for his new dynasty. On his list of priorities, rites and constitutions ranked highest and the most important.[62] Zhu saw the necessity and urgency in setting up a new set of rites and laws, because he had a clear vision of what his future empire should be like. Devoting his government to the establishment and promotion of rites and music, he hoped to restore the glory and prosperity of the Three Dynasties (大興禮樂, 復三代之舊).[63]

Regardless of whether he succeeded in his project of restoration, Zhu Yuanzhang was certainly serious about the rites. Soon after he took the throne, he ordered to learned Confucians to gather to begin his project on rites and music.[64] In 1370, merely three years into his reign, the book *Ming jili* (明集禮), or *Complete Rites of the Ming*, was completed to offer detailed instructions on all five rites, laboriously laying out many rigid and complicated rules for rituals for officials of all ranks to follow on formal and informal occasions.[65] Concerning the rite of hospitality, *Complete Rites* devotes three chapters to the topic, regulating and describing different procedures of Ming diplomacy.[66]

Of the three chapters discussing the rite of hospitality for various diplomatic occasions, the first two set up the protocols for the Ming court's reception of the visiting tributary kings and delegations, while the third chapter describes and lays out details of the ceremonies that the tributary countries must follow to welcome and receive the Ming delegations sent to them.[67] The chapters all begin with reminiscences of how the ancient Middle Kingdom treated foreign delegates and how it went around to different areas to transform the barbarians so that they were moved to follow specific ceremonies and rituals needed for various circumstances. To see how hospitality was expected to serve as a powerful tool for domination in Ming foreign relations, here are some examples from these chapters on hospitality.

In the first chapter on hospitality, it states that, when a tributary king comes to China, there will be an official welcome to him at the border and a banquet in the capital. But before the Ming emperor's audience to the king can be scheduled, the foreign king must be stationed in Tianjie Si (天界寺), a famous Buddhist temple in Nanjing, for a three-day training on Ming ceremonies (習儀).[68] In the third chapter, there are repeated instructions, down to the smallest details, to the tributary countries on proper ceremonies to be followed for the reception of the visiting Ming delegations. For instance, when a Ming imperial edict is to be delivered to a country, this country must go through elaborate formalities, ranging from its king welcoming the Ming emissary outside the capital to the king kneeling down on a specific spot in his palace to listen to the edict read out to him.[69]

The examples from the *Complete Rites* should have made clear that Ming hospitality, like that from any other dynasty in Chinese history, retains first of all the same view as elaborated in the *Spring and Autumn Annals* concerning China's relation with foreign barbarians. But it is likely a unique Ming design that the regime's rite of hospitality should generate and guarantee for the empire an absolute authority both at home and abroad in the regime's dealings with its foreign neighbors. With a hospitality rite in place, foreigners—both those traveling to China to pay tribute and those receiving Ming visiting delegates to their countries—must follow without exception the ceremonies set up by the Middle Kingdom, the ultimate host and master with the utmost power and highest authority.

Turning to the relationship between the Ming and the Jesuits, it has been made clear that the missionaries, no matter how much admiration they had for the Chinese civilization, remained dedicated to their evangelizing mission. Though there were moments and events at which some missionaries expressed their readiness and willingness to be of service to the Chinese authority, a close reading of their words and deeds often reveals that what actually happened was often different. Here, the point is not at all that the missionaries were dishonest, saying one thing but meaning or doing another. Instead, what must be revealed is that the missionaries, by soliciting and receiving the Ming hospitality take the Ming authority and Confucian host hostage, so that the latter is caught in a dilemma where not only the authority or the host becomes dependent on the stranger but also the host's subjectivity shows passivity in its own house. To explain, let me use again the example of Ricci.

For a good part of his career, Ricci lived in China as a famous and popular missionary. This was the case because many of his activities were construed as affirming the domination and authority of the Confucian way of thinking. Like the deeds of many famous Buddhist missionaries who flourished in China centuries before, Ricci's immersion in the Chinese language and customs, including his acceptance of some Confucian doctrines—superficial or not—was taken as his tribute to the "cultural kingdom." Well trained in the modern science of the West and at the same time quite at home with Chinese classics, Ricci seemed to become a walking example of how a foreigner could be both of service to the empire, by bringing Western scientific knowledge, and at the same time be transformed thoroughly by the great civilization of China.[70] Here, a memorial written by Ricci in 1601, when he presented some local trifles (土物) to Emperor Wanli (萬曆; 1573–1620), is typical.

In the memorial, Ricci enlisted his trifles or gifts as including a world map by him, an alarm clock, a Western musical instrument, and, most important of all, some Christian items such as two pictures of Saint Mary, a jewel-studded cross, and a holy book.[71] He also emphasized in the same memorial his reason and goal for having come all the way to China: "When I heard from far away about the fame of the great teachings and the marvelous culture in your Heavenly Kingdom, I began to desire that I immerse myself in this great civilization and remain for the rest of my life a subject of China."[72] Ricci's words, nothing short of a total submission, should account in part for his popularity in China at the time. His memorial virtually presented himself as a human gift, among his other and material gifts, to the Ming emperor. It is then hardly surprising that, despite suggestions that for national security he be kept away from Beijing, he soon received the royal permit to stay in the capital, where he remained until his death in 1610.[73]

With this much said, I now turn to the next chapter to begin discussing the Chinese response or hospitality to the Jesuits.

4

Situating the Middle Kingdom

Matteo Ricci's World Map, the Wobbling Center, and the Undoing of the Host

The heavens are above [us], the earth below. What resides in the middle is China; those occupying the four ends of the heaven and earth are the barbarians. The reality that the barbarians should remain outside and China inside is determined by the heavens and the earth which set the limit or distinction. (天處乎上, 地處乎下, 居天地之中者曰中國, 居天地之偏者曰四夷。四夷外也, 中國內也, 天地為之乎內外, 所以限也。)

—Shi Jie (石介; 1005–1045)

Nowadays, a reflection on hospitality presupposes, among other things, the possibility of a rigorous delimitation of thresholds or frontiers: between the familial and the non-familial, between the foreign and the non-foreign, the citizen and the non-citizen, but first of all between the private and the public, private and public law.

—Jacques Derrida, *Of Hospitality*

The reason to choose Ricci's world map as the first subject for the analysis of Confucian hospitality toward the missionaries is not simply that this map was among the earliest Jesuit works to gain popularity in late Ming China. The map, and what happened around it, marked off an ideological high ground where the Confucian host and the Jesuit stranger enacted the essential and paradoxical types of hospitality theorized and discussed in the previous chapter. In the Confucian-Jesuit encounter, the map and the issues generated by it represented some of the most vigorous and highly complicated cultural negotiations or accommodations that arose, and both sides would, knowingly or not, cross back and forth over the boundaries that they themselves had set up. Both sides would keep smearing the demarcation of the inside and the outside, or the distinction between the Self and the Other, the host and the stranger. Without any doubt, each side attempted to claim authority over the other—the Confucians with their Sino-centrism and the Jesuits with their map and new geographic information, plus Catholic faith in the omnipotence of God. The foregoing discussion has revealed how the missionaries' work in China breached their Catholic universalism. The task of this chapter and the next two chapters is to demonstrate how the seemingly closed Ming circle of the Same is not only infiltrated by the missionaries but also torn apart by a series of Jesuit works starting with the world map. What the map makes manifest first of all are the limits of the Ming empire. These imperial limitations in turn reiterate the fact that Ming China, like the missionaries, exists and functions in a world where innate heterogeneity grants no stability to the roles of host, stranger, or hostage.

It is certainly justifiable to see Ricci's act of presenting the world map to the Chinese as a certain form of self-introduction or self-identification. A complete stranger, uninvited guest, and thus unexpected visitor to the Chinese, he had to tell his host where he and his fellow missionaries were from. To this end, a map would be an appropriate instrument.[1] At the same time, Ricci and his fellow missionaries had in mind another more important agenda for the map. As mentioned earlier, the Jesuits at the beginning of their mission decided to keep a check on their religious fervor. Refraining from preaching too readily and bluntly so as to avoid offending their Chinese host, they turned to various kinds of cultural products from Europe hoping these products could inspire among the Chinese interest in Western civilization and eventually in the Christian religion. Such missionary practices, known as cultural accommodation, began early. Soon after they arrived in Zhaoqing (肇慶), a small county near Canton in south China, and set up their mission house there, Ricci and Ruggieri wasted no time in laying out on display

> the treasures of their small European library—tomes on astronomy, cosmography, and other learned subjects, beautifully printed and exquisitely bound—to men who all their lives had lived under the influence of books. From the first the Jesuits realized the value and influence of the printed page; the picture, the engraving, the map, and the textbook were throughout the history of the

mission a powerful aid to propaganda. . . . He [Ricci] had in his room a map of the world (probably the "Typus orbis terrarum" from the *Theatrum mundi* of Ortelius).[2]

As expected, the missionary exhibits, especially the map, drew much attention from the Chinese.[3] When a local governor by the name of Wang Pan (王泮) visited the Jesuits, he too was fascinated by the Western perception of the world, particularly by the graphic representation of a brand-new world.

As the well-known story continues, Wang suggested that Ricci, with the assistance of an interpreter, "make his map speak Chinese, assuring him that such a work would bring great credit and favor with everyone."[4] Ricci obliged readily. He put out his map, initially entitled "Complete Geographical Map of the Mountains and Seas" (輿地山海全圖) but ultimately named "Complete Map of All Ten Thousand Countries on Earth" (坤輿萬國全圖). As soon as it came out in 1584 as the very first modern world map in the Chinese language,[5] it saw immediate success, earning Ricci instant fame and popularity,[6] not to mention the continuous praise of scholars regarding his solid training in mathematics and geographical knowledge, both crucial in mapmaking.[7]

Ricci's knowledge and use of geographic and cartographic science impressed many of his Chinese contemporaries. But it is important to bear in mind that his map was primarily a requisite of the Jesuit cultural accommodation. It was a tool utilized to serve the Jesuit mission. As Ricci was never shy to admit, the priority of many of his scientific projects, his map included, was to have some impact on the Confucian ideology. In his own words, "When the Chinese see [from the map] that their country is so small in size in comparison with those other countries, this fact will knock off some of their pride and encourage them to form some relationship with other countries."[8] With his map and other objects like the clock and the globe that he made for the Chinese, he intended to teach them a lesson more ideological than scientific and technological. Of course, the advanced scientific and technological knowledge that he possessed helped in rendering his lesson much more powerfully and with long-lasting effect. His map provides a telling example of how Jesuit ideology and science were combined to put forward some questions, both challenging and detrimental, to the Chinese traditional view of the world.

The first of its kind available to the Chinese,[9] the map models were based, mainly but not exclusively, on the *Theatrum orbis terrarum*, published in 1570 by Abraham Ortelius (1527–1598), a Belgian cartographer and mapmaker. Regarded as one of the first world atlases and consisting of fifty-three map sheets, *Theatrum orbis terrarum* was as extremely popular as it is significant in modern cartography. Believed to be a groundbreaking achievement of modern times unlike any previous cartographic work, Ortelius's map "was based more on contemporary knowledge than on theory and myth. It contained no maps from the classical era and therefore represented a fairly up-to-date picture of how the world looked to educated Europeans in the sixteenth century."[10] Thus guided, Ricci's presentation of the world contains not only new geographical knowledge of his time, but also modern mapmaking techniques.

Of the different geographical and cartographical information conveyed to the Chinese through Ricci's map, two features are particularly relevant to the current discussion. First, the map contributed to the Chinese geographical understanding by bringing about the idea or concept of the world as a globe, unknown to the Chinese up to that time. The idea of the earth as round, to be further addressed later in this chapter, posed a serious problem to Sino-centrism by calling into question the traditional Chinese view of a flat earth with an identifiable center. Second, the map introduced the Chinese to the most advanced Western cartography of the day.[11] To present a three-dimensional globe on a two-dimensional surface of paper or stone, the map employed the so-called equal-area oval projection or orange-peel projection—a technique of modern cartography—with meridians or cursive longitudinal lines converging vertically at the poles while crossing horizontally with straight latitudinal lines. With the meridian lines dividing the surface of the earth into different time zones, the map, besides further confirming a round world, made it possible for its viewers to calculate the time of and distance between areas.[12]

Despite some flawed understanding that Ricci had of the universe, to be briefly discussed later, the idea of the earth as a globe measured and presented with meridian and longitude lines, besides evidently contradicting traditional cartographic knowledge of China, challenged directly the Ming idea of Sino-centrism. This was so primarily because the spherical shape denied the possibility for anyone to identify or locate any single and fixed point on its surface as the central one. But Ricci was tactical enough not to want to confront his host too quickly. As if hoping to mitigate the detrimental impact that his map might have on the Chinese cosmology, or to defer his host's possible negative reaction to his map, Ricci demonstrated his characteristic innovativeness. Despite his contempt toward the Ming self-centered and self-important view of the world, he cleverly maneuvered the two above-mentioned geographic and cartographic features to produce a map that has China positioned in the very middle of the world.[13]

Though mapmakers in traditional China would often place their country's administrative capital near the geometric center of a map,[14] a map with China in the middle of it was unprecedented in the history of European mapmaking. Standard cartographic practice in Europe since the Middle Ages, including the one by Ortelius, always put the so-called first meridian line (meridian origin, or *méridien premier de Canaries*) as the central longitude dividing the map into eastern and western hemispheres.[15] As a result, China is often placed at the very end of the right-hand side of those maps. What Ricci did was move the first meridian line almost 170 degrees to the left. As a result, in his map, the Fortunate Islands (known today as Gran Canaria or Canary Islands) that the meridian goes through now appears on the far left-hand side, while China stands in the center.

Ricci's act of placing China in the center of his map can be seen as an indication of the uncertainty of the roles of the host and stranger. Undoubtedly, Ricci, as the mapmaker, was in charge of what to put in his map and where to do so. And his freedom to move China around in his map, or his authority to decide from what angle he would like his map to present its content to his audience, proves his authority in the matter. In other words, his mapmaker role seems to reverse, as far as his map is concerned, the role of his Chinese host. For a moment, he had his Chinese host in his palm, making the latter's country appear to be a most passive entity at his disposal.

Unaware of the implication, many Ming Confucians found the map with China in the middle to be a welcome thing, a thing deserving hospitality. The map so structured turned out to be a highly presentable gift to Ricci's Chinese host. For example, when he submitted a copy of his map to Emperor Wanli, the latter, so fond of this new trifle of curiosity, ordered ten more copies to be made. According to some scholarly views, it was exactly because quite a number of Confucian officials, like their emperor, took the map for a trifle or toy that the cartographic knowledge that Ricci hoped to disseminate through it was not quickly picked up or absorbed by the Chinese, excepting a handful of them.[16] Of course, the slow reception of cartographic technology and scientific information in China does not mean in any fashion that the Chinese took the map as a mere trifle with no political significance.

Besides the emplacement of China, which certainly went well with the Sino-centric view, Ricci's very act of presenting a world map to the

Chinese should also be a reason for the map's initial popularity among the Confucians. In traditional China, despite the lack of administrative training of professional cartographers until perhaps the middle of the nineteenth century, authorities from very early on fully realized the importance of maps for both military activities and political control. Maps were regarded as crucial to national security and were thus always heavily guarded as top secrets of the state. To present a map of one state to another state was always seen to be an act of submission, surrender, or betrayal.[17] When, after the Han, maps played a more important role in foreign relations,[18] it so happened that, as Cordell D. K. Yee has recently argued, "presentation of *yudi tu* [輿地圖 the Terrestrial Map] to the emperor was apparently part of the ceremonies associated with enfeoffment."[19] Toward this point, Ming history offers its own examples. During the Ming, maps were used in foreign affairs as a powerful aid to symbolize, and even actualize, Chinese hegemony in the world.

From the beginning of the dynasty, Zhu Yuanzhang took maps to be an assuring sign of foreign submission. Zhu would therefore order his empire's tributary countries to provide maps of their territories as well as other state records to be brought to China.[20] For some Confucians in the late Ming who shared this traditional view, the Jesuits presenting maps and books on the geography of the West and other related topics was nothing but a proof of the foreigners' submission, owing to the greatness of the Chinese empire. For example, in his preface to the *Zhifang waiji*, a book on world geography, including cartography, that the Jesuit Aleni wrote in Chinese, Ye Xianggao remarked, "Mr. Aleni has come all the way to China out of his admiration and respect for the righteousness of our country. He [and his fellow Jesuits] submitted hundreds of volumes of new and curious books [as tributary gifts] to the imperial court. Isn't it true that the missionaries have done much more than [in ancient times] the Country of Yueshang had, having its letters to our emperors go through several translations in order to submit their [white] pheasants as their tribute to us?"[21] Unfortunately, what Ye did not realize here is that the Jesuit visitors saw for their tribute some completely different uses in China.

With China occupying its most visible and prominent spot, Ricci's map may seem at first to speak for rather than against the Confucian view of "keeping the barbarians out, and China in the center." It may just as well be true that his presentation actually pleased many Chinese by satisfying their chauvinistic mindsets for many years to come. But in his annotations added to the map, Ricci showed no hesitation in making clear his disagreement with, and even criticism of, the erroneous cosmological views of the Chinese:

> The earth and the seas are both spherical in shape. Together they form a globe, situated in the middle of a bigger globe called the heavens, the same as the yoke of an egg is situated in the middle of the egg white. Those who argue about the earth being square are actually talking about the fixed and unmovable position of the earth not its shape.[22]

Taking the earth to be immobile, Ricci's remarks are obviously marred by his geocentric misconception based on the Ptolemaic system of the cosmos.[23] Regardless of Ricci's presentation of the church-approved cosmology,[24] what he said aimed at discrediting the Chinese misunderstanding of the world. His presentation of the earth as a globe, a proven fact by then to the Europeans,[25] challenged the entire Chinese cosmology—a square earth with a center—that had dominated not only Chinese cartography but also Chinese administrative measures, political thinking, and worldview. To see the significance of this challenge from Ricci and its "devastating" effect, it is necessary to reflect briefly on the history of and theories within traditional Chinese cosmology.

As is known, the Chinese developed early their cosmology that the world was a square made up of four quarters. In the chapter of Yugong (禹貢) from the *Book of Documents* (尚書), one learns how the Great Yu (大禹; c. 2140 BCE), the supposed author of the chapter, divided the Middle Kingdom into nine provinces or states (九州) inhabited peacefully by the Chinese (九州攸同). The Yugong chapter describes five concentric geographical zones emanating outward from the capital: royal domains, princely domains, a pacification zone, the zone of allied barbarians, and the zone of savages. This section of the description also offers minute details concerning the square feet and length of the border of each zone. Though the chapter contains no actual map to indicate the shape of these zones, based on the Confucian cosmological notion of a "square earth," the zones have been depicted as five rectangular squares inside each other.[26] It is true that there were in ancient China three different theories of the cosmos.[27] The traditional maps in China have virtually always been based on the same Confucian cosmic notion of a square earth. Even the map by Pei Xiu (裴秀; 224–271), a project that has won unanimous praise from scholars throughout history for its scientific cartographic techniques, likewise conveys the same idea of the emperor sitting in the center and knowing things in all four quarters. In short, throughout history it was a combination of the Circular-Heaven theory and the Sphere-Heaven theory that remained dominant concerning the traditional cartographic presentation of the general and political understanding of the world in ancient China.[28]

The ancient Chinese had their reasons for believing in a square earth. Only when the earth remained square could a center in the middle of the earth become possible and locatable. What is more important than having a center for the earth is that in the center the Chinese could have a spot from which their emperor could rule all under heaven. The emperor, communicating directly with Heaven to receive mandates from above, could secure his rule over the country. Obviously, the ancient Chinese had no doubt at all that the cosmic assumption of a square earth and a ruler with crowning glory and supreme power were not only interdependent, but also could work to reinforce each other. They therefore launched long ago their search for a spot or place known as *tuzhong* (土中), or *dizhong* (地中), a geographic point or landing exactly on the very center of "all under the heaven."[29] Of the various choices, from the early Mt. Kunlun (崑崙山) to Jian Mu (建木) or the Jian Tree, the Confucian scholars, following years of collaboration and speculation, narrowed down the places to two possible sites in He'nan (河南) as the center of the earth: either Luoyi (雒邑), today's Luoyang (洛陽) and also an ancient capital, or Yangcheng (陽城)—that is, today's city of Dengfeng (登豐).[30]

The Confucian obsession with the center of the earth can be interpreted in line with Mircea Eliade's theory. In *The Myth of the Eternal Return*, Eliade discusses the symbolism of the center, one of which he refers to as *axis mundi*, the center of the world. According to him, such a center, often represented by a sacred city or temple, is regarded as "the meeting point of heaven, earth and hell."[31] Though Eliade does not reference China in this instace, Eliade's point that the center often serves as a "Bond of Heaven and Earth" applies well to the Chinese understanding and significance of a center. Here is an exemplifying passage in *Huainanzi* describing the Jian Tree, the supposed center of the earth during the early Han: "The Jian Tree on Mt. Duguang, by which the gods ascend and descend (to and from Heaven), casts no shadow at midday. If one calls (from the place), there is no echo. This is so because this is the center of the earth."[32]

Undoubtedly, the attempt to locate the center of the earth should be seen first of all as part of the Chinese effort to form its own political cosmology. And the formation or acquisition of this identification of a cosmological center will in turn grant ideological support to the Confucian world order or ethnocentrism. Here, the assertion from Xunzi serves as a good testimony: "To be close to all four quarters, there is no place better than the center. As the rite has it, the king must stay in the very center."³³ Seeing the religious, ideological, and political importance of the center, Ban Gu (班固; 32–92) gives the following statement in response to the question "Why must the king, for his capital, select [a place in] the center of the earth?":

> It is in order that he may maintain an equipoise of [the effects of his spiritual] teaching, and equalize the distance to and from the [capital]; that he may easily be informed of the good and the evil that is committed. It indicates that he should always be careful and diligent in the observation of [the people's] good and evil [deeds]. The *Shang shu* says: "May the king come [in the new capital] to continue [the work] of the Lord on High, and undertake himself [the duties of government] in the center of the land."³⁴

Clearly, the myth of and desire for a center in traditional China resembles what Derrida has called the "fascination of totality."³⁵ For the Chinese, only when the capital or the throne is placed in the very middle of the earth can the Son of Heaven as the master or host of his world rule all four quarters.

Given the ideological and hegemonic importance embedded within the theory of the center of the earth, the challenge from the new world map should strike one as all the more crucial and significant. When the earth was presented to be nothing but round, the world map now tended to eliminate the fact of a center once and for all. What the world map showed to the Ming audience was the complete absence of the center that had been understood from the traditional Confucian point of view. Though Ricci's map still had China placed in the middle, as if the center could still be located, that middle point was already desacralized, with its importance and significance severely deflated. In short, with his map, Ricci supplanted the center. By moving China to the middle, he already implied that on a round earth the center could be anywhere, or that any spot could be used or viewed as center or as margin. In his book on geography for the Chinese, Aleni has the following succinct message: "On the surface of a sphere, any point can be the center."³⁶

Once realizing the tremendous danger that the spherical earth in Ricci's map could bring to Chinese Sino-centrism, the Confucians were quick to voice their disagreement and anger. While some Chinese scholars found it distasteful that the position of China on Ricci's map was not central enough,[37] others saw clearly the threat Ricci's new geography posed to the Chinese hegemony. For example, in a letter to his friend, Li Suiqiu (黎遂球; 1602–1646), a famous painter and accomplished poet from Guangdong, expressed his concern about Ricci's presentation of the earth as a globe:

> The strange theory [of the Westerners] is that on our earth there are no such directions as east, west, south, north and thus no up and down. If one follows such idea, then humans [standing on the surface of the earth] are all hanging with their heads down, and what the *Book of Changes* has called to be the high heaven and the low earth, and the hierarchy of ranks will all become uncertain. If people are convinced by this idea, there will be no end to our trouble. This is what disturbs me deeply. . . . What worries me more and more is that once this idea gains popularity and causes the world disasters, this idea will be a stepping-stone to a world without distinction between ruler and subjects, or between high and low.[38]

Li's tone indeed sounds grave. For someone who took the teachings from the *Book of Changes* as the way the world must be, or how the world should be ordered, the possibility of finding a center everywhere on the face of the earth must have been truly terrifying.

If Li only worried about the possible loss of hierarchy, for Yang Guangxian (楊光先; 1597–1669), an official in the early Qing Dynasty (1644–1911), the hierarchy between China and the rest of the world was already destroyed by Ricci's round earth theory. To believe that what Ricci said in his map was right would mean, Yang pointed out, that China had already lost its status as the authority in and master of the world. He elucidates thus:

> The theory [from Ricci] about the earth being in the shape of a ball, and humans on [different halves of] the earth standing with the bottom of their feet towards each other, is extremely upsetting to me. It is a fact that the sun at noon is up high, and that the moon at noon is down low. They are saying literally

that our Middle Kingdom is underneath the Western Ocean [continent] for the people there to stamp on with their feet. This is the worst insult to our Middle Kingdom!³⁹

To be sure, Yang's reasoning would strike a modern reader as naive and laughable. But what both he and Li said about the end of hierarchy represents a genuine and serious concern of the Confucians at the time. For these Confucians, the idea of a geographic and cartographic center occupied by China constituted, among other things, the dichotomy or distinction of the Self and the Other—not just the distinction separating the ruler and his subjects within the country but also a dichotomy distinguishing the master and his vassals, or civilization and barbarism around the world. When the idea and fact of a round earth significantly diluted the importance and the meaning of the center, what became immediately questionable for the Confucians was their sense of hierarchy and the separation of China and the outside (華夷之辨).

As one can see, the hierarchy and separation of China and the outside indeed became problematic when Ricci's world map put into question the host status of the Great Ming. It is true that losing the center might already have meant to the host or master the loss of his place, where his authority and power were generated and protected. But one must drive the matter in hand to a greater depth. As one knows, China from early on entertained the belief and hope not only of itself as being at the center but also of having under its control the entire earth, a belief and hope best illustrated in the poetic lines from the *Book of Songs*: "Under the wide heaven, / All is the king's land, / Within the sea-boundaries of the land, / All are the king's servants."⁴⁰ As can be inferred from these lines, China, from the Confucian point of view, equaled exactly the world. Or the size of the world was the precise size of China, no more and no less. To describe this Confucian mentality by borrowing the Heideggerian term, China's *Dasein*, or its Being-in-the-world, was simply China's being-the-world. With its emperor claiming mastery or ownership of all people and the entire world, the Chinese Empire sat on top of its hierarchy as, to quote the phrase from a modern scholar, "an empire without neighbours."⁴¹ The Chinese Empire had no neighbors because, as the Confucian doctrine purported, all China's neighboring countries and peoples existed only as fiefs of the Chinese master or host. Such Confucian hierarchy or separation meant to maintain a world of one meaning and a singular history for China. In a country without otherness like the Chinese Empire, no wonder so many Confucians found it appalling and unthinkable the small size of the Middle Kingdom in Ricci's map and the many peoples and countries unknown before.

Throughout history, the Confucians had hoped to sustain China's hegemony by having their empire remain one of no-otherness and with a singular history. The Chinese, especially the Confucians, entertained the conviction that, with more and more known countries entering China's tributary system,[42] their empire stood as the only master or host of the world, a master or host who had the entire world as his house. But this otherwise ideal kingdom began to tumble when it suddenly came before a modern world map. More by accident than by Ricci's design,[43] the map ripped open this closed and limited world that the Confucians had imagined for themselves centuries earlier and had sustained until the time when Ricci emplaced China in the middle of what one can call, borrowing a Foucauldian phrase, a "heterogeneous space,"[44] a space with numerous countries previously unknown and unheard of to the Chinese. When the map introduced China as a new member—instead of as a parent, master, or host—into a world family, the relation between Ming China and the rest of the world stopped being the usual hierarchical one, with the Middle Kingdom on top of everyone else. In this world family, China's existence, by the Confucian view, as a "perfectly detached, distinct and closed" Self—or, as has been mentioned above, its "being-the-world"—turned irreversibly into what Heidegger has referred to as the *Mitsein*, the Being-with other beings or countries.[45] In this world family where one seems to find only a kind of coexistence, that would mean, as Jean-Luc Nancy argues, "finitude existence to finitude existence,"[46] with no sign or existence of head, owner, host, or master. In the map, the Confucians saw only different countries and peoples spread as far and wide as the surface of the earth could allow.[47]

If Franco Moretti is right to point out that "a map is . . . a connection made visible—[which] will allow us to see some significant relationships that have so far escaped us,"[48] then the relationship that became visible, almost palpable, through Ricci's map had some alarming effects in China. This relation or coexistence—a heterogeneous existence or inhabiting of a world full of difference and diversity, a world so entangled and out of control—predetermined the futility of any human attempt to distinguish one thing from another, and it even implied a certain incapability of Ricci's Almighty God.[49] To the Confucians, this vast and seemingly endless new world without the China-determined order and hierarchy certainly caused much frustration and anxiety. For example, Xu Dashou (許大受), a late Ming anti-Christian author whose work will be discussed in greater detail later in this book, accused Ricci of "feigning the distance [between China and the West] (詐遠)."⁵⁰ To Xu, Ricci's claim that he had come from a country more than eighty thousand *li* away had no veracity but served as a ploy to secure the West by placing it beyond the reach and power of the Ming Empire's cultural transformation (化外) and beyond its political control.⁵¹ Besides protecting the West from the transforming power of Chinese civilization, the distance also prevented the Chinese from verifying the stories and statements expressed by the missionaries. This lack of verification then pointed to a problem much more serious than the possibility that the missionaries could tell the Chinese just about anything that struck their fancy. This lack of knowledge of the other or "non-knowledge," as Derrida has called it, translated readily into the singularity of the other, an Other impossible to appropriate or reduce to a subordinate part of the Ming Self.⁵² In short, any existence of singularity, as Xu and other Confucians knew in their own way, meant certain irreducible difference, or simply interruption, to the Confucian history of totality, a history of self-sufficient subjectivity. With the other remaining far beyond transformation, beyond reach, and, most importantly, outside knowledge to the Self—and singular and thus irreducible to the Self—the Self ceases to be the master or host.

If the discussion of Ricci's map so far has revealed to a certain degree the devastation that the missionary map had brought for the Confucian hierarchy, what rendered the Ming Self so incomplete, or the Ming host so futile in the encounter, even dependent on the missionaries as a hostage, involves more—much more—to come. As the China-Jesuit encounter and exchange continued, the Confucian attempt to keep separate the Self and the Other by maintaining the China-foreign hierarchy began to crack. Some Confucians began to concede that there might be some truth in the concept of a round earth. Here is a good example. A Confucian by the name of Zhou Xing (周星), a scholar passing in 1640 his *jinshi* (進士) or Metropolitan Graduate examination, wrote an essay with the following conclusions about the missionaries and their science:

> The saints detect and take [what is reasonable out of] ravings from madmen. Now it is known to us that there are the so-called scholars of learning from the Western land, people truly ridiculous and not worth mentioning. But what is correct beyond any doubt and unalterable are their theories of the shape of the earth and heaven, including theories of the eclipse of the sun and moon. These theories state that the earth is surrounded by

heaven with the earth sitting in the very center of heaven; that the shape of the earth is like a big globe with the sea flowing around on its surface, and that humans live all over it.[53]

It would be hard for a reader to miss the condescending tone in Zhou's remarks. Designating the missionaries as madmen while commenting positively on their knowledge of geography, Zhou showed how his hospitality could be both dismissive and receptive at the same time. To put it differently, he made his approval of Western geography and astronomy in the passage sound like a limited and reluctant hospitality, a kind of hospitality displaying more caution than openness or welcome toward the Other. It seems that with his reserved hospitality he was, instead of praising the usefulness and accuracy of Western science, suggesting actually the good fortune for the Jesuit visitors before their Chinese host. That is, observing Confucius's instruction of not dismissing anyone,[54] the Ming Confucian saints actually rescued the otherwise completely unworthy missionaries, these strangers, by discovering some value in their senseless and ridiculous ravings. Given these facts, one is certainly justified in reading and critiquing the above passage as another example of Confucian Sino-centrism. However, there is more to Zhou's words.

Zhou's partial and guarded hospitality is by no means the same as the wholehearted praises that Christian converts like Xu Guangqi (徐光啟; 1562–1633) and Li Zhizao (李之藻; 1571–1630) would sing about the Jesuit science.[55] But what he said in the quoted passage was already different in a fundamental fashion from the harsh criticism and total rejection uttered by Li Suiqiu, Yang Guangxian, and Xu Dashou. Unlike those Confucians, who rejected everything from the Jesuits, Zhou saw the use of Western science, which he thought could at least be supplementary to what China already had. As far as his remarks are concerned, his rather patient and detailed description of Western geography and astronomy demonstrate more than a sober recognition of the validity of Western science and technology. He pointed to an epistemological as well as practical need for the Confucians to make use of Western science. Furthermore, his acceptance of Jesuit science, though granted condescendingly, signaled, however implicitly, a changed view of the Sino-foreign relationship, a view that ultimately pointed to the weakness and incompleteness of the Confucian subjectivity that had become aware of otherness.

The next chapter will relate more details to show how the Ming empire's increasing dependence on Western astronomy and other sciences confirmed further the weak and incomplete subjectivity of the Chinese host. In the remaining pages of the current chapter, I hope to demonstrate further how the world map and knowledge of geography, besides expanding the Chinese worldview in a scientific way, also deconstructed the authority of Confucian ideology. Supplying new knowledge of a greater world with many more peoples previously unknown to the Chinese, the world map and geography from the West stimulated rethinking of this Confucian ideology, a fact that shows that Confucianism, traditionally claiming to represent the universal, ultimate, and complete truth of both nature and culture, could be, and was being, supplemented. One example to be examined in the following paragraph is the reinterpretation of the neo-Confucian concept known as the Principle or *li* (理)—an important concept formulated in the Song (宋; 960–1279) and further developed in the Ming. Here is what happened.

Realizing gradually but certainly the validity of cartographic and geographic science from the West, the Confucians found themselves facing a dilemma. They had, on the one hand, to provide a satisfactory answer to the embarrassing question of why strangers from what was believed to be some barbaric part of the world had better and more knowledge of the earth than the Chinese. On the other, aware of the service that missionary science could grant late Ming society, they had now to search for a theory that could justify and legitimize China's making use of the so-called *xixue* (西學), that is, Western science and learning.[56] Interestingly, several Confucian scholars, most of them Christian converts and friends of the Jesuits, came up with converging arguments by resorting to viewpoints concerning the mind or *xin* (心) and the Principle of Lu Jiuyuan (陸九淵; 1139–1193), a Confucian thinker in the Southern Song (1127–1279).[57] Quoting virtually word for word Lu's well-known theory of the universality and union of the mind and Principle, these Confucians and Christian converts attempted to negotiate the China-West difference by insisting that China and the West shared a common Truth that both sides would know through the same epistemology. Here are a few examples. In his introduction to the last edition of Ricci's world map, Li Zhizao told his reader, "Looking now at this [world] map, without exchanging a word [with the mapmaker], I know that what I have thought of [the world] is the same as what is presented here. As the saying goes, 'In the Western Ocean as in the Eastern Ocean, the minds are the same and there is only one Principle.' Isn't this map a proof of that saying?"[58] Another scholar, Wang Jiazhi (王家植), who passed the state examination in 1604, wrote a preface to Ricci's *Ten Chapters of a Strange Man*, where he first pointed out the vast distance between China and the West. Then he asserted that the teachings and mores that Ricci had learned and preached did not contradict those put out by past Chinese sage kings, like Yao, Shun, King Wen, and Confucius (不詭於堯舜周孔大指). For Wang, it would be impossible for the Ming and the West to think differently, because "the world does not have two Principles; humans do not have two minds; a thing does not have two meanings. Looking up, one sees only one heaven, and Heaven does not have two masters."[59] It seems that Li Zhizao was particularly fond of quoting Lu's phrase of assimilation for his own emphasis on the sameness between China and the West as far as the human pursuit of Principle/Truth was concerned. In his introduction to a new edition of Ricci's *The True Meaning of the Lord of Heaven*, he states, "Lo! In the Eastern Sea as in the Western Sea, the minds are the same and the Principle remains one. What makes these facts seem different are only the words from different languages used to express them."[60]

Whether the Confucian Christians with what they said in effect wished to assimilate the missionaries, or hoped to stimulate some Chinese tolerance toward the strangers, one thing is certain: their insistence on a same mind and Principle shared by China and the so-called Far West represented by the Jesuits was unprecedented. To understand what the reference to Lu Jiuyuan actually meant about China's Self or Ming subjectivity, or what the applicability of Western science in the Chinese context suggested about the Confucian sense of cultural supremacy, one needs first to look at Lu's philosophy and his use of the concept of Principle, one of the most important concepts in neo-Confucian discourse since the Song, particularly the Southern Song.

Simply put, Principle as a concept in neo-Confucian thinking depicted in a metaphysical sense the Way of Heaven (*tianli* 天理). Though the meaning of the Principle could vary slightly in the discussions of different neo-Confucian philosophers,[61] it is a consensus among these philosophers that Principle as the Way of Heaven did much more than merely describe the movement and existence of the universe. It also served as the ultimate guide for, as well as the loftiest mode of, human righteousness to be understood and observed by all. In short, with its assumed universality for both the natural world and human society, Principle stood for the very essence of everything and everyone. Of all these thinkers who discussed Principle, no one seemed to be more forceful and relevant to the present discussion than Lu Jiuyuan, the founder of the Learning of the Heart or Idealistic thought (心學), who believed the Heavenly Principle to be *innate* in the human mind.[62]

Like virtually all other neo-Confucian thinkers, Lu treated Principle as both the Heavenly Way and the ultimate Confucian moral. But what made him unique was that, with the fundamentals of his philosophy based on Mencius's thought,[63] he believed that all humans possessed in a transcendental fashion standards of virtue and righteousness, which he called the original mind (本心).[64] For him the original mind was the same as [the Heavenly] Principle (本心即理).[65] To summarize Lu's philosophy of mind and Principle by borrowing a contemporary scholar's words, Lu's thought was simply that "there was nothing outside the [original] mind (一心無外)," or "there was nothing outside Principle (一理無外)."[66] Lu's point was that for anyone wanting to learn how to be a good human being, it was essential that he or she maintain the original mind or retrieve it.[67] Every time a person did something immoral was as a matter of fact the time when this person would lose his or her original mind (失其本心). A person seeking self-elevation would need to look into his or her mind for the moral guide for his or her behavior. Firmly convinced by his own idea of the identification of the human mind and Principle, Lu went through life philosophizing and advocating his point, repeatedly and tirelessly making catchy and often palindromic remarks like the following ones: "Those affairs which are within the universe are those which fall within my duty; those affairs which fall within my duty are those which are within the universe"; "The universe is my mind, and my mind is the universe"; and "The Principle permeates the universe. This is what is meant by saying that beyond the Truth (Dao), nothing exists; outside of things no Truth exists."[68]

Lu sometimes expressed doubt whether foreign barbarians could ever comprehend and learn the right Way of living.[69] He was completely certain that the Confucian Principle could and should serve both as guide and guarantee of an ideal form of human existence in which all people and all cultures could come together. The following are his own well-known words, words that late Ming converts quoted frequently, which express his conviction of the universality of Principle:

> The universe is my mind, and my mind is the universe. If in the Eastern Sea there were to appear a sage, he would have this same mind and this same Principle. If in the Western Sea there were to appear a sage, he would have this same mind and this same Principle. If in the Southern or Northern Seas there were to appear sages, they (too) would have this same mind and this same Principle. If a hundred or a thousand generations

ago, or a hundred or a thousand generations hence, sages were to appear, they (likewise) would have this same mind and this same Principle.⁷⁰

Doubtlessly, Lu's vision of unifying all people and cultures under Principle or the Confucian Way was consistent with Confucius's assertion that "there is one single thread binding my Way together" (吾道一以貫之; *Analects* 4.15). Moreover, Lu's universal applicability of the Confucian Way was inherited and developed by his Ming disciple Wang Yangming, who pushed Lu's theory to its extremity.⁷¹ Dismissing Buddhist and Daoist teachings as heresies,⁷² Wang shared Lu's conviction that Confucian doctrines represented the only and final truth. What is more, both Lu and Wang believed that this Truth—this Principle—must be what every person of every culture strove to pursue and obtain in order to live a perfect life.⁷³ The question now, however, is whether the Confucian Principle is indeed as far-reaching and all-encompassing as these Song and Ming philosophers believed and promoted it to be. One must ask whether this Principle, as the ultimate host, truly welcomes all and whether it, as the imperial signifier denotes, is precisely the holiest message from the divine that would meet every need of everyone in every corner of the earth. Most importantly, is the Principle truly so ultimate, final, and complete? These questions should take one back to the late Ming context, where Lu's argument of a shared mind and a common Heavenly Way was quoted word-for-word and repeated in the discussion of the missionaries and their introduction of European science to the Chinese.

Quoting Lu frequently, these late Ming Confucian Christians seemed at first to be making a straightforward point that the missionaries should be no strangers to the Chinese because they shared the same mind with them and upheld the same Confucian Principle. At least, Lu's words, plus the Confucian view behind his concept of Principle, may give the reader the impression that these Confucians intended to assimilate the missionary strangers. With their assertion of the same-mind and same-Principle, it may look like they took the scientific exchange between China and the missionaries as marking a memorable moment in cross-cultural history at which the East and West came together to see in each other a common mindset that sought and found a "common or shared truth" (普遍真理).⁷⁴ When the Jesuits traveled all the way to China to offer gifts of their most recent knowledge and technology, plus other curious trifles, what else could it be but that they had come to know and learn the Chinese mind, to immerse themselves in Chinese culture, and, in short, to seek transformation by and from Chinese civilization (嚮化).

But a close inspection should reveal that, despite their frequent references to Lu's theory and concepts, the late Ming Confucian Christians were by no means promoting the Confucian Principle as the only truth. On the contrary, they were inserting their subtle and yet definite differences into the meaning of the terms "mind" and "Principle." Discussing approvingly Jesuit science, knowledge, technology, and the Catholic deity, they were pointing out that the missionaries had in them their own mind and their own principle, both quite different from those of the Confucians. With their repetition of Lu's shared mind and shared Principle for people both in the Eastern Sea and the Western Sea, these Confucian Christians were actually saying that both the mind and principle that the missionaries had were different and, as a matter of fact, absent from the Confucian repertoire of possessions. Worse still, such absence, rather than an indication of a certain moral impediment on the side of the Jesuits, pointed to a certain incompleteness of the Confucian Principle, an incompleteness signaling the need of as well as the possibility for supplement. Despite the fact that Lu, Wang, and virtually all other Confucian thinkers argued for the universality and totality of the Confucian Way, the missionaries, suggested these Chinese converts, had proved that they and their science represented something both valid and exterior to the Confucian system. This argument that the stranger from a barbaric and uncivilized part of the world could possess some truth missing in Confucianism certainly went against the grain of the Confucian worldview and ideology. But the late Ming converts had two points they wanted to make.

First, besides undermining the universality of the Confucian Way, the reality that the stranger from far away should manage to discover all by himself truth not included in the Confucian Principle would call into question the distinction between China and the barbarians. If this distinction for the Ming Confucians represented first of all a hierarchy based on high moral standards and cultural superiority, then the stranger with high moral standards of his own clearly posed a threat to the superiority and authority of the Ming empire by upsetting the China-barbarian hierarchy that the Confucians always hoped to sustain. The late Ming Confucians became aware of the uncertain ground on which the missionary work in China had placed Confucianism. Here are the words of Qu Shigu (瞿式穀; 1593–?), Qu Rukui's son and a Catholic convert:

When looking for evidence from our past masters, they have stated: "In the Eastern Sea and the Western Sea, people's minds are the same and Principle is the same." Who can be sure that out of the same mind and the same Principle people [at different places] will not radiate their own excellence? The stubborn people [in China] who believe themselves to be right and others [from abroad] wrong are truly mistaken. Furthermore, how can the distinction between China and the barbarians be constant without the possibility of change? If a people is trustworthy and righteous . . . , this people then is part of China no matter how faraway it is. If a people has no sense of morality and has no shame . . . , it is barbaric even when it may be right beside us.[75]

Using some Confucian moral concepts to demarcate civilized and uncivilized behaviors, or determine who qualified to be Chinese and who did not—to be exact, a reshuffling of host and guest—Qu was by no means endorsing the argument that Confucianism was the only moral standard. Instead, he pointed out the fact that the Jesuit strangers who never received any Confucian education could still have their own high moral values. To be sure, some may have a counterargument that Qu's statement, and similar ones by others, simply proved the neo-Confucians' theory that Principle indeed existed and waited for anyone from any place to understand and follow. It is therefore no surprise at all that the Confucian Principle could be picked up by strangers. Furthermore, the strangers' scientific knowledge and technological dexterity only worked to make them better supporters and promoters of the Confucian doctrines. While the next chapter will focus on what the missionary service did for Confucianism and the Ming empire, the task for the moment is to show that the differences between the Confucians and the Jesuits observed and revealed by the late Ming converts have posed a thorny problem, not only to the supposed China-foreign hierarchy but also to the argument concerning the universality and totality of the Confucian Principle. And it is amidst this inconvenient reality for Confucianism that the late Ming converts made their second point.

Whether the Confucian distinction tumbled down completely in the presence of the strangers with equally high moral standards, these Chinese Christians during the late Ming dynasty seemed to be certain of one thing in their discussion of the missionary activities in China. Given the fact that the missionary strangers could obtain their own truth and fare well in the world, they believed that what must happen next was not that the strangers should identify themselves with the Confucian values; on the contrary, it was the Chinese or Confucians who needed to open up to the strangers. They had to do so not only to welcome and accept the strangers' new science, technology, and knowledge in various fields but also to understand and even accept their new values, ideologies, and faith. Concerning this need facing the Chinese, Yang Tingyun (楊廷筠; 1562–1627), one of the first Confucians to be baptized, made a most forceful argument. In the preface that he wrote to Aleni's *Zhifang waiji*, Yang pointed out that the missionaries have more knowledge than the Confucians. He first alluded to an episode in *Chuci* (楚辭), or *The Songs of the South*, by Qu Yuan (屈原; 340–278 BCE), where a Confucian scholar was asked about the whereabouts of the end of the world but could not answer.[76] He continued on to say that the missionaries had responded to this ancient question by showing the Chinese that the globe had no [geographical] beginning or end, center or margin.[77] Yang told the reader that the missionaries knew more than the Chinese, because the West still retained many books that had escaped the fire of the First Emperor of China, and there were many extraordinary men who had traveled extensively to accumulate knowledge.[78] Though he mentioned that owing to some divine design the people living in one area could be self-sufficient without having to acquire the knowledge owned by the people in other areas, he nevertheless urged the Chinese to try to understand and learn what a wonder the earth was as told by the Jesuits. More importantly, when the Chinese opened up to the missionaries, they would do well if they did not allow themselves to be simply taken in by the curious things told by the foreign missionaries but to try to discern the meaning behind what was said. Using Aleni's book as an example, Yang called it "a book that hopes to touch the reader's heart and soul through its enjoyable materials that please the ears and eyes of the reader." But unless a Chinese reader took into his heart what Aleni and other Jesuits actually meant to say beneath their stories (i.e., the divine message from the Christian deity), light-hearted reading would be the same as keeping what was unimportant but missing the treasure.[79]

Calling on the Chinese to open up to the missionaries not only for science but also for religion, the Confucian Christians quoted so far would certainly have been denounced by Han Yu (韓愈; 768–824), who had in his essay "On the Way" (原道) expressed his animosity toward the attempt at "imposing ideas of the barbarians on the teachings from our ancient kings" (舉夷狄之法，而加之先王之教上). Nevertheless, these Confucian Christians' discussion serves as evidence that there emerged a new understanding of the relation between Ming China and the missionaries. Their assertion that the Jesuits came to China already having discovered their own truth, truth with no less validity but not as part of the Confucian Principle, seemed to question the universality of Confucianism. It simply undermined the self-claimed host and master status of the Confucians.

5

Reforming the Calendar

The Ming Empire's Stairway to Heaven through the Jesuits

> For an agricultural economy [like that in ancient China], astronomical knowledge as regulator of the calendar was of prime importance. He who could give a calendar to the people would become their leader.
>
> —Joseph Needham, *Mathematics and the Science of Heaven and Earth*

If Ricci's world map, as argued in the previous chapter, took away symbolically from the Ming its self-appointed master status and removed China from its imaginary center of the world by leading and re-emplacing the country as a newcomer into a family of human races, the calendar reform undertaken by the Jesuits during Chongzhen's (崇禎) reign (1628–1644) went even farther. The reform converted the Ming host into a virtual hostage, a hostage whose chance for its social, religious, and, more importantly, political well-being depended literally and squarely on the assistance and work of foreigners, the missionaries from the West. The following is an explanation.

As some scholars have pointed out, the Ming saw continued interest in so-called correlative cosmology, an interest revived by some Song neo-Confucian philosophers.[1] Toward the end of the Ming, however, such interest mutated into a sense of necessity, even of urgency, owing to what was going on in the country at the time. What generated this metamorphosis was that the Ming calendar, an entity of centrality in imperial politics, rituals, and administration, not to mention agriculture, was in need of immediate rectification.

135

As is well known, the calendar in use through the years of the Ming dynasty was the Datong calendar (大統曆). A modified version of the Yuan dynasty's Season-Granting calendar (授時曆), the Datong calendar sometimes received needed rectifications from the Muslim calendar, known in China as the *Huihui li* (回回曆).[2] By the beginning of the seventeenth century, however, the Datong calendar, already in use for nearly three centuries, was becoming increasingly inaccurate.[3] Long before Jesuit involvement,[4] Chinese officials had suggested adjustment and attempted some rectification. As early as 1579, for instance, an official by the name of Fan Shouji (范守己; 1542–1611) organized renovation of the astronomical instruments in disrepair at the Nanjing observatory. In 1595, the prince Zhu Zaiyu (朱載堉; 1536–1611) made suggestions for an astronomical reform in his book *Shengshou wannian li* (聖壽萬年曆; Sagely Longevity Ten-Thousand-Year Calendar).[5] But owing to lack of enthusiasm and motivation from the officials in the imperial court and the Imperial Astronomical Bureau (欽天監), the agency overseeing calendric matters, no action was taken to reform the calendar until 1610, when another inaccurate prediction of a lunar eclipse occurred.

According to historical records from this period, the Ministry of Rites responded to this miscalculation by both acknowledging the need for a calendar reform and actually grouping together some officials, including Xing Yunlu (邢雲路; 1549–?), Fan Shouji, Xu Guangqi, and others, to initiate the project. At the same time, suggestions were made that the Jesuits, having by then been active in the capital for about ten years, be employed to translate Western astronomical books so as to complement the Chinese classics.[6] It took nearly twenty more years before the reform eventually began. Finally, it happened following another inaccurate prediction of a solar eclipse in 1629 by the Imperial Astronomical Bureau.[7] Because Xu Guangqi, who had worked with the missionaries since his conversion in 1603, had showed his more accurate calculation using the Western astronomical methods, he was put in charge of the Calendar Office (曆局), established especially for the reform, under the Imperial Astronomical Bureau. Xu took his opportunity to recommend that Jesuits join the program, such as Niccolò Longobardo (1559–1654) or Long Huamin (龍華民), Jean Terrenz (1576–1630) or Deng Yuhan (鄧玉函), and, later, Jacques Rho (1593–1638) or Luo Yagu (羅雅谷)and Johann Adam Schall von Bell (1592–1666) or Tang Ruowang (湯若望).[8] He also recruited some Chinese both knowledgeable of astronomy and interested in Christianity to work in the Calendar Office.[9] As a result, Xu put together a strong team for the reform. In other words, thanks to his arrangement, the calendar reform turned out to be a Jesuit-controlled project from beginning to end.

Between 1629 and 1634, the Jesuits worked on the reform persistently and efficiently. In early 1634, they completed their entire 137-*juan*, or chapter, book known as the *Chongzhen Calendar* (崇禎曆書).[10] A work of collaboration between Jesuit missionaries and Chinese scholars, the *Calendar* was a seventeenth-century encyclopedia of Western astronomy. It contained almost all of the astronomical knowledge available in Europe at the time. Despite its fundamental structure founded on by then already questionable Tychonic cosmography, and its explanation of the movements of the planets from a heliocentric point of view, the Calendar presented many new astronomical methods previously unknown to the Chinese.[11] For example, Western and more scientific methods of calculation and charts of observation were introduced to replace the traditional Chinese twenty-eight lunar lodge (二十八宿) system for precise measurement and observation.[12] In short, the many inclusions and improvements would have made the *Calendar* a useful tool for China at the time, had it been put into use.

The *Calendar* was never issued to the public during the Ming. As soon as the Jesuits finished the book, the Confucian conservatives, unhappy about foreigners' involvement in the reform, became vocal with their contempt of the *Calendar* and exerted strenuous efforts to prevent its issue. According to *Ming shi*, the debates between the two groups grew so intense that eight official tests were held to verify the viability of the *Chongzhen Calendar*, either alone or in a face-to-face fashion with the forecasts by the Confucian astronomical officials.[13] The Western methods every time proved more accurate with their calculation of the time for the eclipses. But the Confucians, for the first seven tests, managed to persuade the authorities, especially the emperor, to prolong the use of the Datong calendar. It was not until late 1643 when, following another failure of a solar eclipse prediction, that the emperor was finally convinced of the accuracy of the Western methods (深知西法之密). He therefore ordered that, beginning the following year, the *Chongzhen calendar* be made the official calendar of the Ming Empire.[14] However, before the royal order could be implemented, the dynasty fell, in March 1644.

Though the *Chongzhen calendar* never saw its use in the Ming, the significance of the very production of this calendar cannot be overestimated. The significance lies in the fact that the calendar offered in this multivolume book was a result of the Jesuits' entering the Imperial Astronomical Bureau and reforming the calendar for the Ming empire. This Jesuit breakthrough into Ming astronomy alone is particularly exceptional. This successful missionary penetration into one of the most sensitive and most important imperial agencies will not be recognized fully without some reflection on a few historical facts concerning the use of calendar in the political and religious life of traditional China—first of all, during the Ming period.

Since the beginning of the dynasty, the Imperial Astronomical Bureau had been, by the order of Zhu Yuanzhang, staffed on a hereditary basis. This fact, while making the bureau inaccessible to anyone from the outside, also means that the official astronomers could work only for the bureau and did so for life.[15] Furthermore, the hereditary rule determined that the astronomers' children—and children's children as well—were not allowed to choose for themselves any other subject of study but astronomy in order to inherit their fathers' jobs. According to the *Da Ming lü* (大明律), or the *Ming Code*, anyone violating this rule by studying other subjects or pursuing professions other than astronomy would be exiled to Nanhai (today's Hainan [海南]), the remotest and allegedly most uninhabitable place at the time.[16] Another fact, related to the rules concerning the Astronomical Bureau, is that during the Ming the state set up harsh laws banning private study of astronomy and any unauthorized calendar making.[17]

There is no doubt that the Ming imposed restrictions on astronomy and calendars. But government control of astronomical matters, including calendars, was by no means a Ming invention. It was a rather standard practice of authorities throughout Chinese history, and they had good reasons for doing so. The earliest example for this, in fact, comes from the *Book of Documents*, which mentions how Emperor Zhuanxu (顓頊) "commissioned [the astronomers] Zhong and Li to make an end of the communications between heaven and earth, and [as a result] the descent of spirits ceased."[18] From a well-known passage in *Discourse of the States*, or *Guoyu* (國語), one learns that Zhuanxu decided to sever heaven-earth communication (絕地天通),[19] because he wanted to deny the common people any direct contact with heaven so that the access to heaven and to heavenly messages could be reserved as an imperial monopoly. It is such a monopoly of astronomy and calendars as seen in this passage that provides convincing evidence that kings and emperors in traditional China ruled the state as the "head shaman" or "priest-king."[20] In other words, such a royal monopoly determined what Joseph Needham refers to as the "official character" of astronomy and calendars in old China.[21]

There is no doubt that astronomy and the calendar have always been important in the eyes of Chinese rulers. But it was during the Western Han dynasty that, with his effort to promote the ideas of the Yin-Yang school, particularly his own concept of *Tianren heyi* (天人合一), or "Heaven-man integration," Dong Zhongshu (董仲舒; 179–104 BCE) perpetuated as well as theorized the centrality of astronomy and the calendar in the dynastic politics of China. In *Chunqiu fanlu* (春秋繁露), a book traditionally attributed to him, Dong perceives Heaven to be, among other things, an entity possessing cognition and consciousness.[22] He sees that Heaven, like humans, experiences all kinds of emotions:

> Exactly like human beings, Heaven also possesses the feelings of joy and anger, or the mood of grief and pleasure. . . . Those who act according to [the way of] Heaven will achieve great order; while those who act against Heaven will see great disorder. Therefore the Way of the ruler lies most obviously in the premise of making use of whatever his body and acts do to follow Heaven, and of making manifest his happiness and anger at the right moment.[23]

Thus interpreted, the text argues that the way in which the king can provide instruction to his subjects is to "carry forward the purpose of Heaven" (承天意). That is why his work proposes with all seriousness that the king "models himself on its (Heaven's) numerical (categories) and uses them when initiating affairs" (法其數以起事). His book contains a list from which one sees that the governmental structure and posts are to be patterned after the four seasons and the spread of the stars in the sky.[24] The purpose of such an arrangement or juxtaposition in the imperial court is, of course, to better run the country by following the Way of Heaven, just as one reads in the *Han shu*, "What is astronomy? It is to watch the pattern of the Twenty-Eight Lunar Mansions, observe and measure the [movements of] the Sun, Moon and the Five Planets; it therefore makes manifest the images of the good and bad omens, following which the sage kings run their states."[25] What must be pointed out here is that such an arrangement later on became the standard understanding among the Confucian officials concerning their duty in the government. To give an example, in his conversation with his emperor, Chen Ping (陳平; ?–178 BCE) describes his responsibility as the prime minister "to be an aid to the Son of Heaven above, to adjust the forces of the yin and yang, and to see that all proceed in accordance with the four seasons while striving to nourish the best in all creatures."[26]

Given all the crucial roles that they had to play in state politics, religious rituals, divination, the administration, and many other things—including

140 / FRIENDSHIP AND HOSPITALITY

the economy, owing to their use in agriculture—it is not difficult at all to see why astronomy and the calendar had to be administered exclusively by the central government and be in good shape. To reiterate this point, here are the remarks of Richard J. Smith, who stresses the tight relation between calendar and politics in traditional China, but also on the importance of keeping the calendar accurate for the imperial government:

> From earliest times the Chinese calendar exemplified the notion of cosmological kingship. According to long-standing political beliefs in China, a sovereign had to understand the processes of change in the universe so as to assure that the social order and the natural way (*Dao*), would be fully congruent. An inaccurate calendar, like the failure of designated officials to predict cosmic events such as eclipses, became a sign of moral imperfection, a warning that the monarch's virtue was not adequate to keep him in touch with celestial rhythm. Anomalies, including the gap between solar years (365.2422 days) and synodic months (29.53059 days), had to be reconciled, or at least explained. This accounts for the seemingly insatiable demand on the part of Chinese rulers for precision in calendrical calculations that far exceeded normal agricultural, bureaucratic, and economic requirements.[27]

In summary, the calendar was in the past expected to do much more than simply provide the right dates for the people in China. Just as Smith asserts in another of his studies, "Chinese astrology, astronomy, divination and calendric science coalesced into a single administratively grounded science."[28]

As a final reflection on their history, and to bring the discussion back to the Ming dynasty, I would like to point out that the calendar and astronomy as "administratively grounded science" were not merely crucial in domestic politics in traditional China. The calendar was expected to function in such a way that it helped achieve and sustain China's hegemony, symbolically or not, in the international arena as well. It is mentioned briefly in a foregoing chapter that, at the beginning of his dynasty Zhu Yuanzhang sent emissaries to some South Asian countries to deliver Ming letters of credence—in other words, Zhu's edicts—to announce the dynasty change of the Middle Kingdom. Besides revoking any existing diplomatic ties between the recently overthrown Yuan dynasty with these countries, the letters would often mention issuing copies of the Ming Datong calendar to the rulers and kings of these countries. For example, in what seems to be a state letter Zhu wrote to the king of Java, delivered sometime in 1369, it reads:

> Following the mandate of Heaven, I, the Emperor of China, am now ruling this Kingdom. . . . I am distributing to you a copy of the Datong calendar. Once Your Majesty could learn the dates promulgated by me, you will follow them as the mandate from Heaven so that your subjects will live in peace and Your Majesty will be guaranteed to pass your fortune and good luck to your descendants. May you strive [to do what I said here] without slacknesss.[29]

It should not be difficult for one to see what lay behind Zhu's urging of the Java king to run his state by observing the dates determined in the Datong calendar. With what he said, he was declaring Java's and other countries' inclusion in a new fiefdom under the Great Ming. In traditional China, including during the Ming empire, giving the calendar to other countries was supposedly an act meant to secure China's suzerainty in the international arena. Those utilizing the Chinese calendar would be following the Chinese calculation of time, including the dates for all of the Chinese political and ritual ceremonies. Such use of the Chinese calendar would be understood as a submissive gesture traditionally referred to as *feng zhengshuo* (奉正朔)—to observe the calendar promulgated by the [Chinese] emperor.[30] In this way, the ancient Chinese could see the ruler with his calendar bringing together his subjects from far and wide.[31]

Bearing in mind the centrality of astronomy and the calendar in the political and religious life of traditional China, one must say that the Jesuit involvement in the calendric reform was no mean feat. With their accurate calculation and prediction of the lunar and solar eclipses dependent on them, the Jesuits apparently became for the Ming emperor and his empire akin to the ancient royal astronomers Zhong and Li. The Jesuits with their skills served as the staff who would be channeling the communication between Heaven and the emperor. Because of their ability to calculate with accuracy the eclipses, the dependence of the emperor's normal political function landed on their shoulders. To put it differently, no longer uninvited or complete strangers, the missionaries had turned themselves into useful people with important skills that the imperial host needed for his well-being—or at least for the routine running of his administration. Given the fact that in Chinese history the "failure of a predicted eclipse to occur as scheduled was the result of [the flawed] imperial virtue having influenced the heavens,"[32] one cannot emphasize enough the significance and indispensability of the Jesuit work on the Ming calendar. As has been mentioned, the calendar made by the Jesuits in the late Ming was not put to use. But the revised and improved edition of this calendar by Johann Adam Schall and some later missionaries, renamed as the *Xiyang xinfa lishu* (西洋新法曆書) or *The Book of the New Western Calendric System*, served as the basis for Qing calendar making for about 260 years.[33]

To further interpret the roles of and relation between the Ming authority and the Jesuits in the calendric reform, it can be said that the Ming host's hiring and welcoming of the missionary stranger into its bureau of astronomy resembles Oedipus's consulting of the blind old man, a stranger, for assistance in saving his country from the horrible plague. The Ming used the Jesuits for a new and accurate calendar, just as Oedipus used the stranger to rescue him, which is, to quote Derrida, akin to relying on "the stranger to save the master, and liberate the power of his host."[34] Whether the host's power is liberated or impeded is a matter on which I will have more to say in the next chapter. Here, it is important to make clear the irony of the master's dependence on, or the host's welcome to, the stranger for the sake of the Self. In his effort to deconstruct the concept of hospitality, Derrida points out the paradox of the host, which in the French *hôte* means both the one to give, *donner*, and the one to receive, *reçoire*. This fact predetermines that, on the one hand, hospitality must, in his words, "be ready to welcome [*accueillir*], to host and shelter, to give shelter and cover, it must prepare itself and adorn itself [*se préparer et se parer*] for the coming of the *hôte*; it must even develop itself into a culture of hospitality."[35] On the other, he continues,

> to be hospitable is to let oneself be overtaken [*surprendre*], *to be ready to not be ready*, if such is possible, to let oneself be overtaken, to not even *let oneself* be overtaken, to be surprised, in a fashion almost violent, violated/raped [*violée*], stolen [*volée*] (the whole question of violence and violation/rape and of expropriation and de-propriation is waiting for us), precisely where one is not ready to receive—and not only *not yet ready* but *not ready*, *unprepared* in a mode that is not even that of the "not yet."[36]

Unfortunately, to "let oneself be overtaken" appeared to be exactly what the Ming government did. Recruiting the Jesuits to work on the calendar in its stead, the government certainly claimed and displayed its authority by, first of all, assigning jobs to the strangers, confirming the government's master status, a master or a host who could get the visitors to work for the benefit of the empire. But what ended up happening at the same time was that the Ming authority let the missionaries come "where one [the host] is not ready to receive." Allowing the Jesuits to come into its Imperial Astronomical Bureau—a highly sensitive, political, and completely religious agency where the strangers were put in charge and given trust—meant, particularly to some anti-Jesuit Confucians, an utter violation to the Chinese host.

To be sure, it is possible to regard the Jesuit involvement in calendar reform as another link in a historical continuity. Indeed, Chinese authorities throughout history often had foreign specialists working in the bureaus of astronomy to help reform their calendars.[37] But the Jesuit case in the late Ming generated some relatively new and thus significant thinking among the Confucians regarding the host-guest relation. What such Ming "hospitality" to the missionaries would mean to the Confucians and the Ming empire will be the subject of discussion in the remaining pages of this chapter. But here one can make a quick point by invoking the tragedy of Oedipus again. In the play, the stranger clearly brings about the end of Oedipus by helping him end the plague ravaging his country—that is, by helping him find out that he is the person to be punished for having caused the terrible ordeal to his country and people. Likewise, the Jesuits, by helping preserve and regenerate the power of the late Ming authority by rectifying its calendar concurrently weakened the very same authority by showing that the authority, together with its ideology and rituals, rested on a material base provided by foreigners. To put this point in general terms, the host or master indeed emerged, each time after according hospitality to the Other, regenerated and with his or her power liberated, but, at the same time, the host was undermined, his or her authority significantly reduced. Just as Levinas has argued, the master's welcoming of the stranger always turns out to be a welcoming of the alterity, a welcoming of the latter obligatorily, willingly, and openly.[38] Thus, finding one's Self in the trace of the Other not only points to a lack in the Self or the Self's need to consistently open up to the Other, but also shows that the Self's welcome turns the master or the host, the Ming empire at large, into a virtual hostage.

Without any doubt, one cannot expect the late Ming Confucians to be, in any shape or form, aware of the deconstructive nature of the late Ming–missionary interaction. But some scholars—the anti-Christian ones in particular—indeed saw fairly keenly the irony that the Great Middle Kingdom should blur the distinction between China and the barbarians (夷夏之大防) by trusting its calendar to strangers from countries far away and little known. In the case of these Confucians, their concern was therefore not how useful the missionary-assisted calendar project could be. Finding that the missionaries' presence in China itself—let alone their activities in science and religion—was already a threat to Confucian values, these Confucians called for a total rejection of the strangers, who they argued should not be allowed to be in China at all, much less to throw influence on such sensitive and ideological tasks as calendar reform and similar projects. To give an example, according to Xu Dashou, one of the most famous anti-Christian authors mentioned in the previous chapter, the Ming, by having the Jesuits participate in its calendric reform, was simply allowing these foreign barbarians to kidnap the "authorized calendar" (正曆) of China and in its place sneak in their "unwarranted calendar" (私曆). The Jesuit calendar was unofficial because it had nothing to do with the official Ming calendar.[39] In Xu's view, the missionaries' activities in China—"imposing their unwarranted calendar, stealing omens, plotting rebellions, and much more—were done to commit the greatest sedition ever known since antiquity."[40] Xu was obviously fully conscious of the importance of the calendar in Chinese politics, religion, and economy. As his remarks indicate, the issue circling around the Jesuit involvement in the calendric reform had to do with who was the boss or host—not just the boss or host managing the reform but the boss or host governing China.

    Xu Dashou by no means stood alone. There were others in the anti-Christian group who shared his opinion. Here are a couple more examples. Xie Gonghua (謝宮花), a Confucian against the missionaries, stated in his pamphlet entitled "On Calendrics," "China has its own way for making its own calendar. There is no need for the Western barbarians to say anything."[41] Another and later Confucian, Yang Guangxian, who became known for his passionate attacks on the Jesuit involvement in calendric management, went so far as to say, "[I would] rather that China have no good calendar than it host men from the Western Oceans."[42] His reason for saying so, as he pointed out, was that "a great country will not receive the first day in its first month promulgated by a petty country."[43] In short, for the Confucians concerned with the distinction between China and the barbarians, or the host and the stranger, the Western calendar techniques had to be rejected simply because, to repeat and paraphrase Mencius's teaching, the Great Middle Kingdom should not allow itself to be converted to the barbarian way!

Apart from the anti-Christian scholars and their belligerence, there were others seeking a different interpretation of the clash between the host and the stranger, or the Self and the Other, in their defense of Confucian values. Perhaps owing to their realization that the dexterous as well as unruly missionary strangers could not be expelled from China due to the fact that the imperial house was now dependent upon them for its normal functioning, some Confucians tried a different, though not entirely new, approach in their thinking of the relation between Confucian ideology and Western science. As a result, they formulated a theory—later on referred to as the argument called *Xixue Zhongyuan* (西學中源) or "Chinese origin of Western learning"—with which they argued that Western science and technology, mainly astronomy, originated from ancient China. In other words, Western science as a whole was an export from China in antiquity.[44]

Despite the fact that such an export did not leave any plausible and traceable records, the idea or assumption that the Western knowledge of science had its origin in ancient China must have brought quite some comfort to the Sino-centric mentality shared by many in China at the time. Those who supported this theory, or expressing similar views, include Huang Zongxi (黃宗羲; 1610–1695), Fang Yizhi (方以智; 1611–1671),[45] and Wang Fuzhi (王夫之; 1619–1692), to mention a few. Huang, believed by some to be the first to advocate this theory, spoke about the algebraic Pythagorean theorem, known in China as *gougu dingli* (勾股定理), with these words: "*Gougu dingli* was handed down from the Duke of Zhou (周公) and Shang Gao (商高), but lost by later [Chinese] mathematicians, an opportunity for the Westerners to steal it and [ever after] pass it on."[46] If Huang's comment is too brief, the following is another example with more elaboration on the topic by Fang Yizhi:

> During Wanli's reign, with the world transformed by Chinese civilization, some scholars from the Far West came to our land. When their theory that the earth in the universe was like a bean hanging in the middle of an air balloon matched what had been said in the oracle charts (*tu*), the [Confucian-perceived] Principle became manifest immediately. The people stuck with their biases found this situation strikingly surprising, because they did not know that what was happening had been prophesized by sages. . . . The Master said: "When the [Zhou or Lu] rulers' canons and codes lie in ruin and get lost [from the central

government], kings of remote and small countries still preserve and remember them."⁴⁷

The Master's words quoted in the passage come from *Zuo's Commentary* (左傳).⁴⁸ According to Zuo, after hearing that the lords in some small faraway countries still kept the records and retained certain customs from the time of the ancient sage kings of China, Confucius uttered these words in praise of these lords for their work in preserving the ancient and lost records from China. Obviously, Fang here was applying the Master's remarks to the entire world in the seventeenth century. More than simply being joyful about the viability and longevity of Chinese achievements in knowledge and science, he was arguing that the scientific knowledge now being imported by the scholars from the West—the missionaries—had been introduced to the West from China in the first place. That was why Fang sneered at people who, not knowing that only one and the same Principle applied to everything and had originated in and spread from China, subjected themselves to surprise at the missionaries' skills and technology.

To be sure, such chauvinistic appropriation of the Other, as Huang and Fang tried to do, was hardly anything new. Similar tactics and arguments had been commonplace in cross-cultural relations and interreligious history. One well-known example is the book called *Laozi huahu jing* (老子化胡經), or *The Classic of Laozi's Transformation of the Foreigners*, a book forged by Wang Fu (王浮), a Daoist in the Western Jin dynasty (266–315), to combat the fast-spreading and flourishing Buddhism in China at the time. The book argues that Laozi had traveled to India as early as the time of King You (幽王; 781–771 BCE) during the Western Zhou not only to promote Daoism but also to become the Buddha (浮屠) himself.⁴⁹ Undoubtedly, as the book goes on, what Laozi had done in India, including teaching the people there, evolved into Indian Buddhism and was later on introduced back to China.⁵⁰ While the goals of these arguments concerning Laozi in India are apparent, it is still necessary to discuss what the late Ming "Chinese origin for Western learning" theory hoped to achieve. Two points are to be reiterated.

First, and simply, as has been mentioned, the Confucian appropriation of Western learning was meant to help the Ming Self by erasing the otherness that was the Jesuit stranger. This effort of erasing the otherness—that is, making the stranger disappear into the Self, or into the history of the Self, as seen in the remarks of Huang and Fang—coincided with a process in which the Self was assumed to have emerged with a complete, independent, and self-sufficient, not to mention enhanced, identity or subjectivity. It was a process out of which the subjectivity of the Self took form in a continuous history or an uninterrupted history. Just as Foucault has pointed out, "Continuous history is the indispensable correlative of the founding function of the subject."[51] Specifically, the late Ming theory of Chinese origin for Western learning was formulated to grant the possibility for a grand narrative that in turn suggested a complete and uninterrupted history of the Chinese empire. It was through the assumption and discourse of such a history, one taken to be ethnocentric and Sino-centric, that the Ming Confucians hoped both to build and maintain the empire's subjectivity.

Second, also already suggested in the foregoing discussion, formulating the subjectivity of the Self by granting it a continuous history, the argument of Western learning coming from China was meant to allow the Self to make legitimate and unlimited use of the missionary science. Once the Confucians were assured that all knowledge from the West in fact originated in China, they could without apologies take advantage of the latter's technology and skills. Just as the argument that Laozi was the founder of Buddhism would present Buddhism as a native religion, which would in turn serve as justification for many Chinese in the third and fourth centuries to become Buddhists, the late Ming Confucians found themselves, armed with and protected by their own theory of all science originating from China, capable of absorbing Western knowledge without losing an ounce of their subjectivity; nor had their Self been disturbed in any fashion. To put the matter frankly, the theory of the Chinese origin for Western learning appeared to be a Confucian reversion of what happened with Ricci's world map. If, as discussed in the previous chapter, the Jesuit map intended to lead Ming China and its people into the world family, the idea or argument of China as the source of Western knowledge represented the Confucian effort and attempt to drag the outside world back into the house of China.

The possibility of a theory of Chinese civilization containing the seeds for Western learning indeed inspired self-confidence among Confucian scholars. At least, convinced that Western learning was the long-lost child from China, the Confucians appeared less reluctant to accord welcome upon the child's homecoming. Here is a mid-Qing example. In his preface to the book *A Pictorial Explanation of the Globe* (地球圖說), written by the French Jesuit Michel Benoist (1715–1774), known as Jiang Youren (蔣友仁) in China, Ruan Yuan (阮元; 1764–1849) made the following observation:

> As for the ideas in this herewith translated volume of *A Pictorial Explanation of the Globe*, they are all copies and studies of the ancient rules and knowledge [of China]. This is what one would call the disciples and descendants of the [ancient] mathematicians being now scattered around the four borders. . . . This idea [of the earth being a globe] is no other but the old idea already advanced by Duke of Zhou, Shang Gao, Confucius, and Zengzi. Scholars now should accept this idea not just because they find it new. It is likewise unnecessary for them to shun the idea just because their suspicion is raised by its novelty.[52]

In this paragraph, besides claiming again the Chinese origin of Western learning, Ruan called on his readers to feel free and relaxed in their acceptance and use of the knowledge from the West. He assured his readers that, though the knowledge and technology recently made available by the missionaries might strike some as new, they were actually old ideas that China had once had but had lost centuries ago. The right thing for a Chinese scholar to do now, in Ruan's view, was to embrace and use this knowledge and technology as the master would welcome the return of his stolen treasure. What Ruan's passage implied was a Confucian view or mentality possibly summarized in the phrase "retrieving the lost rituals from the barbarians' countries" (禮失而求諸野). Attributed to Confucius,[53] the phrase has represented a Confucian attitude toward the Other. But it has also served as a method of appropriation and tantalization for the Self. To put it in the present context of late imperial China, with this approach devised by the Master, the Confucian Self could take possession of the Jesuit science needed for the Middle Kingdom and at the same time make its taking or appropriation look like a most forgiving and particularly generous display of hospitality, or a specific culture of Confucian hospitality.

The discussion so far should leave little doubt about the totalizing nature of the Confucian theory of the "Chinese origin for Western learning." Blatantly and bluntly imperialistic and chauvinistic, the theory presents China as the center of the earth and civilization, not only the center attracting with centripetal force Jesuit admirers and tributary countries alike, but also a source or fountain distributing in some centrifugal fashion science and knowledge all over the world. The task now, however, is to situate the center of the Middle Kingdom by demonstrating and questioning what can be called the center's pivotability. It is important to examine further to what extent the Ming pivot depends on external influences, or how squarely the Ming center depends on the peripheries, particularly the Jesuit strangers. To this end, I would like to discuss one last example in this chapter, another effort mounted by the late Ming Confucians to negotiate the Confucian-Jesuit difference in defense of the values of the former.

Let me begin again with Fang Yizhi. In the preface to his *Wuli xiaozhi* (物理小識), Fang stated, "The Western scholars arriving in China during Wanli's reign were specialized in observation and measurement, but weak in philosophy. But some wise men [in our country] praised them. However, the Western science of observation and measurement is not that perfect."[54] While Fang may be expressing some reservation regarding Western science, Sun Lan (孫蘭), an early Qing scholar once studying under Johann Adam Schall's tutorship, made it more clear by praising Western science and ridiculing Christian teachings. His observation goes as follows:

> Men from the Far West . . . , who refer to themselves as Western scholars, have their religion in the doctrine of seven victories [over the deadly sins], a doctrine seemingly resembling the Confucian teaching of "disciplining the self and restoring the rites." But through interacting with these Western men and listening to their words, we know that every one of them is good at calendrics and math. That is what makes them perfect for the jobs of making instruments and serving with reverence the natural world. However, what particularly renders them as misbelievers are their worship of a Heavenly God and their bragging about Heaven and Hell.[55]

These remarks show a dialectic vision that some Confucians formulated to help identify the Western Other whom they tended to divide into two halves, the welcomed half and the unwelcomed half. These Confucians viewed the Western stranger's scientific half as obviously useful to the Ming empire and its Confucian institution, whereas the other half, religious or doctrinal, they viewed as potentially harmful and dangerous.

With such distinctions arising out of discretion and highly conscious self-interest, what Fang, Sun, and others upholding the same opinion about the West were arguing here seemed to be a herald of a later and similar debate that took place with much more intensity and on a much larger scale during the late Qing dynasty. What is foreshadowed here in the words of the late Ming Confucians is the late Qing debate on the relation between *ti* (體), or a "base substance," and *yong* (用), or a "practical application" or "function." Stimulated by China's defeat in the Opium Wars of 1840 and 1842, this debate, one of the many since this time, circled around what was to be done to strengthen China before the foreign powers. Should China abandon its Confucian institutions, something of absolutely no avail during the war, to adopt the Western military and political system? Or should China retain its traditions and remain on its old course? Of the many opinions and theories suggested, there is one that argued for a balance, a distinction between a "base substance" and "practical application." This theory insisted that China must remain a Confucian country, or hold on to Confucianism as the country's base structure, while making use of Western science and technology as "practical applications" in order to make the country militarily strong. This theory, later known as the theory of "Chinese base, Western function" (中體西用),[56] quickly became the topic of a heated discussion in the late nineteenth century.[57] But from what one sees in the quoted remarks by the late Ming and early Qing scholars so far, this debate began much earlier, as a result of the Ming-Jesuit encounter.[58] And the key in this debate since the late Ming,[59] announced or not, has been nothing else but Sino-centrism.

It is by no means surprising that some late Ming Confucians should think like their colleagues over two hundred years later. The two different times faced similar problems, in kind if not in degree: both were in decline, had dwindling economies, and faced threats from abroad. Concerning the Ming, as is known to many, though its rulers from the beginning made every effort possible to protect their empire from the world without, the country was never free from challenges from the outside. Besides the ever-present brigandage by Japanese pirates on the southern coast, the Ming continuously sustained border harassments in the north from the Mongols throughout its history and later from the Manchus.[60] These and the many other military confrontations that persisted and worsened certainly contributed to the final fall of the dynasty to the Manchus invading army in 1644. It was against this background that the late Ming Confucians, compelled to deal with and think of the question of the Jesuit stranger, began adopting their "substance-function" dialectic concerning the Jesuit mission in China.

Conceived against such a tumultuous background, this late Ming dialectic of a "Chinese substance" and "Western function" as a part of the Confucian response to the Jesuit mission represented nothing accidental. On the contrary, like the "Chinese origin for Western learning" and other previously mentioned theories, this dialectic represented a Chinese reaction dictated by the same Confucian Sino-centrism. At a time when they were facing various types of threats from the outside world, it was a way to sustain the hierarchical relation or distinction between China and what was foreign. Before proceeding to discuss where it led the Ming Confucians and their empire, it is necessary to place this dialectical thinking in the context of the philosophical thinking of the Confucians.

It must be made clear that "base" or "substance" and "function" represent terms and concepts frequently discussed in Confucian thinking throughout history. These terms, and a few of their substitutes like "body," "base structure," "application," and so forth, are loosely interchangeable with a series of other paired terms often seen in traditional Chinese philosophy, such as Dao (道) and "tool" (器), "Principle" (理) and "image" (象) or *qi* (氣) or ether, the "fundamental" or *ben* (本), the "incidental" or *mo* (末), and so forth.[61] It goes without saying that these terms are paired to mark, to borrow a set of philosophical ideas from the West, metaphysics and its opposite.

One outstanding characteristic of the substance-function dichotomy in Confucian thought is the hierarchy determining the relation between the two terms while at the same time keeping the two separated. Such hierarchical relation is recognized and defined as early as the *Book of Changes*, where it states, "What is above form is called Dao; what is within [under] form is called tool."[62] Though, as it will soon become clear, the above and underneath positions are changeable, what remain persistent and unalterable are the fundamental and the accidental entities in the relation. Using the *Book of Changes* statement above to illustrate the issue at hand, one must say that the concept of *Dao* is the fundamental that determines the nature and essence of the tool that can stand for anything in life, while the tool functions and follows to enact faithfully with every movement it makes the meaning or power of the presiding Dao. When it comes to the discussion on the relationship between substance and function, a similar argument is frequent. Here is an example from Zhu Xi. In response to a disciple who asks him whether substance and function have their fixed positions or roles (定所), Zhu affirms, "[The places or roles of] substance and function are fixed. What lies at [or as] the base is substance, and what comes after [and thus on top] is function. This body [of mine] is substance, my actions and movements are functions."[63]

Zhu's theory of the relation between substance and function seen in his remarks bears certain resemblance to ideas from Chinese Buddhism. For instance, Sengzhao (僧肇; 384–414?) in his works exercises similar thinking by pointing to the interdependence of substance and function with these words: "The lamp is the substance of the light, while the light is the function of the lamp."[64] But no matter how and where Zhu forms his understanding of substance and function, he does not, like many other Confucian thinkers on this topic, deny the fact that their substance is not an empirical entity. Therefore, rather ironically named, substance or body, very much like the Dao, does not have its own substance but can make its being known only through its function or the tool. Though substance may as the central structure or fundamentality determine the nature and essence of what is called function, substance is by nature invisible but manifests each time only through function. Just as the Song neo-Confucian Cheng Yi asserts, "Substance and function come from the same origin; their integration is one of mutual illumination and without interruption."[65] It is based on this consensus of the interdependence between substance and function that Confucian philosophers, including Zhu Xi, see that the two entities represented by these two terms or concepts form an economy or circle of reciprocity within which function serves and illuminates substance while being determined and assimilated by substance.

Such a closed circle must appear particularly useful to the late Ming and early Qing scholars who proposed the theory of "Chinese substance, Western function." To them, the China-Jesuit exchange could be an event of ambivalence. Unless fully controlled and well supervised, this encounter might bring to China and its people much harm, with Christian teachings being the most dangerous. It must be partly out of this concern or recognition of the potential danger of the religion from the West that the late Ming Confucians showed little interest in appropriating Christianity, while they had no hesitation in claiming ownership of Western science and technology. When they tried to take over Western scientific learning with their theories like "Chinese origin for Western learning" and "Chinese substance, Western function," the late Ming scholars did not make any serious attempts at a systematic takeover of the Christian religion, a takeover similar to what one has read in the argument of Laozi's founding of Buddhism in India. Quite the contrary, excepting some converts, even Confucians receptive to Western science often at the same time denied any merits of Christian religion and expressed concern about its dissemination in China. This simultaneous acceptance of science and rejection of Christianity seem to culminate in the theory of "Chinese substance, Western function," a theory or effort to contain the missionaries by keeping them servile and subordinate to China. As another example of the partial or limited hospitality of the Confucians, the theory aims at justifying and legitimizing substance's or the Self's use and abuse for its own gain of the function or the Other as a mere tool, an insignificant inferior, an absolute nonself, without the Self running the slightest risk, or sustaining the smallest sacrifice, or even bearing the faintest sense of responsibility. This, one must admit, appears to be a perfect way for the Ming Self to fare through the China-West encounter.

Indeed, the substance-and-function economy must have struck the Chinese as so philosophically inspiring and practically convenient that even some Christian converts resorted to its argument. For instance, in his endeavor to promote the use of the Jesuit-assisted calendar, Xu Guangqi would go so far as to quote the words of Zhu Yuanzhang to point out the usefulness of the foreign science:

> The First Emperor of our dynasty . . . ordered that the official Wu Bozong and his colleagues translate the three-chapter *Calendar Book from the Western Marches*, and have the book recorded in the state annals. He also gave face-to-face the following order to the Minister Li Chong and others: "Recently *yin-yang* diviners from the Western Marches have done computations of celestial phenomena, which have been found to be accurate. These diviners' methods for the latitude have never been acknowledged in any Chinese books. Because this [capability of knowing celestial phenomena] concerns both Heaven and humans in an important way, it will be beneficial to translate their books so that they are available for my consultation at all times, and so that in observing celestial phenomena I will be able to examine myself, cultivate my virtues, and run the country for my people by following Heaven's disposition."[66]

Emphasizing the benefit to be gained from the foreigners, Xu's words here offer a small example for why he involved the Jesuits in the Ming calendric projects.

As a convert, however, Xu would have liked to see more Christian triumphs in China. To this end, he sought and seized every opportunity to praise and promote Christian teachings as vigorously as he did Western science. More relevant to the discussion here, he would use from time to time the very substance-and-function method of reasoning to present Christianity as function or the tool fit to be employed to serve the Chinese substance or Dao. In his "Memorial on Learning," an appeal for and defense of missionaries and converts submitted to the emperor following what is known as the Nanjing Persecution (南京教案) from 1616 to 1617, Xu argued that Christian teachings only aimed at making people moral beings. As he insisted, the teaching propagated by the emperor's "foreign subjects" (陪臣)—the missionaries—would help China in many ways. It would "truly supplement and reinvigorate the imperial transforming power; it will assist the Confucian doctrines, rectifying what has gone wrong with Buddhist teachings."[67] He continued, if the emperor could as a test give permission for such great teachings to disseminate without restriction in China for some time, just as Buddhism and Daoism had been allowed through history, one would in a few years' time watch China, with all its ancient Confucian values restored, enter a most peaceful and strong time, a time even better than the best of all times in Chinese history, the time of Yao and Shun and the Three Dynasties (唐虞三代).[68]

Unlike Xu, however, most Chinese scholars and officials at the time knew that they had to keep separate what was seen as the complementary Western science from the harmful teachings of Christianity. They would not mind if the missionaries' science and technology contributed to the improvement and enhancement of the Confucian Way. But they would not want at all, or give in any way, any opportunity for these strangers to undermine the state doctrine. Convinced that their empire could benefit from these strangers but that the strangers' erroneous and detrimental religion must be kept at bay, they would not hesitate to cut off completely the missionaries' scientific function or service to the Confucian substance at any time when Christianity tended to spill over to challenge the Confucian orthodoxy. In short, what the Chinese authorities as well as Confucians would want was an absolutely harmless but useful stranger.[69] Following this Confucian rationale, or Confucian culture and politics of hospitality, the theory of "Chinese substance, Western function" meant that the missionary function could and should easily be molded into a handy and docile tool that would in turn work neatly and tirelessly to meet all the needs that the Ming empire might have, just as the Confucian thinking believed and expected any function would and should do.

What calls for further investigation into the matter is the fact that, owing to a worsening border situation during the late Ming, the Confucian notion of "Chinese substance, Western function" did not remain mere speculation or theory. It was put to the test at a time when, as part of the overall effort to defend and save the empire, the Ming again sought help from strangers—Jesuits or other foreigners. As is known, beginning in 1618, with the loss of Fushun (撫順) in northeast China to the Manchus, the Ming experienced in consternation consecutive defeats in battles and suffered the loss of various places of strategic importance.[70] As their solution to the problem, in 1621 both Xu Guangqi and Li Zhizao submitted memorials to suggest that the empire call to the capital from Macao some foreign experts, including Jesuits, to help cast modern cannons and train artillery forces.[71] Accepting their suggestions, the imperial court welcomed in December of the same year the arrival of the first shipment of four cannons purchased from Portuguese businessmen in Macao. By 1627, owing to their adoption of Western cannons, the Ming army was inflicting heavy casualties on Manchu troops.[72] Unfortunately, the modern military weaponry and skills were not enough to save the already moribund dynasty,[73] whose luck would soon run out.

For this discussion, it matters little how and why the Western cannons failed to save the Ming. A more important point is that the way in which the Ming resorted to and relied on the arms and technology from the Far West for its survival, just like the regime's reliance on Jesuit calendric knowledge, reveals the very nature of the empire: the empire depended more than not on the Other for its well-being and even its very existence. Some may argue, and it is true, that the Ming regime's use of Western technology for national security served as just another example proving the Confucian substance-function discourse discussed a moment ago. Only this time, it is the foreign function that came to the aid of the Great Ming substance by securing the latter's manifestation. Besides the irony that the great Chinese empire had to cling to one stranger in order to fight off another stranger, the most challenging and troubling aspect of this argument is that, when called upon by the Confucian substance during the late Ming, the foreign function did not, as it did not at any other time in Chinese history, come alone. Instead, it brought along with it the baggage of Christian ideology, the part of the foreign import that the "Chinese substance, Western function" slogan hoped to block or filter out. As one knows, when the Ming authority opened its door to the cannon-casting technology, it also invited into its capital the bearers of the technology, namely "foreign businessmen" (夷商) and "foreign subjects" or Jesuit missionaries.[74] Among these experts were Longobardo, and Emmanuel Diaz Jr. (1574–1659), known in China as Yang Ma'nuo (陽瑪諾). While Longobardo was known for opposing Ricci's accommodation policy and denouncing Confucianism as a cult to be rejected,[75] Diaz was designated as a dangerous enemy whom the Ming government had convicted in Nanjing and would have liked to deport from China.[76] In short, one "side effect" of this hiring of Western personnel for technology was the revival of Christian missions in inland China.[77]

To conclude this chapter's discussion, one must say that it is by no means accidental that the Ming empire opened its Self to the Jesuit Other, or extended its hospitality to the stranger from the West. Indeed, the imperial solicitation and utilization of the much-needed foreign knowledge and technology were meant to be self-serving or, as has been mentioned, to enhance the empire by keeping its administration normal and its border safe. In a way, the foreign knowledge and technology did serve this goal. While the calendar had the potential to help enable the imperial court to sustain its ritual and administrative routine, the cannons likewise postponed the demise of the dynasty. To wit, the Jesuit function, in fact, did work to make it possible for the Ming substance to manifest. But there is no doubt that this manifestation came at a price. While the foreign function served as the condition of possibility for the empire, it also undermined and put into question the empire by exposing and highlighting its weakness, lack of purity, and reliance on the Other for its own subjectivity. In short, the Ming's hospitality to the Jesuits, no matter how partial and conditional, points unmistakably to a ruptured subjectivity, a state described by Levinas as "an incessant alienation of the ego."[78]

6

The Confucian Hospitality

Responding to the Jesuits

> To apprehend oneself from within—to produce oneself as I—is to apprehend oneself with the same gesture that already turns toward the exterior to extra-vert and to manifest—to respond for what it apprehends—to express; it is to affirm that the becoming-conscious is already language, that the essence of language is goodness, or again that the essence of language is friendship and hospitality. . . . The fundamental scission into same and the other is a non-allergic relation of the same with the other.
>
> —Emmanuel Levinas, *Totality and Infinity*

> We must then ask ourselves what a decision is and *who* decides. And if a decision is—as we are told—active, free, conscious and voluntary, sovereign. What would happen if we kept this word and this concept, but changed these last determinations?
>
> —Jacques Derrida, *The Politics of Friendship*

The discussion in the two previous chapters should have made clear how both the status and identity of the Ming host, together with its Confucian Sino-centrism, became uncertain before the Jesuits' infiltration with their world maps, calendric science, and other technologies. This chapter will examine the Jesuit challenge sustained by Confucianism when Christian ideology and theology clashed directly and drastically with Confucian rituals, doctrines, and concepts. Focusing on anti-Christian Confucian responses to the missionaries, the discussion will demonstrate how the Confucian Self confirmed its own limits and undermined its own subjectivity as it attempted to claim univocality and sole authority for Confucianism.

Compared with many of the Confucians discussed in the preceding chapters, the anti-Christian Confucians to be examined in the following pages represent a most obstinate group that insisted on an outright rejection of the missionary strangers, their Christian religion and Western science included. These Confucians began to openly oppose the missionaries in the 1610s, when some Jesuits became increasingly critical of Confucianism, especially Confucian rituals.[1] They were convinced that what the missionaries planned to do was, as Mencius has put it, "convert the Chinese to the barbarian way."[2] To them, the missionaries posed a danger to everything and everyone Chinese, because with their Christian teachings they sought to eradicate fundamental Confucian doctrines and practices. The anti-Christian Confucians therefore called for the expulsion of the Jesuits. Assuming the role of an inhospitable host, this group used first of all governmental intervention—the most famous example being the so-called Nanjing Persecution that led to the arrest and trial of some Jesuits and their deportation to Macao between 1616 and 1617.[3] Besides resorting to administrative means to end the missionary presence in China, the Confucians also picked up their brushes and produced a number of writings using harsh rhetoric to defend and clarify Confucian doctrines and refute ideology and religion from the West. Out of these Confucian apologetic writings, this chapter chooses to examine two examples, both written in 1623, as representatives of the Confucian responses to the Jesuits and Christianity: *Shengchao zuobi* (聖朝佐辟), or *Assisting the Holy Dynasty in the Refutation [of Heterodoxy]*, by Xu Dashou (許大受),[4] and *Qingshu jingtan yiji* (清署經談・一集), or *Discourse on the Canons in the Clear Studio, Volume 1*, by Wang Qiyuan (王啟元).

In their works, both authors expressed grave concerns with the Jesuits' proselytical activities, which they believed were posing a serious threat to Confucianism. They apparently had good reason to be worried, because the spreading foreign religion was setting up a new hierarchy under the Christian God, in which the Great Middle Kingdom became subordinate. My discussion earlier in this book pointed out how Ricci in his *The True Meaning of the Lord of Heaven* hoped to naturalize the Christian hierarchy by presenting God as the "common father" of all Chinese, including the state ruler and all biological fathers. To clarify this fact and also facilitate the discussion that follows, here are some remarks with which Ricci explained to his Chinese interlocutor the obedience expected from humans to God using the Confucian concept of filial piety:

I would now like to define the theory of filial piety. To define the meaning of filial piety, one must first define the relationship between father and son. In this world, every man has three fathers: the first being the Lord of Heaven, the second the sovereign of the state, and the third the father of one's family. To disobey these three fathers is to be unfilial. As there is the Dao under heaven, the will of the three fathers are in no conflict, because what the father of the lowest rank will command his own son to do is obey and serve the father or fathers of the higher rank or ranks.[5]

Making everyone, including the emperor, a filial and thus ideal son before God, Ricci's argument did not go well with the Confucians. They found it particularly offensive that the missionaries should be trying to impose on them a foreign God. In the view of these Confucians who had their own deities, the idea that they must now bow to the Christian God as the one and the only God for all people and nations was unthinkable. The very idea was particularly hateful to the Confucians in the sense that a submission to the Christian God would first and foremost be detrimental to the Chinese social and political structures. Xu Dashou's response represents a typical example of the Confucian response concerning the matter of who the host or master should be.

A late Ming Confucian supposedly well-versed in Confucian canons and Buddhist and Daoist teachings,[6] Xu opened his anti-Christian treatise *Shengchao zuobi* by devoting an entire section to the untrustworthiness of the Jesuits. In Xu's eyes, it was not just that the missionaries could not be trusted owing to the religious faith they were preaching. Questionable was the very existence of the Daxiyang guo (大西洋國), or the countries of the Great Western Ocean, from which the missionaries claimed to have come. He took this stance because these countries were not mentioned in such books as the *Shanhai jing* (山海經), *Soushen ji* (搜神記), *Xianbing lu* (咸賓錄), *Xiyu zhi* (西域志), or *Taiping guangji* (太平廣記).[7] More important, he asserted, no one should think that the missionary Lord of Heaven, also called Jesus, could have anything worthwhile to offer China. Jesus was born as late as Emperor Aidi's (哀帝) reign (6 BCE–1 CE) in the Western Han (206 BCE–25 CE), a time much later than Confucius and Laozi, who had already founded and expressed all the morals about the *Dao* or the Way. Therefore, by the time Jesus came to this world, what good ideas could still be left out there for him to discover or to offer? From this perspective, what would qualify him to morally surpass all the Chinese sages?[8]

An opening rebuttal based on the lack of knowledge of the Trinity should indeed, in the eyes of Christian theologians, weaken and even annul completely the Confucian argument.[9] But one would be naive to believe that Xu was more interested in historicity than he was in the authority and dominance contained in the discussion of history.[10] Here, like many other Confucians making similar statements in this collection of anti-Christian writings and elsewhere, Xu was not as concerned with the primacy in history as he was with the practical use of history. To put it differently, if the Jesuit concept of the Christian God as the "common father" could be seen as Christian hospitality and an invitation to the Chinese Other to submit to the omnipotent God, for Xu and other Confucians, their insistence on the seeming late coming of Jesus was a use of history as a method both to reject the missionary strangers and to present or identify the Self as the master or host of the empire. As a matter of fact, from Xu's work, as from Wang Qiyuan's work to be discussed later, one clearly sees that for which both the Confucians and the Christians contended: nothing other than totalization in the sense of who had the authority and power over the other, or who was the host, the hegemon, or the master.

In Xu's view, the consequences of submitting to the Christian God, or accepting even a tiny portion of what the Jesuits were professing to China, would be extremely severe and most devastating. If the Christian God became the God of China, it would mean a loss of imperial authority and privilege. This God would relegate the Chinese rulers to the role of mere subordinates, because, as Xu related, the missionary barbarians had made clear that "compared with all kings and emperors, with all the sages and worthies, the Lord of Heaven stood as the sole authority."[11] With this argument, the missionaries were imposing their God on the Chinese emperor. As Xu saw it, the Chinese had always worshipped Heaven. According to the examples of the works by Zisi (子思; 483–402 BCE), Dong Zhongshu, and others, the concept of Heaven discussed by the Jesuits had in fact been a crucial as well as common concept in Confucian thinking and practice. What was important was that the Heaven understood and worshipped by the Chinese, including the Confucians, should not be confused with what the Jesuits were promoting, because the Confucian Heaven was not at all similar to the Lord of Heaven from the West.[12] The missionaries from the West, Xu continued, were trying not only "to appropriate Heaven by claiming the Lord of Heaven" but also "by appropriating Heaven to dominate the Son of Heaven."[13] And when the Chinese emperor came under the domination of a foreign God, he would also lose both his authority and privilege, or his special relationship with Heaven, a relationship or privilege that he alone had.

If China became a Christian nation, Xu believed that the Chinese would see Christian churches everywhere in the country, which would in turn mean that everybody could go to the churches to worship Heaven.[14] This would be a drastic change, because in traditional China, Tian or Heaven was regarded as holy, and the emperor alone had the right to worship it. As Huang Zongxi put it, "Only those who have the kingdom can worship heaven; the princes and others do not dare to do so."[15] Because offering sacrifice to Heaven was reserved for the emperor, during the Ming any such undertaking in private by individuals was considered a sacrilegious engagement prohibited by law.[16] Now, the missionaries were encouraging the Chinese converts to violate this law by encouraging congregations every few days to attend Mass and offer their sacrifices to Heaven.[17]

As Xu saw it, reducing the imperial power by imposing on it the Lord of Heaven represented only part of the problem that the missionaries were causing the Ming empire. The missionaries were also trying to promote their concept of friendship. Because their friendship argued for a kind of Christian brotherhood under God, the missionaries gave the Chinese the impression that, in Xu's words, "in their part of the world the kings and ministers treat each other like brothers."[18] Although, as has been discussed in chapter 2, Ricci did not present his Jesuit understanding of union with God, the Chinese throughout the years did learn enough about Christian brotherhood from the works by missionaries.[19] But for Xu, as for many other Confucians, this Christian brotherhood between the emperors and their ministers was particularly harmful to China in more than one way. He therefore asserted, "The kings and lords are needed to exercise control of all things and people under Heaven, parents are needed to have control of a home, and the masters are needed to control the slaves. Today's barbarians don't understand these fundamentals of ours. Why do they think that the high and low can be leveled by forcing on everyone the word or idea of 'friendship'?"[20] Xu's warning here is clear: The Jesuits were attempting to reduce all social groups and classes to one with an illusory equality, or to reduce all relationships to a singular one, which the Jesuits called friendship.

To Xu, it is obvious that the equality promised in the Christian kinship—all people under God—would radically upset the Chinese social and political order by destroying at least four of the five cardinal relationships in China. If China allowed these relationships to be replaced by the Christian kinship, there would be no more hierarchies and differences between emperor and minister, father and son, husband and wife, and elder and younger brother.[21] To Xu and other Confucians, the promotion of a community under a "common father" would be especially detrimental to the Chinese idea of the filial son.[22] If everyone were to share God as the common and ultimate Father, a son would not regard his biological father as a true father but only as another human being. In that situation, if an unbaptized father died, the son, no matter how filial, would not be able to do anything to help his father but would watch him sink into hell for damnation.[23]

Speaking of damnation, one should mention that, by the Christian standards that the missionaries set up for the Chinese, it was not merely that people might helplessly watch their loved ones go to hell. What was graver is that even the country's past sage kings and saints might be condemned to suffering as well, simply because these ancient dignitaries followed the Confucian way of life. As is known, one Confucian practice that the Jesuits vigorously criticized and vehemently opposed was polygamy, a life style typical in male-dominated societies and common among Confucian scholars and officials, including the emperors. Though the Confucians defended this sexist and male chauvinistic deed by insisting that they kept concubines to procreate male descendants to continue the family lineage, the missionaries found their polygamy distasteful. They therefore set as a prerequisite for all those wanting to be baptized that they first give up their concubines, because for the missionaries carnal lust is first and foremost, to borrow from Saint Augustine, "in tension with the law of the mind."[24] Because of this rule, some Confucians interested in Catholicism but reluctant to alter their polygamist lives were unable to receive baptism. Furthermore, the missionary requirement that a Christian could not have concubines also made the Chinese wonder about their past kings and sages. Given the fact that these past kings and sages lived their lives surrounded by concubines, the Chinese wanted to know how these ancient people, often hailed as the loftiest and holiest dignitaries in Chinese history, were faring in the afterlife. This was a truly difficult question for the missionaries, who had always argued that the ancient Confucians knew the Christian God.[25] After some hesitation, they told the Chinese that these sage kings and people had to now be full of regret and sorrow, because of the suffering they were now damned to for their sin of polygamy.[26] Witnessing the pain that the missionaries' "no-concubine" rule (不妾之道) had caused some Confucian families,[27] Xu could hardly hold back his indignation. His verdict on these uninvited and unwanted strangers reads:

> They [the missionaries] are nowadays running more amuck, not knowing nor caring much for our law. They came [to our country] without being summoned, and they entered without being permitted. What they have done is called unlawful entry. They don't follow the edicts and orders from our government to leave our country; also they resist with resilience our effort to expel them. What they have done is called defiance of imperial command.[28]

Given their deeds in China, Xu in the last part of his treatise proposed what he regarded as both logical and appropriate punishments for the Jesuits, who seemed to have only plans of destruction for China and the Chinese. Besides burning their books and penalizing their followers, he suggested that the missionaries be executed, clubbed to death, or expelled from China:

> We must arrest these strangers, the missionary leaders residing in the provinces, namely Aleni, Longobardo and others, simply either to flog them to death, or deport them. What must also be done is our border officials at the exit port must sign documents of deportation as their reports to be filed with the imperial court to make sure that these strangers are never ever again allowed entry into our country! If they are ever allowed entry again, the border officials who signed the documents, including the guards who escorted the strangers to the border in the first place, will be executed.[29]

As the passage indicates, Xu would go so far as to suggest that the Ming court should hold their border officials responsible in order to keep the missionaries out of the country.

The proposal to expel the foreigners aimed at nothing short of a radical separation, a separation that would, by cutting the tie between the Self and the Other, ultimately guard the univocality or closure of the Ming Empire, including Confucian subjectivity. According to the Confucian literati, China already had self-sufficiency, completeness, purity, and superiority, all supplied and sustained by Confucianism. There was therefore no need for the country to open to an ill-willed Other with the intention to disrupt. Masters in this house called China, Confucians did not need to be hospitable to the missionaries by opening doors to them or granting them a place in the Middle Kingdom. In the eyes of the anti-Christian Confucians, it was better that the outsiders were kept outside. At least, this was the plan.

However, the outsider always proves to be more resilient than expected, and the Jesuits, who turned out to be hard to get rid of, were no exception. Despite the Confucian project and effort to expel them from the country, they continued their stay in China. Furthermore, their physical presence in the country was often coupled with the ideological impact they had on the Confucians. Though the missionaries had limited success in changing the minds of the anti-Christian Confucians, their activities in China developed to the extent that the Confucians found themselves compelled from time to time to think of and respond to the Christian teachings preached and promoted by the Jesuits. The examples quoted above from Xu Dashou's book should already make clear the Confucian awareness of the Jesuit presence and mission. Such Confucian need, as well as the actions they undertook, to respond to the missionaries and their evangelical activities should be seen as an opening, a yielding, or simply a hospitality on the part of the Confucian host to the Jesuit stranger, because, as Derrida has argued, the self who makes a decision cannot actually call the decision his or her own. Quite the contrary, according to Derrida, the decision and responsibility concerning the other take place through the other already in the self, or, in other words, their taking place "in me" indicates something about the other (*alterity*) in me.[30]

To see the extent to which the Confucian response to the missionaries took place through the missionary stranger, one should quickly point out the fact that the anti-Christian writings by Xu and others contain numerous details of Christian teachings with which they familiarized themselves through their reading of Jesuit writings. Such patience or such an approach in Confucian apologetic works had been virtually unprecedented. It is true that the anti-Christian Confucians still employed the harsh and denigrating rhetoric typical in traditional Confucian polemics of other religions.[31] But what makes these late Ming Confucians somewhat different from their predecessors is that they did not choose to attack Christianity only from institutional and political perspectives, as their predecessors often did.[32] Rather, they in their writings paid more attention to the religious aspects of this foreign religion—its doctrines, rituals, and so forth—by relating details that they had picked up from their reading of the missionary works.[33] From this perspective, they were not like Han Yu, the Tang essayist and adamant anti-Buddhist author who, as some claimed, refused to honor Buddhism by giving perusal to Buddhist writings, be they sutras or other documents.[34] In the case of the late Ming Confucians, they never showed much hesitation in their works against the missionaries when they needed to support their argument with examples of Christian ideologies that they had read of and learned from the missionaries. To be sure, like Han Yu's refusal to familiarize himself with the erroneous teachings of Buddhism, the Confucian reading of the Christian doctrines preached by the Jesuits did not mean to honor or glorify the heretical religion of the missionary strangers. Obviously, the Confucians knew that, as Levinas points out, "subjective existence derives its features from separation."[35] But as the Confucian case has shown clearly all the same, the subject's existence, its gaining individuation, or its coming into being, had to come out of the subject's familiarity—that is, relation—with the Other. In short, the Confucians, in order to separate themselves from the missionaries, or to prove themselves to be the host or master, had initially to open themselves up to the missionary strangers.[36] And there is more.

From the writings collected in the *Poxie ji*, the reader sees that the anti-Christian Confucians were not just opening to the Jesuit Christians. In their pursuit of Confucian purity, the Confucians proved in an ironical fashion and with their own deeds as well as arguments that they became willing to open themselves up to more equivocality. Here is the example of Xu again. Writing his treatise to reject the Christian strangers, Xu let certain Others to Confucianism—Buddhism and Daoism—sneak into his argument. In his preface, there is a paragraph entitled "To Refute Heterodoxy so as to Revere the Three [Chinese] Teachings" (辟邪而崇三教) that reads as follows:

> One may ask: "If you who are honorable are against the Christians, why in your apologetics do you not argue for Confucianism alone, but at the same time defend Buddhism?" My answer: "Because the foreign barbarians have talked about the life after death. So if I do not relate Confucianism and Buddhism, there will not be a strong enough argument to refute successfully their erroneous argument.[37]

The preface continues to assert that Christianity had no comparison with Confucianism because it was even inferior to both Buddhism and Daoism.[38] But as indicated in the quoted passage, Xu saw it necessary for a union between Confucians and Buddhists, because Confucians alone would not be strong enough to reject the Christian missionaries.[39] Such acknowledgment itself, that Confucians alone lacked the strength or means needed to defeat the foreign religion from the West, is a topic worthy of attention and further examination. But given the concerns of the discussion here, it is more relevant to point out that the union with Buddhism suggested by Xu provides another example of the host welcoming, even inviting, into the Confucian domain a stranger usually regarded as a threat in order to fight off another stranger believed to be more dangerous. Xu's remarks in the quotation indicate his conviction that without assistance from this Confucian-Buddhist union, the cause against the Jesuits might not succeed as hoped. Here, one must make clear what Xu's or the Confucian hospitality to Buddhism may mean to the Confucian subject and subjectivity.

As the reader notes, references to Buddhism in Xu's book can be seen everywhere.[40] But many of them are concentrated in section 8, and it is no accident that, out of the ten sections in his book, this eighth one is the longest. In this section, Xu shows how Catholicism stole Buddhist ideas, insisting that "Buddhism, as well as Confucianism, were both most powerful doctrines," and he also rushes to the defense of the Buddha under Jesuit attack.[41] The fact that Xu as a Confucian apologist should come to the defense of Buddhism or recourse to Buddhist teachings must not be explained away by saying that it was common in Xu's time to mix Confucianism and Buddhism in one's work, particularly in the works of many neo-Confucians. Also, it is not enough to say that Xu's use of Buddhism was a mere reaction to the Jesuits, who in their works often exercised the strategy of separating Confucianism and Buddhism, accepting the former while completely rejecting the latter. To be sure, some may say, and rightly so, that the entire *Poxie ji* was put together by Xu Changzhi (徐昌治; 1582–1672),[42] known to be a disciple of the well-known Buddhist monk Yuanwu, who engaged in direct debate with the missionaries.[43] Therefore, it is not surprising that the compiler was willing to include Buddhist sympathizers' works in the volume. While all these may be reasonable as well as true, it is still important to make clear that Xu Dashou's use and defense of Buddhism are more significant than it may at first appear.

I mentioned at the opening of this chapter that Dashou's father was Xu Fuyuan.[44] A famous Confucian philosopher, Xu Fuyuan owed his fame to a large degree to his harsh criticism of the neo-Confucians' mixing of Confucian teachings with Buddhist ideas.[45] For instance, in his work "On Learning" (辯學錄), he mounted a vigorous argument to prove that Confucianism had everything it needed, and it was therefore both redundant and detrimental if anyone should attempt to supplement it with Buddhist or Daoist ideas. On the contrary, according to him, no matter how useful and profound some of the Buddhist and Daoist ideas might be, they were already included and discussed in Confucianism. In short, what Xu Fuyuan tried to do in his essay was reconfirm the hierarchy between Confucianism and the other two religions.[46]

Given Xu Fuyuan's criticism of Buddhism and Xu Dashou's effort to have a united front with Buddhism against the Jesuits, it is interesting that the father's enemy, Buddhism, should become the son's comrade. But it would not be adequate to merely say that friends and enemies change as time goes by. Xu Dashou's recourse to Buddhism before the missionaries seems to constitute a betrayal on his part of the ideology of his father, who would perhaps take any tolerance toward any religions outside Confucianism as an interruption of the Confucian Self.[47] Far from a philosophical fantasy or a display of religious luxury, Xu Dashou's recourse to Buddhism was done first of all out of political necessity. More importantly, his recourse or his hospitality to Buddhism came from the sense of instability within and inability of Confucianism itself. It revealed the dependence of the Self on the Other, a kind of dependence that is by nature the Derridean paradox in which the subject claiming to have a sovereign-presence has its sovereignty dwell, and often squarely so, on some inferior and unworthy Other. In other words, what becomes clear out of Xu's call for a united front between Confucians and Buddhists is not only the ongoing and irreducible interruption from the Other but also the need of the Self for such interruption to sustain the Self. And such interruption of the Self, or invitation of the Other into one's own house or territory, as Derrida has called it, is hospitality.[48] In Xu Dashou's case, it was not just hospitality toward Buddhism at a time of fear and anger but hospitality stronger than fear and anger, because he showed that, in the presence of the missionaries, he did not mind going out of his way—even though it meant that both he and his doctrine had to open their Self, double their Self, and even wound their Self.

In comparison with Xu Dashou's passionate apologetic treatise, Wang Qiyuan's *Discourse on the Canons in the Clear Studio*, volume 1, certainly entertains similar anti-Christian sentiment. However, discussing various issues concerning Confucianism, deemed to be the most urgent in his time, Wang did not devote his entire book to the missionary question. Also, he did not share Xu's idea of uniting Confucianism with Buddhism, or with any other religious schools in China. In fact, from time to time in his book, Wang showed little or no hesitation to denounce, or at least disparage, Buddhism, Daoism, and other religions in China for their fallacies. But in his book, he made it clear that attacking these religions would not be worth his time, given these religions' innate inferiority in comparison with Confucianism. As declared in the preface, his sole task was to restore Confucianism to its original form as Confucius had founded it. It was for this goal alone that Wang saw the need to rebut other religions, including Christianity.

To help understand Wang Qiyuan's book, it is necessary to say a few words about his background. Wang Qiyuan's exact date of birth remains unknown. But it is clear that he was from a prominent family in Liuzhou (柳州), Guangxi (廣西), with both his grandfather and father being high-ranking officials.[49] His mother, also from an important family in Liuzhou, received by imperial edict the title of Virtuous and Notable Lady (節烈婦).[50] Growing up in this family, Wang became a provincial graduate (孝廉) in 1585. After passing his metropolitan graduate examination in 1622, he worked as an examining editor (檢討) in the Hanlin Academy.[51] From his preface dated 1623, he finished writing his *Discourse*, volume 1, in Beijing, shortly before he retired and returned to his hometown. Although Wang continued to write in his hometown, there is no evidence that he worked on volume 2 of his *Discourse*.[52] The published volume 1 did not seem to see wide circulation, as its title did not appear in most bibliographic catalogs from the late Ming and Qing,[53] and today only one copy of the book is extant.

Not widely known, and thus not much discussed,[54] since its publication, Wang Qiyuan's *Discourse* is nevertheless an important book for its effort, seriously made, to restore the original Confucianism by presenting it as a revealed religion. Written around the same time as Xu Dashou's anti-Christian treatise, Wang's *Discourse* has a wider vision and graver concern to discuss. What initially motivated Wang to undertake his project was the overall dire situation of Confucianism at the time. It was true that the late Ming intellectual scene was believed to be, in general, "stable but not static."[55] On closer inspection, however, the society at the time, as was often the case in traditional China, harbored many other activities and trends contesting and threatening the authoritative status of Confucianism. Xie Zhaozhe's *Wuzazu*, for instance, mentions repeatedly how corrupt and clueless many Confucian scholars were at the time.[56] The book also gives vivid descriptions of how Buddhist and Daoist rituals, not to mention those of countless folk religions, enjoyed enormous popularity with people in virtually all walks of life in the country's capital and elsewhere. To illustrate how gods from various religions shook the authority of Confucianism, here is a passage from the book:

> Nowadays no deity receives more sacrifices and enjoys more temples built for him than the Lord of Guan. . . . The other true gods [also] customarily worshipped today include Guanyin or Avalokiteśvara, the High Lord of Zhenwu and the Lord of Bixia. These three lords enjoy as many joss sticks and burning candles at temples as the Lord of Guan does. As a result, on hillsides nearby as well as in valleys faraway, there are people offering sacrifices and worshipping. Take a woman or a young lady, and mention to her the Lord of Zhou and Confucius, and she may not know about them. But she would so profoundly esteem and so firmly believe in the four gods that her piety would not allow her to have disrespect even in her mind or to talk about the gods with any words of contempt. These four gods therefore will be as eternal as Heaven and Earth!⁵⁷

It was against this historical, cultural, social, and religious background that many Confucian scholars began to discuss the importance as well as necessity of restoring the old Confucian rituals and values.⁵⁸ Judging by its contents and thesis, Wang's book was clearly produced to answer this call for restoration. But for the author, the return to the original Confucianism of ancient times meant not only to jettison the Confucian corruption and heretical thinking of some neo-Confucian philosophers, but also to reject the Christian ideas and concepts, most importantly the Lord of Heaven.⁵⁹

Wang believed that Confucian restoration would require first of all the restoration of the absolute authority of the Lord-on-High or Shangdi. He therefore saw the Christian God as the worst obstacle for his project. This God or, as the strangers called it, the Lord of Heaven must be rejected, for the Jesuits were working to identify their God with the Chinese and Confucian Lord-on-High. This identification, for Wang both a missionary conspiracy against and an imminent threat to a fundamental concept in Confucianism, should account for his animosity toward the missionaries and their theology. Soon after his book opens, Wang elucidates his point: "The men from the Western Oceans are here to promote their theory of the Lord of Heaven. That has resulted in the virtual impossibility to differentiate [their God from] the Lord-on-High that China has been worshipping all these years. Alas!"⁶⁰

In chapter 15 of his book, a chapter concentrating on the missionary problem, Wang explains why Christianity was more dangerous and thus more despicable than the teachings of Buddhism:

> It is true that Buddhism claims for itself some authority higher than Lord-on-High. But the Buddha after all does not identify himself with Lord-on-High, and thus he and Lord-on-High stay as two different deities. However, when the Lord of Heaven addresses himself with the same name as Lord-on-High, he in a confusing fashion mixes himself up with the Chinese god so that the two seem to be one. What should the Chinese worshippers do? Do they remain reverent to the indigenous Lord-on-High of China, or do they worship the foreign Lord of Heaven? . . . When we discuss the matter of the name of the Lord, a distinction must be made.[61]

As the above passage shows, Wang spared the Buddhists harsh criticism because they, as rivals to Confucians, would compete in the open as outsiders and strangers. The differences between the two schools, therefore, remained readily visible to all.[62] When it came to the Jesuits, however, the situation looked drastically different as well as particularly treacherous. The Jesuits intently sought to erase, or at least smudge, the difference that separated the deities of the West and China so that their Lord of Heaven would cease to be a strange or foreign God but appear to be a Chinese one. In Wang's view, such hijacking of the authority and status of the Chinese Lord-on-High had to be treated with all seriousness.[63]

The Chinese could certainly not have two gods over them, because, in Wang's words, "a nation does not have two kings, a household does not have two masters. In the past, over a few thousand years ago, there was already a god. If a few thousand years later there came another god, it would mean that we have two sources [of authority]—which one is the human mind to follow?"[64] Here, Wang obviously shared Xu Dashou's idea that China had its own god and thus did not need another one, particularly a foreign one.[65] If China allowed the Christian God to be superimposed upon its Lord-on-High, there would be, among other things, confusion among people about who the master was and who the stranger, guest, or subject. In short, if Wang would not mind granting limited and occasional hospitality toward Buddhism and Daoism, which for him were second- or third-rate religions posing no genuine threat to Confucianism, he felt nothing similar toward Christianity. Hostility and opposition were what he had in store for the religion of the Lord of Heaven, a sophisticated and thus dangerous enemy.[66]

Just as Wang's book hoped to restore original Confucianism, one method that he used to combat the Christian God was to place the Chinese god at the beginning of time and in a virgin place, where the actuality as well as authority of the god would stand and remain before and beyond any possible dispute and contradiction. In the section "An Open Discussion on the Lord of Heaven" (天主公論篇) in chapter 15, Wang asserted in the following passage the supremacy of the Lord-on-High while discrediting the Lord of Heaven:

> Lord-on-High is the god who has existed since the beginning of time, when Heaven and Earth were created. He is the one whom the *Rites of Zhou* has called "the Lord-on-High of the vast Heaven." His existence [in relation to Heaven and Earth] resembles that of mankind because, when a person is born, he is born with a mind as well. The two [body and mind] come simultaneously. . . . But the theory from the Western Ocean states that Heaven and Earth had existed for a few thousand years before the Lord of Heaven came. If one uses the analogy of the human body [and mind], one sees how absurd this theory is. . . . The master [mind] must exist as long as the human body exists and it remains as one and unchanged at all. [According to the Western theory,] the Lord of Heaven existed as soon as the Heaven and Earth came into being, then he came again a few thousand years later. Was he then the same god, or another one? Also, if the Lord of Heaven was born [later than Heaven and Earth], who had then been there to take care of Heaven and Earth before he was born?[67]

Pushing the date of the Confucian Lord-on-High to the very beginning of time, Wang intended to reconcile authority, temporality, and space. He seemed to assume the origin to be a time and place where his god not only stood alone as the highest deity free from any relation, interruption, and influence but also possessed all divine power and absolute authority. In his argument—the restoration project he undertook—there is clearly some nostalgia, a certain homesickness, or a desire for origin, a closure or simply a holy place of godhead where a supposedly undisturbed god from the past lays his claim on the present and future for the Ming empire and the Confucian Self. In other words, his call to go back in tradition aimed at refuting the missionary God from the West. Like Xu Dashou, Wang was equally unaware of the complex Trinitarian theology and Christology. He therefore assumed that Lord-on-High's anteriority vis-à-vis the late-coming

Jesuit Lord of Heaven alone would prove the Confucian god to be the absolute deity both above and beyond the Christian God. In his view, the Lord-on-High's earlier existence in China already affirmed its status as the real master, the true host, or the ultimate god of China. What Wang hoped to do was establish or reestablish the term Lord-on-High as an ancient and ultimately proper name, or as an old and perennial exemplarity that would mark both the beginning and the end—or, as can be said, the telos—of Confucianism, this proper name granting and preserving the Confucian cultural memory as well as identity.

As discussed so far, the project that Wang undertook was as apologetic and ambitious as it was orthodox. But at the same time, his attempt and effort to restore the original Confucianism by going all the way back to the ultimate deity, Lord-on-High, may strike the reader as somewhat untraditional. Undoubtedly, he appeared to be following the previous Confucian thinkers in his definition and presentation of the nature and features of Lord-on-High.[68] But his almost exclusive use of the name Lord-on-High instead of the term Heaven—a term more commonly employed since the Western Zhou dynasty (1046–256 BCE) as the Confucian designation of the state deity—appears to be rather out of character in traditional discourse on Confucian religion.[69] To put it differently, it looks rather odd that Wang should suddenly find it necessary to stick to the more ancient name of the god in his book.[70] It seems that he preferred the name Lord-on-High primarily to combat the Christian Lord of Heaven. Still, one should add that the term and concept of Lord-on-High might also seize Wang as useful in his effort to refute the erroneous neo-Confucian thinking—Wang Yangming's innate moral knowledge in particular.[71] Leaving aside for the moment the domestic dispute among the Ming Confucians, one must ask the question of why Wang did not call on Heaven or any other divine being from the repertoire of the Confucian religion to oppose the Lord of Heaven. What propelled him to resort to Lord-on-High not only as the ultimate godhead of the Confucians but also as the archenemy to the Christian God?

To answer this question, one must begin by acknowledging that the term or concept of Lord-on-High that goes back to very ancient times indeed designates a deity worshipped and revered by the Chinese. It is from this religious tradition of Confucianism that Wang drew the theoretical underpinning for his argument against the missionaries.[72] Speaking of the ancient tradition of the Confucian Lord-on-High could and must be seen as an effort on his part to defend as well as define the Confucian identity before the missionary strangers and their God. Just as Herman Rapaport has pointed out in a different context, "Speaking a language . . . is a means of dwelling or remaining within one's political identity."[73] Nevertheless, the very fact that he needed religious language to identify his or the Confucian Self already points to an identity crisis he and his fellow Confucians were experiencing, a crisis partly brought about by the missionary stranger and the foreign God.[74]

It was in this undesirable context that he found in the Lord-on-High the needed and possible savor of the Confucian identity, and he also realized that, in order for his god to grant and protect his Self, he must first of all rescue this so-called Lord-on-High who had been kidnapped or appropriated by the missionaries. But by the time the *Discourse on the Canons in the Clear Studio* was published, this Confucian Lord-on-High, supposedly an indigenous god of the Shang dynasty (c. 1600–1046 BCE),[75] had sustained much missionary representation or misrepresentation. As has been discussed, Ricci and other missionaries had argued to identify Lord-on-High with the Christian God, the Lord of Heaven. To quote Ricci again, "The only distinction between the Lord-on-High and the Lord of Heaven is that they are the same deity bearing two different names."[76] When Wang began to write his book over forty years after Ricci's arrival in China, the Lord-on-High, presented and represented through repeated missionary interpretations, had become a name revived and popularized because of the Jesuits. Even his feature as a personal god had been revitalized in the missionary writings. Needless to say, Wang himself never admitted in his book that he had to take his god back from the Christians. But his restoration project certainly served as a good example of what Derrida calls "the decision of the Other in me."[77] Let me explain.

One outstanding feature in Wang's argument, especially the part against the missionaries, is that he treated Confucianism as a revealed religion and Confucius himself as the godfather. The following passage is crucial for understanding his idea of how and why its revelation confirmed Confucianism to be a unique religion superior to others:

> The Great Commentary [of the *Changes*] also states: "The Yellow River brought forth a map and the Luo River brought forth a writing, which the holy men took as models." There has not been even one case since antiquity when a supernatural being would itself pass on the doctrines to help establish a religion. Regarding the map and writing from the rivers, aren't they the secrets that Heaven itself granted to the holy men? Concerning

> the two other religions [Daoism and Buddhism] and other various schools, they in general rose after the middle of the classical period; Confucianism, therefore, is the only one from the very beginning of history.... Within the other two religions and the hundred schools, their teachings are handed down only from the patriarchs to the disciples, while the Confucian school stands as the only one receiving its doctrines directly from Heaven and Earth. This fact requires that the philosophers of the Holy Dao interpret and explicate Confucianism in a context as broad as Heaven and Earth. They must also mention specifically that the Holy Dao, after coming originally and directly from the Heaven and Earth, later on formed the fundamentals of Confucianism.[78]

Without inserting the term Lord-on-High in the passage, Wang nevertheless made clear the give-and-receive relation between the divine and Confucianism. There are two things worth noting. First, revelation or the Mandate of Heaven predetermined the holiness of Confucianism that in turn, as Wang illustrated elsewhere in his book, proved the holiness of Heaven or Shangdi;[79] second, this holiness thereby defined the superiority of Confucianism to other religious and philosophical schools. Strictly speaking, as far as the first point in the passage is concerned, if one sees it as part of the traditional view often expressed from the time of Confucius on down to the Han dynasty when many would write or talk about prognostication, apocrypha, numerology, and so forth, then it may seem that Wang was saying nothing new. However, Wang's sudden return to early Confucianism, which supposedly worshipped Shangdi, along with his reopening of the question of the Confucian legitimacy mandated by Heaven seem for a moment to be out of place at a time when most Confucian thinkers would concern themselves with concepts like *li* (Principle), *xin* (Mind), *xing* (性; Nature), and so on. Reading Wang's discussion of the Mandate of Heaven, his presentation of Confucianism as a revealed religion—with Confucius himself as the patriarch (教主)[80]—indicating the relation between the holy and the ordinary, one should be able to say with good reason that Wang's words must bear some influence from Christian theology, as seen in the many Jesuit works about creation and the omnipotence of God. What is different with Wang is that he clearly states that the Confucians do not want a foreign god to be superimposed on China. But despite his worries about and anger at the Jesuits, his thinking or his decision that they must be got rid of comes from the beginning from the Jesuits.

To recapitulate what has been said in this chapter about Wang's argument against the missionaries through his emphasis on Lord-on-High and the religious nature of Confucianism, I would like to refer again to a point raised by Derrida in his *Politics of Friendship*. Derrida argues that no subject can keep its subjectivity undisturbed. A subject can remain intact only when it does not have to decide on any event. But, as Derrida sees it, there is always an event, as an undesirable or uninvited guest, to intrude into the subject's closed space and to force "a passive decision" out of the subject—"passive" in the sense that the subject does not come up with the decision but is compelled by the event to take responsibility or extend hospitality in the situation. This passive decision is always in the subject and is always the decision of the other that surprises the very subjectivity of the subject.[81]

Conclusion

> To say that the other can remain absolutely other, that he enters only into the relationship of conversation, is to say that history itself, an identification of the same, cannot claim to totalize the same and the other. The absolutely other, whose alterity is overcome in the philosophy of immanence on the allegedly common plane of history, maintains his transcendence in the midst of history. The same is essentially identification within the diverse, or history, or system. It is not I who resist the system, as Kierkegaard thought; it is the other.
>
> —Emmanuel Levinas, *Totality and Infinity*

At the point of concluding this project, and having been immersed for so long in thinking about and discussing the China-West, mainly Jesuit-Confucian, encounter that began four hundred years ago, one is more tempted to look forward rather than turn back to what the preceding pages have said. One tends to keep one's eyes on the future, or what is to come, because the subjects discussed and interpreted in this book, the Jesuits and Confucians, are two representative groups who demonstrate both in their works and lives a particular obsession with the past.

Their past or pasts, so distant and different from each other and yet so strikingly similar, were obviously a tremendous attraction to the Jesuits and Confucians, often regarded to be times of glory and harmony, representing the time before the fall, before Reformation, or during the Three Dynasties, a period lasting two thousand years roughly from 2140 to 250 BCE, or the time of "original Confucianism." Such nostalgia on the part of these Jesuits and Confucians, therefore, does not speak of a shared fear of the future but rather of a common hope, longing to somehow return to and reunite with their past. And their awareness of time's constant movement forward certainly helped intensify this longing. As Ricci wrote to a friend in one of his letters, "Though still a young man, I have already taken on the trait of the elderly, who are always praising time past."[1]

To praise the past certainly confirms one's nostalgia or shows the tenacity of human memory. But in the case of Ricci and the Confucians, such nostalgia or memory or longing translated itself into action, effort, and a certain work ethic with which attempts were made and work was undertaken to reconstruct or recreate the past. As has been mentioned, Ricci's and the Confucians' pasts are pasts of harmony and universality. Simply, their history is history of One. Thinking of the time they lived in, perhaps one should refrain from bombarding with hasty criticism the enthusiasm that the Jesuits and Confucians showed for the past. With the separation of the church, the weakened papal authority, and the declining Ming dynasty on the verge of a fall, one wonders how many could remain happy, and how so many could pass up the opportunity of enlisting in the Jesuit order, in which spiritual exercises were designed to bring fallen souls back to God in a divine union. One would certainly understand why Wang Qiyuan, the late Ming Confucian with anti-Christian sentiments examined in the previous chapter, would not relent in his book in calling to restore Confucianism to its original and religious state.

However, that these intentions to return to a past of purity are understandable does not mean that they were guaranteed to produce harmony and peace or universality. Quite the contrary, the Jesuit and Confucian examples treated in this book alone should have made clear that the projects claiming to lead to the return to such a past or a restoration of universality always had as their condition of possibility the oppression and repulsion of many deemed to be different and other to the ideal of the One. This was as true with the Jesuit mission as it was with the Confucian institution. To be sure, the Jesuits and the Confucians alike would, from time to time, as has been discussed, see the need to establish friendship with and extend hospitality to one another. But their friendship and hospitality, as convincingly argued by Schmitt in his discussion based on biblical examples and examples from other sources, were again and again reserved only for their identified groups and kept with clearly maintained distinctions.[2] For instance, available records show it is true that the Jesuits had announced that they would not mind granting pardons to Reformation heretics, particularly those believed to be just followers.[3] At the same time, one may need to be reminded of the principal reason why the Society of Jesus was founded in the first place. To this end, these words will help:

It was an evil day for new-born Protestantism when a French artillery-man fired the shot that struck down Ignatius Loyola. . . . The soldier gave himself to a new warfare. In the forge of his great intellect, heated but not disturbed by the intense fires of zeal, was wrought the prodigious enginery whose power has been felt to the uttermost confines of the world. . . . The Church to rule the world; the Pope to rule the Church; the Jesuits to rule the Pope, such was and is the programme of the Order of Jesus.[4]

Speaking here of the clash between the Jesuit vocation and the Confucian tradition dating to four centuries ago, one cannot help but feel the resemblance, and thus the philosophical relevance, that this historical event has with present-day politics, culture, and international relations. Watching the events in the past few decades and present day in the political arena and the scholarly one, including, for instance, the military, ideological, and economic conflicts, and the theories put out by different scholars, who would be so bold-faced and oblivious as to say that history does not repeat itself? No matter how inviting and charming one history, or one culture, or one civilization may look, completely free from or exclusive of alterity, the strife that arises from this desire is dangerous and detrimental.

To be sure, as has been argued throughout this book, the danger posed by those determined to establish the One also haunts the promoters themselves. To repeat a point made in one of the previous chapters, the Jesuit spirituality aimed at purifying the Jesuits, including their very self, so as to qualify them for union with God—like the friendship promoted by Ricci in China—proves that its practitioners often have to execute it at the price of sacrificing the very fundamentals of the spirituality itself. Such dilemma and paradox of and for the One, no matter what it stands for, is by no means accidental. Its contradiction is predetermined by what Derrida has called the concept of *différance*. Instead of referring to the definition of *différance*, one can quote Derrida's words from his *Archive Fever*, which offers a good explanation of the troubling nature of the One:

> As soon as there is the one, there is murder, wounding, traumatism. *L'Un se garde de l'autre*. The one guards/keeps some of the other, it protects *itself* from the other, but, in the movement of this jealous violence, it compromises in itself, thus guarding it, the self-otherness or self difference (the difference from within oneself) which makes it the One. The "One differing, deferring

from itself." The One as the Other. At once, at the same time, but in a same time that is out of joint, the One forgets to remember itself to its self, it keeps and erases the archive of this injustice that it is. Of this violence that it does. *L'Un se fait violence.* The One makes itself violence. It violates and does violence to itself but it also institutes itself as violence. It becomes what it is, the very violence—that it does to itself. Self-determination as violence. *L'Un se garde de l'autre pour se faire violence* (*because* it makes itself violence and *so as* to make itself violence).[5]

Diagnosing the problem disturbing the One as innate because of "the entwinement of the-other-in-the-same which is the condition of the same itself (*le même même*),"[6] these words can also help explicate why there are so many troubling moments for the missionary friendship promoted by the Jesuits and the hospitality displayed by the Confucians in their dealings with the missionary strangers.

The first encounters between the Jesuits and the Confucians are long over. But the legacies are still with us today. Furthermore, what still continue are the growing interest in these fascinating stories and the thriving scholarly enterprise of discussion of them. It is hoped that the interpretations produced as well as understanding thus achieved will open for the future a series of potentially endless recoils within the canonical history of friendship and hospitality in regard to the communications, conversations, and exchanges that take place between cultures and between religions.

Notes

Introduction

1. David Lonsdale, *Eyes to See, Ears to Hear: An Introduction to Ignatian Spirituality*, rev. ed. (Maryknoll, NY: Orbis, 2000), 13.

2. Lonsdale, *Eyes to See*, 13.

3. Quoted in Friedrich Wulf, "Ignatius as a Spiritual Guide," in *Ignatius of Loyola: His Personality and Spiritual Heritage, 1556–1956; Studies on the 400th Anniverary of His Death*, ed. Friedrich Wulf, SJ (St. Louis: Institute of Jesuit Sources, 1977), 7.

4. See John W. O'Malley, *The First Jesuits* (Cambridge, MA: Harvard University Press, 1993), 70.

5. George L. Harris, "The Mission of Matteo Ricci, S. J.: A Case Study of an Effort at Guided Culture Change in the Sixteenth Century," *Monumenta Serica* 25, no. 1 (1966): 2. To commend his extraordinary achievements in his mission to China, a dossier on Ricci's beatification was sent to the Congregation for the Causes of Saints in Rome in January 2014. See R. Po-chia Hsia, *Matteo Ricci and the Catholic Mission to China, 1583–1610: A Short History with Documents* (Indianapolis: Hackett, 2016), 36.

6. Harris, "Mission of Matteo Ricci," 2.

7. According to Pasquale M. d'Elia, when it was first put together in 1595, *On Friendship* contained about seventy-six sayings, whose main source was the *Sententiae et exempla* (various editions in 1569, 1572, 1585, and 1590) by Andreas Eborensis, viz. Andrea de Rèsende Eborensis, born in Evora in 1498. It was only in its later editions from 1601 on that the number of aphorisms was brought to one hundred. See d'Elia, "Il trattato sull'amicizia 交友論: Primo libro scritto in cinese da Matteo Ricci S. I. (1595)," *Studia Missionaia* 7 (1952): 464–66. See also d'Elia, "Further Notes on Matteo Ricci's De amicitia," *Monumenta Serica* 15, no. 2 (1956): 366.

8. This relation is illustrated among others in the words of Jesus when he reminds the Christians, "Just as you did it to one of the least of these who are members of my family, you did it to me" (Mt 25:40). All biblical citations in English are from the NRSV.

9. The Christian tradition of charity can be seen in such commands in the Old Testament as "Open your hand to the poor and needy neighbor in your land" (Dt 15:11). In Jesus's teachings from the New Testament, the topic of charity appears more frequently. For example, one reads in Mark, "You shall love the Lord your God with all your heart, and with all your soul, and with all your mind, and with all your strength. . . . You shall love your neighbor as yourself'" (12:30–31). There are other scriptural passages preaching similar teachings in Matthew 25:31–46, John 13:35, 15:17, and Acts 4:32, 34, to name only a few. In addition to the scriptural teachings, there have been numerous works on charity by church fathers and theologians. One outstanding work on this topic is Saint Augustine's *On Christian Doctrine*. For Augustine, the principle of first importance is charity, which is the gift of the Holy Spirit sent by Christ by means of which an order for the world can be established, if not in the temporal world, at least in the spiritual world of the Church made up of those united in Christ. For brief discussions on the scholarly consensus that the meaning of *agapē* emerges primarily from Paul's "Hymn to Love" (1 Cor 13) and from the identification of God and *agapē* in 1 John 4:8, 16, see David L. Norton and Mary F. Kille, eds., *Philosophies of Love* (New York: Rowman and Littlefield, 1983), 82, 153.

10. In works by early Christian fathers, like Basil the Great, Paulinus of Nola, and Augustine, classical values concerning friendship were often transformed in the context of uniquely Christian values.

11. *Summa Theologica* I–II, q. 65, art. 5. Thomas Aquinas, *Summa Theologica*, trans. Fathers of the English Dominican Province, 3 vols. (London: Burns and Oates, 1947–48), 1:865.

12. In one discussion, Derrida has also pointed out such political use of friendship by quoting the remarks of Carl Schmitt: "Rationally speaking, it cannot be denied that nations continue to group themselves according to the friend and enemy antithesis, that the distinction still remains today, and that this is an ever present possibility for every people existing in the political sphere." Derrida, "Politics of Friendship," *American Imago* 50, no. 3 (1993): 356. See also his "The Politics of Friendship," *Journal of Philosophy* 85, no. 11 (1988): 641–42. It should be mentioned that thinkers in traditional China had a similar perception of the political and ethical importance of friendship. Confucius, who himself perceived this importance, declared in the *Analects*: "There is no point for people who follow different ways to take counsel together" (15.40).

13. For a summary of how the Greeks used their language of friendship for foreign relations, see David Konstan, *Friendship in the Classical World* (Cambridge: Cambridge University Press, 1997), 9, 33–37, 83–87.

14. A catechism, *The True Meaning of the Lord of Heaven*, first appeared in a xylographic edition in 1603, though Ricci started writing the first draft of the book in 1595–1596. See Douglas Lancashire and Peter Hu Kuo-chen, SJ, translators'

introduction to Matteo Ricci, *The True Meaning of the Lord of Heaven*, ed. Edward J. Malatesta, SJ, trans. Douglas Lancashire and Peter Hu Kuo-chen, SJ (St. Louis: Institute of Jesuit Sources, 1985), 19.

15. Ricci, *The True Meaning of the Lord of Heaven*, 375 (translation modified).

16. Ricci, *The True Meaning of the Lord of Heaven*, 559.

17. The biblical example of hospitality comes as early as the book of Genesis, where it tells of Abraham welcoming three strangers traveling by his tent (18:1–9).

18. Elizabeth Newman, *Untamed Hospitality: Welcoming God and Other Strangers* (Grand Rapids, MI: Brazos, 2007), 141.

19. In his discussion of charity, Saint Thomas receives much influence from the Aristotelian view of friendship, particularly the idea that "shared good" provides the basis for love and friendship. See Paul J. Wadell, CP, *Friends of God: Virtues and Gifts in Aquinas* (New York: Peter Lang, 1991), 8–9.

20. Quoted in Hannah Arendt, *Love and Saint Augustine*, eds. Joanna Vecchiarelli Scott and Judith Chelius Stark (Chicago: University of Chicago Press, 1996), 43.

21. The story of Beelzebul in Mark 3:22–27 is often used to present how Satan controls the entire demonic realm. See Hans Schwarz, *Evil: A Historical and Theological Perspective*, trans. Mark Worthing (Minneapolis: Fortress, 1995), 68–85.

22. This statement appears twice in the New Testament, in Matthew 5:44 and Luke 6:27.

23. See Carl Schmitt, *The Concept of the Political*, trans. George Schwab, expanded ed. (Chicago: University of Chicago Press, 2007), 28–29.

24. The following shows that, as the general opinion goes, having personal or private enemies is not glorious. In his speech delivered on March 17, 1883, at the burial of Karl Marx at Highgate Cemetery, London, Frederick Engels showered Marx with words of praise before concluding thus: "I make bold to say that, though he may have had many opponents, *he had hardly one personal enemy*." Engels, "Speech at the Graveside of Karl Marx," in Robert C. Tucker, ed., *The Marx-Engels Reader* (New York: Norton, 1978), 682 (emphasis added).

25. To show that Schmitt is by no means the only one to see the importance of the friend-enemy distinction in politics, one may use the example of Mao Zedong (1893–1976), the communist leader of modern China. Mao's article "Analysis of the Classes in Chinese Society," written in 1926—a year before the first communist-led uprising—opens with the following remarks:

> Who are our enemies? Who are our friends? This is a question of the first importance for the revolution. The basic reason why all previous revolutionary struggles in China achieved so little was their failure to unite with real friends in order to attack real enemies. . . . To ensure that we will definitely achieve success in our revolution and will not

lead the masses astray, we must pay attention to uniting with our real friends in order to attack our real enemies. To distinguish real friends from real enemies, we must make a general analysis of the economic status of the various classes in Chinese society and of their respective attitudes towards the revolution.

Collected Works of Mao Tse-tung, 9 vols. (Arlington, VA: Joint Publications Research Service [JPRS], 1978), 1:91.

26. It was only in 1861, after China's defeat in the Second Opium War (1856–1860), that the Qing government decided to establish a new agency, Office in Charge of Affairs of All Nations, *Zongli geguo shiwu yamen* (總理各國事務衙門), a special board or subcommittee under the Grand Council, to be responsible for foreign affairs (洋務). China established its *Waiwu bu* (外務部), a genuine ministry of foreign affairs, in 1901. See Ssu-yu Teng and John K. Fairbank, eds., *China's Response to the West: A Documentary Survey, 1839–1923* (Cambridge: Harvard University Press, 1979), 47. See also Masataka Banno, *China and the West, 1858–1861: The Origins of the Tsungli Yamen* (Cambridge: Harvard University Press, 1964).

27. Pheng Cheah, "To Open: Hospitality and Alienation," in The Conditions of Hospitality: Ethics, Politics, and Aesthetics on the Threshold of the Possible, ed. Thomaz Claviez (New York: Fordham University Press, 2013), 57.

28. See Mark Mancall, *China at the Center: 300 Years of Foreign Policy* (New York: Free Press, 1984), 80.

29. Mancall, *China at the Center*, 80.

30. Here are two examples. Arriving in Beijing in 1601, Ricci offered Emperor Wanli (萬曆; 1563–1620) various gifts. After he received imperial permission to stay in the capital, many high-ranking officials began to befriend him (公卿以下重其人，咸與晉接). Zhang Tingyu 張廷玉 et al., *Ming shi* 明史, 28 vols. (Beijing: Zhonghua shuju, 1974), *juan* 326, 28:8460. When the Jesuits were seen to confuse people's minds and gather many concerts to worship the foreign God, officials ordered that the missionaries be expelled from Nanjing to Guangdong (煽惑群眾，朔望朝拜....。令...俱遣赴廣東). Chen He 陳鶴, *Ming ji* 明紀, 48.10b, vol. 6, set 6 of *Siku weishou shu jikan* 四庫未收書輯刊 (Beijing: Beijing chubanshe, 2000), 720.

31. Derrida, "Hostipitality," in *Acts of Religion*, ed. Gil Anidjar (New York: Routledge, 2002), 360.

Chapter 1

1. Javier Osuna, SJ, *Friends in the Lord: A Study in the Origins and Growth of Community in the Society of Jesus from St. Ignatius' Conversion to the Earliest Texts of the Constitutions (1521–1541)*, trans. Nicholas King, SJ (London: The Way, 1974), 4, 5.

2. Osuna, *Friends in the Lord*, 8.
3. See Hans Wolter, "Elements of Crusade Spirituality," in *Ignatius of Loyola: His Personality and Spiritual Heritage, 1556–1956; Studies on the 400th Anniversary of His Death*, ed. Friedrich Wulf, SJ (St. Louis: Institute of Jesuit Sources, 1977), 97. I will return to this point shortly.
4. For the so-called "active ministry" or evangelization of the Jesuit order, see John W. O'Malley, SJ, "To Travel to Any Part of the World: Jeronimo Nadal and the Jesuit Vocation," *Studies in the Spirituality of Jesuits* 16, no. 2 (1984): 1–20.
5. According to H. Outram Evennett, of all the challenges posed to the Catholic Church during the Reformation period, the most urgent was "the challenge of the discovery of new races of men to be evangelized." See his *The Spirit of Counter-Reformation* (Notre Dame, IN: University of Notre Dame Press, 1968), 42.
6. The founding of the Society was confirmed on September 27, 1540, when Pope Paul III accepted Cardinal Gsparo Contarini's (1483–1542) proposal and promulgated the bull *Regimini militantis Ecclesiae*. More about the bull later.
7. One should mention that, according to the biblical tradition, Christians are often said to be "soldiers." See 2 Timothy 2:3 and 1 Peter 2:11.
8. See Cándido de Dalmese, SJ, *Ignatius of Loyola, Founder of the Jesuits: His Life and Work*, trans. Jerome Aixalá (St. Louis: Institute of Jesuit Sources, 1985), 149.
9. Quoted in O'Malley, *First Jesuits*, 69.
10. General Congregation 32, decree 2, ss. 15–16. *Society of Jesus, Documents of the Thirty-second General Congregation of the Society of Jesus, December 2, 1974–March 7, 1975: An English Translation* (Washington, DC: Jesuit Conference, 1975), 9–10.
11. The General Congregation is a formal Jesuit gathering where policymaking takes place for the Society. It is, as O'Malley observes, "the Jesuit equivalent of the General Chapters of the mendicant orders." *First Jesuits*, 52.
12. It is said that the phrase "church militant" is an Augustinian idea that Ignatius of Loyola took over and gave new life to by deepening it profoundly and making it widely known.
13. See Wolter, "Elements of Crusade Spirituality," 97.
14. "Friends in the Lord" (*amigos en el Señor*) is an expression used by Ignatius before the founding of the Society, in a letter to Juan Verdolay, dated July 1537. See Ignatius, *Epistolae et instructiones*, 12 vols, first series of *Monumenta Ignatiana, S. Ignatii* (Rome: Monumenta Historica Societatus Iesu, 1964–1968), 1:119. See Antonio M. de Aldama, SJ, *Constitutions of the Society of Jesus: The Formula of the Institute, Notes for a Commentary*, trans. Ignacio Echániz, SJ (St. Louis: Institute of Jesuit Sources, 1990), 28.
15. In this book, gendered language will be followed, as it appears in the works by Jesuits and other authors from the past, to keep the discussion consistent with the ancient discourse on friendship and on other topics, which, in both the West and China, usually excluded women. For a discussion on whom friendship includes

and excludes, see Derrida, "The Politics of Friendship," *Journal of Philosophy* 85, no. 11 (1988): 642. See also his *Politics of Friendship* (London: Verso, 1997), 153–54.

16. See Steven Ozment, *The Age of Reform, 1250–1550: An Intellectual and Religious History of Late Medieval and Reformation Europe* (New Haven, CT: Yale University Press, 1980), 409.

17. Repeated over one hundred times in the *Constitutions* of the Jesuit order, this phrase, mostly appearing as "for the greater glory of God" (*ad maiorem dei gloriam*), has been regarded as an unofficial motto of the Society.

18. See John O'Malley, "Early Jesuit Spirituality: Spain and Italy," in *Christian Spirituality: Post-Reformation and Modern*, eds. Louis Dupré and Don E. Saliers (New York: Crossroad, 1991), 18.

19. To be exact, Jesuit spirituality, seen from Ignatius's works, is Christocentric. See Wolter, "Elements of Crusade Spirituality," 122.

20. One can reflect on the words about Christian mysticism from the beginning of Christianity to the sixteenth or seventeenth century:

> For sixteen centuries, Christian discipleship had been understood as creaturely dependence transformed into friendship: from being subjects of the king of heaven we became his kin. To "know God" was to know oneself drawn by love outpoured in Christ towards the heart of that imponderable mystery of life and truth "quod omnes dicunt deum" (as Aquinas put it): "which everyone calls God."

Nicholas Lash, *The Beginning and End of Religion* (Cambridge: Cambridge University Press, 1996), 168–69. Lash's translation of Aquinas's phrase in the quotation has been modified.

21. Jean-Luc Nancy, *The Inoperative Community*, trans. Peter Connor, Lisa Garbus, Michael Holland, and Simona Sawhney (Minneapolis: University of Minnesota Press, 1991), 10.

22. See O'Malley, *First Jesuits*, 25.

23. See his *Spiritual Exercises*, in Ignatius of Loyola, *Spiritual Exercises and Selected Works*, ed. George E. Ganss, SJ (New York: Paulist Press, 1991), 98. Further references to *Spiritual Exercises* will be from this book and given in the text abbreviated as *SpEx* with section numbers.

24. Wolter, "Elements of Crusade Spirituality," 123.

25. Roland Barthes, *Sade, Fourier, Loyola*, trans. Richard Miller (Berkeley: University of California Press, 1976), 54.

26. This is a term that Mark C. Taylor uses to describe Martin Luther's turn to religious devotion of the individual self. Though Luther's theology is drastically different from, and in certain parts even completely opposite to, that of Ignatius, this term points to a fundamental concern of Jesuit spirituality to be discussed shortly.

For Taylor's use of this term, see his introduction to *Critical Terms for Religious Studies*, ed. Mark C. Taylor (Chicago: University of Chicago Press, 1998), 2–3.

27. Paul Dudon, *St. Ignatius of Loyola*, trans. William J. Young (Milwaukee: Bruce, 1949), 227. The biblical passages referenced can be found in Matthew 16:24, Mark 8:34, and Luke 9:23.

28. For the ways that individualism and individuality is related to Protestant reformers, see Paul Tillich, *A History of Christian Thought*, ed. Carl Braaten (New York: Harper and Row, 1968), 178–79; Reinhold Niebuhr, *The Nature and Destiny of Man*, vol. 1, *Human Nature* (New York: Charles Scribner's Sons, 1964), 57–65; and Mark C. Taylor, *After God* (Chicago: University of Chicago Press, 2007), 53–55. It is interesting to note that, according to Max Weber, one result of the individualism generated in Calvinism is that "loving of one's neighbor," often promoted by the Catholic Church, "died out" among the Protestants, particularly Puritans. From this perspective, one may say that the Society's emphasis on friendship can be seen as a Counter-Reformation act on the part of the Jesuits, regardless of whether this was meant to be a conscious choice against the Protestants. For Weber's discussion on Calvinism, see his *The Protestant Ethic and the Spirit of Capitalism*, trans. Talcott Parsons (New York: Routledge, 1992), 225–26n34.

29. This is Hannah Arendt's comment on Saint Augustine's fear of death in his early years. See Arendt, *Love and Saint Augustine*, 78.

30. Augustine, *Confessions*, trans. William Watts, Loeb Classical Library, 2 vols. (Cambridge, MA: Harvard University Press, 1977–88), 1:41. Further references from this book will be given in the text with book and chapter numbers.

31. Augustine, *Tractates on John's Gospel*, 65.1. Quoted in Arendt, *Love and Saint Augustine*, 78.

32. See Arendt, *Love and Saint Augustine*, 78–79. See Peter Brown, *The Making of Late Antiquity* (Cambridge, MA: Harvard University Press, 1978), 56.

33. It is known that the Jesuits and their theology came under the influence of Franciscans and Dominicans. Franciscan influence is even reflected in *The Spiritual Exercises*. O'Malley, *First Jesuits*, 94–95, 146–47. Both Franciscans and Dominicans had theologians who argued for individualism: for instance, John Duns Scotus (1266–1308), a Scottish Franciscan friar, who discussed individualization in his work and John Crathorn (fl. c. 1340–1346), an English Dominican, who disagreed with Scotus on this topic. For Scotus's rather complicated theory on individualism, see C. Balic and T. B. Noone, "John Duns Scotus," in *New Catholic Encyclopedia*, ed. Thomas Carson and Joanne Cerrito, 2nd ed., 15 vols. (Detroit: Gale Research, 2002), 4:936. For Crathorn's view and work on individuation, see A. B. Emden, *A Biographical Register of the Scholars of the University of Oxford to A.D. 1500*, 3 vols. (Oxford: Oxford University Press, 1957–59), 1:511. To some, it is necessary to mention, Scotus's individuality is by no means as autonomous as some would like to assume. In his discussion, Heiko Oberman points out that Scotus's theory, like that of Aquinas, actually denies individualism, because, as Scotus sees it, whether

a man realizes his potential does not depend on the effort he makes but on God's predestination. See Oberman, *Forerunners of the Reformation: The Shape of Late Medieval Thought, Illustrated by Key Documents* (Philadelphia: Fortress, 1981), 130.

34. One should point out that the effort to argue for individualism in Ignatius's work continues to the present day. By Moshe Sluhovsky's view, for example, the *Spiritual Exercises* has been a part of an "enduring contribution of Catholic practices of belief to modern notions of selfhood." Sluhovsky, *Becoming a New Self: Practices of Belief in Early Modern Catholicism* (Chicago: University of Chicago Press, 2017), 146.

35. Quoted in Philip Endean, *Karl Rahner and Ignatian Spirituality* (Oxford: Oxford University Press, 2004), 13.

36. Thomas Worcester, introduction to *The Cambridge Companion to the Jesuits*, ed. Thomas Worcester (Cambridge: Cambridge University Press, 2008), 3.

37. Saint Ignatius of Loyola, *The Constitutions of the Society of Jesus*, trans. George E. Ganss, SJ (St. Louis: Institute of Jesuit Sources, 1970), 813 (p. 332). Further references to the *Constitutions* will be from this edition, and abbreviated as *Const*, followed by the section and page numbers given in the text. For an elaboration on how the Jesuit mission is to be taken and how its effectiveness and success were assured, see George E. Ganss, SJ, general introduction to *Spiritual Exercises and Selected Works*, 43.

38. See O'Malley, "Early Jesuit Spirituality," 5.

39. Ignatius, *The Constitutions of the Society of Jesus*, 66. Further references will be given in the text with the *Formula Instituti*'s own paragraph number.

40. Drafted by Ignatius, the *Formula Instituti* or *The Formula of the Institute* has been the rule of the Society. It was approved by Pope Julius III on July 21, 1550, through the bull *Exposcit debitum* that includes the *Formula* in full.

41. For a discussion of the history of the vow of obedience from the early monastics to the time of Ignatius, see David Knowles, *From Pachomius to Ignatius: A Study in the Constitutional History of the Religious Orders* (Oxford: Clarendon, 1966), 69–94. Concerning the vow of poverty, the scholarly consensus is that this comes to the Jesuits through Ignatius from the Franciscans. Ignatius takes Saint Francis and Saint Dominic as his saints. See O'Malley, *First Jesuits*, 348; Ozment, *Age of Reform*, 410.

42. Recently, Giorgio Agamben discussed the importance of vows and communal—that is, monastic—life in the eyes of the early church fathers. See his *The Highest Poverty: Monastic Rules and Form-of-Life*, trans. Adam Kotsco (Stanford, CA: Stanford University Press, 2015), 3–27.

43. Bernard McGinn, *The Growth of Mysticism: Gregory the Great through the 12th Century*, vol. 2 of *The Presence of God: A History of Western Christian Mysticism* (New York: Crossroad, 1996), 26–27.

44. Grover A. Zinn, "The Regular Canons," in *Christian Spirituality: Origins to the Twelfth Century*, ed. Bernard McGinn, et al. (New York: Crossroad, 1987), 218.

45. See Evennett, *Spirit of the Counter-Reformation*, 67.

46. Joseph de Guibert, SJ, *The Jesuits, Their Spiritual Doctrine and Practice: A Historical Study*, trans. William J. Young, SJ (St. Louis: Institute of Jesuit Sources, 1972), 593.

47. See Ignatius's *Autobiography*, 38–48, in *Spiritual Exercises and Selected Works*, 83–88. Originally entitled *Acta Patis Ignatii*, the *Autobiography* is the last of Ignatius's books. An unfinished work covering only eighteen of his sixty-five years of life, it is a book that he dictated to a fellow Jesuit, Luis Gonçalves da Câmara (1520–1575), who wrote down the narrative. Owing to this, the autobiographer in the book is referred to, in the third person singular, as "he." For a recent discussion on this book and Luis Gonçalves da Câmara, see McGinn, *Mysticism in the Golden Age of Spain, 1500–1650*, vol. 6, pt. 2, of *The Presence of God: A History of Western Christian Mysticism* (New York: Crossroad, 2017), 63, 85.

48. See Ignatius, *Autobiography*, 35, in *Spiritual Exercises and Selected Works*, 82–83.

49. Cándido de Dalmases, *Ignatius of Loyola: Founder of the Jesuits, His Life and Work*, trans. Jerome Aixalá (St. Louis: Institute of Jesuit Sources, 1985), 109.

50. De Dalmases, *Ignatius of Loyola*, 121.

51. De Guibert, *Jesuits*, 593.

52. It is a point emphasized by Ignatius that a person will be free from earthly desires, "when some interior motion is caused within the soul through which it comes to be inflamed with love of its Creator and Lord. As a result[,] . . . it can love no created thing on the face of the earth in itself, but only in the Creator of them all" (*SpEx* 316).

53. Teresa of Avila, *The Interior Castle*, trans. Kieran Kavanaugh and Otilio Rodriguez (New York: Paulist, 1979), 59.

54. See Hugh S. Pyper, "World," in *The Oxford Companion to Christian Thought*, ed. Adrian Hastings, Alistair Mason, and Hugh Pyper (Oxford: Oxford University Press, 2000), 761.

55. "Love Hates Evil" is the title of a chapter in Lewis B. Smedes, *Love within Limits: A Realist's View of 1 Corinthians 13* (Grand Rapids, MI: Eerdmans, 1978), 73–84.

56. Ignatius, *Spiritual Exercises and Selected Works*, 406.

57. There are many passages in the *Spiritual Exercises* elaborating how serving God should be the only end for humans. See, for instance, 23.

58. Concerning the term "wholly other" in the religious traditions of both the East and West, Rudolf Otto mentions that the term saw its use in ancient India, while it also appeared in Saint Augustine's works as the *Aliud valde* or the *Disimile*. See Otto, "The 'Wholly Other' in Religious History and Theology," in *Religious Essays: A Supplement to "The Idea of the Holy,"* trans. Brian Lunn (London: Oxford University Press, 1931), 78–94.

59. Rudolf Otto, *The Idea of the Holy: An Inquiry into the Non-rational Factor in the Idea of the Divine and Its Relation to the Rational*, trans. John W. Harvey (New York: Oxford University Press, 1950), 10.

60. Otto, *Idea of the Holy*, 11.

61. Otto, *Idea of the Holy*, 12. See also 5–7 for Otto's discussion of the necessity for this coined word.

62. Otto, *Idea of the Holy*, 13.

63. Otto, *Idea of the Holy*, 26.

64. Otto, *Idea of the Holy*, 28.

65. See Otto, "Wholly Other."

66. Francis Schüssler Fiorenza and Gordon D. Kaufman, "God," in *Critical Terms of Religious Studies*, ed. Mark C. Taylor (Chicago: University of Chicago Press, 1998), 139–40. The biblical references the authors give include passages from John 3:16 and 1 John 4:12.

67. John Panteleimon Manoussakis, introduction to *After God: Richard Kearney and the Religious Turn in Continental Philosophy*, ed. John Panteleimon Manoussakis (New York: Fordham University Press, 2006), xvii.

68. For an interesting discussion on God's transcendence and immanence, see Thomas G. Weinandy, *Does God Suffer?* (Notre Dame, IN: University of Notre Dame Press, 2000), 41–42.

69. The phrase *mysterium tremendum* from Otto served as the theoretical underpinning for the Czech philosopher Jan Potacka's argument for the superiority of Christianity in his book *Heretical Essays in the Philosophy of History* (Chicago: Open Court, 1995).

70. Derrida points out how important the term *sans* or "without" is in the thought of Blanchot, who often says "*X without X*" to mark the external and internal catastrophe of a concept or argument. See Derrida, "Of an Apocalyptic Tone Newly Adopted in Philosophy," in *Derrida and Negative Theology*, ed. Harold Coward and Toby Foshay (Albany: State University of New York Press, 1992), 67.

71. Derrida's point as presented at a roundtable discussion at Villanova University in October, 1994. See John D. Caputo, ed., *Deconstruction in a Nutshell: A Conversation with Jacques Derrida* (New York: Fordham University Press, 1997), 14.

72. One example comes from Derrida, *Specters of Marx*, trans. Peggy Kamuf (New York: Routledge, 1994), 22–28. In this book, Derrida debates Heidegger's concept of *Versammlung*, "gathering." Finding it a problem that Heidegger grants privilege to gathering, Derrida points out that Heidegger does not see what must "be rendered to the singularity of the other, to his or her absolute *precedence* or to his or her absolute *previ*ousness, to the heterogeneity of a *pre-*, which, to be sure, means what comes before me, before any present, thus before any past present, but also what, for that very reason, comes from the future or as future: as the very coming of the event" (27–28).

73. Many of these words are included in at least three series—Religion and Postmodernism, edited by Mark C. Taylor, and published by University of Chicago Press since the late 1980s; Perspectives in Continental Philosophy, with John D. Caputo as editor for Fordham University Press, since the 1990s; and the Indiana

Series in the Philosophy of Religion, under the general editorship of Merold Westephal, from Indiana University Press.

74. John D. Caputo, "The Experience of God and the Axiology of the Impossible," in *The Experience of God: A Postmodern Response*, ed. Kevin Hart and Barbara Wall (New York: Fordham University Press, 2005), 24, 25.

75. In Caputo's own words, what he hopes to do by writing his *The Prayers and Tears of Jacques Derrida: Religion without Religion* (Bloomington: Indiana University Press, 1997) is show "how to put deconstruction to work in the service of religious faith." B. Keith Putt, "What Do I Love When I Love My God: An Interview with John D. Caputo," in *Religion without Religion: The Prayers and Tears of John D. Caputo*, ed. James H. Olthuis (New York: Routledge, 2002), 157. See also 150–79, esp. 164–65.

76. For an example of scholarly disagreement with Caputo, see Richard Kearney, "Enabling God," in *After God: Richard Kearney and the Religious Turn in Continental Philosophy*, ed. John Panteleimon Manoussakis (New York: Fordham University Press, 2006), 39–54. See also Kearney's discussion of the God of possibility in his *The God Who May Be* (Bloomington: Indiana University Press, 2002).

77. See John D. Caputo, "Introduction: Who Comes after the God of Metaphysics?," in *The Religious*, ed. John D. Caputo (London: Blackwell, 2001), 1–19.

78. Hugo Rahner, *Ignatius the Theologian*, trans. Michael Barry (New York: Herder and Herder, 1968), 5. Rahner notes here that, in a 1545 letter to a friend, Ignatius refers to God as the *fuente universal* of all good things.

79. See Jean-Luc Marion, *God without Being: Hors-texte*, trans. Thomas A. Carlson, 2nd ed. (Chicago: University of Chicago Press, 2012).

80. Barthes, *Sade, Fourier, Loyola*, 50.

81. See also *SpEx* 213–17. One should say that Ignatius does call for caution with most dietary matters, including drinks. But he does not regard bread to be food. See *SpEx* 210.

82. The call for total submission to God is virtually everywhere in the book. Here is one more example from the opening of the book: "The persons who receive the Exercises will benefit greatly by entering upon them with great spirit and generosity towards their Creator and Lord, and by offering all their desires and freedom to him so that his Divine Majesty can make use of their persons and of all they possess in whatsoever way is according to his most holy will" (*SpEx* 5).

83. *Spiritual Exercises and Selected Works*, 419.

84. Here it may not be entirely superfluous to refresh one's memory with a familiar passage from Mark: "He [Jesus] called the crowd with his disciples, and said to them, 'If any want to become my followers, let them deny themselves and take up their cross and follow me'" (8:34).

85. See similar verses in Luke 9:24 and 17:33.

86. See David M. Stanley, SJ, *A Modern Scriptural Approach to the Spiritual Exercises* (St. Louis: Institute of Jesuit Sources, 1967), 211.

87. Derrida's use of "gift of death" is quite complicated. It first of all means that the gift is from God to humans in the sense that the Divine bestows goodness—through his gifts of grace—in the converted so that the latter cut their ties with worldly desires. Also, among other meanings, it points to what the self can give to others—that is, to die for the other. See Jacques Derrida, *The Gift of Death and Literature in Secret*, trans. David Wills, 2nd ed. (Chicago: University of Chicago Press, 2008), 36–53.

88. See David Lonsdale, *Eyes to See, Ears to Hear: An Introduction to Ignatian Spirituality*, rev. ed. (Maryknoll, NY: Orbis, 2000), 107.

89. For details, see *Confessions* 10.30. See also Peter Brown, *Augustine of Hippo* (Berkeley: University of California Press, 2000), 173. For a succinct discussion on the early Christian view of bodily desires and moral problems, see Wayne A. Meeks, *The Origins of Christian Morality: The First Two Centuries* (New Haven, CT: Yale University Press, 1993), 130–49.

90. See O'Malley, *First Jesuits*, 348.

91. See O'Malley, *First Jesuits*, 348.

92. Derrida, *Gift of Death*, 41.

93. Derrida, *Gift of Death*, 41.

94. For Patočka's discussion, see Derrida, *Gift of Death*, 41.

95. Quoted in Derrida, *Gift of Death*, 42–43.

96. Derrida, *Gift of Death*, 43.

97. Derrida, *Gift of Death*, 44.

98. Derrida, *Gift of Death*, 45.

99. Derrida, *Gift of Death*, 46.

100. See Derrida, *Gift of Death*, 51–52.

101. See *SpEx* 169–74. It is in section 172 where Ignatius expresses his concern about "bad choice" and election "not made properly."

102. See O'Malley, *First Jesuits*, 348.

103. It must be added that what the Jesuits did for their mission was much more than just relax their vow of poverty. To finance their mission, Jesuits, as Charles R. Boxer points out, had economic activities that eventually were "far greater in scope than those of either the Dutch or the English East India Companies." Boxer, *Portuguese India in the Mid-Seventeenth Century* (New Delhi: Oxford University Press, 1980), 50. For a focused and extended study on Jesuit finances and missions to the world, see Dauril Alden, *The Making of an Enterprise: The Soceity of Jesus in Portugal, Its Empire, and Beyond* (Stanford, CA: Stanford University Press, 1998). See also Fred Vermote, "Finances of the Missions," in *A Companion to Early Modern Catholic Global Missions*, ed. Ronnie Po-chia Hsia (Leiden: Brill, 2018), 267–400.

104. In the words of Pierre Favre, obedience serves virtually as "'the foundation (*fundamentum*) of the whole Society' and 'its most manifest vocation.'" Quoted in de Dalmases, *Ignatius of Loyola*, 121.

105. De Dalmases, *Ignatius of Loyola*, 287.

106. William J. Young, trans. and comp., *Letters of St. Ignatius of Loyola* (Chicago: Loyola University Press, 1959), 288.

107. O'Malley, *First Jesuits*, 352.

108. *Const* 547 (p. 249). In his discussion of this section of the *Constitutions*, Ganss warns the reader against the simplistic interpretation of Ignatius's call for "blind obedience" as his intention that "the subject should abdicate his judgment, responsibility, and initiative," because this is, in Ganss's words, "something which no man may do and which is incompatible with the dignity of the human person."

109. Jacques Derrida, *The Other Heading: Reflections on Today's Europe*, trans. Pascale-Anne Brault and Michael B. Nass (Indianapolis: Indiana University Press, 1992), 41.

110. Emmanuel Levinas, *Entre Nous: On Thinking-of-the-Other*, trans. Michael B. Smith and Barbara Harshav (New York: Columbia University Press, 1998), 13.

111. See Levinas, *Entre Nous*, 13–15.

112. Levinas, *Entre Nous*, 20.

113. Derrida, *Gift of Death*, 82. In fact, Derrida both introduces and discusses this concept before his developed discussion referenced here.

114. Derrida, *Gift of Death*, 83.

115. Derrida, *Gift of Death*, 78.

116. Derrida, *Gift of Death*, 83.

117. Derrida, *Gift of Death*, 83–84.

118. Derrida, *Gift of Death*, 84.

119. Derrida, *Gift of Death*, 87.

120. Derrida, *Gift of Death*, 87.

121. Derrida's words from another book should help clarify his dictum: "The other, that is, God or no matter who, precisely, any singularity whatsoever, as soon as every other is wholly other. For the most difficult, indeed the impossible, dwells there; there where the other loses his name or is able to change it in order to become no matter what other." Jacque Derrida, *On the Name*, trans. David Wood, John P. Leavey, Jr., and Ian McLeod (Stanford, CA: Stanford University Press, 1995), 74.

122. Derrida, *Gift of Death*, 108.

123. Caputo, *Prayers and Tears*, 51–52.

124. For similar biblical examples, see Isaiah 45:7, Psalms 139:7–10, *Romans* 11:36, Acts 17:28, Galatians 1:15–17, to name a few.

125. Mark C. Taylor, *Erring: A Postmodern A/theology* (Chicago: University of Chicago Press, 1984), 35.

126. Taylor, *Erring*, 35.

127. Young, *Letters of St. Ignatius*, 240.

128. Tillich, *History of Christian Thought*, 234.

129. See Ozment, *Age of Reform*, 414.

130. Heiko A. Oberman, *Luther: Man between God and the Devil*, trans. Eileen Walliser-Schwarzbart (New York: Image, 1982), 193.

131. Quoted in Oberman, *Luther*, 193.
132. O'Malley, *First Jesuits*, 296 (emphasis added).
133. Wolter, "Elements of Crusade Spirituality," 97.
134. Knowles, *From Pachomius to Ignatius*, 91.
135. Knowles, *From Pachomius to Ignatius*, 91.
136. According to Ignatius, "He first saw the *Gergonçito* [*The Imitation of Christ*], and never afterwards did he wish to read another book of devotion. He recommended it to all those with whom he dealt, and read a chapter or two every day." See Ganss, general introduction to *Spiritual Exercises and Selected Works*, 28. See also *SpEx* 27–28.
137. O'Malley, *First Jesuits*, 264. O'Malley mentions that the popularity of the book among the Jesuits, a result of the endorsement from the Society, in turn drove up the price of the book. In addition, the Jesuits' love of the book even led to its Chinese translation as early as around 1680. See Nicolas Standaert, "Jesuits in China," in *The Cambridge Companion to the Jesuits*, ed. Thomas Worcester (Cambridge: Cambridge University Press, 2008), 182.
138. See McGinn, *The Varieties of Vernacular Mysticism, 1350–1550*, vol. 5 of *The Presence of God* (New York: Crossroad, 2012), 102, 103.
139. Thomas à Kempis, *The Imitation of Christ*, trans. Leo Sherley-Price (London: Penguin, 1952), 30. Further references to this book will be given in the text.
140. Lu Ann Homza, "The Religious Milieu of the Young Ignatius," in *The Cambridge Companion to the Jesuits*, ed. Thomas Worcester (Cambridge: Cambridge University Press, 2008), 18.
141. Georges van den Abbeele, *Travel as Metaphor: From Montaigne to Rousseau* (Minneapolis: University of Minnesota Press, 1992), xiii. See also Northrop Frye, "The Journey as Metaphor," in *Myth and Metaphor: Selected Essays 1974–1988*, ed. Robert D. Denham (Charlottesville: University Press of Virginia, 1991), 212.
142. See Abbeele, *Travel as Metaphor*, xvii–xviii.
143. John Ziesler, *Pauline Christianity* (Oxford: Oxford University Press, 1990), 2.
144. For discussion of the instability of the missionaries in China, see D. E. Mungello, *Curious Land: Jesuit Accommodation and the Origins of Sinology* (Honolulu: University of Hawaii Press, 1989), 49.
145. Quoted in O'Malley, *First Jesuits*, 300.
146. O'Malley, *First Jesuits*, 301 (emphasis added).
147. See O'Malley, "Early Jesuit Spirituality," 8–9.
148. This is what can be discerned from a contemporary Jesuit scholar's elaboration of Nadal's view of the world as a dwelling for the missionaries. See James F. Keena, SJ, "Jesuit Hospitality?," in *Promise Renewed: Jesuit Higher Education for a New Millennium*, ed. Martin R. Tripole (Chicago: Loyola University Press, 1999), 236–39.

149. Evennett offers a fitting description of this crucial time in history, during which the Catholic Church was faced with shrinking authority in Europe and at the same time with new opportunity to expand its power: "While Rome was beginning to lose Germany and Switzerland and Scandinavia, she was simultaneously planting her hierarchies in Mexico and Peru and Central America." *Spirit of the Counter-Reformation*, 122. For recent discussion on European expansion to Asia and China, see Sanjay Subrahmanyam, *The Portuguese Empire in Asia, 1500–1700: A Political and Economic History*, 2nd ed. (London: Wiley-Blackwell, 2012); and John E. Wills, Jr., ed., *China and Maritime Europe, 1500–1800: Trade, Settlement, Diplomacy, and Missions* (Cambridge: Cambridge University Press, 2011).

150. Ignatius of Loyola, *Letters and Instructions of St. Ignatius Loyola*, vol. 1, *1524–1547*, ed. A. Goodier, trans. D. F. O'Leary (New York: Cosimo, 2007), 57.

151. For the entirety of Paul's well-known self-characterization, see 1 Cor. 9:19–23.

152. Quoted in Margaret M. Mitchell, "Pauline Accommodation and 'Condescension' (συγκατάβασις): 1 Cor 9:19–23 and the History of Influence," in *Paul beyond the Judaism/Hellenism Divide*, ed. Troels Engberg-Pedersen (Louisville: Westminster John Knox, 2001), 209.

153. Quoted in Mitchell, "Pauline Accommodation," 203 (emphasis added).

154. See Derrida, "Psyche: Invention of the Other," in *Psyche: Inventions of the Other*, ed. Peggy Kamuf and Elizabeth Rottenberg, 2 vols. (Stanford, CA: Stanford University Press, 2007), 1:1–47.

155. Standaert, "Jesuits in China," 172. For the important role Vaglinano played in the Jesuit accommodation in China, see Gianni Criveller, *Preaching Christ in Late Ming China: The Jesuits' Presentation of Christ from Matteo Ricci to Giulio Aleni* (Taibei: Ricci Institute for Chinese Studies, 1997), 35–36.

156. See Criveller, *Preaching Christ in Late Ming China*, 36.

157. *Siamo fatti Cini ut Christo Sinas lucrifaciamus*. This famous statement was made by Michel Ruggieri (1543–1607), known in China as Luo Mingjian (羅明堅). See Ruggieri's letter of February 7, 1583, collected in Pietro Tacchi Venturi, ed., *Opere storiche del P. Matteo Ricci, SJ*, 2 vols. (Macerata: F. Giorgetti, 1911–13), 2:416.

158. Peterson, "What to Wear? Observation and Participation by Jesuit Missionaries in the Late Ming China," in *Implicit Understandings: Observing, Reporting, and Reflecting on the Encounters between Europeans and Other Peoples in the Early Modern Era*, ed. Stuart B. Schwartz (Cambridge: Cambridge University Press, 1994), 418.

159. See Standaert, "Jesuits in China," 173.

160. As Derrida points out in his essay, the *Oxford English Dictionary* defines the term "invent" to mean "come up, find." See "Psyche," 6.

161. Derrida, "Psyche," 39.

162. See Derrida, "Psyche," 38–39.

163. See Standaert, "Jesuits in China," 183.

164. Derrida, "Psyche," 44. The same paragraph contains Derrida's explanation of why the other invented or found must be the impossible: "Invention invents nothing, when in invention the other [other than the same] does not come, and when nothing comes to the other or from the other."

165. Derrida, "Psyche," 44.

Chapter 2

1. Beginning in 1986 with his book *Memoirs of Paul de Man*, in which he discusses his friendship with de Man, Derrida published a succession of discussions specifically focused on the topic of friendship, including two essays bearing the same title—"The Politics of Friendship," *Journal of Philosophy*, 85, no. 11 (1988): 632–44, and "Politics of Friendship," *American Imago* 50, no. 3 (Fall 1993): 353–91—and a book-length discussion, also named *Politiques de l'amitié* in 1994 (English translation by George Collins as *Politics of Friendship* [London: Verso, 1997]). A book in his later years is *The Work of Mourning*, ed. Pascale-Anne Brault and Michael Naas (Chicago: University of Chicago Press, 2001), a collection of essays commemorating deceased friends and meditating on the issue of death. In addition, there are a few of his other works closely related to the idea and understanding of friendship such as *Adieu to Emmanuel Levinas*, trans. Pascale-Anne Brault and Michael Naas (Stanford, CA: Stanford University Press, 1999), and *Of Hospitality*, trans. Rachel Bowlby (Stanford, CA: Stanford University Press, 2000).

2. Unless otherwise noted, all English passages of this work are from Cicero, *De senectute, De amicitia, De divinatione*, trans. William Armistead Falconer, Loeb Classical Library (Cambridge, MA: Harvard University Press, 1938).

3. See Derrida, *Politics of Friendship*, 3.

4. Derrida, *Politics of Friendship*, 3.

5. Derrida, *Politics of Friendship*, 4.

6. Derrida, *Politics of Friendship*, 4.

7. Derrida, *Politics of Friendship*, 4.

8. Derrida, "The Politics of Friendship," 641–42. As has been mentioned, Confucians also saw the political and ethical importance of friendship. To offer one more example, here is a statement from *Mencius*: "in making friends with someone you do so because of that person's virtue" 友也者，友其德也 (V.B.3).

9. Derrida, *Politics of Friendship*, viii.

10. Derrida, *Politics of Friendship*, viii. See further discussion in 153–54.

11. Derrida, *Politics of Friendship*, viii.

12. Derrida, *Politics of Friendship*, 99.

13. This is a point first taken up by Carl Schmitt. See Derrida, *Politics of Friendship*, 99–100.

14. Derrida, *Politics of Friendship*, 89.

15. Schmitt, *Concept of the Political*, 29n9.

16. Derrida points out that Plato in book 5 of his *Republic*, after identifying the opposition between a public enemy and a private one, added the following remarks, insisting that the Greeks should treat the barbarians as they would treat their fellow Greeks:

> I, he said, agree that our citizens ought to deal with their Greek opponents in this wise [*semblable doit être*, "their policy must be similar"] (*omologô outō dein*), while treating barbarians as Greeks now (*ōs nun*) treat Greeks. Let us then lay down this law also (*tithōmen dè kai touton ton nómon*), for our guardians, that they are not to lay waste the land or burn the houses. Let us so decree (*thomen*), he said, and assume that this and our preceding prescriptions are right. (471b–c)

Quoted in *Politics of Friendship*, 90 (brackets Derrida's). See also 296–305 for more of Derrida's discussion of the Greek view of lineage, race, and family, as well as their relationship with the barbarians. It must be emphasized here that the Greek idea of friend and other is highly intricate and complicated. How ancient Greeks applied the language of friendship to foreign relations can serve as an interesting example of this view and use of interhuman relationships. Studies have shown that in Greek usage beginning at least in the sixth century BCE, *philia*, an abstract noun commonly rendered as "friendship," was the normal word for a treaty or alliance between states. See Konstan, *Friendship in the Classical World*, 33–37, 83–87. For an interesting linguistic discussion of the dichotomy between the Greek terms or concepts of *phílos* or a friend, and *xénos* or a guest-stranger, see Emile Benveniste, *Indo-European Language and Society*, trans. Elizabeth Palmer (London: Faber and Faber, 1973), 278–88.

17. Derrida, *Politics of Friendship*, 91–92.

18. The ancient Greeks were not alone in using ethnic distinction to divide friends and foes. In traditional China, the Confucians would also divide people by their clans. For example, as narrated in the Confucian classic *Zuo's Commentary on the Spring and Autumn Annals*, when in 587 BCE Duke Cheng of Lu was contemplating setting up a friendly relationship with the State of Chu, one of his ministers doubted whether the duke of Chu, being no kin to the State of Lu, would actually love the people of Lu (其肯字我乎). As the minister put it, "If he be not of our kin, he is sure to have a different mind" (非我族類，其心必異). *Chunqiu Zuozhuan Zhengyi* (春秋左傳正義・成公四年), 26.7a, vol. 6 of *Shisan jing zhushu* 十三經注疏, ed. Ruan Yuan 阮元 (Taibei: Yiwen yinshu guan, 2011), 439. Translation in James Legge, *The Ch'un Ts'ew, with the Tso Chuen*, vol. 5 of *The Chinese Classics* (Taibei: SMC, 1994), 355.

19. Samuel P. Huntington, *The Clash of Civilizations and the Remaking of World Order* (New York: Simon and Schuster, 2003), 13, 21.

20. Huntington, *Clash of Civilizations*, 42.
21. Huntington, *Clash of Civilizations*, 42.
22. Huntington, *Clash of Civilizations*, 42.
23. See Derrida, *Politics of Friendship*, 154.
24. Huntington, *Clash of Civilizations*, 20–21.
25. See Francis Fukuyama, *The End of History and the Last Man* (New York: Simon and Schuster, 2006), 46. It is a known fact that Fukuyama first articulated his theory in his essay "The End of History?," *National Interest* 16 (Summer 1989): 3–18, before developing and expanding it in his book-length discussion.
26. Fukuyama, *End of History*, 55.
27. For a summary of Fukuyama's theory from which this paragraph of discussion has borrowed, see Josef Teboho Ansorge, "The (International) Politics of Friendship: Exemplar, Exemplarity, Exclusion," in *Derrida: Negotiating the Legacy*, eds. Madeleine Fagan, Ludovic Glorieux, Indira Hasimbegovic, and Marie Suetsugu (Edinburgh: Edinburgh University Press, 2007), 122.
28. Before he ridicules again Fukuyama's argument in his *Clash of Civilizations* (31), Huntington has an essay, "No Exit: The Errors of Endism" published in *National Interest* 17 (Fall, 1989): 3–11, as his response to and criticism of Fukuyama's view. For more criticisms of the end-of-history argument by Fukuyama, see *The New Shape of World Politics: Contending Paradigms in International Relation*, rev. ed. (New York: Foreign Affairs, 1999). Without sharing the arguments by many of Fukuyama's critics, one nevertheless sees Fukuyama's argument that the collapse of communism means once and for all the end of the ongoing battle of ideologies to be formulated by neglecting the reality of world politics and by reflecting little, likely not at all, on the development of history. Though Mark C. Taylor in his recent book gives praise to Fukuyama for his "solid understanding of both Hegel and [Alexandre] Kojève," it must be noted that his theory receives scathing treatment from Derrida (*Specters of Marx*, 56). For Taylor's discussion of Fukuyama's view of history and democracy, see his *Abiding Grace: Time, Modernity, Death* (Chicago: University of Chicago Press, 2018), 26–29. In his discussion on Fukuyama's 2006 book, *America at the Crossroads: Democracy, Power and Neoconservative Legacy*, Perry Anderson observes that Fukuyama, deeming US foreign policies in the Middle East to be ineffective and counterproductive, "remains fully committed to the American mission of spreading democracy round the world." Anderson, *American Foreign Policy and Its Thinkers* (London: Verso, 2015), 250.
29. See Derrida, *Politics of Friendship*, 92.
30. Derrida, *Politics of Friendship*, 155.
31. Derrida, *Politics of Friendship*, 232 (emphasis in original).
32. John D. Caputo, *More Radical Hermeneutics: On Not Knowing Who We Are* (Bloomington: Indiana University Press, 2000), 61.
33. Here it should be helpful to quickly mention Ricci's life and work. Born on October 6, 1552, in Macerata, a town some twenty-five miles southwest

of Ancona, near the Adriatic coast, Ricci entered the Society of Jesus in 1571 at the age of nineteen. While completing a thorough education in theology, the humanities, law, and sciences, Ricci traveled extensively through Rome, Florence, Portugal, Spain, Cochin, and Goa (where he was ordained in 1580). In 1582, two years after his ordination, he arrived in Macao, China, to begin his missionary work. He remained in China till his death in 1610. Shortly after his arrival in China, Ricci and his fellow missionary Ruggieri, who had arrived in China earlier, established the first mission station in Canton Province—a remarkable feat, as no other Catholic missionaries, including Jesuit, had been granted permission to remain in interior China for more than a few weeks, with the vast majority being allowed only a couple days' residence. Though many had made strenuous efforts to preach in China, none of them had been favored by Ricci's luck. Of those who had tried up to the time when Ricci left for China, some had not even had the chance to step on Chinese soil. In this way, Ricci's extended stay in itself already exemplified a great achievement, which in turn marked his mission as special and different. For more details of Ricci and his work in China, see Carrington Goodrich and Chaoying Fang, eds., *Dictionary of Ming Biography*, 2 vols. (New York: Columbia University Press, 1976), 2:1136–37.

34. It has been mentioned earlier that, according to d'Elia, Ricci took many of his maxims from Andreas Eborensis's *Sententiae et exempla*. Jonathan Spence points out that, in writing *On Friendship*, Ricci might have drawn heavily and freely on authors anthologized in de Resende's work. He discusses Ricci's lack of books in China, which compelled him to rely on his memory when composing some of his other works. See Spence, *The Memory Palace of Matteo Ricci* (New York: Penguin, 1984), 142, 127.

35. Li Madou [Matteo Ricci], *Jiaoyou lun*, in *Tianxue chuhan* 天學初函 [*The First Collection of Catholic Teachings*], ed. Li Zhizao 李之藻, 6 vols. (Taibei: Xuesheng shuju, 1965), 1:299. All translations of *On Friendship* in this book are mine. In translating, I have consulted Matteo Ricci, *On Friendship: One Hundred Maxims for a Chinese Prince*, trans. Timothy Billings (New York: Columbia University Press, 2010). Here I must mention two earlier translations of *On Friendshp* that I have found most useful: Stanislas Yen, SJ, "Traité de l'amitié par Li Ma-T'eou d'Europe" (1947), in *Une rencontre de l'Occient et de la Chine: Matteo Ricci: Colloque public en l'honneur du 4e centenaire de l'arrivée en Chine du Père Ricci* (Paris: Centre Sèvres, 1983), 63–72; d'Elia, "Trattato sull'amicizia," 425–515.

36. 荷［建安王］不鄙，許之以長揖賓序，設醴驩甚。王乃移席握手而言曰：" 凡有德行之君子辱臨吾地，未嘗不請而友且敬之。西邦為道義之邦，願聞其論友道，何如？"竇退而從述暴少所聞，輯成友道一帙，敬陳於左。*Jiaoyou lun*, 299–300. In his letter of November 4, 1595, Ricci talked about his friendship with this prince and his writing of *On Friendship*. In the letter, he also mentioned that the prince called him "*signor maestro*" (xiansheng), a title that surprised Ricci and made him proud.

37. 吾友非他, 即我之半, 乃第二我也。當視友如己焉. *Jiaoyou lun*, 300. D'Elia identifies the source for this maxim in his "Trattato sull'amicizia," 470.

38. One can also compare Augustine's words with those of Horace to identify friend as the better half of my soul (*dimidium animae meae*). See Caputo, *More Radical Hermeneutics*, 62.

39. See Christopher Norris, *Derrida* (Cambridge, MA: Harvard University Press, 1987), 230.

40. It has been argued that, for Augustine, love, among other things, represents a "path by which the soul ascends or descends" (*amando ascendis, negligendo descendis* [homily on Ps 85, par. 6]). By his view, each person is what he loves (*talis est quisque, quails ejus dilectio est* [homily on 1 Jn 2, par. 14]), and love is the "glue" by which humans adhere to whatever they truly desire (*The Trinity* 10.8.11). For Christians, as he insists, charity is the true glue that binds humans to God (homily on Ps 62, par. 17). See McGinn, *The Foundation of Mysticism: Origins to the Fifth Century*, vol. 1 of *The Presence of God: A History of Western Christian Mysticism* (New York: Crossroad, 1995), 258–59.

41. For Ricci's trip to Nanjing and his stay in Nanchang, including the troubles he had with the local Nanjing officials during his first stay, see Ricci, *China in the Sixteenth Century: The Journals of Matthew Ricci, 1583–1610*, trans. Louis J. Gallagher, SJ (New York: Random House, 1953), 258–86.

42. For in-depth discussions of the threats to the late Ming from the surrounding outside areas, see chapters 4 and 5 in Denis Twitchett and Frederick W. Mote, eds., *The Ming Dynasty, 1368–1644* (pt. 2), vol. 8 of *The Cambridge History of China* (Cambridge: Cambridge University Press, 1998).

43. Li Zhi's approving words about Ricci read, "言我此間之言, 作我此間文字, 行此間之儀禮." Li, "A Letter to a Friend" 與友人書, in his *Xu fenshu* 續焚書 [*More Books to Burn*] (Beijing: Zhonghua, 1975), 35.

44. 其欲以所學易吾周、孔之學, 則又太愚. Li, *Xu fenshu*, 35. Li's opinion was by no means accidental but shared by many others at his time. For example, Shen Defu (沈德符; 1657–1642), a virtual contemporary of Li and Ricci, held a similar view. See Shen, *Wanli yehuo bian* 萬曆野獲編, 3 vols. (Beijing: Zhonghua, 2004), 3:784.

45. Harris, "Mission of Matteo Ricci," 55.

46. For a discussion of how Ruggieri and Ricci changed their Buddhist-style robes to Confucian-style ones, see Harris, "Mission of Matteo Ricci," 69–70; Twitchett and Mote, *Ming Dynasty, 1368–1644* (pt. 2), 793–98.

47. Quoted in Spence, *Memory Palace of Matteo Ricci*, 54. See also Ricci, *China in the Sixteenth Century*, 89.

48. 友之與我, 雖有二身, 二身之內, 其心一而已. *Jiaoyou lun*, 300.

49. The Greek original of this Aristotelian dictum is first recorded in Diogenes Laertius's biography of Aristotle in which one reads the following: "To the query, 'What is a friend?' his [Aristotle's] reply was, 'A single soul dwelling in two

bodies.'" Diogenes Laertius, *Lives of Eminent Philosophers*, vol. 1, trans. R. D. Hicks Loeb Classical Library (Cambridge, MA: Harvard University Press, 1972), 5.1.20.

50. Aristotle, *Nicomachean Ethics*, in *The Complete Works of Aristotle*, ed. Jonathan Barnes, 2 vols. (Princeton, NJ: Princeton University Press, 1984), 2:1827.

51. See Paul Schollmeier, *Other Selves: Aristotle on Personal and Political Friendship* (Albany: State University of New York Press, 1994), 37.

52. Aristotle, *Eudemian Ethics*, in *The Complete Works of Aristotle*, 2:1958.

53. Aristotle's philosophy of friendship has continued to generate scholarly studies. Here are a few recent works on Aristotle's theory of friendship: Lorraine Smith Pangle, *Aristotle and the Philosophy of Friendship* (Cambridge: Cambridge University Press, 2003); Ann Ward, *Contemplating Friendship in Aristotle's Ethics* (Albany: State University of New York Press, 2016); John von Heyking, *The Form of Politics: Aristotle and Plato on Friendship* (Montreal: McGill-Queen's University Press, 2016); and Kevin Vost, *The Four Friendships: From Aristotle to Aquinas* (New York: Angelico, 2018).

54. 友者與友，處處時時一而已. Li [Ricci], *Jiaoyou lun*, 304.

55. 徒試之于吾幸際，其友不可恃也. *Jiaoyou lun*, 309, 302.

56. 吾之真友，則愛我以情，不愛我以物也, and 交友使獨知利己不復顧。蓋其友是商賈之人耳. *Jiaoyou lun*, 305.

57. 友之饋友而望報，非饋也。與市易者等耳. *Jiaoyou lun*, 301.

58. 友之職至於義而止焉. *Jiaoyou lun*, 308.

59. 德志相似，其友始固. *Jiaoyou lun*, 303.

60. 永德，永友之美餌矣. *Jiaoyou lun*, 316.

61. 友之樂多於義，不可久友也. *Jiaoyou lun*, 306.

62. 各人不能全盡各事，故上帝命之交友，以彼此胥助。若使除其道於世者，人類必散壞也. *Jiaoyou lun*, 303.

63. 上帝給人雙目、雙耳、雙手、雙足，欲兩友相助，方為事有成矣. *Jiaoyou lun*, 309.

64. See d'Elia, "Trattato sull'amicizia," 491.

65. See d'Elia, "Trattato sull'amicizia," 410–11.

66. Cicero, *Orations*, trans. John Henry Freese (Cambridge, MA: Harvard University Press, 1930), 95 (translation modified). Here, the words of Steven M. Cerutti could be helpful: "For Cicero the moral obligation of *officium* and *amicitia* are closely linked, the primary distinction between the two being that consular *officium* was a public obligation, *amicitia* was a private obligation. But in the political world of the late republic, the dividing line between the two was often blurred." Cerutti, *Cicero's Accretive Style: Rhetorical Strategies in the Exordia of the Judicial Speeches* (Lanham, MD: University Press of America, 1996), 88).

67. "Ipsi quoque homini duplices manus, socias, aures, oculos geminos Deus tribuit, ut robustius peragaretur officium, quod duorum fuerat societate complendum." Quoted from *Letters of Cassiodorus, Being a Condensed Translation of the Variae Epistolae of Magnus Aurelius Cassiodorus Senator*, trans. Thomas Hodgkin (London: Henry Frowde, 1886), 417.

68. For Cassiodorus's conversion, see James J. O'Donnell, *Cassiodorus* (Berkeley: University of California Press, 1979), ch. 4.

69. Plutarch, "On Brotherly Love," in *Moralia*, vol. 6, trans. W. C. Helmbold, Loeb Classical Library (Cambridge, MA: Harvard University Press, 1957), 249.

70. See Jack Mahoney, "Casuistry," in *The Oxford Companion to Christian Thought*, ed. Adrian Hastings, Alistair Mason, and Hugh Pyper (Oxford: Oxford University Press, 2000), 98; Benjamin N. Nelson, *The Idea of Usury: From Tribal Brotherhood to Universal Otherhood*, 2nd ed. (Chicago: University of Chicago Press, 1969), 24, 25.

71. John O'Malley, "How the First Jesuits Became Involved in Education," in *A Jesuit Education Reader: Contemporary Writings on the Jesuit Mission in Education, Principles, the Issue of Catholic Identity, Practical Applications of the Ignatian Way, and More*, ed. George W. Traub, SJ (Chicago: Loyola Press, 2008), 44.

72. Aldo Scaglione, *The Liberal Arts and the Jesuit College System* (Philadelphia: Benjamins, 1986), 2.

73. Scaglione, *Liberal Arts*, 3–4.

74. For the influence on the Jesuits from Renaissance humanism, see O'Malley, "Renaissance Humanism and the Religious Culture of the First Jesuits," in *Religious Culture in the Sixteenth Century: Preaching, Rhetoric, Spirituality, and Reform* (Brookfield, VT: Variorum, 1993), 471–87. For the Thomistic tradition in the Society, see O'Malley, "How the First Jesuits Became Involved in Education," 48.

75. Michael J. Buckley, SJ, *The Catholic University as Promise and Project: Reflections in a Jesuit Idiom* (Washington, DC: Georgetown University Press, 1998), 95.

76. Nadal suggested this reading list for the Jesuit college in his 1548 directive of humanistic studies. See Sangkeun Kim, *Strange Names of God: The Missionary Translation of the Divine Name and the Chinese Responses to Matteo Ricci's Shangti in Late Ming China, 1583–1644* (New York: Peter Lang, 2005), 40. According to the Jesuit records, Erasmus's name was removed from later versions of the *Ratio Studiorum*, as Kim observes (44).

77. See Young, *Letters of St. Ignatius*, 133–34; Buckley, *Catholic University*, 95.

78. Paul Oskar Kristeller, *Eight Philosophers of the Italian Renaissance* (Stanford, CA: Stanford University Press, 1964), 149–50.

79. Ignatius used the phrase "the spoils of Egypt" more than once. See Scaglione, *Liberal Arts*, 52.

80. Scaglione, *Liberal Arts*, 2.

81. Buckley, *Catholic University*, 68.

82. According to d'Elia, in 1588, when Ricci translated a letter from Pope Sixtus V to the Chinese emperor, he used the term Lord-on-High for God. But in *On Friendship* it was the first time that this term appeared in print to signify the Christian God. See d'Elia, "Trattato sull'amicizia," 476n2. In addition, Ricci used Lord-on-High in his *The True Meaning of the Lord of Heaven* as well, an important and complicated topic to be treated at another time.

83. Here is Ricci's own Italian translation of the Ciceronian maxim: "Non può ogn'huomo per se stesso far ogni cosa, et però Iddio commandò l'amicitia, acciò s'aiutasse l'un l'altro. Onde se si toglie l'amicitia dal mondo, senza dulio ch'il mondo si disfarà." Quoted in d'Elia, "Trattato sull'amicizia," 476–77. For the translation of the maxim by Plutarch and Cassiodorus, see "Trattato sull'amicizia," 491. The modern translation offered by d'Elia for Lord-on-High in both quotations is *Supremo Dominatore*. Also, d'Elia (476) has in his comments, "Se già nella prime edizione del 1595 si trouvava questa espressione Sciamti 上帝 = Supreme Dominatore, questa sarebbe la prima volta che il Ricci se ne sarebba servito in un libro nel sense di Dio; la stessa espressione ricorre più sotto al numero 56. Se ne era già servito nel 1588 nel suposto Breve di Sisto V all'imperatore di Cina . . . , ma questo era restato manoscritto. Le edizioni dell'*Amicizia* che non contengono questa espressione sono certamente di data posteriore." (If already in the first 1595 edition one could find that this expression Sciamti = Supreme Dominator, this would be the first time Ricci would use it in a book in the sense of God; the same expression appears again below in number 56. He had already used it in 1588 in the "Suposto Breve" by Sixtus V sent to the emperor of China . . . , but this remained in his handwritten version. The edition of the *De amicitia* not containing this expression certainly came later).

84. Caputo, *Prayers and Tears of Jacques Derrida*, 191. See Derrida, *Gift of Death*, 28–29.

85. Paul Oskar Kristeller, *Renaissance Thought: The Classic, Scholastic, and Humanistic Strains* (New York: Harper, 1961), 18. See p. 14 on the rediscovery of some of Cicero's lost works.

86. John W. O'Malley, introduction to *The Jesuits II: Cultures, Sciences, and the Arts, 1540–1773*, ed. John W. O'Malley (Toronto: University of Toronto Press, 2006), xxxii. The Cicero passage, in O'Malley's own translation, reads as follows: "We are not born for ourselves alone. . . . Everything that the earth produces is created for our use, and we, too, as human beings are born for the sake of other human beings, that we might be able mutually to help one another, we ought therefore to take Nature as our guide and contribute to the common good of humankind by reciprocal acts of kindness, by giving and receiving from one another, and thus by our skill, our industry, and our talents work to bind human society together in peace and harmony."

87. O'Malley, introduction to *The Jesuits II*, xxxii.

88. O'Malley, introduction to *The Jesuits II*, xxxii.

89. See Maryks, *Saint Cicero and the Jesuits: The Influence of the Liberal Arts on the Adoption of Moral Probabilism* (Burlington, VT: Ashgate, 2008), 1.

90. Maryks, *Saint Cicero*, 7.

91. Maryks, *Saint Cicero*, 7.

92. Maryks, *Saint Cicero*, 3–4.

93. The Jesuit use of Cicero will be discussed later. An additional example is that of the Protestant reformer John Calvin (1509–1564), who, to form his theology of revelation, employed the term "accommodation." Moreover, following Erasmus, an admirer of Cicero, he "extended this idea to include God's communication to humanity. God speaks to us in a way in which we can understand." Stephen H. Webb, "Reviving the Rhetorical Heritage of Protestant Theology," in *A Companion to Rhetoric and Rhetorical Criticism*, ed. Walter Jost and Wendy Olmsted (Malden, MA: Blackwell, 2004), 419.

94. Cicero, *De oratore*, trans. E. W. Sutton, Loeb Classical Library (Cambridge, MA: Harvard University Press, 1959), 151.

95. Cicero, *De oratore*, 313.

96. Cicero, *De partitione oratoria*, trans. H. Rackham, Loeb Classical Library (Cambridge, MA: Harvard University Press, 1997), 319.

97. See Maryks, *Saint Cicero*, 91, also 4. Some years ago, another Jesuit scholar considered *On Friendship* to be "fundamentally Stoical" because Ricci saw "in Chinese Confucianism and in Western Stoicism a common 'natural philosophy.'" See Christopher A. Spalatin, SJ, *Matteo Ricci's Use of Epictetus* (Taegu, Korea: Waegwan, 1975), 21.

98. For the use of Cicero by early Christian authors, see Carolinne White, *Christian Friendship in the Fourth Century* (Cambridge: Cambridge University Press, 1992).

99. For the Aristotelian view of the rarity of true friendship, see *Nicomachean Ethics*, 9.10, 1171a. For some incisive comment on this Aristotelian view, see W. R. Johnson, *A Latin Lover in Ancient Rome: Readings in Propertius and His Genre* (Columbus: Ohio State University Press, 2009), 49.

100. Haseldine, "Friendship, Equality and Universal Harmony: The Universal and the Particular in Aelred of Rievaulx's *De Spiritali Amicitia*," in *Friendship East and West: Philosophical Perspectives*, ed. Oliver Leaman (Richmond, UK: Curzon, 1996), 193.

101. Haseldine, "Friendship, Equality and Universal Harmony," 194.

102. Haseldine, "Friendship, Equality and Universal Harmony," 194.

103. For a short discussion of how Cicero was Augustine's teacher of rhetoric, see Michael J. Scanlon, "The Humiliated Self as the Rhetorical Self," in *Questioning God*, ed. John D. Caputo, Mark Dooley, and Michael J. Scanlon (Bloomington: Indiana University Press, 2001), 268–69.

104. *Confessions*, 1:157–59 (translation modified).

105. Derrida, *Politics of Friendship*, 186.

106. Arendt, *Love and Saint Augustine*, 98.

107. Vost, *Four Friendships*, 101.

108. See Vost, *Four Friendships*, 114.

109. Paul J. Wadell, CP, *Friendship and the Moral Life* (Notre Dame: University of Notre Dame Press, 1989), 101 (emphasis added).

110. See Paul J. Wadell, CP, *Becoming Friends: Worship, Justice, and the Practice of Christian Friendship* (Grand Rapids, MI: Brazos, 2002), 78.

111. See Wadell, *Becoming Friends*, 79.

112. Marie Aquinas McNamara, OP, *Friendship in Saint Augustine* (Fribourg, Switzerland: University Press, 1958), 202.

113. Gilbert Meilaender, *Friendship: A Study in Theological Ethics* (Notre Dame, IN: University of Notre Dame Press, 1981), 16.

114. "Friends are similar to brothers. That is why a friend is referred to as elder brother. Those who are closer than brothers are friends" (友與昆倫邇。故友相呼為兄, 而善於兄弟者為友). *Jiaoyou lun*, 306. According to d'Elia, this maxim, a translation of *Fratres homines omnes inter sese*, comes supposedly from book 2 of *Contra academicos* by Augustine. But it cannot be found there. See d'Elia's discussion, "Trattato sull'amicizia," 483.

115. 友與仇如樂與鬧, 皆以和否辯之耳。故友以和為本焉, 以和, 微業長大。以爭, 大業消敗。*Jiaoyou lun*, 301. The Latin original for this maxim reads, "Concordia in civitate est quod harmonia in musica." According to d'Elia, this quotation is from *The City of God* 2. "Trattato sull'amicizia," 473–74. Discussing the same saying (written as Concordia in *civitate est, quod harmonia in musica*) included in Queen Elizabeth I's *Sententiae*, Jane Mueller and Joshua Scodel point out that it is actually "[a] close quotation of Augustine's *De civitate Dei*, 2.21: '*et quae harmonia a musicis diccitur in cantu, eam esse in civitate concordim*' (the agreement that the musicians call harmony in singing is known as concord in the body politic)." See Mueller and Scodel, eds., *Elizabeth I: Translations, 1544–1589* (Chicago: University of Chicago Press, 2009), 384n165.

116. 友之譽與仇之訕, 並不可盡信焉. *Jiaoyou lun*, 304.

117. Meilaender, *Friendship*, 17.

118. 友之饋友而望報, 非饋也。與市易者等耳. *Jiaoyou lun*, 301.

119. 平時交好, 一旦臨小利害, 遂為仇敵, 由其交之未出於正也。交既正, 則利可分, 害可共矣. *Jiaoyou lun*, 311.

120. 仇之饋, 不如友之棒也. *Jiaoyou lun*, 315.

121. 友者過譽之害, 較仇者過譽之害猶大焉. *Jiaoyou lun*, 304.

122. Nicolas Standaert, "Jesuit Corporate Culture as Shaped by the Chinese," in *The Jesuits: Cultures, Sciences, and the Arts, 1540–1773*, ed. John O'Malley, Gauvin Alexander Baily, Steven J. Harris, and T. Frank Kennedy, SJ (Toronto: University of Toronto Press, 1999), 353. The Jesuit evangelical activities in China since Ricci, being shaped by the Chinese, is a point Standaert has repeatedly discussed in various works, including his recent essay "Matteo Ricci: Shaped by the Chinese," *China Heritage Quarterly* 23 (September 2010), http://www.chinaheritagequarterly.org/features.php?searchterm=023_standaert.inc&issue=023.

123. Ruggieri, letter of January 25, 1584. Quoted in Jacques Gernet, *China and the Christian Impact: A Conflict of Cultures*, trans. Janet Lloyd (Cambridge: Cambridge University Press, 1985), 15.

124. This is how Derrida interprets Aristotelian friendship. See Derrida, *Politics of Friendship*, 222–23.

125. Derrida, *Politics of Friendship*, 155.

126. Derrida, *Politics of Friendship*, 236.

127. Derrida, *Politics of Friendship*, 178.

128. For Zhang's life, thought, and work, see *juan* 283 in Zhang Tingyu et al., *Ming shi*, 28 vols. (Beijing: Zhonghua shuju, 1974), 24:7293; Huang Zongxi 黃宗羲, *Ming ru xue'an* 明儒學案, rev. ed., 2 vols. (Beijing: Zhonghua, 2012), 2:570–71; L. Carrington Goodrich and Chaoying Fang, eds., *Dictionary of Ming Biography*, 1:83–85.

129. See John Meskill, *Academies in Ming China: A Historical Essay* (Tucson: University of Arizona Press, 1982), x–xii.

130. For a quick introduction to and samples of Wang's teaching, see W. Theodore de Bary and Irene Bloom, comps., *Sources of Chinese Tradition*, 2nd ed., 2 vols. (New York: Columbia University Press, 1999), 1:842–46.

131. See Lü Miaw-fen (呂妙芬), *Yangmingxue shiren shequn—Lishi, sixiang yu shijian* 陽明學士人社群—歷史、思想與實踐 (Taibei: Jindaishi yanjiu suo, Academia Sinica, 2003), and her *Chengsheng yu jiating renlun—zongjiao duihua mailuo xia de Ming qing zhiji ruxue* 成聖與家庭人倫—宗教對話脈絡下的明清之際儒學 (Taibei: Liangjing, 2017).

132. There are three important points concerning the five relationships. First, they are all about the relationships between humans; second, as relationships, they are by nature binary, with two parties involved, just as the term *lun* (倫) signifies, customarily translated as "cardinal," as it is used in *wulun* in the sense of matching or peering; third, most of the five relationships, as it will become clear, do not regard the parties involved to be equal. For a recent and in-depth discussion of the Confucian view of human relations and the complex role ethics expected of each individual, see Roger T. Ames, *Confucian Role Ethics: A Vocabulary* (Hong Kong: Chinese University Press, 2011), esp. 159–210. For a recent discussion of friendship through examples from literary works during the late Ming, see Maria Franca Sibau, *Reading for the Moral: Exemplary and the Confucian Moral Imagination in Seventeenth-Century Chinese Short Fiction* (New York: State University of New York Press, 2018), 139–58.

133. Lü Miaw-fen, "Yangming xuezhe de jianghui yu youlun" 陽明學者的講會與友論, *Han xue yanjiu* 漢學研究 17, no. 1 (June 1999): 103.

134. 古人謂父子兄弟不責善，以責善歸之朋友者，為不同志者言也。若文王之於周公，明道之於伊川，即父子兄弟為師友。家庭唯諾，尤一毫躲閃不得。此志苟同，千百年之遠，尚得相應；志苟不同，堯舜之於朱，均亦徒然耳。Wang Ji, "Tianxin shoushou ce" 天心授受冊, in Wang Ji, *Longxi Wang xiansheng quanji* 龍谿王先生全集, published in 1615, 15.31a–32b. For a similar but much more radical example, see "On Friendship" 論友 by He Xinyin (何心隱; 1517–1579) in *He Xinyin ji* 何心隱集 (Beijing: Zhonghua, 1960), 28. In his article, Joseph P. McDermott warns

against the simple conclusion that the friendship discussed by these Confucians "entailed the outright rejection of family ties." McDermott, "Friendship and Its Friends in the Late Ming," in *Jinshi jiazu yu zhengzhi bijiao lishi lunwen* 近世家族與政治比較歷史論文, ed. Zhongyang yanjiu yuan jindai shi yanjiu suo 中央研究院近代史研究所 (Taibei: Zhongyang yanjiu yuan jindai shi yanjiu suo, 1992), 77. In the same article, McDermott offers various examples of the late Ming discussion of friendship, including that by Zhu Tingdan (朱廷旦), to insist that the relationship between ruler and minister be treated as friendship (66, 78–79).

135. See McDermott, "Friendship and Its Friends," 70.

136. See *Wulun shu*, vols. 935–36 of *Xuxiu siku quanshu* 續修四庫全書 (Shanghai: Shanghai guji, 2002), 499–852, 1–373.

137. Martin Huang, "Male Friendship in Ming China: An Introduction," in *Male Friendship in Ming China*, ed. Martin Huang (Leiden: Brill, 2007), 2–3. For the general history and the late Ming history of factionalism, see Zhu Ziyan 朱子彥 and Chen Shengmin 陳生民, *Pengdang zhengzhi yanjiu* 朋黨政治研究 (Shanghai: Huadong daxue chubanshe, 1992); Xie Guozhen 謝國楨, *Ming Qing zhiji dangshe yundong kao* 明清之際黨社運動考 (Beijing: Zhonghua, 1982).

138. See Martin Huang, "Male Friendship and *Jiangxue* (Philosophical Debates) in Sixteenth-Century China," in *Male Friendship in Ming China*, ed. Huang (Leiden: Brill, 2007), 156.

139. In the most famous dictum from *Mencius*, "A benevolent person loves human beings" (仁者愛人; 4.B.28), the point made is that a man's benevolence is seen from his love of other men, not from his love of God.

140. See Pasquale M. d'Elia, SJ, ed., *Fonti Ricciane* (Rome: Libreria dello Stato, 1942–49), 1:337n4. See also Rule, *K'ung-Tzu or Confucius? The Jesuit Interpretation of Confucianism* (Sydney: Allen and Unwin, 1986), 19n100.

141. See Rule, *K'ung-Tzu or Confucius?*, 19–20.

142. See Venturi, ed., *Opere storiche*, 2:230. Even when he did talk to his Chinese friends about the Christian faith, he skipped the Trinity and other topics.

143. On October 12, 1595, he wrote to a friend explaining, "As we have banished [from use in our regard] the name of [Buddhist] bonze, which is equivalent among [the Chinese] to the word friar among us . . . , we shall not in these beginnings establish either church or chapel, but conversation hall." Quoted in George H. Dunne, *Generation of Giants: The Story of the Jesuits in China in the Last Decades of the Ming Dynasty* (Notre Dame, IN: University of Notre Dame Press, 1962), 46.

144. For Ricci's holding back from the Chinese such Christian concepts as Trinity, incarnation, and redemption and for the criticism of such omission in his mission, see Dunne, *Generation of Giants*, 96–97.

145. Quoted in Dunne, *Generation of Giants*, 44.

146. One such example comes from Jiao Hong (焦竑; 1540–1620). A high-ranking official who met Ricci in Nanjing around 1599, Jiao recorded in his work a brief exchange he had with a student of his. The student complained to Jiao that

"wild thoughts" (妄念), which would disappear from him when he was with friends at discussion meetings, would again come to disturb his mind after he left the meetings, to which Jiao responded, "Who asked you to leave?" Having reminded his student of the Master's words "A gentleman cultivates his benevolence through friends" (以友輔仁) in *The Analects*, Jiao went on to say, "Mr. Li [Ricci] from the West said: 'My friend is a second me.' These words are as wonderful as they are appropriate" (西域利君言:'友者, 乃第二我也.' 此語甚希, 亦甚當). Jiao, *Danyuan ji* 澹園集, 2 vols. (Beijing: Zhonghua, 1999), 2:735. See also Edward T. Ch'ien, *Chiao Hung and the Restructuring of Neo-Confucianism in the Late Ming* (New York: Columbia University Press, 1986), 236–37.

147. 西泰子間關八萬里, 東游于中國, 為交友也。其悟交道也深, 故其相求也切, 相與也篤, 而論交道獨詳⋯. 有味乎其論, 而益信東海西海, 此心此理同也. Feng, preface to Ricci, *Jiaoyou lun*, 291–92.

148. It seems that even the format of aphorism in *On Friendship* contributes to the book's warm reception among the Confucians. As it is known to all, aphoristic discussions on morals and doctrines has a long tradition in Confucian writings, and the *Analects* were particularly popular during the late Ming. That is why the aphoristic presentation in *On Friendship* and other works by Ricci got noticed. For instance, in part of a poem written for the Jesuits (贈西國諸子詩), Ye Xianggao (葉向高; 1559–1627), once a senior Grand Secretary of the imperial court in the 1620s, describes Ricci thus: "In his works there are many aphorisms, in his company, many elegant gentlemen. I also got to know him, learning with happiness things profound" (著書多格言, 結交皆賢士. 我亦與之遊, 泠然得深旨). Quoted in Liu Tong 劉侗, *Dijing jingwu lüe* 帝京景物略 (Beijing: Beijing guji chubanshe, 2000), 154.

149. See Henri Bernard, *Le père Matthieu Ricci et la société chinoise de son temps (1551–1610)*, 2 vols. (Tientsin: Hautes études, 1937), 1:248. Quoted in Rule, *K'ung-tzu or Confucius?*, 21.

150. An alternate reading of IHS, specifically for the Jesuits, is *iesus humiis societas*, humble Society of Jesus.

151. For a summary of the discussions on passive or unconscious decision by Levinas and Derrida, see Critchley, *Ethics, Politics, Subjectivity: Essays on Derrida, Levinas and Contemporary French Thought* (London: Verso, 1999), 183–97, 254–86.

152. Critchley, *Ethics, Politics, Subjectivity*, 263.

153. Derrida, *Adieu*, 23.

154. *Politics of Friendship*, 67.

155. The exact dates of Qu's birth and death have for long remained unknown. In an article, Qu Guoxing (瞿果行) mentions that Qu Rukui was born in 1549, without producing any textual evidence. See Qu, "Qu Rukui xingshi fawei" 瞿汝夔行實發微, *Qi Lu zazhi* 齊魯雜誌 1 (1994): 99–101; see also Huang Yi-Long 黃一農, "Qu Rukui (Taisu) jiashi yu shengping kao" 瞿汝夔（太素）家世與生平考, *Dalu zazhi* 大陸雜誌 89.5 (1994): 1–3.

156. 利公⋯ 頌聖謨、遵王度、受冠帶、祠春秋、躬守身之行, 以踐真修, 申敬事天之旨, 以裨正學. Qu, "Preface to *On Friendship* by Master Li from the Far West" 大西域利公友論序, in *Jiaoyou lun*, 295.

157. Paul Rule, *K'ung-Tzu or Confucius?*, 48.

158. Ricci, *China in the Sixteenth Century*, 335–36. The English translation of the book was based on *De Christiana expeditione apud Sinas suscepta*, the Latin translation by Nicolas Trigault (1577–1628) of Ricci's memoirs, entitled *Storia dell'introduzione del Christianesimo in Cina*, which he drafted in Italian from 1609 to a few months before his death in 1610. Compared with the corresponding passage in *Storia*, the quotation above appears to have altered the order of Ricci's narrative but retains most of the details of Ricci's story about the ritual, including the temple for the sacrifice, the *tansu* priests who carried out the ceremony, description of Chinese music, and so on. For the passage in Latin, see Trigault, *De Christiana expeditione apud Sinas suscepta ab Societate Iesu* (Augsburg, 1615), 368–69; for its Italian original in *Storia*, see d'Elia, ed., *Fonti Ricciane*, N. 553, 2:70–71. Theodore N. Foss offers an extended and in-depth discussion on the lack of faithfulness of Trigault's Latin translation in "Nicolas Trigault, SJ—Amanuensis or Propagandist? The Rôle of the Editor of *Della entrata della Compagnia di Giesù e Christianità nella Cina*," in *International Symposium on Chinese-Western Cultural Interchange in Commemoration of the 400th Anniversary of the Arrival of Matteo Ricci, SJ, in China*, suppl. (Taibei: Fu Jen University Press, 1983), 1–94.

159. In his memoirs, which later gained popularity in Europe, Ricci persisted in presenting Confucius as a philosopher and Confucianism as a school of morals. He tried hard to deny any religious dimension there was in Confucius's teachings and Confucian practice of rituals, sacrifices and cultus. Here is an example of how Ricci wanted his readers in the West to see Confucius and Confucians:

> One of the sciences they [the Confucians] know well is morals. . . . The greatest philosopher among them is Confucius, who was born 551 years before Christ. And he lived a good life for over seventy years, teaching the nation with his words, deeds and writings. Hence, everybody has held and venerated him as the most saintly man who has ever descended to this world. . . . In every city and school where the *literati* gather, there is, following an old law, a much decorated temple of Confucius, where his statue stands with his name and title. All days of new and full moon through the seasons of the year, the *literati* offer to him a certain kind of sacrifice of *profumi* [incense and candles] and dead animals, though they do not recognize him as a divinity or ask him for anything. Therefore one cannot call this offering a true sacrifice.

D'Elia, *Fonti Ricciane*, N. 55, 1:39–40. Such presentation of Confucius and Confucianism in Ricci's *Storia* led to the scholarly consensus, for long popular and influential in the West, that China had no religion. For criticism of this erroneous view, see Anthony C. Yu, *State and Religion in China: Historical and Textual Perspective* (Chicago: Open Court, 2005), 5–6; see also Jordan Paper, *The Spirits are Drunk: Comparative Approaches to Chinese Religion* (Albany: State University of New York Press, 1995), 10–12.

160. The Chinese term that d'Elia supplied in Ricci's memoirs is *Dasi dian* (大祀殿), namely *Dasi tan* (大祀壇) or, simply, *Tiantan* (天壇). See *Fonti Ricciane*, N. 553, 2:70.

161. See Zhang Tingyu, *Ming shi*, juan 47, 5:1225.

162. See Zhang Tingyu, *Ming shi*, juan 47, 5:1227–28. For the layout of the temple, see *Jingcheng tuzhi* [洪武]京城圖志, vol. 24 of *Beijing tushuguan guji zhenben congkan* 北京圖書館古籍珍本叢刊 (Beijing: Shumu wenxian chubanshe, 2000), 4.

163. As for how a sacred space stands in opposition to "all other space, the formless expanse surrounding it," see Mircea Eliade, *The Sacred and the Profane: The Nature of Religion* (New York: Harcourt Brace, 1957), 20. For Eliade's extended discussion on temple, palace and center of the world as "sacred places," see *Patterns in Comparative Religion*, trans. Rosemary Sheed (London: Sheed and Ward, 1997), 367–85.

164. Concerning the exclusive use of the Temple of Heaven for sacrifice to Confucius conducted by Daoist priests, see *Jinling xuanguan zhi* 金陵玄觀志, 13.1a–b, vol. 719 of *Xuxiu siku quanshu*, 182. More about the Daoist priests for Confucian sacrificial ritual later.

165. See Joseph Henninger, "Sacrifice (First edition)," in *Encyclopedia of Religion*, ed. Lindsay Jones, 2nd ed., 15 vols. (Detroit: Macmillan Reference USA, 2005), 12:8001.

166. For how a sacred space such as a church or temple relates the human world to the other one, see George Galavaris, *The Icon in the Life of the Church: Doctrine, Liturgy, Devotion* (Leiden: Brill, 1981), 8.

167. The term *Tansu* in both English and Latin tsranslation seems to be a misspelling of *Tausu* used in Ricci's *Storia*. See d'Elia, *Fonti Ricciane*, N. 553, 2:70.

168. For a recent and focused discussion of the Daoist priests from the Imperial Music Office in both Nanjing and Beijing from the Ming to Qing, see Yonghua Liu, "Daoist Priests and Imperial Sacrifices in Late Imperial China: The Case of the Imperial Music Office (Shenyue guan), 1379–1743," *Late Imperial China* 33, no. 1 (2012): 55–88.

169. See Liu, "Daoist Priests and Imperial Music Office," 69.

170. See Dunne, *Generation of Giants*, 27.

171. Mungello, *Curious Land*, 70.

172. Hugh Trevor-Roper, *From Counter-Reformation to Glorious Revolution* (London: Pimlico, 1992), 6.

173. Ricci, *The True Meaning of the Lord of Heaven*, 245 (translation modified).

174. Thomas A. Wilson points out that, starting with Ricci, the worship of Confucius has remained "one of the least understood aspects of Confucianism" by

scholars in the West. See his introduction to *On Sacred Grounds: Culture, Society, Politics, and the Formation of the Cult of Confucius*, ed. Thomas A. Wilson (Cambridge, MA: Harvard University Press, 2002), 3.

175. Derrida, *Adieu*, 35.

176. For the religious importance of music in virtually every aspect of society from government to ordinary people's everyday life, see Xunzi's 荀子, "Yuelun (On Music)" 樂論, in *Xunzi jijie* 荀子集解, 2 vols. (Beijing: Zhonghua, 1988), 2:379–85. See also the section on "Li yue (Rites and Music)" (禮樂), in Ban Gu 班固, Baihu Tong shuzheng 白虎通疏證, 2 vols. (Beijing: Zhonghua, 1997), 2:93–128. For the ritual use of music at the Ming court, see Zhang Tingyu, *Ming shi, juan* 61–63, 5:1499–1586.

177. Michael Nylan, *The Chinese Pleasure Book* (New York: Zone, 2018), 61.

178. *Xunzi: The Complete Text*, trans. Eric L. Hutton (Princeton, NJ: Princeton University Press, 2014), 218 (translation modified).

179. *Xunzi*, 219.

180. *Xunzi*, 221 (translation modified).

Chapter 3

1. The exchanges that the Buddhists and Daoists had with the missionaries will be mentioned when and where necessary, but detailed investigation will be left for another project.

2. Confucians interested in what the Jesuits were doing in China form the biggest group and include such high ranking officials and prominent scholars as Ye Xianggao, Tang Xianzu (湯顯祖; 1550–1610), the three Yuan brothers (Yuan Zongdao 袁宗道 [1560–1600], Yuang Hongdao 袁宏道 [1568–1610], Yuan Zhongdao 袁中道 [1570–1623]), Dong Qichang (董其昌; 1556–1637), and many more. For a longer partial list of these Confucian scholars and officials, see Lin Jinshui (林金水), *Li Madou yu Zhongguo* (利瑪竇與中國) (Beijing: Zhongguo shehui kexue chubanshe, 1996), 286–316.

3. Of course, the resistance to Christianity did not come from the Confucians alone. Buddhists also engaged in debates with the Jesuits. For instance, the book *Poxie ji* 破邪集 (1639) contains the anti-Christian works of several influential Buddhist monks at the time, such as Zhuhong (株宏; 1535–1615), Yuanxian (元賢; 1578–1657), Yuanwu (圓悟; 1566–1642), a lay devotee by the name of Yu Chunxi (虞淳熙), and others. See *Poxie ji*, vol. 5 of *Mingmo qingchu yesuhui sixiang wenxian huibian* 明末清初耶穌會思想文獻匯編, ed. Andrew Chung (鄭安德 Zheng Ande). 5 vols. (Beijing: Beijing daxue zongjiao yanjiu suo, 2003).

4. Derrida describes his discussion of hospitality as being "in the name or under the title of the opening [openness (*l'ouverture*)]." See his *Adieu*, 19. On the same page of the book, he remarks that "Levinas suggests the opening in general on the basis of hospitality or welcoming, and not the other way around." According to

Derrida, one must try to think of openness to the Other as arising from hospitality, not vice versa (and this is how Derrida believes Levinas thinks of hospitality and the Other). See *Adieu*, 44.

5. Emmanuel Levinas, *Otherwise than Being; or, Beyond Essence*, trans. Alphonso Lingis (The Hague: Martinus Nijhoff, 1981), 79.

6. Emmanuel Levinas, *Totality and Infinity: An Essay on Exteriority*, trans. Alphonso Lingis (Pittsburg: Duquesne University Press, 1969), 79.

7. Levinas, *Totality and Infinity*, 51.

8. Derrida's exposition of Levinas. Derrida, *Adieu*, 22.

9. See Levinas, *Totality and Infinity*, 168–74.

10. Levinas, *Otherwise than Being*, 82–83.

11. Levinas, *Totality and Infinity*, 152, 157.

12. Levinas, *Totality and Infinity*, 152. Concerning the isolation and protection that home offers to the subject, see also Martin Heidegger, "Building Dwelling Thinking," in his *Poetry, Language, Thought*, trans. Albert Hofstadter (New York: Harper & Row, 1971), 147.

13. Levinas, *Totality and Infinity*, 158; see also 164–65.

14. Levinas, *Totality and Infinity*, 162. See also Derrida, *Adieu*, 45.

15. Levinas, *Totality and Infinity*, 171.

16. Levinas, *Totality and Infinity*, 170–71.

17. Levinas, *Totality and Infinity*, 172–73.

18. See Derrida, "Hostipitality," 364. In the same article, Derrida insists that "all cultures compete in this regard of [extending hospitality] and present themselves as more hospitable than others." He therefore concludes, "Hospitality—this is culture itself" (361). See also Caputo, *Deconstruction in a Nutshell*, 109–10.

19. *Adieu* consists of two parts, the first, "Adieu to Emmanuel Levinas," being the eulogy Derrida gave at Levinas's funeral, and the second, a sustained discussion on *Totality and Infinity*.

20. Derrida, *Adieu*, 33.

21. Immanuel Kant, "Perpetual Peace: A Philosophical Sketch," in *Kant: Political Writings*, trans. H. B. Nisbet, ed. Hans Reiss, 2nd exp. ed. (Cambridge: Cambridge University Press, 1991), 358.

22. See Derrida, *Adieu*, 86–88.

23. Derrida, *Adieu*, 97.

24. Derrida, *Adieu*, 91.

25. Derrida, *Adieu*, 87. See also O. Custer, "Making Sense of Derrida's Aporetic Hospitality," in *Jacques Derrida*, ed. Leonard Lawlor and Zeynep Direk, 3 vols. (London: Routledge, 2002), 3:200.

26. Derrida, *Adieu*, 100–101.

27. See Derrida, *Of Hospitality*, 149–56.

28. Paul Patton and Terry Smith, eds., *Jacques Derrida: Deconstruction Engaged, the Sydney Seminars* (Sydney: Power Institute Publications and the Research Institute for Humanities and Social Sciences at the University of Sydney, 2001), 98.

29. See Derrida, "The Deconstruction of Actuality," in his *Negotiations: Interventions and Interviews, 1971–2001*, ed. and trans. Elizabeth Rottenberg (Stanford, CA: Stanford University Press, 2002), 95.

30. See Derrida, *Of Hospitality*, 118–20. See also "Hospitality, Justice and Responsibility: A Dialogue with Jacques Derrida," in *Questioning Ethics: Contemporary Debates in Philosophy*, ed. Richard Kearney and Mark Dooley (London: Routledge, 1999), 67–73.

31. For the idea of gift, see Derrida, *Politiques de l'amitié*, 388; for forgiveness, see his *On Cosmopolitanism and Forgiveness*, trans. Mark Dooley and Michael Hughes (London: Routledge, 2001). It is also out of his belief in the necessity of absolute hospitality that Derrida expresses his suspicion about the concept of tolerance, because tolerance, according to him, "remains a scrutinized hospitality, always under surveillance, parsimonious and protective of its sovereignty." Giovanna Borradori, ed., *Philosophy in a Time of Terror: Dialogues with Jürgen Habermas and Jacques Derrida* (Chicago: University of Chicago Press, 2003), 128.

32. See Derrida, *Of Hospitality*, 25–27.

33. Derrida, *Of Hospitality*, 83.

34. Derrida, "Débat: Une hospitalité sans condition," in *Manifeste pour l'hospitalité, aux Minguettes: Autour de Jacques Derrida*, ed. Mohammed Seffahi (Grigny: Paroles d'aube, 1999), 137. Quoted in Mireille Rosello, *Postcolonial Hospitality: The Immigrant as Guest* (Stanford, CA: Stanford University Press, 2001), 11–12. When discussing the September 11 attack, Derrida reiterates his point from a different perspective: "This visit [of the foreigner] might actually be very dangerous, and we must not ignore this fact, but would a hospitality without risk, a hospitality backed by certain assurances, a hospitality protected by an immune system against the wholly other, be true hospitality?" Borradori, *Philosophy in a Time of Terror*, 129.

35. Derrida himself is fully aware of the impracticality challenging his unconditional hospitality. He admits that "one cannot in any case, and by definition, organize it [unconditional hospitality]. . . . No state can write it into its laws." But at the same time, he insists that "without at least the thought of this pure and unconditional hospitality, of hospitality *itself*, we would have no concept of hospitality in general and would not even be able to determine any rules for conditional hospitality. . . . Without this thought of pure hospitality (a thought that is also, in its own way, an experience), we would not even have the idea of the other, of the alterity of the other, that is, of someone who enters into our lives without having been invited." In short, he argues that his unconditional hospitality, though neither juridical nor political, "is nevertheless the condition of the political and the juridical" (Borradori, *Philosophy in a Time of Terror*, 129). When thinking of the viability of unconditional hospitality, however, it may be helpful to bear in mind the frequent warning from Derrida that his reader should not be too quick to dismiss the futurity of Derridean politics—such as democracy to come—to dream, to imagination, to utopia. See, for instance, Derrida, "The University without Condition," in *Without Alibi*, ed. and trans. Peggy Kamuf (Stanford, CA: Stanford University Press, 2002),

210. Such warning is valid as well when considering Derrida's thought of hospitality. For questions and answers about Derridean hospitality, see the session transcript for "Politics and Friendship: A Discussion with Jacques Derrida," Centre for Modern French Thought, University of Sussex, December 1, 1997, http://www.dariaroithmayr.com/pdfs/assignments/Politics%20and%20Friendship.pdf.

36. Derrida explains his thought of unconditional hospitality thus: "I have always, consistently and insistently, held *unconditional hospitality*, as *impossible*, to be *heterogeneous* to the *political*, the *juridical*, and even the *ethical*. But the impossible is not nothing. It is even that which happens, which comes, by definition. I admit that this remains rather difficult to think but that's exactly what preoccupies what is called thinking, if there is any and from the time there is any." Jacques Derrida, *Rogues: Two Essays on Reason*, trans. Pascale-Anne Brault and Michael Naas (Stanford, CA: Stanford University Press, 2005), 172n12.

37. Caputo, *More Radical Hermeneutics*, 71.

38. See Jacques Derrida, *Points . . . : Interviews, 1974–1994*, ed. Elisabeth Weber (Stanford, CA: Stanford University Press, 1995), 201.

39. Derrida, *Of Hospitality*, 3.

40. The two deviations from the Latin word *hostis*, stranger and enemy, should give some hint to the dubious nature of the foreigner and the foreigner's potential threat to the subject or host. See Derrida, *Of Hospitality*, 45, 55–56. But for Derrida, the threat or danger coming with or from the stranger, the unknown visitor, must be seen as the essence of hospitality.

41. In *Otherwise than Being*, Levinas writes, "In responsibility for another, subjectivity is only [the] unlimited passivity of an accusative . . . [reducible] to the passivity of a self only as a persecution . . . that turns into an expiation" (112). A few pages later, he remarks that "the self of this passivity . . . is a hostage" (114). Relevant in the present context is the sacrifice, the becoming hostage of that which is held dear. For Levinas, as pointed out by one scholar, "the primordial act of expiation is the willingness to substitute for the other. Is this acceptance of being hostage for the other not also the very law of hospitality?" Edith Wyschogrod, "Autochthony and Welcome: Discourse of Exile in Levinas and Derrida," *Journal of Philosophy and Scripture* 1, no. 1 (2003): 37.

42. Derrida, *Adieu*, 41–42.

43. *Of Hospitality*, 47–48; see also 125.

44. See Caputo, *More Radical Hermeneutics*, 63–64. See also Jean-Luc Nancy, *Inoperative Community*, 31. More will be said about community momentarily.

45. Derrida, *Of Hospitality*, 55.

46. For an extended discussion of the Qing government's use of hospitality rites in foreign affairs, see James L. Hevia, *Cherishing Men from Afar: Qing Guest Ritual and the Macartney Embassy of 1793* (Durham, NC: Duke University Press, 1995).

47. According to Zheng Xuan (鄭玄; 127–200), the five rites include "the Rite of Sacrifice, the Rite of Misfortune, the Rite of Army, the Rite of Hospitality,

and the Rite of Kindness" (吉[禮], 凶[禮], 軍[禮], 賓[禮], 嘉[禮]). See *Zhou li* 周禮, 19.6a–b, vol. 3 of *Shisan jing*, 292.

48. 大宗伯之職, 掌建邦之天神人鬼地示之禮, 以佐王建保邦國。…以賓禮親邦國, 春見曰朝, 夏見曰宗, 秋見曰覲, 冬見曰遇, 時見曰會, 殷見曰同, 時聘曰問, 殷頫曰視. *Zhou li*, 18.12a–b, vol. 3 of *Shisan jing*, 275. All translations from this book will be mine unless otherwise acknowledged.

49. In antiquity, all five rites, including the rite of hospitality, were court rituals. They were designed and used for state affairs involving the kings, government officials, and feudal princes. To be sure, this fact does not mean that there were not rites for the commoners; it is that such rites were developed at a later time.

50. 親, 謂使之相親. *Wuli tongkao*, 230.2a, vol. 141 of *Yingyin Wenyuange siku quanshu* 影印文淵閣四庫全書 (Taibei: Shangwu yinshu guan, 1986), 141–42. To support his interpretation, Qin quotes a comment by Zheng E (鄭鍔; active in the twelfth century) that uses the term *qin* in the same way (以賓禮親之, 彼安得不吾親哉?). A contemporary Chinese scholar also observes that the word *qin* in this very sentence from the *Rites of Zhou* should be read as "to generate affectionate affiliation [among the princes to the king]" (使親附). See Li Wuwei 李無未, *Zhongguo lida binli* 中國歷代賓禮 (Beijing: Beijing tushuguan chubanshe, 1998), 1. One more example of such use of *qin* comes from "The Rule of the King" (王制) by Xunzi: "Concerning the way of making friends and foes, a king will treat feudal lords with reverence, then the feudal lords will be pleased. The reason they have affection for the king is that he does not try to take them over. If there should be any appearance of taking them over, then the feudal lords will distance themselves from him" (修友敵之道, 以敬接諸侯, 則諸侯說之矣. 所以親之者, 以不并也; 并之見, 則諸侯疏矣). *Xunzi*, 72 (translation modified).

51. Causative verbs were commonly used in classical Chinese and their function was well understood by ancient China scholars. For example, concerning the text that says that officials of rites would make the visiting princes cherish the king by offering food and wine to them (以飲食之禮, 親宗族兄弟), Zheng Xuan's well-considered note reads, "The term *qin* means to make the princes cherish [the king]. The king held the rite of offering food and wine to members of his family. He thus made people cherish him" (親者, 使之相親. 人君有食宗族飲酒之禮, 所以親之也). *Zhou li*, 18.15b, vol. 3 of *Shisan jing*, 277. Despite the long history of causative verbs in China, the study of them began only a little over one hundred years ago. In chapter 5 of his *Mashi wentong* (馬氏文通; 1898), the first book on Chinese grammar, Ma Jianzhong (馬建中; 1845–1900) mentioned the causative use of verbs and gave a partial explanation. The first Chinese grammarian to define and discuss classical Chinese causative verbs was Chen Chengze (陳承澤; 1885–1922) in his *Guowenfa caochuang* (國文法草創; 1922). See Chen, *Guowenfa caochuang* (Beijing: Shangwu yinshu guan, 1982), 36–37. To give one more ancient example of such use of causative verbs, here is "武丁朝諸侯, 有天下" in *Mencius* (2A.1). Seeing clearly the causative use of the term 朝 (*chao*)

in the phrase, D. C. Lau was absolutely right to translate the phrase into "Wu Ting commanded the homage of the feudal lords and maintained the possession of the Empire." *Mencius*, trans. D. C. Lau (London: Penguin, 1970), 75.

52. 朝覲, 所以教諸侯之臣也. *Li ji*, 48.12a, vol. 5 of *Shisan jing*, 824; translated in James Legge, trans., *Li Chi: Book of Rites*, 2 vols. (Whitefish, MT: Kessinger, 2003), 2:231. See similar quotations stating that "the king gives audiences at court so that the princes know why they are subjects and ministers" (朝覲, 然後諸侯知所以臣), and "the ceremonies at the court audience of the different seasons were intended to illustrate the righteous relations between ruler and subject" (朝覲之禮, 所以明君臣之義也). *Li ji*, 39.16a, 50.5a, vol. 5 of *Shisan jing*, 697, 847. Translated in Legge, *Li Chi*, 2:124, 258 (translation modified).

53. Gil Anidjar, "A Note on 'Hostipitality,'" in Jacques Derrida, *Acts of Religion*, ed. Gil Anidjar (New York: Routledge, 2002), 356.

54. Derrida, *Adieu*, 15. According to Gil Anidjar, for the purpose of describing this violence from the host, Derrida has coined his neologism "hostipitality." See Anidjar, "A Note on 'Hostipitality,'" 356–57.

55. Undoubtedly, the rite of hospitality was always used in foreign relations. For examples of how hospitality was applied to strike up international relations in the early history of China since the Shang dynasty (1711–1066 BCE), see chapter 5 in Li Wuwei, *Zhongguo lidai binli*.

56. Some scholars have pointed out that during the Han, the rite of hospitality was almost exclusively preformed for emissaries to the capital from remote and barbarian tribes. See Yang Zhigang 楊志剛, *Zhongguo yili zhidu yanjiu* 中國儀禮制度研究 (Shanghai: Huadong shifan daxue chubanshe, 2001), 398–409; and Li Wuwei, *Zhongguo lidai binli*, 30–32.

57. For discussion on the Chinese worldview, see John K. Fairbank, ed., *The Chinese World Order: Traditional China's Foreign Relations* (Cambridge, MA: Harvard University Press, 1968). For a recent discussion of the development and use of this China-centered view through the ages, see Fang Tie 方铁, "古代'守中治边'、'守在四夷'治边思想初探," *Zhongguo bianjiang shidi yanjiu* 中国边疆史地研究 6, no. 4 (2006): 1–8.

58. Phrases like "keeping the barbarians out, and China in the center" (內夏外夷), "venerating China and warding off the barbarians" (尊夏攘夷), and similar ones from the text, as well as the annotations in *Chunqiu gongyang zhuan* (春秋公羊傳), have become common expressions in Chinese. See 1.22a, 5.5a, 12.3a, and 18.1b, vol. 7 of *Shisan jing*, 16, 61, 149, 228. For a brief history of the theoretical discussion of the Confucian totality, see Yang Xiangkui 楊向奎, *Dayitong yu rujia sixiang* 大一統與儒家思想 (Beijing: Zhongguo youyi chuban gongsi, 1989).

59. It is necessary to point out the patriarchal use of language by Confucians. Again, in the discussion that follows, I will not always try to change the male pronouns found in Confucian works.

60. James Legge, trans., *The Doctrine of the Mean*, vols. 1 and 2 of *The Chinese Classics* (Taibei: SMC, 1991), 409.

61. 夷狄進至乎爵，天下遠近大小若一（隱公元年十二月），*Chunqiu gongyang zhuan* 春秋公羊傳, 1.22b, vol. 7 of *Shisan jing*, 17.

62. See *Taizu shilu* 太祖實錄 or *The Veritable Records of Taizu Emperor*, in *Ming shilu* 明實錄 (Taibei: Zhongyang yanjiu yuan lishi yuyan yanjiu suo, 1962–66), 14.1b–2a, ce 1, pp. 176–77; see also 73.1b–2a, ce 4, pp. 1336–37.

63. See *Taizu shilu*, 15.1a–1b, ce 1, pp. 195–96.

64. See *Taizu shilu*, 44.10a, ce 3, p. 875. See also *Ming shi*, juan 136, 13:3926, and *juan* 47, 5:1223.

65. See *Ming shi*, 5:1223 and *Ming jili*, vol. 650 of *Yingyin wenyuange siku quanshu*.

66. It is worth mentioning that the Ming authorities did not forget that their rite of hospitality should not be followed by officials alone. That is why the reader can see two particular sets of the hospitality ritual: the rite of greetings for ranked officials (品官相見禮) and the rite of greetings for commoners (庶人相見禮). For content of the two rites, see *Ming shi*, juan 56, 5:1427–28.

67. The titles of the three chapters indicate the three respective topics: "Reception for Kings from Tributary Countries" (蕃王朝貢), "Reception of Delegates from Tributary Countries" (蕃使朝貢), "Reception of Delegates from the Ming" (遣使). See *Ming jili*, juan 30–32, vol. 650 of *Yingyin wenyuange siku quanshu*, 18–73. See summaries of the Ming rite of hospitality in *Ming shi*, juan 5:1421–26, and Shen Shixing 申時行 et al., comps., *Da Ming huidian* 大明會典, 5 vols. (Taibei: Huawen shuju, 1964), *juan* 58, 2:1001.

68. 前朝禮部告示，侍儀司諸執事，引蕃王及蕃國從官，具服于天界寺習儀三日。擇日朝見. *Ming jili*, 30.15a–b, vol. 650 of *Yingyin wenyuange siku quanshu*, 25.

69. See *Ming jili*, 32.3b–16b, vol. 650 of *Yingyin wenyuange siku quanshu*, 69–70.

70. The so-called inculturation has been the topic of many studies. One recent example is Nicolas Standaert, *The Interweaving of Rituals: Funerals in the Cultural Exchange between China and Europe* (Seattle: University of Washington Press, 2008).

71. See Ricci's memorial to the throne in *Zhengjiao fengbao* 正教奉褒 (Shanghai: Shanghai cimutang, 1904), 6b. As for the specific items from Ricci's list, see d'Elia, *Fonti Ricciane*, 2:114, 123n5, 124n1. See also Shen Defu, *Wanli yehuo bian*, 3:783–84. For a discussion of Ricci's gift-giving in the hope of favors from the Ming imperial court, see Spence, *Memory Palace of Matteo Ricci*, 194–95. See also Li Sher-shiueh, *Yishu: Ming mo Qing chu yesuhui fanyi wenxue lun* 譯述—明末清初耶穌會翻譯文學論 (Hong Kong: Hong Kong Chinese University Press, 2012), 36.

72. 迷聞天朝聲教文物，竊欲霑被其餘，終身為氓. *Zhengjiao fengbao*, 4b.

73. According to *Ming shi*, Emperor Wanli did not meet Ricci in person. However, pleased by Ricci's gifts, he ordered that Ricci be allowed to stay in Beijing

and granted him a piece of land to build a residence where he could live and preach (帝嘉其遠來，假館授業，給賜優厚). See *Ming shi, juan* 326, 28:8460.

Chapter 4

1. Ricci used the map as his self-introduction to the Chinese. The fact finds testimony in the words of Li Zhizao (李之藻): "萬曆辛丑，利氏來賓，余從寮友數輩訪之。其壁間懸有大地圖，畫線分度甚悉。利氏曰：'此吾西來路程也 . . . .'" Li, "刻《職方外紀》序," in Ai Rulue 艾儒略 (Giulio Aleni; 1582–1649), *Zhifang waiji jiaoshi* 職方外紀校釋, ed. Xie Fang 謝方 (Beijing: Zhonghua, 1996), 6. See also Theodore N. Foss, "Ricci's World Map: The 1602 *Kunyu Wanguo Quantu*," in *China at the Center: Ricci and Verbiest World Maps*, ed. Natasha Reichle (San Francisco: Asian Art Museum, 2016), 19.

2. Arnold H. Rowbotham, *Missionary and Mandarin: The Jesuits at the Court of China* (Berkeley: University of California Press, 1942), 56.

3. As testified by Ricci's own words, "one of the primary products of European intellectuals to attract the attention of the Chinese" was a "cosmographical chart of the universe." Ricci, *China in the Sixteenth Century*, 165.

4. Ricci, *China in the Sixteenth Century*, 166. The corresponding part in *Fonti Ricciane* does not differ much in meaning. See d'Elia, *Fonti Ricciane*, N. 262, 1:207.

5. Though various editions of the world map made by Ricci in different years have extant copies, these do not include any copies of the 1584 edition. The one used for this discussion is a copy, made in 1604, stored currently in the British Museum. For the most recent and extended survey of the existing copies of the map, see Huang Shijian 黃時鑒 and Gong Yingyan 龔纓晏, *Li Madou shijie ditu yanjiu* 利瑪竇世界地圖研究 (Shanghai: Shanghai guji, 2005), 136–60.

6. Hung Ye (洪葉; William Hung) discusses the repeated requests from the Chinese for copies of the map in his "Kao Li Madou de shijie ditu" 考利瑪竇的世界地圖, in *Hung Ye lunxue ji* 洪葉論學集, ed Weng Dujian 翁獨健 et al. (Beijing: Zhonghua, 1981), 150–52. Kenneth Chen points out the tremendous interest that the Chinese took in Ricci's map in his "Matteo Ricci's Contribution to, and Influence on, Geographical Knowledge in China," *Journal of the American Oriental Society* 59, no. 3 (1939): 325.

7. See Henri Bernard, *Le père Matthieu Ricci et la société chinoise de son temps (1551–1610)*, 2 vols. (Tiantsin: Hautes études, 1937). See also Huang and Gong, *Li Madou shijie ditu yanjiu*, 87–93.

8. D'Elia, *Fonti Ricciane*, N. 893, 2:474.

9. Strictly speaking, Ricci's was not the first world map introduced into China. In 1267, during the Yuan Dynasty, the Persian missionary Jamaluddin (扎馬魯丁), who served as a director at the Beijing Observatory under the Yuan Shizu

(1215–1294), made a globe for the Chinese. This and other projects by Jamaluddin are recorded in Song Lian 宋濂 et al., *Yuan shi* 元史, 8 vols. (Beijing: Zhonghua, 1977), *juan* 48, 4:998–99.

10. Rebecca Stefoff, *The British Library Companion to Maps and Mapmaking* (London: British Library, 1995), 209.

11. See Cordell D. K. Yee, "Reinterpreting Traditional Chinese Cartography and the Myth of Westernization," in *The History of Cartography*, vol. 2, bk. 2, *Cartography in the Traditional East and Southeast Asian Societies*, ed. J. B. Harley and David Woodward (Chicago: University of Chicago Press, 1994), 170–202. See also Yee, "Space and Place: Ways of World Making," in *Space and Place: Mapmaking East and West: Four Hundred Years of Western and Chinese Cartography from the Library of Congress, Geography and Map Division, and the Collection of Leonard and Juliet Rothman*. Exhibition Catalogue by Cordell D. K. Yee (Annapolis, MD: Elizabeth Myers Mitchell Art Gallery, 1996), 7–16.

12. The map adds some new place or country names to Chinese vocabulary, a number of which are still in use today. Here are some of the place names listed in Kenneth Chen's article: *diqiu* (地球; earth), Nanbeiji (南北極; North and South Poles), Luoma (羅馬; Rome), Daxiyang (大西洋; Atlantic), Jianada (加拿大; Canada). See Chen, "Matteo Ricci's Contribution," 339.

13. See d'Elia, *Fonti Ricciane*, NN. 262–63, 1:208–11.

14. See Richard J. Smith, *Chinese Maps: Images of "All under Heaven"* (New York: Oxford University Press, 1996), 5.

15. Such cartographic presentation in world maps began with Mercator, whose map would, rather than center on Jerusalem, have Europe at the top center. See Jeremy Black, *Maps and Politics* (Chicago: University of Chicago Press, 1997), 30. Aleni in his Chinese book on world geography mentions this cartographic tradition in the West. *Zhifang waiji*, 28–29.

16. Kenneth Chen points out that the Confucian treatment of Ricci's map as an amusing toy represents what prevented China from utilizing the Western knowledge and cartographic techniques introduced by Ricci and other missionaries. See Chen, "Matteo Ricci's Contribution," 357–58.

17. The military importance of the map was first clearly emphasized by Guanzi (管子; 719–645 BCE) in the chapter "Maps" (地圖) in his work. See *Guanzi xiaozhu*, 3 vols. (Beijing: Zhonghua, 2004), *juan* 10, 2:528–35. As for the political importance of maps in the well-being of a state, see *Book of Zhou*, 10.1a–2a, vol. 3 of *Shisanjing*, 149. See also chapter "Wudu" (五蠹) in *Han Feizi jishi* 韓非子集釋, ed. Chen Qiyou 陳其猷, 2 vols. (Shanghai: Shanghai renmin, 1975), 2:1067. Recently, Cordell D. K. Yee pointed out the utility of maps in warfare in Chinese history. See Yee, "Chinese Maps in Political Culture," in *The History of Cartography*, vol. 2, bk. 2, *Cartography in the Traditional East and Southeast Asian Societies*, ed. J. B. Harley and David Woodward (Chicago: University of Chicago Press, 1994), 83–84.

18. Yee, "Chinese Maps in Political Culture," 77.

19. Yee, "Chinese Maps in Political Culture," 82; see 83–84 for discussion of how China banned any of its people from sending maps abroad.

20. See *Taizu shilu*, 48.4b, ce 3, p. 954.

21. "今艾君輩乃慕義遠來，獻其異書數千种於朝，其視越裳之重譯獻雉，不啻過之." Ye, "Zhifang waiji xu" 職方外紀序, in Aleni, *Zhifang waiji*, 13–14.

22. 地與海本是圓形而合為一球，居天球之中，誠如雞子，黃在青內。有謂地為方者，乃語其定而不移之性，非語其形體也. These are the opening remarks from the description on the right-hand side of the map. See Matteo Ricci, *Li Madou kunyu wanguo quantu* 利瑪竇坤輿萬國全圖 (Beijing: Yugong xuehui, 1936), 1, 2.

23. Ricci's map shows his cosmological understanding to be in line with the Catholic Church. In the explanatory remarks he put in his map, he stated that the sun completed one revolution around the earth every twenty-four hours (日輪一日作一週). More importantly, the two charts that he had in the upper left-hand corner of his map to illustrate eclipses of the moon and the sun placed the earth in the center of the universe with the sun orbiting around it. Because he made his first map forty or so years after Copernicus's (1473–1543) book *De revolutionibus orbium coelestium* (1543) had become available, Ricci has been criticized for intentionally hiding Copernicus's dispute of Ptolemy, the astronomer accepted by the church. But to conceal Copernicus's revolutionary theory and its supporter Galileo from the Chinese was the consensus among the Jesuits at the time. Aleni continued to spread the same geocentric view in China. See his *Zhifang waiji*, 27.

24. For a succinct and powerful discussion on the Jesuit introduction of modern astronomy to China that began with Ricci, see Nathan Sivin, "Copernicus in China," in *Science in Ancient China* (Great Yarmouth, UK: Variorum, 1995), 4:63–122. See also Benjamin A. Elman, *On Their Own Terms: Science in China, 1550–1900*. (Cambridge, MA: Harvard University Press, 2005).

25. As a matter of fact, by 1582, the time of Ricci's arrival in China and exactly sixty years after the completion of the first circumnavigation around the world (1519–1522) led by Magellan (1480–1521), the idea of a round earth was already common knowledge in Europe.

26. See Smith, *Chinese Maps*, 23–25.

27. Namely, the Circular-Heaven theory (蓋天說), describing the heavens to be round like a canopy, and the earth square like a chessboard; the Sphere-Heaven theory (渾天說) summarized by Zhang Heng (張衡; 78–139); and the Empty-Space theory (宣夜說), a theory that comes closest to the medieval understanding of the universe in the West. For these three and other minor cosmological conceptions in traditional China, see Chen Zungui 陳遵媯, *Zhongguo tianwen xue shi* 中國天文學史, 2 vols. (Shanghai: Shanghai, 2016), 2:1307–18.

28. 渾蓋合一說. See Chen Zungui, *Zhongguo tianwen xue shi*, 2:1313–17.

29. As stated in *Rites of Zhou*, "One needs to find the straightened shadow in order to locate the center of the earth.... Where there is the midday shadow

of the sun, whose length is one foot and five inches, that spot would be the center" (正日景以求地中. . . . 日至之景,尺有五寸,謂之地中 [周禮・地官・大司徒]). On this passage, Sun Yirang (孫詒讓; 1848–1908) comments that this refers to "the center of the earth, that is the center or middle of the four quarters and all nine areas outside the imperial capital" (地中者,為四方九服之中也). Both to support and elaborate his point, Sun goes on to quote multiple examples from the Confucian classics and other works. Sun, *Zhouli zhengyi* 周禮正義, 14 vols. (Beijing: Zhonghua, 1987), 2:721.

30. For a discussion of the different places as the center of the earth, see Guan Zengjian 关增建, "Zhongguo tianwen xue shang de dizhong gainian" 中国天文学史上的地中概念, *Ziran kexue shi yanjiu* 自然科学史研究 19, no. 3 (2000): 251–63.

31. Mircea Eliade, *The Myth of the Eternal Return; or, Cosmos and History*, trans. Willard R. Trask (Princeton, NJ: Princeton University Press, 1991), 15. For an extended discussion of the concept or the symbolism of the "center," see Eliade, *Images and Symbols: Studies in Religious Symbolism*, trans. Philip Mairet (Princeton, NJ: Princeton University Press, 1991), 37–51.

32. 建木在都廣,眾帝所自上下,日中無影,呼而無響,蓋天地之中也. *Huainanzi jishi* 淮南子集釋, 3 vols. (Beijing: Zhonghua, 1998), 1:328–29. Modified translation in John S. Major, *Heaven and Earth in Early Han Thought: Chapters Three, Four, and Five of the* Huainanzi (Albany: State University of New York Press, 1993), 158.

33. 欲近四旁,莫如中央。故王者必居天下之中,禮也 (大略). Modified translation in *Xunzi*, 288.

34. (王者京師必擇土中何?). 所以均教導,平往來,使善易以聞,為惡易以聞,明當懼慎,損于善惡。《尚書》曰:"王來紹上帝,自服於土中." Chapter on the Capital (京師) in *Bahu tong shuzheng* 白虎通疏証, 2 vols. (Beijing: Zhonghua, 1994), 1:157. Modified translation from *Po Hu T'ung: The Comprehensive Discussions in the White Tiger Hall*, trans. Tjan Tjoe Som, 2 vols. (Westport, CT: Hyperion, 1952), 2:424.

35. Derrida, *Adieu*, 147.

36. 地形既圓,無處非中. Aleni, *Zhifang waiji*, 27. One must bear in mind that Aleni's statement about the missing of the center does not mean he thinks there is no center. The same is true with Ricci. In fact, their geocentric understanding of the universe already indicates it clearly.

37. In his anti-Christian pamphlet, Wei Jun (魏濬) states, "It is only reasonable that China occupies the very center. But this map gives [China] a position slightly to the west. This is utterly ridiculous!" (中國當居正中,而圖置(中國)稍西,全屬無謂). Wei, "Li shuo huangtang huoshi tijie" 利說荒唐惑世題解 in *Poxie ji, juan* 8, in *Mingmo qingchu yesuhui sixiang*, 5:6.

38. 造為奇論,謂無東西南北上下之分。推而究之,若人皆倒懸於世,而《周易》所稱天尊地卑以為貴賤之位者,皆無可定。使世人皆信之,其禍將不可底止。此吾之所深憂也⋯. 吾益憂其說之流以禍世,將來無君臣上下之分,皆此之階矣. Li Suiqiu, "Yu Chen Qiaosheng tan tian shu" 與陳喬生談天書, in his *Lianxu ge ji* 蓮鬚閣集, 13.1a–6b, vol. 183 of 四庫禁燬書叢刊・集部 (Beijing: Beijing Chubanshe, 2000), 137–39.

39. 大地如球, 足心相踏之說, 益令人傷心焉. 午陽在上, 丑陰在下, 明謂我中夏是彼西洋腳底所踹之國. 其輕賤我中夏其已. Yang Guangxian, *Budeyi* 不得已, in *Mingmo qingchu yeshuhui sixiang*, 5 vols., 5:425–26. It is worth mentioning that the idea of the earth being a globe and the people on its surface standing "with the bottom of their feet towards each other" was disturbing even to scientists in China at the time, not just to Confucians. For instance, Song Yingxing (宋應星; 1587–1666), whose encyclopedic book *Tiangong kaiwu* (天工開物) earned him praises from Joseph Needham, who calls Song "the Diderot of China," expressed his indignation about Ricci's point thus: "The Westerners take it that the earth, in a spherical shape, hangs in the middle of a void [the universe] with its surface occupied by things and humans like ants. They also believe that the inhabitants in Mabazuo (Mapazo or Maparo) and those in China stand with the bottoms of their feet towards each other. This is truly a denigration of the cosmos much worse than those we have heard of in the Empty-Space theory and in the *Zhou bi* or *The Zhou Classic of Calculation*" (西人以地形為圓球, 虛懸於中, 凡物四面蟻附. 且以瑪八作之人與中華之人足行相抵. 天體受誣, 又酷於宣夜與周髀矣). Song, *Ye yi, Lun qi, Tan tian, Silian shi* 野議, 論氣, 談天, 思憐詩 (Shanghai: Shanghai renmin, 1975), 101. For a discussion on Song Yingxing's scientific contributions in the late Ming period, see Needham, *Science and Civilization in China*, vol. 5, *Chemistry and Chemical Technology*, pt. 7, *Military Technology; the Gunpowder Epic* (Cambridge: Cambridge University Press, 1986), 102.

40. 溥天之下, 莫非王土, 率土之濱, 莫非王臣 (诗. 小雅. 北山). Translated in Legge, *The She King*, vol. 3 of *The Chinese Classics*, 360. These lines also appear with minor variations in 左傳. 昭公七年, 44.3b, vol. 5 of *Shisan jing*, 759; and 孟子. 萬章上 (*Mencius*, 5.B.4).

41. The phrase is used in the title of an essay by Vadime Elisséeff and Hans Kaal, "The Middle Empire, a Distant Empire, an Empire without Neighbours," *Diogenes* 42 (Summer 1963): 60–64.

42. Xie Zhaozhe (謝肇淛), to give an example, talked with pride about the Chinese empire's expansion as new and previously unheard of countries joining the tributary system under the Ming (前代史冊所不載[之外國來貢]). Xie, *Wuzazu* 五雜組. 地部二, 2 vols. (Shenyang: Liaoning jiaoyu chubanshe, 2001), *juan* 4, 1:85.

43. In addition to my discussion in previous chapters of how Ricci and his fellow missionaries planned to unite China under Roman Catholicism, I would like to say that Ricci's vision of the world as presented in his map is no less hierarchical than that of the Confucians. The world in his map is clearly divided, among other things, by civilized peoples (such as the Chinese and Europeans) and less civilized ones (such as some South Americans wearing no clothes and dieting on human flesh, and those from what were clearly countries of fantasy such as Ox-hoofs Land 牛蹄國, where humans grow hooves). See Ricci, *Li Madou kunyu wanguo quantu*, 2, 10, 11, 13, 16. In his annotations to the map, Ricci also makes sure that he

attacks Buddhism by denigrating the latter's mathematic achievements. As he admits in a letter to Rome, his dogmatism results in counterattacks from the Chinese, both Buddhists and Confucians.

44. Michel Foucault, "Different Spaces," in *Aesthetics, Method, and Epistemology*, vol. 2 of *Essential Works of Foucault, 1954–1984*, ed. James D. Faubion (New York: New Press, 1998), 172.

45. See Nancy, *Inoperative Community*, 4.

46. Nancy, *Inoperative Community*, xl.

47. Of course, the Chinese were both unhappy to see this fact and slow to accept it. That was why, in the late nineteenth century, a time after the Western powers broke down China's door through a series of armed conflicts and various unequal treaties, James Legge, a British missionary, sinologist, and translator, still had the reason to complain thus:

> During the past forty years her [China's] position with regard to the more advanced nations of the world has been entirely changed. She has entered into treaties with them upon equal terms; but I do not think her ministers and people have yet looked this truth fairly in the face, so as to realize the fact that China is only one of many independent nations in the world and that the "beneath the sky," over which her emperor has rule, is not *all* beneath the sky, but only a certain portion of it which is defined on the earth's surface and can be pointed upon the map.

(Legge, "Prolegomena," in *The Ch'un Ts'ew, with the Tso Chuen*, vol. 5 of *The Chinese Classics*, 52).

48. Franco Moretti, *Atlas of the European Novel* (New York: Verso, 1998), 3.

49. It will not be too far-fetched to say that the finitude-to-finitude existence would apply well to the world Ricci tried to portray in his map and through his mission. Though Ricci hoped for a union of the world based on the Christian faith in God and vision of the like, the divided world in his map seemed to call into question the power of his God, a deity said to be omnipotent and omniscient. This is so because, as one annotation in the map relates, Christianity is practiced in only some countries in Europe, which means God has power over a small percent of people occupying a small portion of the world. See Ricci, *Li Madou kunyu wanguo quantu*, 13.

50. Xu, *Shengchao zuobi* 聖朝佐辟, *juan* 4, in Xu Changzhi, comp., *Poxie ji*, in *Mingmo qingchu yesuhui sixiang*, 5 vols., 5:128.

51. Interestingly, according to Hung Ye, Ricci and Aleni indeed wrongly calculated the distance between China and Europe. See Hung, "Kao Li Madou de shijie ditu," in *Hung Ye Lunxue ji*, 151. Concerning the distance, Ricci ironically thought that the fact that the West was far away from China should make the Chinese

feel safe, for the distance would reduce any potential threat to the Ming from the West.

52. Here, I am borrowing the phrase "non-knowledge" or *non-savoir*, but I am doing so without much of the complicated meaning it carries concerning the "apophatic secret" or the "messianic" discussed in part by Derrida in his *On the Name*, 131–32n1. Caputo offers a clear and detailed introduction to the phrase or concept of nonknowledge or secret elaborated in various works by Derrida. Caputo, *Prayers and Tears of Jacques Derrida*, 101–10. Derrida has an extended discussion of the religious or nonreligious awe or "trembling" stimulated by the nonknowledge or "secret" in his *The Gift of Death*, some points from which have received treatment in chapter 1 of this book.

53. 狂夫之言, 聖人擇焉, 世聞有所謂西土之學者, 誠荒誕不足道, 然其論天地之形與日月食之理, 則至當而不易。曰天包地外, 地居天中, 地形如大圓球, 海水繞球而流, 人物環球而生. Zhou, "Tiandi yu riyue shi lun" (天地與日月食論), in his *Jiuyan xiansheng yiji* 九煙先生遺集, 1.5a–b, vol. 1399 of *Xuxiu siku quanshu*, 390.

54. "The Master said: 'Even when walking in the company of two other men, I am bound to be able to learn from them'" (三人行, 必有我師焉; *Analects*, 7.22]). Confucius thus urges his disciples to learn from others, including strangers.

55. For an early biography of Xu, see Zha Jizuo 查繼佐, *Zuiweilu* 罪惟錄, vol. 101 of *Sibu congkan sanbian* 四部叢刊三編 (Shanghai: Shangwu, 1939), *juan* 11c, n. p. See Ruan Yuan 阮元, *Chouren zhuan* 疇人傳, 32.1b–5b, vol. 516 of *Xuxiu siku quanshu*, 311–13. See also Fang Hao, *Zhongguo tianzhujiao shi renwu zhuan* 中國天主教史人物傳 (Beijing: Zongjiao wenhua chubanshe, 2007), 80–88.

56. To be accurate, *xixue* as a generic term to mean Western learning in general gains its popularity in the late Qing. During the late Ming period, the Chinese seem to give specific names to different branches of scientific knowledge introduced by the missionaries, such as *lisuan* (曆算) for calendar and math, *shuifa* (水法) for irrigation, *jihe* (幾何) for geometry, and so forth. It must be made clear here that Christianity—viewed as *xijiao* (西教), the Western doctrine—was not included in the meaning of *xixue*. I will return to this point in the next section of discussion.

57. Lu's philosophy in the late Song Dynasty has recently been regarded as one of the two new types of "universalism which argues that 'all beings are endowed with the same moral nature.'" See Peter Bol, *New Confucianism in History* (Cambridge, MA: Harvard University Asian Center, 2008), 14–15.

58. 今觀此圖, 意與暗契, 東海西海, 心同理同, 於茲不信然乎? Li, preface to Ricci, *Li Madou kunyu wanguo quantu*, 8.

59. 世無二理, 人無二心, 事無二義, 仰無二天, 天無二主. Wang Jiazhi, "Ti Jiren shipian xiaoyin" (題畸人十篇小引), in *Tianxue chuhan*, 1:112.

60. 信哉! 東海西海, 心同理同, 所不同者, 特言語文字之際. Li Zhizao, "*Tianzhu shiyi* chongke xu"《天主實義》重刻序, in *Tianxue chuhan*, 1:357.

61. Almost all major neo-Confucian thinkers of the Song, including Zhou Dunyi (周敦頤; 1017–1073), Cheng Hao (程顥; 1033–1085), Cheng Yi (程頤;

1033–1107), Zhu Xi (朱熹; 1130–1200), Lu Jiuyuan, and others, gave their attention to this concept.

62. See Fung Yu-lan, *A History of Chinese Philosophy*, trans. Derk Bodde, 2 vols. (Princeton, NJ: Princeton University Press, 1953), 2:573.

63. Lu drew the essence of his theory from Mencius's argument that "for a man to give full realization to his heart is for him to understand his own nature, and a man who knows his own nature will know Heaven" (盡其心者知其性, 知其性則知天矣; 7.A.1]). For a discussion of the Mencian source for Lu's thinking, see Chen Lai 陳來, *Song Ming lixue* 宋明理學 (Shanghai: Huadong shifan daxue chubanshe, 2005), 147–49.

64. As Lu states, "孟子曰'所不學而知者, 其良知也。所不學而能者, 其良能也。'此天之所與我者, 我固有之…。故曰'萬物皆備於我矣。'此吾之本心也." Lu, *Lu Jiuyuan ji* 陸九淵集 (Shanghai: Shanghai guji, 1982), 5.

65. In his letter to a friend, Lu states sternly, "Mind, there is only one; Principle, there is likewise one. They both are simply one, with no distinction in essence and meaning. For this mind and this Principle, there is no room for two. That is why the Master says: 'There is a single thread binding my Way together.'" (心, 一心也; 理, 一理也; 至當歸一, 精義無二。此心此理, 實不容二。故夫子曰: "吾道一以貫之"). Lu, "Yu Zeng Zhaizhi" 與曾宅之, in *Lu Jiuyuan ji*, 4–5.

66. See Rao Zongyi 饒宗頤, *Cong Lu Xiangshan dao Liu Jishan* 從陸象山到劉蕺山 (Shanghai: Shanghai guji, 2001), 8. I will return to Lu's point shortly.

67. See *Lu Jiuyuan ji*, 237.

68. 宇宙內事, 乃己份內事; 己份內事, 乃宇宙內事, 宇宙便是吾心, 吾心便是宇宙; and 此理充塞宇宙, 所謂道外無事. In *Lu Jiuyuan ji*, 273, 483. Translated in Fung Yu-lan, *History of Chinese Philosophy*, 2:593.

69. By Lu's view, not only foreigners did not observe the Principle. Even Buddhists who had been in China for centuries likewise failed to follow the Heavenly Way. To give an example, in a letter he wrote to Wang Shunbo (王順伯), a Confucian scholar famous for his collection of calligraphy and seals, Lu claimed that Buddhist teachings had made people selfish and were thus inferior to Confucian doctrines, which taught people to be altruistic toward others and toward their state. See *Lu Jiuyuan ji*, 17.

70. 東海有聖人出焉, 此心同也, 此理同也; 西海有聖人出焉, 此心同也, 此理同也; 南海有聖人出焉, 此心同也, 此理同也; 千百世上, 有聖人出焉, 此心同也, 此理同也; 千百世下, 有聖人出焉, 此心同也, 此理同也. Lu's observation was recorded in his disciple Yang Jian's 楊簡 *Biographical Sketch of Master Xiangshan* 象山先生行狀, in *Lu Jiuyuan ji*, 388. Translated in Fung Yu-lan, *History of Chinese Philosophy*, 2:573.

71. For a quick summary of Wang's relation to the Song neo-Confucians, particularly his "the mind itself is Principle" (心即是理), and his other ideas, see Fung Yu-lan, *History of Chinese Philosophy*, 2:603–8.

72. See Wang, "Jian ying Fo shu" 諫迎佛疏, in *Wang Yangming quanji* 王陽明全集, 2 vols. (Shanghai: Shanghai guji, 1992), 1:293–96.

73. See Lu, "Yizhang xian xueji" 宜章縣學記, in *Lu Jiuyuan ji*, 229.

74. See Ge Zhaoguang 葛兆光, "Yige pubian zhenli guannian de lishi lüxing: Yi Lu Jiuyuan 'xintong litong' shuo wei li tan guannian shi de yanjiu fangfa" 一個普遍真理觀念的歷史旅行——以陸九淵"心同理同"說為例談觀念史的研究方法, *Dongyue luncong* 東岳論叢 25, no. 4 (July 2004): 11.

75. 曷徵之儒先, 曰東海西海, 心同理同。誰謂心理同而精神之結撰不各自抒一精彩, 顧斷斷然此是彼非, 亦大踳矣。且夷夏亦何常之有？其人而忠信焉..., 雖遠在殊方, 諸夏也。若夫寡廉鮮恥焉..., 雖近於比肩, 戎狄也。Qu, preface to *Zhifang waiji*, 9. If Qu here was insisting that the Chinese acknowledge the possibility that the strangers from the West knew the truth, Yao Lü (姚旅), Qu's contemporary and a Fujian (福建) native, went farther. In his *Lou shu* (露書), after quoting a few maxims from Ricci's *On Friendship*, Yao made the remarks that "living in different continents, humans nevertheless share the same Dao and the same emotion" (人有異域, 其道其情一也). Next, he continued to state that those who would slight other cultures or countries should feel shameful about themselves (世每少異域, 夏蟲耳。然生中華而徒有其胸... 不愧殺乎). Yao, *Lou shu* (Fuzhou: Fujian renmin chubanshe, 2008), 114.

76. Yang, preface to Aleni, *Zhifang waiji*, 4.

77. 無起止, 無中邊。Yang, preface to Aleni, *Zhifang waiji*, 4.

78. 西國有未經焚劫之書籍, 有遠遊窮海之畸人. Yang, preface to Aleni, *Zhifang waiji*, 4.

79. 西士引人歸向天帝, 往往借事為梯, 注述多端, 皆有深意。而是編則用悅耳娛目之玩以觸人心靈。言其近, 指其遠。彼淺嚐者, 第認為輶軒之雜錄, 博物之談資, 則還珠而買櫝者也. Yang, preface to Aleni, *Zhifang waiji*, 5.

Chapter 5

1. See John B. Henderson, *The Development and Decline of Chinese Cosmology* (New York: Columbia University Press, 1984), 119–38.

2. For the use and significance of *Huihui li* in imperial China, see Chen Jiujin 陈久金, *Huihui tianwen xue shi* 回回天文学史研究 (Guilin: Guangxi keji chubanshe, 1996).

3. As early as the middle of the fifteenth century, the Datong calendar began to show problems, and, as a result, erroneous predictions for lunar eclipses increased, which in turn generated debates on the need for reform. See *Ming shi*, *juan* 31, 3:518.

4. Seeing the inaccurate Ming calendar as an opportunity for the missionaries, Ricci suggested to the Society that competent Jesuit astronomers be sent to China. See his letter dated May 12, 1605, in Venturi, ed., *Opere storiche*, 2:285.

5. See *Ming shi*, *juan* 31, 3:520; Willard J. Peterson, "Calendar Reform Prior to the Arrival of Missionaries at the Ming Court," *Ming Studies* 21 (Spring 1986): 49–52.

6. Some details of what happened concerning the decision about inviting the Westerners to participate in the calendar reform can be seen in one of the "Lizhi" (歷志) chapters in *Ming shi, juan* 31, 1:528. See also Xia Xie 夏燮, *Ming tongjian* 明通鑒, 3 vols. (Changsha: Yuelu shushe, 1999), 3:2074; Han Qi, "Astronomy, Chinese and Western: The Influence of Xu Guangqi's Views in the Early and Mid-Qing," in *Statecraft and Intellectual Renewal in Late Ming China: The Cross-cultural Synthesis of Xu Guangqi (1562–1633)*, ed. Catherine Jami, Peter Engelfriet, and Gregory Blue (Leiden: Brill, 2001), 368.

7. This failure on June 21, 1629, to be exact, infuriated Emperor Chongzhen (崇禎), who, as a result, ordered the much-needed reform to be launched. See *Ming shi, juan* 31, 3:529–30.

8. In a memorial written in 1630 following Terrenz's death and Longobardo's withdrawal from the reform, Xu asked for imperial permission to invite Rho and Johann Adam Schall to the office. See his "Gai lifa qing fangyong Tang Ruowang Luo Yagu shu," 改歷法請訪用湯若望羅雅谷疏 in *Xu Guangqi ji*, 2:343–44.

9. Two of the Chinese staff were Jin Sheng (金聲; 1598–1645) and Li Zhizao.

10. *Chongzhen lishu* 崇禎曆書, ed. Pan Nai 潘鼐, 2 vols. (Shanghai: Shanghai guji, 2009). It is unfortunate that no extant version of this book is complete.

11. For the missionaries' scientific contributions to the *Chongzhen Calendar*, see Sun Xiaochun, "On the Star Catalogue and Atlas of *Chongzhen Lishu*," in *Statecraft and Intellectual Renewal in Late Ming China: The Cross-cultural Synthesis of Xu Guangqi (1562–1633)*, ed. Catherine Jami, Peter Engelfriet, and Gregory Blue (Leiden: Brill, 2001), 315–16.

12. Sun Xiaochun, "On the Star Catalogue," 315.

13. See *Ming shi, juan* 31, 3:541–44.

14. *Ming shi, juan* 31, 3:543.

15. It is a scholarly consensus that the Ming had the tightest restriction on astronomy for most of the dynasty. See Chen Zungui, *Zhongguo tianwen xue shi*, 1:159, 160–63.

16. In the *Da Ming huidian*, one reads these words, "洪武六年詔：[欽天監]人員永不許遷動，子孫只習學天文曆算，不許習他業；其不習學者發南海充軍." *Da Ming huidian, juan* 223, 5:2959. See also Long Wenbin 龍文彬, comp., *Ming huiyao* 明會要, 2 vols. (Beijing: Zhonghua, 1956), 1:688.

17. As stated in the *Ming Code*: "凡私家收藏玄象器物天文圖讖者，杖一百。若私習天文者，罪亦如之。並於犯人名下追銀一十兩，給付告人充賞." The collected annotation (集解) under this statute explains that the ban was based on the crucial roles that astronomy and the calendar play in the many aspects of political life of the dynasty from divination to military actions and state institutionalization (象天之物，其理幽玄，如璇璣玉衡之類、天文圖象、讖緯是一項事，皆以調兵、璽玉全完以行制。此皆非私家所宜有). *Da Ming lü*, 12.2a–b, vol. 862 of *Xuxiu siku quanshu*, 490. See Shen Defu, *Wanli yehuo bian, juan* 20, 2:524. See also Henderson, *Development and Decline*, 117; Richard Joseph Smith, *Chinese Almanacs* (New York: Oxford University Press, 1992), 4–5.

18. "乃命重黎，絕地天通，罔有降格." *Shangshu* 尚書, 19.20b, vol. 1 of *Shisan jing*, 297. Translation with modification in Legge, *The Shoo King*, vol. 3 of *The Chinese Classics*, 593.

19. See *Guo yu* 國語, 2 vols. (Shanghai: Shanghai guji, 1988), 2:562.

20. See K. C. Chang, *Art, Myth, and Ritual: The Path to Political Authority in Ancient China* (Cambridge, MA: Harvard University Press, 1982), 45n3; Joseph Needham, *Mathematics and the Science of Heaven and Earth*, vol. 3 of *Science and Civilization in China* (Cambridge: Cambridge University Press, 1959), 189. See also David N. Keightley, "Early Civilization in China: Reflections on How It Became Chinese," in his *These Bones Shall Rise Again: Selected Writings on Early China*, ed. Henry Rosemont Jr. (New York: State University of New York Press, 2014), 51–52.

21. Needham, *Mathematics*, 189. See also Nathan Sivin, "Science and Medicine in Imperial China—the State of the Field," *Journal of Asian Studies* 47, no. 1 (1988): 63.

22. See Fung Yu-lan, *A History of Chinese Philosophy*, 2:19.

23. 天亦有喜怒之氣，哀樂之心，與人相副⋯與天同者大治，與天異者大亂。故為人主之道，莫明於在身之與天同者而用之，使喜怒必當義而出. Dong, *Chunqiu fanlu yi zheng* 春秋繁露義證 (Beijing: Zhonghua, 2002), 341–42.

24. See chapter 24 of Dong, *Chunqiu fanlu*, *juan* 7, 214–19.

25. 天文者，序二十八宿，步五星日月，以紀吉凶之象，聖王所以參政也. Ban Gu 班固, *Han shu* 漢書, 12 vols. (Beijing: Zhonghua, 1961), *juan* 30, 7:1765.

26. 宰相者，上佐天子理陰陽，順四時，下育萬物之宜，陳丞相世家. Sima Qian, *Shiji huizhu kaozheng fu jiaobu* 史記會註考證附校補, 2 vols. (Shanghai: Shanghai guji, 1986), 2:1245. Translated in *The Records of the Grand Historian of China*, trans. Burton Watson, 2 vols. (New York: Columbia University Press, 1961), 1:127.

27. Smith, *Chinese Almanacs*, 2.

28. Richard J. Smith, *Fortune-Teller and Philosophers: Divination in Traditional Chinese Society* (Boulder, CO: Westview, 1991), 19. See also Jiang Xiaoyuan 江曉原, "Zhongguo gudai lifa yu xingzhanshu—jianlun ruherenshi zhongguo gudai tianwen xue" 中國古代曆法與星占術—兼論如何認識中國古代天文學, *Da zirab tansuo* 大自然探索 7, no. 35 (1988): 153–60.

29. 朕奉天命以主中國⋯頒去《大統曆》一本，王其知正朔所在，必能奉若天道，俾爪哇之民安於生理，王亦永保祿位福及子孫. Quoted in Yan Congjian 嚴從簡, *Shuyu zhouzi lu* 殊域周咨錄 (Beijing: Zhonghua, 1993), *juan* 8, 292.

30. It is common knowledge that the traditional calendars—both imperial calendars (皇曆) and people's calendars (民曆)—were usually heavily annotated with detailed instructions concerning specific activities on fixed dates, ranging from administrative undertakings such as royal participation in sacrifice and state banquet to household chores, like kitchen cleaning and visiting one's barber.

31. Some telling examples of an ancient Chinese ruler's use of calendar to confirm his authority in domestic and international politics can be found in *Li ji*, *juan* 34, and *Zhou li*, *juan* 26. Richard Smith discusses how the Qing authority

would distribute Chinese calendars to "tributary states, notably Korea and Annam, as a tangible symbol of sway over these areas." Smith, *Fortune-Tellers and Philosophers*, 75.

32. Henderson, *Development and Decline*, 115–16. Anyone with some knowledge of Chinese political history knows that there are numerous examples of the rulers trusting and using astrology as omens of their political fortune. See Huang Yi-Long (黃一農), "Yesuhui shi dui zhongguo chuantog zhanxingshu de taidu" 耶穌會士對中國傳統星占術的態度, *Jiuzhou xuekan* 九州學刊 4, no. 3 (1991): 7–8. For some further ancient examples in the classics, see Lü Simian 呂思勉, *Qin Han shi* 秦漢史 (Shanghai: Shanghai guji, 2005), 729.

33. See Jiang Xiaoyuan and Niu Weixing, *Tianwen xixue dongjian ji*, 386. For some details of how the *Xiyang xinfa lishu* was used to form calendars in the dynasty, see Chen, *Zhongguo tianwen xue shi*, 1:163–69; 2:1063, 1068–70.

34. Derrida, *Of Hospitality*, 123.

35. Jacques Derrida, *Acts of Religion*, ed. Gil Anidjar (New York: Routledge, 2002), 360–61.

36. Derrida, *Acts of Religion*, 361.

37. See Nathan Sivin, "Science and Medicine in Chinese History," in *Heritage of China: Contemporary Perspectives on Chinese Civilization*, ed. Paul S. Ropp (Berkeley: University of California Press, 1990), 174; Harriet T. Zurndrofer, "One Adam Having Driven Us Out of Paradise, Another Has Driven Us Out of China": Yang Kuang-hsien's Challenge of Adam Schall von Bell," in *Conflict and Accommodation in Early Modern East Asia: Essays in Honor of Erik Zürcher*, ed. Leonard Blussé and Harriet T. Zurndorfer (Leiden: Brill, 1993), 146–47.

38. See Levinas, *Totality and Infinity*, 281.

39. See Xu, *Shengchao zuobi* 聖朝佐闢, *juan* 10, in Xu Changzhi, comp., *Poxie ji*, in *Mingmo qingchu yesuhui sixiang*, 5:175.

40. 行私曆, 攘瑞應, 謀不軌, 為千古未聞之大逆. Xu, *Shengchao zuobi*, in *Poxie ji*, in *Mingmo qingchu yesuhui sixiang*, 5:175.

41. 然中國之曆法, 自有一定之論, 不待西夷言之也. Xie Gonghua, 曆法論, in *Poxie ji*, in *Mingmo qingchu yesuhui sixiang*, 5:231.

42. 寧使中夏無好曆法, 不可使中夏有西洋人. Yang Guangxian, "Budeyi" 不得已, in *Mingmo qingchu yesuhui sixiang*, 5:441.

43. 為大國無奉小國正朔之理. Yang, "Budeyi," in *Poxie ji*, in *Mingmo qingchu yesuhui sixiang*, 5:404.

44. Throughout Chinese history, many Confucians had this assumption. For some such examples, see Qian Zhongshu, *Guanzhui bian* 管錐編, 5 vols. (Beijing: Zhonghua, 1980), 2:969–70.

45. Fang was a complex character. As will soon become clear, his attitude toward the missionaries' science by no means remained consistent.

46. 勾股之術, 乃周公、商高之遺, 而後人失之, 使西人竊其傳. Quoted in Quan Zuwang 全祖望, "梨子周先生神道碑文," in his *Jiqiting ji* 鮚琦亭集, *juan* 11, in *Quan Zuwang ji huijiao jizhu* 全祖望集匯校集注, 3 vols. (Shanghai: Shanghai guji, 2000), 1:222. In the calendar section (曆志一), *juan* 31 of *Ming shi*, these remarks are

possibly from Huang Zongxi or one of his disciples who helped draft this section: "The Westerners' astronomy and astronomical instruments, their understanding of the five geographical zones of hot and cold, their mapmaking theory, and their rules of mores, none of these goes beyond what has been covered in our *Zhou bi*. And from this fact one knows the [Chinese] source of the Western learning. For the sake of knowledge, people [in China] must search far and wide to collect as much as possible so as to retrieve the things that were lost hundreds of years ago. This is what the Master's teaching 'finding the lost rites among the barbarians [who had learned them from China and reserved them]' means to say. That is why we write about the Westerners [active in China]" (西人渾蓋通憲之器, 寒熱五帶之說, 地圖之理, 正方之法, 皆不能出周髀. 亦可知其源流之所自矣. 夫人旁搜博採, 以續千百年之墜緒. 亦禮失求野之意也, 故備論之). *Ming shi*, 3:544–45.

47. 萬歷之時, 中土化洽, 太西儒來, 脬豆合圖, 其理頓顯. 膠常見者, 駭以為異, 不知其皆聖人之所已言也…. 子曰: '天子失官, 學在四夷.' Fang Yizhi, "游子六天經或問序," in 浮山文集後編, 2.16b, vol. 113 of *Siku jinhui shu congkan* 四庫禁毀書叢刊·集部 (Beijing: Beijing chubanshe, 2000), 679.

48. See *Zuo zhuan* (Zhao 17), 46.9a, vol. 6 of *Shisan jing*, 838.

49. See the two extant chapters of Wang's book in vol. 54 of *Daizōkyō*, no. 2139, pp. 1267–70.

50. See Erik Zürcher, *The Buddhist Conquest of China: The Spread and Adaptation of Buddhism in Early Medieval China*, 3rd ed. (Leiden: Brill, 2007), 293–307.

51. Michel Foucault, *Archaeology of Knowledge and the Discourse on Language*, trans. A. M. Sheridan Smith (New York: Pantheon, 1972), 12.

52. 此所譯地球圖說 • • • 則皆沿習古法, 所謂疇人子弟散在四夷者也 • • • 。是說也, 乃周公, 商高, 孔子, 曾子之舊說也; 學者不必喜其新而宗之, 亦不必疑其奇而璧之可也. Ruan Yuan, "*Diqiu tushuo* xu," in Jiang Youren, *Diqiu tushuo*, 3b, vol. 1035 of *Xuxiu siku quanshu*, 2. See also his preface to Luo Shilin 羅士琳, *Xu Chouren zhuan* 續疇人傳, 2b., vol. 516 of *Xuxiu siku quanshu*, 458.

53. Ban Gu, *Han shu*, juan 30, 6:1746.

54. 萬曆年間泰西學人, 詳于質測而拙于通幾. 然智士推之, 彼之質測猶未備也. Fang Yizhi, preface to his *Wuli xiaozhi* (物理小識. 自序), vol. 867 of *Yingyin wenyuange siku quanshu*, 742.

55. 泰西之人…自號西儒以七克為教, 似近于孔門克己復禮. 然接其人, 聆其論, 咸精于曆數, 合于制器尚象之旨; 獨膜拜天神, 奢言天堂地獄, 則異教也. Sun Lan, *Liuting yudi yushuo* 柳庭輿地隅說, 1.9b, vol. 88 of *Congshu jicheng xubian* 叢書集成續編 (Shanghai: Shanghai shudian, 1994), 429.

56. The idea or discussion of 中學為體, 西學為用 (Chinese studies [learning, culture, values] for the base [fundamental structure, framework], Western studies for use [practical application]) is a phrase first put out by Zhang Zhidong (張之洞; 1837–1909) in his book *Quanxue pian* (勸學篇; 1898). For details of this suggestion by Zhang, see chapter 3 (設學) in the Outer Chapters (外篇) of that book. See also chapters 7 (變法) and 13 (會通). *Zhang Zhidong Quanji* 張之洞全集, 12 vols.

(Shijiazhuang: Hebei renmin chubanshe, 1998), *juan* 271, 12:9739–42. Of course, Zhang was by no means the earliest scholar/official during the late Qing period to make this distinction. A few others had done the same before him. For example, Feng Guifen (馮桂芬; 1809–1874) in his "On the Adoption of Western Knowledge (采西學議)" (1861) insisted that China would be strong if the Chinese could "make the Chinese ethics and [Confucian] doctrines the fundamental basis and supplement it with the technologies that have helped various [Western] countries gain prosperity and strength (以中國倫常名教為原本, 輔以諸國富強之術)." Feng, *Jiaobinlu kangyi* 校邠廬抗議, 2.39a, vol. 952 of *Xuxiu sikuquanshu*, 541. Like Feng, Zheng Guanying (鄭觀應; 1842–1922) stated in an essay, "On Western Learning (西學)," written in 1892, "Taking the two together, one must say that Chinese learning represents the base whereas Western learning the minor end" (合而言之, 則中學其本也, 西學其末也). Zheng, *Shengshi weiyan* 盛世危言, in *Zheng Guanying ji* 鄭觀應集, ed. Xia Dongyuan 夏東元, 2 vols. (Shanghai: Shanghai renmin, 1988), 1:276.

57. Pressured by many factors including its need for foreign aid in its crackdown war against the Taiping rebellion, the Qing government began the so-called Movement of Westernization (洋務運動) in the mid-1850s. But the debate on how to retain Confucianism while importing Western technology remained ongoing without ever reaching a unanimous conclusion at that time or later. In fact, issues raised in the debate then have continued to concern the Chinese up to the present day. For some recent discussion on this topic, see Ding Weizhi 丁偉志 and Chen Song 陳崧, *Zhong ti xi yong zhijian: wan Qing wenhua sichao shulun* 中體西用之間—晚清文化思潮述論 (Beijing: Shehui kexue wenxian chubanshe, 2011). Last but not least, the communist leader Deng Xiaoping's (鄧小平) catchy phrase "the socialist modernization with Chinese characteristics" (中國特色的社會主義現代化) also seems to follow the same thought since the late Qing. See Deng, "Build Socialism with Chinese Characteristics, June 30, 1984," and "Interview of Deng Xiaoping by Robert Maxwell on Current Affairs," in Deng, *Speeches and Writings*, 2nd extended ed. (Oxford: Pergamon, 1987), 95–98, 108–12.

58. See Qian Zhongshu, "漢譯第一首英語詩《人生頌》及有關二三事," in his *Qizhui ji* 七綴集 (Shanghai: Shanghai guji, 1985), 121n21.

59. Sun Lung-kee 孫隆基 takes Sino-centrism to be the focal point in the debate in the late Qing period, a period under discussion in his *Lishi xue jia de jing xian: Lishi xinli wenji* 歷史學家的經線—歷史心理文集 (Guilin: Guangxi shifan daxue chubanshe, 2004), 7.

60. Here one does not need to enumerate the many losses—lives and properties—on the Ming side because of the pirates from Japan, or to describe details about the final fall of the dynasty to the Manchus. The Mongols alone caused enough trouble to the Ming empire, because, after the fall of the Yuan, they remained resilient with their harassment and threat to China in spite of a variety of strategies Ming rulers used to pacify them, including maintaining border garrisons. To give a couple of examples, during the Zhengtong's (正統) reign (1436–1449), there was the well-known Tumu

debacle (土木之變; 1442), during which the Mongols captured Emperor Yingzong (英宗; 1427–1464); and a few years later, in the Gengxu debacle of 1550, Mongol troops, led by Altan (俺答), besieged the Ming capital and looted its suburbs. See Twitchett and Mote, *Ming Dynasty, 1368–1644* (pt. 2), 475–76; *juan* 59 in Gu Yingtai (谷應泰), *Mingshi jishi benmo* 明史紀事本末, 4 vols. (Beijing: Zhonghua, 1985), 3:899–910. The Manchus began to become strong during Wanli's reign. It was in the forty-sixth year of Wanli or 1618 when they took Fushun. See Meng Sen 孟森, *Mingdai shi* 明代史 (Taibei: Jicheng tushu gongsi, 1957), 299; *Ming shi*, 28 vols., *juan* 21, 2:291, and also 2:280, 285. For the records of Japanese pirates during the Ming, see *juan* 55 in Gu Yingtai, *Mingshi jishi benmo*, 3:839–70.

61. See 陳榮捷 (Wing-tsit Chan), "Tiyong" 體用, in *Zhongguo zhexue cidian daquan* 中國哲學辭典大全, ed. Wei Zhengtong 韋政通 (Taibei: Shuiniu chubanshe, 1997), 853–56.

62. 形而上者謂之道, 形而下者謂之器 ("Xi ci" 繫辭). The commentary by Kong Yingda 孔穎達 (574–648) goes, "道在形之上, 形在道之下." *Zhou yi zhengyi* 周易正義, 7.32b–33a, vol. 1 of *Shisan jing*, 158. Translated in *The I Ching or Book of Changes*, trans. Richard Wilhelm, English rendition by Cary F. Baynes (Princeton, NJ: Princeton University Press, 1977), 323.

63. 體用也定。見在底便是體, 後來生底便是用。此身是體, 動作處便是用. Li Jingde 黎靖德, comp., *Zhuzi yulei* 朱子語類, 8 vols. (Beijing: Zhonghua, 1986), *juan* 6, 1:101.

64. 燈是光之體, 光是燈之用. *Liuzu dashi fabao tunjing* 六祖宗大師法寶壇經, vol. 48 of *Daizōkyō*, no. 2008, p. 352c.

65. 體用一源, 顯微無間. Cheng Yi, "Yi zhuan xu" 易傳序, in Cheng Yi and Cheng Hao, *Er Cheng ji* 二程集, 2 vols. (Beijing: Zhonghua, 1981), 2:689.

66. 我高皇帝⋯欽命儒臣吳伯宗等翻譯西域曆書三卷, 載在掌故。又面諭詞臣李翀等曰: 邇來西域陰陽家推測天象, 至為精密有驗, 其緯度之法, 又中國書之所未備, 此其有關於天人甚大。宜譯其書, 隨時披閱, 庶幾觀象可以省躬修德, 順天心, 立民命焉. Xu, "Lishu zongmu biao" 曆書總目表, in *Xu Guangqi ji*, 2:373–74. Translated with modification quoted in Han Qi, "Astronomy, Chinese and Western," 364.

67. [事天之學]真可以補益王化, 左右儒術, 救正佛法者也. Xu, "Bianxue zhangshu" 辯學章疏, in *Xu Guangqi ji*, 2:432.

68. *Xu Guangqi ji*, 2:433.

69. Even the missionaries realized that being scientifically and technologically useful to the Chinese might not help their mission. That was why, despite their intention and plan to use science as a bait, they often appeared reluctant to answer questions concerning only science and technology. Xu Guangqi mentioned this Jesuit reluctance in his "Bianxue zhangshu." See *Xu Guangqi ji*, 2:433. See also Fang Yizhi, *Wuli xiaozhi*, 28. It should be mentioned in passing that the Jesuits' unwillingness to discuss science more than talk about their religious ideology offers yet another piece of evidence that the missionaries used science, like maps, math, and astronomy, as their "tool" or "function" for their mission or their Christian "substance" or "Dao."

70. See Gu Yingtai, *Mingshi jishi benmo*, *juan* 1 of supplement (補遺), 4:1409–16; *Xizong shilu* 熹宗實錄, 8.1a–26b, pp. 367–418. The biographies of several Ming officials in charge of the military actions at the time can provide an outline of the dire situation. See *Ming shi*, *juan* 259, 22:6685–723.

71. Xu Guangqi, "Taichong shiyi shu" 臺銃事宜疏, in *Xu Guangqi ji*, 1:187–89; Li Zhizao, "Zou wei zhisheng wuxu xichong qichi suqu shu" 奏為制勝務須西銃乞勑速取疏, in *Xu Guangqi ji*, 1:178–82.

72. For instance, in 1626, the Ming army with its powerful cannons delivered such a heavy blow to the Manchu troops that Nurhachi died broken-heartedly as a result. See records for January 1626 in *Xizong shilu*, 79.19b–20b, pp. 3838–40. See also Huang Yi-long, "Sun Yuanhua (1581–1632)," in *Statecraft and Intellectual Renewal in Late Ming China: The Cross-cultural Synthesis of Xu Guangqi (1562–1633)*, ed. Catherine Jami, Peter Engelfriet, and Gregory Blue (Leiden: Brill, 2001), 235.

73. Ironically, the use of the cannon in a way accelerated the fall of the Ming. The fate of the dyansty was sealed when the Manchus not only turned captured cannons around against the Ming but also imitated the technology. See Ma Chujian 馬楚堅, "Xiyang dapao dui Ming Jin taishi de gaibian" 西洋大砲對明金態勢的改變, in *Mingmo qingchu Huanan diqu lishi renwu gongye yantaohui lunwenji* 明末清初華南地區歷史人物功業研討會論文集, ed. Luo Bingjin 羅炳錦 and Liu Jianming 劉健明 (Hong Kong: Xianggang zhongwen daxue lishi xi, 1991), 11–30. For a discussion of the Manchu imitation of the cannons, see Huang Yi-long 黃一農, "Hongyi dapao yu Ming Qing zhanzheng—yi huopao cezhun jishu zhi yanbian weili" 紅夷大砲與明清戰爭——以火砲測準技術之演變為例, *Tsinghua Jounral of Chinese Studies* 26 (1996): 60.

74. See Li Zhizao, "Zou wei zhisheng wuxu xichong qichi suqu shu," in *Xu Guangqi ji*, 1:180–81.

75. For Longobardo's life and works, see Joseph Dehergne, *Répertoire des Jésuites de Chine de 1552 à 1800* (Rome: Institutum Historicum S. I., 1973), 153–54.

76. Diaz was indicted together with three other missionaries during the Nanjing Persecution. Though at least two of the missionaries were deported following the trial, Diaz somehow evaded the same fate. In fact, the government chased him but could never find, much less arrest, him. His indictment was therefore given *absente reo*. See *Poxie ji*, in *Mingmo qingchu yesuhui sixiang*, 5:32, 37, 40, 41, 43; for the record of Diaz as not one of the two to be deported, see 5:43, 50, 51. For other missionaries' involvement in gun-founding during the late Ming, including cannons and other weaponry such as handguns and portable culverins, see Joseph Needham, *Science and Civilization in China*, vol. 5, *Chemistry and Chemical Technology* (Cambridge: Cambridge University Press, 1976), 240–41.

77. See Zhang Weihua 張維華, *Mingshi Ouzhou siguo zhuan zhushi* 明史歐洲四國傳注釋 (Shanghai: Shanghai guji, 1982), 186.

78. Levinas, *Otherwise than Being*, 79.

Chapter 6

1. See chapter 1, "From Sympathy to Hostility," in Jacques Gernet, *China and the Christian Impact*, 15–16; Criveller, *Preaching Christ in Late Ming China*, 55–58.

2. These Mencian words (用夷變夏) became a warning repeatedly put out by the Confucians. See *Poxie ji*, in *Mingmo qingchu yesuhui sixiang*, 5:97, 187.

3. Along with what has been covered in a note in the previous chapter, it should be added that the persecution was the plan of Shen Que (沈㴇; ?–1623), vice minister of the Nanjing Ministry of Rites. For historical records of the persecution, see *Shenzong shilu* 神宗實錄, 552.1a–2a, pp. 10425–27; *Ming shi*, juan 326, 28:8460–61.

4. The current copy of Xu's book is included in *Poxie ji* (破邪集), or *A Collection for Destroying Heterodoxy*, a collection of writings by various anti-Christian Confucians published in 1639. But it is believed that Xu wrote his book much earlier. Adrian Dudink dates this book in or before 1623. See Dudink, "The *Sheng-Ch'ao Tso-P'i* (1623) of Hsü Ta-shou," in *Conflict and Accommodation in Early Modern East Asia*, 109–24.

5. Ricci, *Tianzhu shiyi*, in *Tianxue chuhan*, 1:619. Modified translation from *The True Meaning of the Lord of Heaven*, 433.

6. See Andrew Chung's introduction to *Shengchao zuobi*, in *Poxie ji*, in *Mingmo qingchu yesuhui sixiang*, 5:119. Of the information in recent scholarship to tell the reader more about the life and thought of Xu Dashou, the fact that Xu's father was Xu Fuyuan (許孚遠; studio name Jing'an 敬菴; 1535–1604) is crucial to my discussion of Dashou's attack on the Jesuits. I should mention in passing that, for evidence of the father-son relationship between Xu Fuyuan and Xu Dashou, one can see Ye Xianggao, "Xu Jing'an xiansheng muzhiming" 許敬菴先生墓誌銘, in the twenty-*juan* edition of his *Cangxia cao* 蒼霞草 published during the Wanli period (1573–1619), 16.14b, vol. 124 of *Siku jinhui shu congkan* 四庫禁毀書叢刊 · 集部, 414. See also Sun Kuang 孫鑛, "兵部左侍郎贈南京工部尚書許公孚遠神道碑," vol. 3 of Jiao Hong, ed. *Guochao xianzheng lu* 國朝獻徵錄 (Taibei: Mingwen shuju, 1991), 41.26a. In his essay, "The *Sheng-ch'ao tso-p'i*," Adrian Dudink offers additional background information on Xu Dashou and his father (107). The relevant passage he mentions can be found in *juan* 4 of *Shengchao zuobi*, in *Poxie ji*, in *Mingmo qingchu yesuhui sixiang*, 5:123. About Xu Dashou's family and life, Mei Qianli 梅謙立 (Thierry Meynard, SJ) has published a detailed study. See Mei, appendix to Mei Qianli, ed., *Ming Xu Dashou* Shengchao zuobi *jiaozhu* 明許大受《聖朝佐闢》校注 (Gaoxiong: Foguang wenhua, 2018), 177–216.

7. See Xu, *Shengchao zuobi*, in *Poxie ji*, 5:123.

8. Xu, *Shengchao zuobi*, in *Poxie ji*, in *Mingmo qingchu yesuhui sixiang*, 5:123.

9. The Confucians' lack of sufficient knowledge and understanding of the Trinity should in part be attributed to the early Jesuits' reluctance, owing to the theological

difficulty they faced, to preach to the Chinese such basic concepts in Christian theology as the Trinity, incarnation, and redemption. As for how Jesuit missionary work led to criticism and debate, including the famous Rites Controversy, see David Mungello, ed., *The Chinese Rites Controversy: Its History and Meaning* (Nettetal, Ger: Verlag, 1994).

10. See *Poxie ji*, in *Mingmo qingchu yesuhui sixiang*, 5:70, 84. The attempt to use history to discredit Jesus's authority persisted through the years in anti-Christian writings in China. For more examples, see Wang Minglun 王明倫, ed., *Fan yangjiao shuwen jietie xuan* 反洋教書文揭帖選 (Ji'nan: Qilu shushe, 1984), 1. See also Zhang Guiyong 張貴永, ed., *Jiaowu jiao'an dang* 教務教案檔 (Taibei: Zhongyang yanjiuyuan Zhongguo jindaishi yanjiu suo, 1974), 1:916; and 2:861.

11. "一切帝王，一切聖賢，不如天主之獨尊。" *Shengchao zuobi*, in *Poxie ji*, in *Mingmo qingchu yesuhui sixiang*, 5:142.

12. *Shengchao zuobi*, in *Poxie ji*, in *Mingmo qingchu yesuhui sixiang*, 5:126.

13. "捏天主以制天，挾天以制天子。" *Shengchao zuobi*, in *Poxie ji*, in *Mingmo qingchu yesuhui sixiang*, 5:127.

14. *Poxie ji*, in *Mingmo qingchu yesuhui sixiang*, 5:141.

15. Huang Zongxi 黃宗羲, "Poxie lun" 破邪論, in *Huang Zongxi quanji*, 12 vols., 1:194–95.

16. See *Ming Code*, 1.4a, vol. 862 of *Xuxiu siku quanshu*, 488.

17. See the relevant passage on Christian mass and its violation of the law in an announcement (拿獲邪黨後告示) issued by the Nanjing Bureau of Rites (南京禮部), *Poxie ji*, in *Mingmo qingchu yesuhui sixiang*, 5:70.

18. 彼國之君臣皆以友道處之. *Shengchao zuobi*, in *Poxie ji*, in *Mingmo qingchu yesuhui sixiang*, 5:137. More on this later.

19. In his essay, Mei Qianli (Meynard Thierry) uses some statistics from *Dadao jiyan* (達道記言) or *Recorded Sayings* by Alfonso Vagnoni (1568–1640), a Jesuit in China, to demonstrate how Vagnoni tactically and tacitly put most of the sayings about the ruler-minister relationship in the section on friendship in his work. See Mei, "Ming Qing zhiji de youyi zhengce" 明清之際的友誼政策, 西學東漸研究 3 (2010): 95–122. See also *Jesuit Chreia in Late Ming China: Two Studies with an Annotated Translation of Alfonso Vagnone's Illustrations of the Grand Dao*, trans. Thierry Meynard and Li Sher-shiueh (Bern: Peter Lang, 2014).

20. "有帝王以主天下，有親以主家，有家督以主臧獲。今夷不識此義，爾反欲以"友"之一字強平之。" *Shengchao zuobi*, in *Poxie ji*, in *Mingmo qingchu yesuhui sixiang*, 5:137. Here Xu's complaint may not be too far off the mark, given the previous discussion in this book on the historical fact that an early Christian as a "friend of God" flaunted his *nomen Christianum* to exclude the current names of kin and township. Raised by his friendship with God above the identity of his fellow men, an early Christian would not bother to give others his name, race, or the city he was from except by saying laconically and repeatedly: "I am a Christian." See Brown, *Making of Late Antiquity*, 56. At the same time, it seems that Xu was

not aware of, or he chose to ignore, the tendency among some Confucian scholars and officials during the late Ming to promote friendship between the rulers and ministers, a topic discussed in Joseph P. McDermott, "Friendship and Its Friends in the Late Ming," in *Jinshi jiazu yu zhengzhi bijiao lishi lunwen ji* 近世家族與政治比較歷史論文集, ed. Zhongyang yanjiu yuan jindaishi yanjiu suo 中央研究院近代史研究所, 67–96. For an extended bibliography of the recent studies on the topic of Confucian friendship during the late Ming period, see Huang, ed., *Male Friendship in Ming China* (Leiden: Brill, 2007), 179–184.

21. See *Shengchao bizuo*, in *Poxie ji*, in *Mingmo qingchu yesuhui sixiang*, 5:137–39.

22. Besides "Common Father," God has also been referred to as *Dazhu* (大主), the Ultimate Master, vis-à-vis the master within a specific household or *jiazhu* (家主). See Jiang Dejing 蔣德璟, preface to *Poxie ji*, in *Mingmo qingchu yesuhui sixiang*, 5:85.

23. See *Shengchao zuobi*, in *Poxie ji*, *Mingmo qingchu yesuhui sixiang*, 5:137.

24. Augustine's words in his letter to a friend. Quoted in Peter Brown, *The Body and Society: Men, Women, and Sexual Renunciation in Early Christianity* (New York: Columbia University Press, 1988), 424.

25. This is an argument Ricci made when he identified the Chinese Lord-on-High or Shangdi (上帝) with God or the Lord of Heaven in his *The True Meaning of the Lord of Heaven* (121–27). Ricci's identification of the two deities will be referenced again later in this chapter, but an in-depth treatment of this topic to reveal its complexity and significance will have to wait for another project.

26. In *Poxie ji*, the editor Huang Zhen (黃貞), a lay Buddhist, mentioned a conversation he once had with Aleni. According to Huang, when he asked what would happen to Wenwang or King Wen (文王; c. 1152–1056 BCE), one of the greatest kings in early China, given his life style—an indisputable violation of the "rule of not having concubines" in the Ten Commandments—Aleni's response, following much hesitation came as follows: "I never wanted to talk about this. . . . But to you, my old friend, I will say what I would not say at all to others—I am afraid that King Wen has been damned to hell as well!" Huang, "A Letter to Petition Mr. Yan Zhuangqi to Refute the Doctrines of the Lord of Heaven" 請顏壯其先生辟天主教書, in *Poxie ji*, in *Mingmo qingchu yesuhui sixiang*, 5:93. It is worth pointing out that, from the above conversation, one can see that the Ten Commandments preached by the missionaries to the Chinese were tailored to suit the situation in China.

27. Xu offered one example: "A friend of mine by the name of Zhou Guoxiang was both old and poor. But he was fortunate to own a concubine and they produced a son. When the baby was two years old, the barbarian missionaries told Zhou: 'In our country, we regard people without concubines as virtuous. And it is not our gravest concern whether we have progenies.' Heeding the words of the missionaries, Zhou expelled his son's mother from the house. Today I wonder whether this motherless child survived." (吾友周國祥, 老貧無子, 幸買一妾, 舉一子,

才二歲。夷教之曰:"吾國以不妾為賢,不以無後為大。"周聽而逐其子之母。今不知此子活否) *Shengchao bizuo*, in *Poxie ji*, in *Mingmo qingchu yesuhui sixiang*, 5:148.

28. "今更橫行,豈知國法。夫不召而來,不遣而入,是謂私通。詔逐不遵,屢除潛蔓,是謂蔑旨。" Xu, *Shengchao bizuo*, in *Poxie ji*, in *Mingmo qingchu yesuhui sixiang*, 5:124.

29. "將省直夷種渠魁,如艾、龍輩,或斃之杖下,或押出口外,而取津吏之回文,疏之朝廷,永永不許再入,入則戮其津吏及押夷者。" *Shengchao bizuo*, in *Poxie ji*, in *Mingmo qingchu yesuhui sixiang*, 5:160. Similar proposals made by other authors appear in *Poxie ji*, in *Mingmo qingchu yesuhui sixiang*, 5:31–38, 168, 190, 195, 197, 219, 223, and so on.

30. This is what Derrida argues in his "Violence and Metaphysics," a discussion of Levinas. See Derrida, *Writing and Difference*, trans. Alan Bass (Chicago: University of Chicago Press, 1978), 52–53. See also Geoffrey Bennington, "Deconstruction and Ethics," in *Deconstructions: A User's Guide*, ed. Nicholas Royle (New York: Palgrave, 2000), 73–74.

31. For examples of the harsh words used in the Confucian denunciation of Buddhism, see Anthony C. Yu, *State and Religion in China: Historical and Textual Perspective* (Chicago: Open Court, 2005), 123–24.

32. This is a fact pointed out by Liu Cunren (柳存仁). See his *Hefeng tang wenji* 和風堂文集, 3 vols. (Shanghai: Shanghai guji, 1991), 2:668.

33. Dudink found in Xu's writing many examples of Xu's obviously good knowledge of Christian ideas. See Dudink, "The *Sheng-ch'ao tso-p'i*," in *Conflict and Accommodation*, 127nn100–101.

34. See Lu Rong 陸容, *Shuyuan zaji* 菽園雜記 (Beijing: Zhonghua, 1985), 19. Indeed, Lu's remarks can be verified by Han Yu's own words in a letter (答李翊書) that he would not venture to inspect books written after the Three Dynasties (Xia, Shang, and Zhou) and the Western Han (206 BCE–9 CE) and the Eastern Han (25–220 CE) (非三代兩漢書不敢觀). But Han also stated elsewhere (答侯繼書) that since his early years he had read, in addition to the five Confucian classics, all the books of other schools that he could find (僕少好學問,自五經以外,百氏之書,未有聞而不求,得而不觀者). To many, Han Yu's familiarity with Buddhist texts was never in doubt. For example, see Sima Guang 司馬光, "Shu xinjing hou zeng Shaojian" 書心經後贈紹鑒, in *Wenguo wenzheng Sima gong wenji* 溫國文正司馬公文集, vol. 841 of *Sibu congkan* 四部叢刊 (Shanghai: Shangwu, 1919), 69.1b. The modern scholar Chen Yinke (陳寅恪) also points out that Han's knowledge of Buddhism might not have been as deliberately meager as he wanted it to appear. As Chen argues, Han's thought could bear substantial Buddhist influence, at least that from Zen Buddhism, a new Buddhist sect in Han's time. Chen argues that Zen Buddhism happened to be popular in Lingbiao (岭表), or today's Guangzhou area, where Han spent his childhood. See Chen, "Lun Han Yu" 論韓愈, in his *Jinming guan conggao chubian* 金明館叢稿初編 (Beijing: Sanlian shudian, 2001), 319–32.

35. Levinas, *Totality and Infinity*, 299.

36. For how Levinas presents the way in which the subject as the host actually relates with and opens to the Other when it attempts to separate itself from the latter, see *Totality and Infinity*, 299–300, 305.

37. "或又曰：'然則子辟言中，何不直崇儒，而乃兼祖佛乎？' 曰 "蠻夷言人有後世，非貫通儒釋，不足以抑妖邪故也." Xu, "Preface to *Shengchao zuobi zixu*" 聖朝佐辟自序, *Shengchao zuobi*, in *Poxie ji*, in *Mingmo qingchu yesuhui sixiang*, 5:120.

38. In Xu's hierarchy, Christianity ranked the lowest. See *Shengchao zuobi*, in *Poxie ji*, in *Mingmo qingchu yesuhui sixiang*, 5:120.

39. Many see Xu's desperate need to seek assistance from Buddhist teachings for his anti–Christian project. For example, see Mei Qianli, introduction to his *Ming Xu Dashou* Shengchao zuobi *jiaozhu*, 53.

40. It should be pointed out here that Xu Dashou was a lay Buddhist who corresponded with some Buddhist monks of his time. For instance, Zhuhong, a renowned Buddhist master and an anti–Jesuit writer, left in his collected writings a letter to Xu Dashou who sought Zhuhong's advice on meditation. See "Da Deqing Xu Kuoru jushi Guangyue" 答德清許廓如居士廣鉞, 8 vols. (Taibei: Dongchu chubanshe, 1991), 8:4571.

41. See *Shengchao zuobi*, in *Poxie ji*, in *Mingmo qingchu yesuhui sixiang*, 5:142, 144, 147.

42. For a biographical note of Xu, see Zhenhua Fashi 震華法師, *Zhongguo fojiao renming da cidian* 中國佛教人名大辭典 (Shanghai: Shanghai cishu chubanshe, 1999), 577. Additional information about Xu can also be seen in *Foguang da cidian* 佛光大辭典, Shi Ciyi 釋慈怡, ed., s.v. "徐昌治," https://www.fgs.org.tw/fgs_book/fgs_drser.aspx.

43. For Yuanwu's work, see the introductory remarks to his anti-Christian work "Bian tian shuo" 辯天說, in *Poxie ji*, in *Mingmo qingchu yesuhui sixiang*, 5:224–25. See also the related entry in Ding Fubo, *Foxue dacidian*, 1169; see also *Foguang da cidian*, s.v. "圓悟," https://www.fgs.org.tw/fgs_book/fgs_drser.aspx.

44. In addition to Ye Xianggao's gravestone inscription on Xu Fuyuan already mentioned, a brief official biography of Xu can be found in *Ming shi, juan* 283, 24:7285–86.

45. For an example of Xu Fuyuan's criticism of Buddhism, see *juan* 41 of Huang Zongxi, *Ming ru xue'an*, 2 vols., 2:972–81. Xu Fuyuan's anti-Buddhist sentiment was so strong and well known that Ye Xianggao reserved some space for its mention in his very short memorial of Fuyuan's death. See Ye, "Ji Xu Jing'an xiansheng wen" 祭許敬菴先生文, in the 28-*juan* edition (published 1573–1627) of his *Cangxia cao quanji* 蒼霞草全集, 10.105a.

46. See in particular the passage in his essay discussing Confucianism being superior to other schools of teaching in *Ming ru xue'an*, 2:974–76.

47. It is true that at Dashou's time, despite the hostility that Buddhism as non-Chinese doctrine often attracted, the men of letters often borrowed, consciously or not, certain ideas from Buddhism and drew analogies on a philosophical level

between Confucianism and Buddhism. See Gernet, *China and the Christian Impact*, 255n80.

48. See Derrida's discussion of how hospitality means an interruption of the Self in *Adieu*, 51–57.

49. Qiyuan's grandfather, Wang Shangxue (王尚學; 1505–1568), studio name Liubin (柳濱), was one of the 222 Associate Metropolitan Graduates (同進士出身) in 1538. See Zhang Chaorui 張朝瑞, *Huang Ming gongju kao* 皇明貢舉考 published during the Wanli period (1573–1619), 7.23a, vol. 828 of *Xuxiu siku quanshu*, 448. The highest office he held was director of Bureau of Operations in the Ministry of War (兵部職方司郎中). For Shangxue's life, see Ye Xianggao's biography of him (柳濱王公傳) in *Cangxia yu cao* 蒼霞餘草, 8.6a–12b, vol. 125 of *Siku jinhui shu congkan* 四庫禁毀書叢刊·集部, 485–87. A recent archaeological discovery of Shangxue's tomb in Liuzhou has provided more information on him and his children. See Chen Jian 陳堅, "Wang Shangxue mu de faxian jiqi yiyi" 王尚學墓的發現及其意義, http://bj.crntt.com/crn-webapp/cbspub/secDetail.jsp?bookid=38201&secid=38247. Qiyuan's father, Wang Hua (王化), studio name Ruzan (汝贊), served in turn as county magistrate (知縣), vice prefect (同知), surveillance vice commissioner (按察副使), and so on. He was known for his bravery and military tactics. For brief biographical notes on him, see *Ming shi, juan* 222, 19:5837; Wang Jin 王錦 et al., comps., *Liuzhou fuzhi* 柳州府志, 25.16a–17a, in *Guangxi fu zhou xian zhi* 廣西府州縣志, 10 vols. (Haikou: Hainan chubanshe, 2001), 3:223. About Wang Hua, a noteworthy biographical essay was written by Jiao Hong, who sang praises of Wang by recounting many of his heroic and virtuous deeds. See "Wang Xianfu Ruzan zhuan" 王憲副汝贊傳, in Jiao, *Danyuan ji, juan* 24, 1:326–30.

50. When Qiyuan was still small, his mother, Lady Ji (計氏) died, committing suicide upon hearing the false report that her husband had been killed in a battle against rebels. Gui Youguang (歸有光; 1507–1571), a famous Ming essayist who was a friend of the Ji family, wrote "Biography of Notable Woman Ji" (計烈婦傳), which recounts Ji's death and pays tributes to her. See Gui, *Zhenchuan xiansheng ji* 震川先生集, 2 vols. (Shanghai: Shanghai guji, 1981), 2:624–25. Gui's essay on Ji is also included in *Liuzhou fuzhi*, 34.43a–44a, in *Guangxi fu zhou xian zhi*, 3:316.

51. Concerning Qiyuan's appointment as examining editor, see Shu Qi 舒啟, comp., *Maping xian zhi* 馬平縣志 (Nanning: Guangxi renmin, 1997), *juan* 7, p. 146; *Liuzhou fuzhi*, 25.21b–22a, in *Guangxi fu zhou xian zhi*, 3:224–25. In his biographical essay on Wang Shangxue, Ye mentioned that Wang Qiyuan at one time also served as an unranked observer (庶吉士) in the Hanlin Academy. See Ye, "Liubin Wang Gong zhuan," in *Cangxia yu cao*, 8.12a, vol. 125 of *Siku jinhui shu congkan* 四庫禁毀書叢刊·集部, 487.

52. See *Liuzhou fuzhi*, 25.21b, in *Guangxi fu zhou xian zhi*, 3:224, vol. 197 of *Gugong zhenben jikan*. It is known that in 1629, when he was about seventy years old, he wrote an essay to mark the renovation of the prefectural school of

Liuzhou. See *Maping xian zhi*, *juan* 8, pp. 191–93; and *juan* 5, p. 67. *Maping xian zhi* records another undated essay by him (p. 195).

53. The only copy of the book we have today has two collector seals impressed in it. The first seal says "Chibei shuku" (池北書庫), indicating that the book was once in the collection of Wang Shizhen (王士禛; 1634–1711). But Wang Shizhen, a leading and prolific literatus in the early Qing who loved to talk about books in his possession, never mentioned this book or Wang Qiyuan in any of his works. The second seal (reading 光緒初書歸黃縣王氏海西閣) shows that the book later on went into the possession of Wang Shouxun (王守訓; 1845–1897), a native from Huang County, Shandong, who passed his metropolitan graduate examination in 1886. The earliest record of the *Discourse* is found in Huang Yuji's (黃虞稷; 1629–1691) catalogue. See Huang, *Qianqing tang shumu* 千頃堂書目 (Shanghai: Shanghai guji, 2001), 84. Only Huang noted the book's title as 清署經談 (without the characters *yiji* 一集 or volume 1) with ten *juan* or chapters instead of sixteen in the copy of the book extant today. This very fact means that, if Huang did not make any typos, there might have been more than one edition of Qiyuan's *Discourse* in circulation. In his bibliographic list of studies of Confucian classics, Zhu Yizun (朱彝尊; 1629–1709) included this book. But he noted that he never saw the book. The information about the book he gave is exactly the same as Huang Yuji's. See Zhu, *Jingyi kao* 經義考, 251.1a–1b, vol. 680 of *Yingyin wenyuange siku quanshu*. It is necessary to add here that scholars have warned about the occasional inaccuracy in Huang's catalogue. For example, see Hung, "Kao Li Madou de shijie ditu," in *Hung Ye lunxue ji*, 173.

54. After the discovery of the book in 1931, Chen Shouyi (陳受頤), a Chicago-trained scholar and comparatist specializing in the literary, cultural, and religious exchanges between China and the West, was the first one to discuss in-depth the *Discourse* over eighty years ago. See Chen, "Sanbainian qian de jianli kongjiao lun" 三百年前的建立孔教論, *Lishi yuyan yanjiu suo jikan* 歷史語言所集刊 6, no. 2 (1936): 133–62. The long silence since the publication of Chen's extended paper was only broken in recent years when Wang Fansen (王汎森) and a student of his had their readings of the *Discourse*. For Wang's brief discussion, see his *Wan Ming qingchu sixiang shilun* 晚明清初思想十論 (Shanghai: Fudan daxue chubanshe, 2004), 52–56; Huang Chuan-hsi 黃譔禧, "Wang Qiyuan *Qingshu jing tan* zai wan Ming sixiangshi shang de yiyi" 王啟元《清署經談》在晚明思想史上的意義 (master's thesis, National Tsing Hua University, 2005).

55. See Willard Peterson, "Confucian Learning and the Late Ming Thought," in Twitchett and Mote, *The Ming Dynasty, 1368–1644* (pt. 2), 709, 770. For a discussion on the development of neo-Confucianism from the Song to the Ming, see Peter K. Bol, *Neo-Confucianism in History* (Cambridge, MA: Harvard University Asian Center, 2008).

56. See Xie Zhaozhe, *Wuzazu*, *juan* 3, 1:45, 52; see also *juan* 13, 2:266, 269–70. For scholarly discussions of the "Chinese pantheon of divinities" throughout history including the late imperial times described in Xie's book, see Meir Shahar

and Robert P. Weller, eds., *Unruly Gods: Divinity and Society in China* (Honolulu: University of Hawaii Press, 1996).

57. "今天下神祇香火之盛,莫過於關壯繆。……世所崇奉正神,尚有觀音大士,真武上帝,碧霞元君三者。與關壯繆香火相埒。遐陬荒谷,無不屍而祝之者。凡婦人女子,語以為周公孔子,或未必知。而敬信四神,無敢有心非巷議者。行且與天地俱悠久矣。" Xie, *Wuzazu*, 2 vols., *juan* 15, 2:313–14.

58. See Gong Pengcheng 龔鵬程, *Wan Ming sichao* 晚明思潮 (Yilan: Foguang, 2001), 1–20, and Li Tiangang 李天綱, "Zaoqi Tianzhujiao yu Ming Qing duoyuan shehui wenhua" 早期天主教與明清多元社會文化, *Shin lin* 史林 4 (1999): 45.

59. To attack the theory or theories by Lu Jiuyuan and Wang Yangming is an important part of Wang's book. See Chen Shouyi, "Sanbainian qian de jianli kongjiao lun," 139–44; Zhu Qianzhi 朱謙之, "Yesuhui duiyu Songru lixue zhi fanxiang" 耶穌會對於宋儒理學之反響, *Shixue zhuankan* 史學專刊 3, no. 1 (1936): 32–33. In his essay, Zhu makes the point that Wang Qiyuan, driven by his dissatisfaction with the philosophy by Lu Jiuyuan and Wang Yangming, hoped to restore Zhu Xi's *lixue* theory, which struck Wang as consistent with the ancient Confucian thought.

60. "而西洋之人,復倡為天主之說至使中國所素尊之上帝亦幾混而莫辨。嗚呼!" Wang, *Qingshu jingtan*, preface, 2b–3a.

61. "佛之教雖自以為尊於上帝,然上帝與佛為二,人頗能辨之也。天主自謂上帝矣,與中國者混二為一矣,人將奉中國原有之上帝也,抑或奉彼之天主耶?…以帝號論之,不可不辯。" Wang, *Qingshu jingtan*, 15.45b–46a. See also "Zhaogao Shangdi pian" 昭告上帝篇, 16.1a–1b.

62. See Wang, *Qingshu jingtan*, 15.47a.

63. As Wang put it, "the Saintly Teachings [of Confucianism] are by nature the holiest. If it is to contend with Buddhism, Daoism, and hundreds of other schools for authority, Confucianism just generates for itself some enmity and as a result makes its own authority depreciate" ([儒者…所處既然高…,何至自貶其高,與之爭勝?] 聖品本尊,而與二氏百家爭勝,自生一敵國,是自貶其尊也). Wang, *Qingshu jingtan*, 15.24b–25a.

64. "國無二王,家無二主,昔前數千年有一帝,後數千年有一帝,是二本也。人心將何從適?" Wang, *Qingshu jingtan*, 15.43b.

65. Wang's view of Lord-on-High, one must say, resembles what Ricci said about the Lord of Heaven in his *The True Meaning of the Lord of Heaven*. The sole difference between the two is that Ricci saw his God to be in charge of the entire world and human race, while Wang, together with Xu Dashou and many other anti-Christian Confucians, tended to divide gods by assigning to them ethnicity.

66. By Wang's view, what made the Jesuits more dangerous was that, as he put it, "the teachings of the Lord of Heaven . . . have quite solid doctrines" (天主之教…其理論其實), or, elsewhere in the same chapter, "I tend to think that what the Buddha preaches is quite easy to comprehend, while the teachings of the Lord of Heaven have a depth hard to see" (愚以為佛氏之說易知,而天主之教難測). Wang, *Qingshu jingtan*, 16.2a, 23a.

67. "上帝是天地開闢所即有者，《周禮》所謂'昊天上帝'是也。如人有身即有心，乃是同時俱有者⋯。如西洋之說，則又是先有天地數千年，而後始有天主也。以人身例之，殆不其然⋯。人身體之主，自生至死，一而已矣。既開闢時已有之，數千年後又復有之，是一人乎？二人乎？如以為果降生，則未降生年間，又誰為天之主乎？" Wang, *Qingshu jingtan*, 15.45a–45b.

68. For instance, in chapter 2 of his book, there is a section called "On Lord-on-High's Authority over Heaven" (上帝統天篇), in which one reads this observation: "Some minor difference likely exists between Heaven and Lord-on-High. One reasonable way to talk about the two terms is that the unnamed and inactive is Heaven, while the other with mastery and authority is Lord-on-High" (天與上帝，似當有微異。以理推之，則無名無為者為天。有主有權者，宜屬上帝). Wang, *Qingshu jingtan*, 2.5b. Wang's argument here echoed clearly what was typical in Confucian discussion on the deity known both as Lord-on-High and Heaven. In fact, his remarks here remind one of Zhu Xi's well-known statement about how the two terms—Lord-on-High and Heaven—denote the two different features or aspects of the very same absolute Being: "Concerning its existence or Being, this [god] should be called Heaven whereas concerning its function as the master it should be called the Lord" (其體即謂之天，其主宰即謂之帝). Zhu, *Zhuzi yulei*, juan 25, 2:621. It is worth pointing out that in the same passage where this quotation comes from, Zhu Xi, like Cheng Yi, also identifies Heaven and *li*, or Principle. According to some scholars, there emerged the trend in the Song dynasty to regard Lord-on-High, Heaven, and Principle as representing three different aspects of the same highest supernatural Being of the state. See Li Shen 李申, *Shangdi—Rujiao de zhishang shen* 上帝—儒教的至上神 (Taibei: Dongda tushu gongsi, 2004), 112–14. Again, adopting the view shared by Zhu Xi, Cheng Yi, and other Confucian thinkers, Wang's discussion seeks not only to define and present the Confucian Lord-on-High as the highest god under whose protection the Confucian Self would formulate and stand, but also oppose, discredit, and eliminate the Christian God of the missionaries.

69. For how during the Zhou the new deity called Heaven replaced the older god, Lord-on-High, see Guo Moruo 郭沫若, "Xian Qin tiandao guan zhi jinzhan" 先秦天道觀之進展, in his *Qingtong shidai* 青銅時代 (Beijing: Kexue chubanshe, 1957), 1–48.

70. Roger Ames points out how the encounter with the "'God-centered' religion" of Christianity has stimulated scholars in China to seek understanding of God. And it is interesting that he points out the Chinese terms such as *tian*, or Heaven, and *di*, or Lord, are often "profoundly abstruse in the Chinese classics, with words such as 'distant' (*yuan* 遠) and 'dark' (*xuan* 玄) being frequently invoked to describe them." Ames, *Confucian Role Ethics*, 221, 224.

71. For Wang's dissatisfaction with and criticism of the thought of Wang Yangming and that of other Confucians, including Lu Jiuyuan, see Wang, *Qingshu jingtan*, 4.7b–8a, 15.24a–27b, 29a–31a.

72. See Wang, preface, *Qingshu jingtan*.

73. Herman Rapaport, *Later Derrida: Reading the Recent Works* (New York: Routledge, 2003), 31. See p. 29 for Levinas's discussion of how language as a house protects one's being.

74. Hent de Vries has argued that resorting to one's own religious tradition is a way through which one hopes to solve some urgent problems. See his *Philosophy and the Turn to Religion* (Baltimore: Johns Hopkins University Press, 1999), xii. This kind of turn seems to apply to all people and all times. As a matter of fact, Wang Qiyuan was certainly just one of those who would turn to religion for a solution to the foreigner problem.

75. See Hu Houxuan 胡厚宣, "Yin buci zhong de Shangdi he Wangdi" 殷卜辭中的上帝和王帝 (上、下), *Lishi yanjiu* 歷史研究 9–10 (1959): 23–50, 89–110; Chen Mengjia 陳夢家, *Yinxu buci zongshu* 殷墟卜辭綜述 (Beijing: Zhonghua, 2004), 561–81.

76. Ricci, *The True Meaning of the Lord of Heaven*, 125.

77. With the words already quoted as this chapter's epigraph, Derrida reminds the reader that a decision that seems to be something free, active, and sovereign is actually not. See Derrida, *Politics of Friendship*, 62–63. See also Critchley, *Ethics, Politics, Subjectivity*, 254–87.

78. "《繫辭》又曰:'河出圖,洛出書。聖人則之。自古立教,未有天人親相授者,則此圖書者,非天所親授於聖人之秘密乎？夫二氏百家大抵興於中古之後,而肇於開闢之初,則惟儒者獨也。二氏百家,自我作祖,特師徒相授受耳。而得之天地之所親授,則又惟儒者獨也。故敘道統者,必推極於天地,而又實指天地之所親授,而後儒者之本原始定。" Wang, *Qingshu jingtan*, 2.2b–3a.

79. In the *Book of Changes*, one reads the following words from the Commentary on the Decision for the hexagram of Guan or View: "The holy man uses the divine way to give instruction, and the whole world submits to him" (聖人以神道設教,而天下服矣). *I Ching, or Book of Changes*, 486.

80. For examples of Wang's apotheosis of Confucius, see *Qingshu jingtan*, 8.2b, 1.8a–b, and 2.2b–3a.

81. See Derrida, *Politics of Friendship*, 68–69.

Conclusion

1. Quoted in Jonathan Spence, *Memory Palace of Matteo Ricci*, 268.

2. See the introduction for a quick reference to Schmitt's argument on the distinction of friends and enemies that determines his *The Concept of the Political*.

3. See O'Malley, *First Jesuits*, 76.

4. Quoted in Scaglione, *Liberal Arts*, 1.

5. Jacques Derrida, *Archive Fever: A Freudian Impression*, trans. Eric Prenowitz (Chicago: University of Chicago Press, 1995), 78.

6. Geoffrey Bennington and Jacques Derrida, *Jacques Derrida*, trans. Geoffrey Bennington (Chicago: University of Chicago Press, 1993), 76.

Selected Bibliography

Primary Texts by Jesuits and Early Missionaries

d'Elia, Pasquale M., SJ, ed. *Fonti Ricciane*. 3 vols. Rome: Libreria dello Stato, 1942–49.

Ignatius of Loyola. *The Constitutions of the Society of Jesus*. Translated by George E. Ganss, SJ. St. Louis: Institute of Jesuit Sources, 1970.

———. *The Spiritual Exercises*. Translated by George E. Ganss, SJ. In *Ignatius of Loyola: Spiritual Exercises and Selected Works*, edited by George E. Ganss, SJ, 113–214. New York: Paulist Press, 1991.

Martini, Martinus. *Qiuyou pian* 逑友篇 [A Treatise on Making Friends]. In *Tianzhujiao dongchuan wenxian sanbian* 天主教東傳文獻三編 [The Third Collection of Catholic Documents in China], edited by Wu Xiangxiang 吳湘湘 and Fang Hao 方豪, 1:1–88. Taibei: Xuesheng shuju, 1984.

Mingmo qingchu yesuhui sixiang wenxian huibian 明末清初耶穌會思想文獻匯編 [An Expository Collection on the Christian and the Anti-Christian Philosophical Manuscripts and Prints in Ming-Qing China], edited by Andrew Chung (鄭安德 Zheng Ande). 5 vols. Beijing: Beijing daxue zongjiao yanjiu suo, 2003.

Ricci, Matteo. *China in the Sixteenth Century: The Journals of Matthew Ricci, 1583–1610*. Translated by Louis J. Gallagher, SJ. New York: Random House, 1953.

———. *Ershiwu yan* 二十五言 [Twenty-Five Discourses]. In *Tianxue chuhan* 天學初函 [The First Collection of Catholic Teachings], edited by Li Zhizao 李之藻 et al., 1:321–50. Taibei: Xuesheng shuju, 1965.

———. *Jiaoyou lun* 交友論 [On Friendship]. In *Tianxue chuhan* 天學初函 [The First Collection of Catholic Teachings], edited by Li Zhizao 李之藻 et al., 1:291–320. Taibei: Xuesheng shuju, 1965.

———. *Le sens réel de "Seigneur du Ciel."* Translated and edited by Thierry Meynard. Paris: Belles lettres, 2013.

———. *Lettere del Manoscritto Maceratese*, edited by Chiara Zeuli. Macerata: Centro Studi Ricciani, 1985.

———. *Li Madou kunyu wanguo quantu* 利瑪竇坤輿萬國全圖 (Matteo Ricci's World-Map in Chinese, 1602). Beijing: Yugong xuehui, 1936.

———. *On Friendship: One Hundred Maxims for a Chinese Prince*. Translated by Timothy Billings. New York: Columbia University Press, 2009.

———. *Tianzhu shiyi* 天主實義 [The True Meaning of the Lord of Heaven]. In *Tianxue chuhan* 天學初函 [The First Collection of Catholic Teachings], edited by Li Zhizao 李之藻 et al., 1:351–636. Taibei: Xuesheng shuju, 1965.

———. *The True Meaning of the Lord of Heaven*. Translated by Douglas Lancashire and Peter Hu Kuo-chen, SJ. Edited by Edward J. Malatesta, SJ. St. Louis: Institute of Jesuit Sources, 1985.

Vagnoni, Alphonsus. *Dadao jiyan* 達道記言 [Recorded Sayings of (Sages Who Have Achieved) Comprehension of the Way]. In *Tianzhujiao dongchuan wenxian sanbian* 天主教東傳文獻三編 [The Third Collection of Catholic Documents in China], edited by Wu Xiangxiang 吳相湘 and Fang Hao 方豪, 2:567–754. Taibei: Xuesheng shuju, 1984.

———. *Jesuit Chreia in Late Ming China: Two Studies with an Annotated Translation of Alfonso Vagnone's Illustrations of the Grand Dao*. Translated by Thierry Meynard and Li Sher-shiueh. Bern: Peter Lang, 2014.

Venturi, Pietro Tacchi, ed. *Opere storiche del P. Matteo Ricci, SJ*. 2 vols. Macerata: F. Giorgetti, 1911–13.

Secondary Texts in Chinese

Ban Gu 班固, comp. *Baihu tong shuzheng* 白虎通疏證. 2 vols. Beijing: Zhonghua shuju, 1994.

Bao Zunpeng 包遵彭, ed. *Mingdai guoji guanxi* 明代國際關係. Taibei: Xuesheng shuju, 1968.

———, ed. *Mingdai zongjiao* 明代宗教. Taibei: Xuesheng shuju, 1968.

Chen Guying 陳鼓應, Xin Guanjie 辛冠潔, and Ge Rongjin 葛榮晉, gen. eds. *Mingqing shixue sichao shi* 明清實學思潮史. 3 vols. Jinan: Qilu shushe, 1989.

Chen Shouyi 陳受頤. "Sanbainian qian de jianli kongjiao lun" 三百年前的建立孔教論. *Lishi yuyan yanjiu suo jikan* 歷史語言所集刊 6, no. 2 (1936): 133–62.

Chen Yuan 陳垣. *Chen yuan xueshu lunwen ji* 陳垣學術論文集. 2 vols. Beijing: Zhonghua shuju, 1980–82.

Chen Zilong 陳子龍, Xu Fuyuan 徐孚遠, and Song Zhengbi 宋征璧, eds. *Ming jingshi wenbian* 明經世文編. 1639. Reprint. Hong Kong: Zhuji shudian, 1964.

Chen Zungui 陳遵媯. *Zhongguo tianwen xue shi* 中國天文學史. 2 vols. Shanghai: Shanghai renmin chubanshe, 2016.

Cheng Hao 程顥 and Cheng Yi 程頤. *Er cheng ji* 二程集. 2 vols. Beijing: Zhonghua shuju, 1981.

Ding Weizhi 丁偉志 and Chen Song 陳崧. *Zhong ti xi yong zhijian: wan Qing wenhua sichao shulun* 中體西用之間——晚清文化思潮述論. Beijing: Shehui kexue wenxian chubanshe, 2011.

Dong Zhongshu 董仲舒. *Chunqiu fanlu* 春秋繁露義證. Beijing: Zhonghua shuju, 1992.

Fang Hao 方豪. *Fang Hao liushi ziding gao* 方豪六十自定稿. 2 vols. Taibei: Published by the author, 1969.

———. *Zhongguo tianzhujiao renwuzhuan* 中國天主教人物傳. Beijing: Zongjiao wenhua chubanshe, 2007.

Fang Yizhi 方以智. *Tong ya* 通雅. Beijing: Zhongguo shudian, 1990.

Feng Youlan 馮友蘭. *Zhongguo zhexue shi* 中國哲學史. 2 vols. Hong Kong: Sanlian shudian, 1992.

Gu Yingtai 谷應泰. *Mingshi jishi benmo* 明史紀事本末. 4 vols. Beijing: Zhonghua shuju, 1985.

Gujin tushu jicheng 古今圖書集成. Compiled by Chen Menglei 陳夢雷 et al. 800 vols. Taibei: Wenxing shudian, 1950.

Han Qi 韓琦. "Bai Jin de Yijing yanjiu he Kangxi shidai de xixue zhongyuan shuo" 白晉的易經研究和康熙時代的西學中源說. *Hanxue yanjiu* 漢學研究 16, no. 1 (1998): 185–201.

———. "Cong *Ming shi* lizhi de zuanxiu kan xixue zai Zhongguo de chuanbo" 從明史歷志看西學在中國的傳播. In *Keshi chuanxin* 科史傳薪, edited by Liu Dunta 劉鈍他, 61–70. Shenyang: Liaoning jiaoyu chubanshe, 1997.

Huang Bolu 黃伯祿. *Zhengjiao fengbo* 正教奉褒. Shanghai: Shanghai cimu tang, 1905.

———, ed. *Zhengjiao fengchuan* 正教奉傳. Shanghai: Shanghai cimu tang, 1908.

Huang Yi-Long 黃一農. *Liangtoushe: Mingmo qingchu de diyidai tianzhu jiaotu* 兩頭蛇—明末清初第一代天主教徒. 3rd rev. ed. Xinzhu: Tsihua University Press, 2014.

Huang Yuji 黃虞稷. *Qianqing tang shumu* 千頃堂書目, edited by Qu Fengqi 瞿鳳起 and Peng Yingzheng 潘景鄭. Shanghai: Shanghai guji chubanshe, 1990.

Huang Yunmei 黃雲眉. *Mingshi kaozheng* 明史考證. 8 vols. Beijing: Zhonghua shuju, 1979.

Huang Zongxi 黃宗羲. *Mingru xue'an* 明儒學案. Rev. ed. 2 vols. Beijing: Zhonghua shuju, 2008.

Huang Zongxi and Quan Zuwang 全祖望. *Song yuan xue'an* 宋元學案. 4 vols. Beijing: Zhonghua shuju, 1986.

Hung Ye 洪業 (William Hung). "Kao Li Madou de shijie ditu" 考利瑪竇的世界地圖. In *Hung Ye lunxue ji* 洪業論學集, edited by Weng Dujian 翁獨健 and Wang Zhonghan 王鍾翰, 150–92. Beijing: Zhonghua shuju, 1981.

Ji Wende 計文德. *Cong Siku quanshu tanjiu Ming qing jian shuru zhi xixue* 從四庫全書探究明清間輸入之西學. Taibei: Hanmei tushu youxian gongsi, 1991.

Jiao Hong 焦竑. *Danyuan ji* 澹園集. 2 vols. Beijing: Zhonghua shuju, 1999.

Li Shen 李申. *Zhongguo rujiao shi* 中國儒教史. 2 vols. Shanghai: Shanghai renmin chubanshe, 1999–2000.

Li Sher-shiueh 李奭學. *Ming qing xixue liu lun* 明清西學六論. Hangzhou: Zhejiang daxue chubanshe, 2016.

———. *Yishu: Mingmo qingchu yesuhui fanyi wenxue lun* 譯述—明末清初耶穌會翻譯文學論. Hong Kong: The Chinese University Press, 2012.

Li Tiangang 李天綱. *Zhongguo liyi zhizheng: Lishi, wenxian he yiyi* 中國禮儀之爭—歷史, 文獻和意義. Shanghai: Shanghai guji chubanshe, 1998.

Li Zhi 李贄. *Feng shu* 焚書, *Xu feng shu* 續焚書. Beijing: Zhonghua, 1974.

Liang Jiamian 梁家勉. *Xu Guangqi nianpu* 徐光啟年譜. Shanghai: Shanghai guji chubanshe, 1981.

Liang Qichao 梁啟超. *Zhongguo jin sanbainian xueshu shi* 中國近三百年學術史. Shanghai: Shanghai sanlian shudian, 2006.

Liu Lu 劉潞, ed. *Qing gong xiyang yiqi* 清宮西洋儀器. Shanghai: Shanghai kexue jishu chubanshe, 1999.

Liu Tong 劉侗 and Yu Yizhen 于奕正. *Dijing jingwu lüe* 帝京景物略. Beijing: Guji chubanshe, 1983.

Long Wenbin 龍文彬, comp. *Ming huiyao* 明會要. 2 vols. Beijing: Zhonghua shuju, 1957.

Luo Guang 羅光. *Li Madou zhuan* 利瑪竇傳. Taibei: Guangqi chubanshe, 1966.

Mei Qianli 梅謙立, ed., Ming Xu Dashou Shengchao zuobi jiaozhu 明許大受《聖朝佐闢》校注. Gaoxiong: Foguang wenhua, 2018.

Meng Sen 孟森. *Ming dai shi* 明代史. Taibei: Zhonghua congshu weiyuan hui, 1957.

Miao Yonghe 繆詠禾. *Mingdai chuban shigao* 明代出版史稿. Suzhou: Jiangsu renmin chubanshe, 2000.

Ming shilu 明實錄. Taibei: Zhongyang yanjiu yuan lishi yuyan yanjiu suo, 1962–66.

Qian Hang 錢杭. "Li Zhi yu Li Madou de jici huijian" Xuelin menlu" 李贄與利瑪竇的幾次會見, *Xuelin manlu* 學林漫錄 3 (1981): 92–97.

Qian Mu 錢穆. *Zhongguo ji sanbainian xueshu shi* 中國近三百年學術史. 2 vols. Taibei: Shangwu yinshu guan, 1997.

Qian Zhongshu 錢鍾書. *Guanzhuibian* 管錐編. 5 vols. Beijing: Zhonghua shuju, 1979.

———. *Qizhuiji* 七綴集. Shanghai: Shanghai guji chubanshe, 1985.

Qu Dajun 屈大均. *Guangdong xinyu* 廣東新語. 2 vols. Beijing: Zhonghua shuju, 1985.

Rao Zongyi 饒宗頤. *Zhongguo shixue shang zhi zhengtong lun* 中國史學上之正統論. Beijing: Zhonghua shuju, 2015.

Ren Jiyu 任繼愈, ed. *Zhongguo fojiao shi* 中國佛教史. 3 vols. to date. Beijing: Zhongguo shehui kexue chubanshe, 1985.

Ruan Yuan 阮元. *Chouren zhuan* 疇人傳. 4 vols. Shanghai: Shangwu yishu guan chubanshe, 1955.

———, ed. *Shisan jing zhushu* 十三經注疏. 8 vols. Taibei: Yiwen yinshuguan, 2011.

Shen Dufu 沈德符. *Wanli yehuo bian* 萬曆野獲編. 3 vols. Beijing: Zhonghua shuju, 1999.

Shen Shixing 申時行, et al., comps. *Da Ming huidian* 大明會典, 5 vols. Taibei: Huawen shuju, 1964.

Su Yu 蘇輿, comp. *Yijiao congbian* 翼教叢編. Shanghai: Shanghai shudian chubanshe, 2002.

Tan Qixiang 譚其驤. *Changshui ji* 長水集. 2 vols. Beijing: Renmin chuanshe, 1987.

———. *Changshui ji xubian* 長水集續編. Beijing: Renmin chubanshe, 1994.
Tang Kaijian 湯開建, ed. *Li Madou: Ming qing Zhongwen wenxian ziliao huishi* 利瑪竇—明清中文文獻資料匯釋. Shanghai: Shanghai guji chubanshe, 2017.
Wang Gang 王崗. *Langman qinggan yu zongjiao jingshen—Wan Ming wenxue yu wenhua sichao* 浪漫情感與宗教精神—晚明文學與文化思潮. Hong Kong: Tiandi tushu youxian gongsi, 1999.
Wang Kentang 王肯堂. *Yugang zhai bichen* 鬱崗齋筆麈. Beiping: Guoli Beiping tushu guan, 1930.
Wang Qiyuan 王啟元. *Qingshu jingtan·yiji* 清署經談·一集. N.p. Preface dated 1623.
Wang Shouren 王守仁. *Wang Yangming ji* 王陽明集. 2 vols. Shanghai: Shanghai guji chubanshe, 1997.
Xia Xie 夏燮. *Ming tongjian* 明通鑑. 3 vols. Changsha: Yuelu shushe, 1999.
Xie Guozhen 謝國楨. *Ming qing zhiji dangshe yundong kao* 明清之際党社運動考. Beijing: Zhonghua shuju, 1981.
———. *Zengding wan Ming shiji kao* 增訂晚明史籍考. Shanghai: Shanghai guji chubanshe, 1981.
Xie Zhaozhe 謝肇淛. *Wuzazu* 五雜組. Shenyang: Liaoning jiaoyu chubanshe, 2001.
Xu Guangqi 徐光啟. *Xu Guangqi ji* 徐光啟集. Edited by Wang Zhongmin 王重民. Shanghai: Shanghai guji chubanshe, 1984.
———. *Zengding Xu Wending gong ji* 增訂徐文定公集. Edited by Li Duo 李杕. Taibei: Zhonghua shuju, 1962.
Xu Zongze 徐宗澤. *Ming qing jian yesuhui shi yizhu tiyao* 明清間耶穌會士譯著提要. Shanghai: Tushanwan yinshuguan, 1938. Shanghai: Shanghai shudian, 1990.
———. *Zhongguo tianzhujiao shi gailun* 中國天主教史概論. Shanghai: Shanghai shuju, 1990.
Xunzi 荀子. *Xunzi jijie* 荀子集解, compiled by Wang Xianqian 王先謙. 2 vols. Beijing: Zhonghua shuju, 1988.
Yong Rong 永瑢 et al., comps. *Siku quanshu zongmu tiyao* 四庫全書總目提要. 2 vols. Beijing: Zhonghua shuju, 1983.
You Tong 尤侗. *Ming shi waiguo zhuan* 明史外國傳. Taibei: Xuesheng shuju, 1977.
Yu Dong [余東]. *Catalogo delle opere cinesi missionarie della Biblioteca Apostolica Vaticana (16–18 sec.)* 梵蒂岡圖書館藏早期傳教士中文文獻目錄 （十六至十八世紀）. Città del Vaticano: Biblioteca Apostolica Vaticana, 1996.
Yu Zhengxie 俞正燮. *Yu Zhengxie quanji* 俞正燮全集. Hefei: Huangshan shushe, 2005.
Zhang Fengzhen 張奉箴. *Fuyin liuchuan Zhongguo shilue* 福音流傳中國史略. 2 vols. Taibei: Fujen University Press, 1970–71.
Zhang Tingyu 張廷玉 et al. *Ming shi* 明史. 28 vols. Beijing: Zhonghua shuju, 1974.
Zhang Weihua 張維華. *Ming qing zhiji zhong xi guanxi jianshi* 明清之際中西關係簡史. Jinan: Qilu shushe, 1987.
———. *Mingshi Ouzhou siguo zhuan zhushi* 明史歐洲四國傳注釋. Shanghai: Shanghai guji chubanshe, 1982.

Zhang Xinglang 張星烺. *Zhong xi jiaotong shiliao huibian* 中西交通史料彙編. 4 vols. Beijing: Zhonghua shuju, 2003.

Zhang Yongtang 張永堂. *Mingmo qingchu lixue yu kexue guanxi zailun* 明末清初理學與科學關係再論. Taibei: Xuesheng shuju, 1994.

Zhou Kangxie 周康燮, ed. *Li Madou yanjiu lunji* 利瑪竇研究論集. Hong Kong: Cuncui xueshe, 1971.

Zhu Weizhi 朱維之. "Yesuhui shi duiyu Songru lixue zhi fanxiang" 耶穌會士對於宋儒理學之反響. *Shixue zhuankan* 史學專刊 3, no. 1 (1936): 5–40.

Secondary Texts in English and Other Western Languages

Acquabiva, Claudio. *The Directory to the Spiritual Exercises* (1599). In *The Spiritual Exercises of Saint Ignatius of Loyola*. Translated by W. H. Longridge, 273–351. London: Mowbray, 1950.

Alles, Gregory D., ed. *Religious Studies: A Global View*. London: Routledge, 2008.

Ames, Roger T. *Confucian Role Ethics: A Vocabulary*. Hong Kong: Chinese University Press, 2011.

Amsler, Nadine. *Jesuits and Matriarchs: Domestic Worship in Early Modern China*. Seattle: University of Washington Press, 2018.

Anderson, Benedict. *Imagined Communities: Reflections on the Origin and Spread of Nationalism*. Rev. ed. London: Verso, 1991.

Aquinas, Thomas. *Summa Theologica*. Translated by Fathers of the English Dominican Province. 3 vols. London: Burns and Oates, 1947–48.

Arendt, Hannah. *Love and Saint Augustine*. Edited by Joanna Vecchiarelli Scott and Judith Chelius Stark. Chicago: University of Chicago Press, 1996.

Aristarkhova, Irina. *Hospitality of the Matrix: Philosophy, Biomedicine and Culture*. New York: Columbia University Press, 2012.

Aristotle. *The Complete Works of Aristotle*. Edited by Jonathan Barnes. 2 vols. Princeton, NJ: Princeton University Press, 1984.

Asad, Talal. *Formations of the Secular: Christianity, Islam, Modernity*. Stanford, CA: Stanford University Press, 2003.

———. *Genealogies of Religion: Discipline and Reasons of Power in Christianity and Islam*. Baltimore: Johns Hopkins University Press, 1993.

Augustine. *Confessions*. Translated by William Watts. 2 vols. Loeb Classical Library. Cambridge, MA: Harvard University Press, 1977–88.

Baker, Donald L. "Neo-Confucians Confront Theism: Korean Reactions to Matteo Ricci's Arguments for the Existence of God." *Journal of the Institute for East Asian Studies* 2 (1983): 157–79.

Bangert, William, SJ. *A History of the Society of Jesus*. St. Louis: Institute of Jesuit Sources, 1972.

Barkas, Janet L. *Friendship: A Selected Annotated Bibliography*. New York: Garland, 1985.
Barthes, Roland. *How to Live Together: Novelistic Simulations of Some Everyday Spaces*. Translated by Kate Briggs. New York: Columbia University Press, 2012.
———. *Sade, Fourier, Loyola*. Translated by Richard Miller. Berkeley: University of California Press, 1976.
Bay, Daniel H. *A New History of Christianity in China*. Malden, MA: Wiley-Blackwell, 2012.
Belloc, Hilaire. *On Translation*. Oxford: Clarendon, 1931.
Bennington, Geoffrey, and Jacques Derrida. *Jacques Derrida*. Translated by Geoffrey Bennington. Chicago: University of Chicago Press, 1993.
Bernard, Henri, SJ. *Le père Matthieu Ricci et la société chinoise de son temps (1551–1610)*. 2 vols. Tientsin: Haute études, 1937.
———. *Matteo Ricci's Scientific Contribution to China*. Translated by Edward Chalmers Werner. Peking: Vetch, 1935.
Bettray, Johannes, SVD. *Die Akkommodationsmethode des P. Matteo Ricci S.I. in China*. Rome: Gregorian University, 1955.
Blanchot, Maurice. *L'amitié*. Paris: Gallimard, 1971.
Blussé, Leonard, and Harriet T. Zurndorfer, eds. *Conflict and Accommodation in Early Modern East Asia: Essays in Honour of Erik Zürcher*. Leiden: Brill, 1993.
Boer, Wietse de, Karl A. E. Enenkel, and Walter S. Melion, eds. *Jesuit Image Theory*. Leiden: Brill, 2016.
Borel, Henri. "Serment d'amitie chinois." *T'oung Pao* 4 (1893): 420–46.
Boxer, Charles R. *The Church Militant and Iberian Expansion, 1440–1770*. Baltimore: Johns Hopkins University Press, 1978.
———. *Portuguese Conquest and Commerce in Southern Asia, 1500–1750*. London: Variorum, 1985.
Boyle, Marjorie O'Rouke. *The Human Spirit: Beginnings from Genesis to Science*. University Park: Pennsylvania State University Press, 2018.
———. *Loyola's Acts: The Rhetoric of the Self*. Berkeley: University of California Press, 1997.
Breitenbach, Sandra. *Missionary Linguistics in East Asia: The Origins of Religious Language in the Shaping of Christianity?* Berlin: Peter Lang, 2008.
Brockey, Liam Matthew. *Journey to the East: The Jesuit Mission to China, 1579–1724*. Cambridge, MA: Harvard University Press, 2007.
Brou, Alexandre, SJ. "Les tatonnements du père Matthieu Ricci." *Revue d'histoire des missions* 15 (1938): 228–44.
Burke, Kenneth. *The Rhetoric of Religion: Studies in Logology*. Berkeley: University of California Press, 1970.
Canclini, Néstor García. *Imagined Globalization*. Translated by Geoge Yúdice. Durham, NC: Duke University Press, 2014.

Caputo, John D. *The Prayers and Tears of Jacques Derrida: Religion without Religion.* Bloomington: Indiana University Press, 1997.
———, ed. *The Religious.* Malden, MA: Blackwell, 2002.
Caputo, John D., Mark Dooley, and Michael J. Scanlon, eds. *Questioning God.* Bloomington: Indiana University Press, 2001.
Caputo, John D., and Michael J. Scanlon, eds. *God, the Gift, and Postmodernism.* Bloomington: Indiana University Press, 1999.
Cartier, Michel. "Aux origines de la politique des lumières: La Chine vue par Matteo Ricci." In *Les rapports entre la Chine et l'Europe au temps des lumiéres: Actes du IIe Colloque international de sinologie*, 39–48. Paris: Les Belles Lettres, 1980.
Cary-Elwes, Columba, OSB. *China and the Cross: A Survey of Missionary History.* New York: Kennedy, 1956.
Cassin, Barbara. *Nostalgia: When Are We Ever at Home?* Translated by Pascale-Anne Brault. New York: Fordham University Press, 2016.
Catto, Michela. "The Tridentine Decrees Interpret the Chinese Rites." In *Trent and Beyond: The Council, Other Powers, Other Cultures*, edited by Michela Catto and Adriano Prosperi, 501–18. Turnhout, Belgium: Brepols, 2017.
Chan, Albert, SJ. *Chinese Books and Documents in the Jesuit Archives in Rome: A Descriptive Catalogue.* Armonk, NY: Sharpe, 2002.
Chan, Sin-wai, and David E. Pollard, eds. *An Encyclopedia of Translation: Chinese-English, English-Chinese.* Hong Kong: Chinese University Press, 2001.
Chapple, Christopher. *The Jesuit Tradition in Education and Missions: A 450-Year Perspective.* London: Associated University Presses, 1993.
Charbonnier, Jean, MEP. "China-Christian Relations in the Spirit of Matteo Ricci." *Tripod* 12 (1982): 102–11.
Chen, Kenneth. *The Chinese Transformation of Buddhism.* Princeton, NJ: Princeton University Press, 1973.
Chen, Sanping. *Multicultural China in the Early Middle Age.* Philadelphia: University of Pennsylvania Press, 2012.
Ching, Julia. *Chinese Religions.* Maryknoll, NY: Orbis, 1993.
Cicero. *De amicitia.* Translated by William Armistead Falconer. Loeb Classical Library. Cambridge, MA: Harvard University Press, 1938.
———. *De oratore.* Translated by E. W. Sutton. 2 vols. Loeb Classical Library. Cambridge, MA: Harvard University Press, 1959.
———. *Tusculan Disputations.* Translated by J. E. King. Loeb Classical Library. Cambridge, MA: Harvard University Press, 1996.
Cigliano, Maria, ed. *Atti del Convegno internazionale di studi ricciani, Macerata-Roma, 22–25 Ottobre 1982.* Macerata, Italy: Centro studi ricciani, 1982.
Clifford, James, and George E. Marcus, eds. *Writing Culture: The Poetics and Politics of Ethnography.* Berkeley: University of California Press, 1986.
Confucius. *The Analects.* Translated by D. C. Lau. London: Penguin, 1979.

Connor, Steven. *Theory and Cultural Value*. Oxford: Blackwell, 1992.
Cooper, John M. "Aristotle on the Forms of Friendship." *Review of Metaphysics* 30, no. 4 (1977): 619–48.
Coward, Harold, and Toby Foshay, eds. *Derrida and Negative Theology*. Albany: State University of New York Press, 1992.
Cracknell, Kenneth. *Justice, Courtesy and Love: Theologians and Missionaries Encountering World Religions, 1846–1914*. London: Epworth, 1995.
Creel, Herrlee G. *The Origins of Statecraft in China*, vol. 1, *The Western Chou Empire*. Chicago: University of Chicago Press, 1970.
Critchley, Simon. *Ethics, Politics, Subjectivity: Essays on Derrida, Levinas and Contemporary French Thought*. London: Verso, 1999.
Criveller, Gianni. *Preaching Christ in Late Ming China: The Jesuits' Presentation of Christ from Matteo Ricci to Giulio Aleni*. Taibei: Ricci Institute for Chinese Studies, 1997.
Cummins, J. S. *A Question of Rites: Friar Domingo Navarrete and the Jesuits in China*. Aldershot, UK: Scolar Press, 1993.
Dalmases, Cándido de. *Ignatius of Loyola, Founder of the Jesuits: His Life and Work*. Translated by Jerome Aixalá. St. Louis: Institute of Jesuit Sources, 1985.
Davis, Walter. *All under Heaven: The Chinese World in Maps, Pictures and Text in the Collection of Floyd Sully*. Edmonton: University of Alberta Libraries, 2013.
Dawson, Christopher. *Mission to Asia: Narratives and Letters of the Franciscan Missionaries in Mongolia and China in the Thirteenth and Fourteenth Centuries*. New York: Harper and Row, 1966.
de Bary, W. Theodore, ed. *Self and Society in Ming Thought*. New York: Columbia University Press, 1970.
Dehergne, Joseph, SJ. *Répertoire des Jésuites de Chine de 1552 à 1800*. Bibliotheca Instituti Historici SI 37. Rome: Institutum Historicum SI, 1973.
Dehergne, Joseph, SJ, and Donald Daniel Leslie. "Le traité de l'amitié de Matthieu Ricci." *Bulletin de l'Université de l'Aurore* 8 (1947): 571–619.
d'Elia, Pasquate M., SJ. "Further Notes on Matteo Ricci's *De amicitia*." *Monumenta Serica* 15, no. 2 (1956): 356–77.
———. *Galileo in China*. Translated by Rufus Suter and Matthew Sciascia. Cambridge, MA: Harvard University Press, 1960.
———. "Il trattato sull'amicizia 交友論: Primo Libro scritto in cinese da Matteo Ricci S. I. (1595)." *Studia Missionalia* 7 (1952): 425–515.
———. "Recent Discoveries and New Studies (1938–1960) on the World Map in Chinese of Father Matteo Ricci SJ." *Monumenta Serica* 20 (1961): 82–164.
de Man, Paul. *The Allegories of Reading: Figural language in Rousseau, Nietzsche, Rilke, and Proust*. New Haven, CT: Yale University Press, 1979.
———. *Blindness and Insight: Essays in the Rhetoric of Contemporary Criticism*. 2nd ed., rev. Minneapolis: University of Minnesota Press, 1983.

Demarchi, Franco, and Riccardo Scartezzini, eds. *Martino Martini: A Humanist and Scientist in Seventeenth Century China*. Trento, Italy: Università degli studi di Trento, 1994.
Derrida, Jacques. *Adieu to Emmanuel Levinas*. Translated by Pascale-Anne Brault and Michael Naas. Stanford, CA: Stanford University Press, 1999.
———. "Des Tours de Babel." In *Difference in Translation*. Edited by Joseph F. Graham, 165–248. Ithaca, NY: Cornell University Press, 1985.
———. *The Gift of Death and Literature in Secret*. Translated by David Wills. 2nd ed. Chicago: University of Chicago Press, 2008.
———. *Mémoires: For Paul de Man*. New York: Columbia University Press, 1986.
———. *Of Hospitality*. Translated by Rachel Bowlby. Stanford, CA: Stanford University Press, 2000.
———. *The Other Heading: Reflections on Today's Europe*. Translated by Pascale-Anne Brault and Michael B. Naas. Indianapolis: Indiana University Press, 1992.
———. *Politiques de l'amitié*. Paris: Galilée, 1994. Translated by George Collins as *The Politics of Friendship* (London: Verso, 1997).
———. *Psyche: Inventions of the Other*. Edited by Peggy Kamuf and Elizabeth Rottenberg. 2 vols. Stanford, CA: Stanford University Press, 2007.
———. *Writing and Difference*. Translated by Alan Bass. Chicago: University of Chicago Press, 1978.
Derrida, Jacques, and Gianni Vattimo, eds. *Religion*. Stanford, CA: Stanford University Press, 1996.
Donohue, John W. *Jesuit Education: An Essay on the Foundations of Its Idea*. New York: Fordham University Press, 1963.
Duddon, Paul. *St. Ignatius Loyola*. Translated by William J. Young. Milwaukee: Bruce, 1949.
Dunne, George H. *Generation of Giants: The Story of the Jesuits in China in the Last Decades of the Ming Dynasty*. Notre Dame, IN: University of Notre Dame Press, 1962.
During, Simon, ed. *The Cultural Studies Reader*. London: Routledge, 1993.
Eco, Umberto. *The Search for the Perfect Language*. Translated by James Fentress. Oxford: Blackwell, 1997.
Eliade, Mircea. *The Myth of the Eternal Return; or, Cosmos and History*. Translated by Willard R. Trask. Princeton, NJ: Princeton University Press, 1991.
———. *Patterns in Comparative Religion*. Translated by Rosemary Sheed. London: Sheed and Ward, 1997.
Eno, Robert. *The Confucian Creation of Heaven*. Albany: State University of New York Press, 1990.
Evennett, H. Outram. *The Spirit of the Counter-Reformation*. Edited by John Bossy. Cambridge: Cambridge University Press, 1968.
Fang Hao. "Notes on Matteo Ricci's *De amicitia*." *Monumenta Serica* 14, no. 1 (1949): 574–83.

Farrell, Allan P. *The Jesuit Code of Liberal Education: Development and Scope of the Ratio Studiorum*. Milwaukee: Bruce, 1938.
Feingold, Mordechai, ed. *Jesuit Science and the Republic of Letters*. Cambridge, MA: MIT Press, 2002.
Fontana, Michela. *Matteo Ricci: A Jesuit in the Ming Court*. New York: Rowman and Littlefield, 2015.
Foss, Theodore Nicholas. "Nicholas Trigault, SJ—Amanuensis or Propagandist? The Rôle of the Editor of *Della entrata della Compagnia di Giesù e Christianità nella Cina*." In *International Symposium on Chinese-Western Cultural Interchange in Commemoration of the 400th Anniversary of the Arrival of Matteo Ricci, SJ in China*, supplement, 1–94. Taibei: Fu Jen University Press, 1983.
———. "Ricci's World Map: The 1602 *Kunyu Wanguo Quantu*." In *China at the Center: Ricci and Verbiest World Maps*, edited by Natasha Reichle, 17–27. San Fransciso: Asian Art Museum, 2016.
Franke, Otto. *Li Tschi und Matteo Ricci*. Berlin: Akademie der Wissenschaften, 1939.
Frye, Northrop. *The Great Code: The Bible and Literature*. London: Penguin, 1983.
———. *Words with Power: Being a Second Study of the Bible and Literature*. London: Penguin, 1990.
Gallagher, Louis Joseph, SJ. *The China That Was: China as Discovered by the Jesuits at the Close of the Sixteenth Century*. Milwaukee: Bruce, 1942.
Gammon, Roland, ed. *All Believers Are Brothers*. New York: Doubleday, 1969.
Gang, Song. *Giulio Aleni, Kouduo richao, and Christian-Confucian Dialogism in Late Ming Fujian*. Monumenta Serica Monograph 69. Abingdon, UK: Routledge, 2019.
Gernet, Jacques. *China and the Christian Impact: A Conflict of Cultures*. Translated by Janet Lloyd. Cambridge: Cambridge University Press, 1985.
———. "La politique de conversion de Matteo Ricci et l'évolution de la vie politique et intellectuelle en Chine aux environs de 1600." *Archives des sciences sociologiques des religions* 36 (1973): 71–89.
Giles, Lionel. "Translation from the Chinese World Map of Father Ricci." *Geographical Journal* 52, no. 6 (December 1918): 367–85; 53, no. 1 (January 1919): 19–30.
Gillman, Ian, and Hans-Joachim Klimkeit. *Christians in Asia before 1500*. Ann Arbor: University of Michigan Press, 1999.
Goodman, Howard L., and Anthony Grafton. "Ricci, the Chinese, and the Toolkits of Textualists." *Asia Major*, 3rd ser., 3, no. 2 (1990): 95–148.
Goodrich, L. Carrington, and Chaoying Fang, eds. *Dictionary of Ming Biography*. 2 vols. New York: Columbia University Press, 1976.
Graham, A. C. *Disputers of the Tao: Philosophical Argument in Ancient China*. La Salle, IL: Open Court, 1989.
Greenblatt, Stephen. *Marvelous Possessions: The Wonder of the New World*. Chicago: University of Chicago Press, 1991.

Grendler, Paul F. *Schooling in Renaissance Italy: Literacy and Learning, 1300–1600.* Baltimore: Johns Hopkins University Press, 1989.

Grossberg, Lawrence, Cary Nelson, and Paula A. Treichler, eds. *Cultural Studies.* London: Routledge, 1992.

Guibert, Joseph de. *The Jesuits: Their Spiritual Doctrine and Practice.* Translated by William J. Young. Chicago: Loyola University Press, 1964.

Habermas, Jürgen. *Religion and Rationality: Essays on Reason, God, and Modernity.* Edited by Eduardo Mendieta. Cambridge, MA: MIT Press, 2002.

Hall, David L., and Roger T. Ames. *Anticipating China: Thinking through the Narratives of Chinese and Western Culture.* Albany: State University of New York Press, 1995.

Hang, Thaddeus T. C. "Ricci's Critique of the Concept of 'Tai-Chi.'" In *International Symposium on Chinese-Western Cultural Interchange in Commemoration of the 400th Anniversary of the Arrival of Matteo Ricci, SJ, in China,* 267–79. Taibei: Fu Jen University Press, 1983.

Hao, Guiyuan. "How Friendship Is Made in the West and in China." In *Martino Martini: A Humanist and Scientist in Seventeenth Century China,* edited by Franco Demarchi and Riccardo Scartezzini, 211–20. Trento: Università degli studi di Trento, 1996.

Harnack, Adolf von. *The Mission and Expansion of Christianity in the First Three Centuries.* 2 vols. New York: Putman, 1908.

Harris, George L. "The Mission of Matteo Ricci, S. J.: A Case Study of an Effort at Guided Culture Change in the Sixteenth Century." *Monumenta Serica* 25, no. 1 (1966): 1–168.

Hart, Roger. *Imagined Civilizations: China, the West, and Their First Encounter.* Baltimore: Johns Hopkins University Press, 2013.

Hastings, Adrian, ed. *A World History of Christianity.* London: Cassell, 1999.

Heidegger, Martin. *The Basic Problems of Phenomenology.* Translated, introduction, and lexicon by Albert Hofstadter. Bloomington: Indiana University Press, 1982.

———. "Die Frage, wo die Freunde sind, und das Wesen der künftigen Freundschaft." In *Hölderlins Hymne "Andenken."* Gesamtausgabe vol. 52, edited by Curd Ochwadt, 166–69. Frankfurt-am-Main: Vittorio Klostermann, 1982.

Henderson, John B. *The Development and Decline of Chinese Cosmology.* New York: Columbia University Press, 1984.

Hermans, Theo. "Images of Translation: Metaphor and Imagery in the Renaissance Discourse on Translation." In *The Manipulation of Literature,* edited by Theo Hermans, 103–35. London: Croom Helm, 1985.

Hevia, James L. *Cherishing Men from Afar: Qing Guest Ritual and the Macartney Embassy of 1793.* Durham, NC: Duke University Press, 1995.

Heyking, John von. *The Form of Politics: Aristotle and Plato on Friendship.* Montreal: McGill-Queen's University Press, 2016.

Horner, Robyn. *Rethinking God as Gift: Marion, Derrida, and the Limits of Phenomenology.* New York: Fordham University Press, 2001.

Horton, Robin. "On the Rationality of Conversion." *Africa* 45 (1975): pt. 1, 219–35; pt. 2, 373–99.
Hucker, Charles, ed. *Chinese Government in Ming Times: Seven Studies*. New York: Columbia University Press, 1969.
———. *The Traditional Chinese State in Ming Times (1368–1644)*. Tucson: University of Arizona Press, 1957.
Hume, David. *Writings on Religion*. Edited by Antony Flew. Chicago: Open Court, 1996.
Hutter, Horst H. *Politics as Friendship: The Origins of Classical Notions of Politics in the Theory and Practice of Friendship*. Waterloo, ON: Wilfried Laurier University Press, 1978.
Hymes, Robert P. *Way and Byway: Taoism, Local Religion, and Models of Divinity in Sung and Modern China*. Berkeley: University of California Press, 2002.
Jami, Catherine. "Imperial Control and Western Learning: The Kangxi Emperor's Performance." *Late Imperial China* 23, no. 1 (2002): 28–49.
Jensen, Lionel M. *Manufacturing Confucianism: Chinese Tradition and Universal Civilization*. Durham, NC: Duke University Press, 1997.
Jordan, Mark. "The Names of God and the Being of Names." In *The Existence and Nature of God*, edited by Alfred J. Freddoso, 161–90. Notre Dame, IN: Notre Dame University Press, 1983.
Jung, Hwa Yol. "*Jen*: An Existential and Phenomenological Problem of Intersubjectivity." *Philosophy East and West* 16, no. 3/4 (July–October, 1966): 169–88.
Kakoliris, Gerasimos. "Jacques Derrida on the Ethics of Hospitality." In *The Ethics of Subjectivity: Perspectives since the Dawn of Modernity*, edited by Elvis Imafidon, 144–56. New York: Palgrave, 2015.
Kao, Karl S. Y. "*Bao* and *Baoying*: Narrative Causality and External Motivation in Chinese Fiction." *Chinese Literature: Essays, Articles, Reviews* 11 (1989): 115–38.
———. "Rhetoric." In *The Indiana Companion to Traditional Chinese Literature*, edited and compiled by William H. Nienhauser, Jr., 121–37. Bloomington: Indiana University Press, 1986.
Keightley, David N. *These Bones Shall Rise Again: Selected Writings on Early China*. Albany: State University of New York, 2014.
Kim, Sangkeun. *Strange Names of God: The Missionary Translation of the Divine Name and the Chinese Responses to Matteo Ricci's Shangti in Late Ming China, 1583–1644*. New York: Peter Lang, 2004.
Konstan, David. *Friendship in the Classical World*. Cambridge: Cambridge University Press, 1997.
Krahmer, Shawn Madison. "Interpreting the Letters of Bernard of Clairvaux to Ermengarde, Countess of Brittany: The Twelfth-Century Context and the Language of Friendship." *Cistercian Studies Quarterly* 27 (1992): 217–50.
Kristeller, Paul Oskar. *Renaissance Thought: The Classic, Scholastic, and Humanist Strains*. New York: Harper Torchbooks, 1961.

Lacouture, Jean. *Jesuits: A Multibiograhpy*. Translated by Jeremy Leggatt. Washington, DC: Counterpoint, 1995.
Lagerwey, John. *China: A Religious State*. Hong Kong: Hong Kong University Press, 2010.
———, ed. *Religion and Chinese Society*. Vol. 1, *Ancient and Medieval China*. Hong Kong: Chinese University Press, 2004.
Lagerwey, John, and Marc Kalinowski, eds. *Early Chinese Religion*. 4 vols. Leiden: Brill, 2010.
Laker, Mary Eugenia, ed. *Aelred of Rievaulx, Spiritual Friendship*. Kalamazoo, MI: Cistercian, 1974.
Latourette, Kenneth Scott. *A History of the Expansion of Christianity*. 7 vols. New York: Harper and Brothers, 1937–45.
Lawlor, Leonard, and Zeynep Direk, eds. *Jacques Derrida*. 3 vols. London: Routledge, 2002.
Leaman, Oliver, ed. *Friendship East and West: Philosophical Perspectives*. Richmond, UK: Curzon, 1996.
Leclercq, Jean. "L'amitié dans les lettres au Moyen Âge." *Revue du Moyen Âge latin* 1 (1945): 391–410.
———. *Monks and Love in Twelfth-Century France*. Oxford: Clarendon, 1979.
Lee, Matthew T., and Amos Yong, eds. *The Science and Theology of Godly Love*. Dekalb, IL: Northern Illinois University Press, 2012.
Lee, Peter K. H., ed. *Confucian-Christian Encounter in Historical and Contemporary Perspective*. Lewiston, NY: Edwin Mellen, 1991.
Lee, Thomas H. C., ed. *China and Europe: Images and Influences in Sixteenth to Eighteenth Centuries*. Hong Kong: Chinese University Press, 1991.
Legge, James. *The Chinese Classics*. 5 vols. Taibei: SMC, 1991.
———, trans. *Li Chi: Book of Rites*. 2 vols. Whitefish, MT: Kessinger, 2003.
Levenson, Joseph R. *Confucian China and Its Modern Fate: A Trilogy*. Berkeley: University of California Press, 1968.
Lévi-Strauss, Claude. *The Elementary Structures of Kinship*. Translated by James Harle Bell and John Ricard von Sturmer. Boston: Beacon, 1969.
Lippiello, Tiziana, and Roman Malek, eds. *"Scholar from the West": Giulio Aleni, SJ (1582–1649) and the Dialogue between Christianity and China*. Nettetal, Ger.: Steyler, 1997.
Liu, Lydia H., ed. *Tokens of Exchange: The Problem of Translation in Global Circulations*. Durham, NC: Duke University Press, 1999.
Lonsdale, David. *Eyes to See, Ears to Hear: An Introduction to Ignatian Spirituality*. Rev. ed. Maryknoll, NY: Orbis, 2000.
Lundbaek, Knud. "Chief Grand Secretary Chang Chü-cheng and the Early Jesuits." *China Mission Studies (1550–1800) Bulletin* 3 (1981): 2–11.
Mahmood, Saba. *Religious Difference in a Secular Age: A Minority Report*. Princeton, NJ: Princeton University Press, 2016.

Malatesta, Edward, SJ. "Matteo Ricci, Friend of China." *Tripod* 12 (1982): 82–95.
Mandair, Arvind-Pal S. *Religion and the Specter of the West: Sikhism, India, Postcoloniality, and the Politics of Translation*. New York: Columbia University Press, 2009.
Manoussakis, John Panteleimon, ed. *After God: Richard Kearney and the Religious Turn in Continental Philosophy*. New York: Fordham University Press, 2006.
Marcocci, Giuseppe, Wietse de Boer, Aliocha Maldavsky, and Ilaria Pavan, eds. *Space and Conversion in Global Perspective*. Leiden: Brill, 2014.
Marion, Jean-Luc. *Negative Certainties*. Translated by Stephen E. Lewis. Chicago: University of Chicago Press, 2015.
———. *Prolegomena to Charity*. Translated by Stephen E. Lewis. New York: Fordham University Press, 2002.
Masini, Federico. *Western Humanistic Culture Presented to China by Jesuit Missionaries (XVII–XVIII Centuries): Proceedings of the Conference Held in Rome, October 25–27, 1993*. Rome: Institutum Historicum SI, 1996.
McEvoy, James. "Anima una et cor unum: Friendship and Spiritual Unity in Augustine." *Recherches de théologie ancienne et médiévale* 53 (1986): 40–92.
McGinn, Bernard. *Mysticism in the Reformation, 1500–1650*. New York: Crossroad, 2017.
McGuire, Brian Patrick. *Brother and Lover: Aelred of Rievaulx*. New York: Crossroad, 1994.
———. *Friendship and Community: The Monastic Experience, 350–1250*. Kalamazoo, MI: Cistercian, 1988.
McInerny, Ralph. *Aquinas and Analogy*. Washington, DC: Catholic University of America Press, 1996.
McNamara, Marie Aquinas. *Friends and Friendship for Saint Augustine*. New York: Alba House, 1964.
Meilaender, Gilbert C. *Friendship: A Study in Theological Ethics*. Notre Dame, IN: University of Notre Dame Press, 1981.
Mencius. *Mencius*. Translated by D. C. Lau. London: Penguin, 1970.
Menegon, Eugenio. *Ancestors, Virgins and Friars: Christianity as a Local Religion in Late Imperial China*. Cambridge, MA: Harvard University Asia Center for the Harvard-Yenching Institute, 2009.
Meynard, Thierry. "Aristotelian Ethics in the Land of Confucius: A Study of Vagnone's Western Learning on Personal Cultivation." *Antiquorum philosophia* 7 (2013): 145–69.
———. *The Jesuit Reading of Confucius: The First Complete Translation of the Lunyu (1687) Published in the West*. Leiden: Brill, 2015.
Miller, Richard B. *Friends and Other Strangers: Studies in Religion, Ethics, and Culture*. New York: Columbia University Press, 2016.
Mish, John L. "Creating an Image of Europe for China: Aleni's *Hsi-Fang Ta-Wen*—Introduction, Translation, and Notes." *Monumenta Serica* 23, no. 1 (1964): 1–87.

Moffett, Samuel H. *A History of Christianity in Asia*. Vol. 1, *Beginnings to 1500*. New York: Harper Collins, 1992.

Montaigne, Michel de. "De l'amitié." In *Les essais de Michel de Montaigne*, edited by Pierre Villey, 1:351–75. Paris: Librairie Félix Alcan, 1930.

Mungello, D. E., ed. *The Chinese Rites Controversy: Its History and Meaning*. Nettetal, Ger.: Verlag, 1994.

———. *Curious Land: Jesuit Accommodation and the Origins of Sinology*. Honolulu: University of Hawaii Press, 1989.

Nancy, Jean-Luc. *Dis-enclosure: The Deconstruction of Christianity*. Translated by Bettina Bergo, Gabriel Malenfant, and Michael B. Smith. New York: Fordham University Press, 2008.

———. *The Inoperative Community*. Translated by Peter Connor, Lisa Garbus, Michael Holland, and Simona Sawhney. Minneapolis: University of Minnesota Press, 1991.

Needham, Joseph. *Chinese Astronomy and the Jesuit Mission: An Encounter of Cultures*. London: China Society, 1958.

Ni, Zhange. *The Pagan Writes Back: When World Religion Meets World Literature*. Charlottesville: University of Virginia Press, 2015.

Nobili, Roberto de, SJ. *Preaching Wisdom to the Wise: Three Treatises*. Translated and Introduced by Anand Amaladass, SJ and Francis X. Clooney, SJ. St. Louis: Institute of Jesuit Sources, 2000.

Norton, David L., and Mary F. Kille. *Philosophies of Love*. New York: Rowman and Littlefield, 1983.

Nygren, Anders. *Agape and Eros: The Christian Idea of Love*. Translated by Philip S. Watson. Chicago: University of Chicago Press, 1982.

Nylan, Michael. *The Chinese Pleasure Book*. New York: Zone, 2018.

Oberman, Heiko A., ed. *Forerunners of the Reformation: The Shape of Late Medieval Thought, Illustrated by Key Documents*. Philadelphia: Fortress, 1981.

———. *The Impact of the Reformation*. Grand Rapids, MI: Eerdmans, 1994.

———. *The Reformation: Roots and Ramifications*. Translated by Andrew Colin Gow. Grand Rapids, MI: Eerdmans, 1994.

Olivera, Bernardo. "Aspects of the Love of Neighbor in the Spiritual Doctrine of St. Bernard." *Cistercian Studies Quarterly* 26 (1991): 107–19, 204–26.

O'Malley, John W. *The First Jesuits*. Cambridge, MA: Harvard University Press, 1993.

———. *Religious Culture in the Sixteenth Century: Preaching, Rhetoric, Spirituality and Reform*. Aldershot, UK: Variorum, 1993.

O'Malley, John, SJ, Gauvin Alexander Baily, Steven J. Harris, and T. Frank Kennedy, SJ, eds. *The Jesuits: Cultures, Sciences, and the Arts, 1540–1773*. Toronto: University of Toronto Press, 1999.

Osuna, Javier. *Friends in the Lord: A Study in the Origins and Growth of Community in the Society of Jesus from St. Ignatius' Conversion to the Earliest Texts of the Constitutions (1521–1541)*. Translated by Nicholas King. London: The Way, 1974.

Otto, Rudolf. *The Idea of the Holy: An Inquiry into the Non-rational Factor in the Idea of the Divine and its Relation to the Rational.* Translated by John W. Harvey. Oxford: Oxford University Press, 1959.
Outka, Gene. *Agape: An Ethical Analysis.* New Haven, CT: Yale University Press, 1972.
Overmyer, Daniel L. "Attitudes toward Popular Religion in Ritual Texts of the Chinese State: *The Collected Statutes of the Great Ming.*" *Cahiers d'Extrême-Asie* 5 (1989–90): 191–221.
Ozment, Steven. *The Age of Reform, 1250–1550: An Intellectual and Religious History of Late Medieval and Reformation Europe.* New Haven, CT: Yale University Press, 1980.
Padberg, John W., SJ. *Together as a Companionship: A History of the Thirty-First, Thirty-Second, and Thirty-Third General Congregations of the Society of Jesus.* St. Louis: Institute of Jesuit Sources, 1994.
Peterson, Willard J. "What to Wear? Observation and Participation by Jesuit Missionaries in Late Ming Society." In *Implicit Understandings: Observing, Reporting, and Reflecting on the Encounters between Europeans and Other Peoples in the Early Modern Era*, edited by Stuart B. Schwartz, 403–21. Cambridge: Cambridge University Press, 1994.
Pfister, Louis Aloys. *Notices biographiques et bibliographiques sur les Jésuites de l'ancienne mission de chine, 1552–1773.* 2 vols. Shanghai: Imprimerie de la Mission catholique, 1932–34.
Plato. *The Collected Dialogues, Including Letters.* Edited by Edith Hamilton and Huntington Cairns. Princeton, NJ: Princeton University Press, 1994.
Plutarch. "On Having Many Friends." In *Moralia*, translated by F. C. Babbitt. Loeb Classical Library. London: Heinemann, 1928.
Quintilian. *Institutio oratoria.* Translated by E. Butler. 4 vols. Loeb Classical Library. Cambridge, MA: Harvard University Press, 1939.
Rahner, Hugo. *Ignatius the Theologian.* Translated by Michael Barry. New York: Herder and Herder, 1968.
———. *The Spirituality of Ignatius Loyola.* Translated by F. J. Smith. Chicago: Loyola University Press, 1953.
Rawlinson, Frank. *Chinese Ideas of the Supreme Being.* Shanghai: Presbyterian Mission, 1927.
Reichle, Natasha, ed. *China at the Center: Ricci and Verbiest World Maps.* San Francisco: Asian Art Museum, 2016.
Renger, Almut-Barbara, and Xin Fan, eds. *Receptions of Greek and Roman Antiquity in East Asia.* Leiden: Brill, 2019.
Ricoeur, Paul. *Figuring the Sacred: Religion, Narrative, and Imagination.* Translated by David Pellauer and edited by Mark I. Wallace. Minneapolis: Fortress, 1995.
———. *Oneself as Another.* Translated by Kathleen Blamey. Chicago: University of Chicago Press, 1992.
Ronan, Charles E., and Bonnie B. C. Oh, eds. *East Meets West: The Jesuits in China, 1582–1773.* Chicago: Loyola University Press, 1988.

Ross, Andrew C. *A Vision Betrayed: The Jesuits in Japan and China, 1542–1742*. New York: Orbis, 1994.
Rossabi, Morris, ed. *China among Equals: The Middle Kingdom and Its Neighbors, 10th–14th Centuries*. Berkeley: University of California Press, 1983.
Rougemont, Denis de. *Love in the Western World*. Translated by Montgomery Belgion. Rev. ed. Princeton, NJ: Princeton University Press, 1983.
Rouner, Leroy S., ed. *The Changing Face of Friendship*. Notre Dame, IN: University of Notre Dame Press, 1994.
Rule, Paul. "The Confucian Interpretation of the Jesuits." *Papers on Far Eastern History* 6 (September 1972): 1–61.
———. "Does Heaven Speak? Revelation in the Confucian and Christian Traditions." In *China and Christianity: Burdened Past, Hopeful Future*, edited by Stephen Uhalley, Jr., and Xiaoxin Wu, 3–79, 364–71. Armonk, NY: Sharpe, 2001.
———. *K'ung-tzu or Confucius? The Jesuit Interpretation of Confucianism*. Sydney: Allen and Unwin, 1986.
Saeki, Yoshirô. *The Nestorian Monument in China*. London: Society for Promoting Christian Knowledge, 1915.
Sahlins, Marshall D. *How "Natives" Think: About Captain Cook, for Example*. Chicago: University of Chicago Press, 1995.
———. *Tribesmen*. Englewood Cliffs, NJ: Prentice-Hall, 1968.
Said, Edward W. *Culture and Imperialism*. New York: Alfred A. Knopf, 1993.
———. *Orientalism*. New York: Vantage, 1979.
Scaglione, Aldo D. *The Liberal Arts and the Jesuit College System*. Philadelphia: Benjamins, 1986.
Schmitt, Carl. *The Concept of the Political*. Translated by George Schwab. Expanded ed. Chicago: University of Chicago Press, 2007.
Schollmeier, Paul. *Other Selves: Aristotle on Personal and Political Friendship*. Albany: State University of New York Press, 1994.
Schwartz, Benjamin I. *The World of Thought in Ancient China*. Cambridge, MA: Harvard University Press, 1985.
Secretariat on Commemoration of the 400th Anniversary of the Arrival of Matteo Ricci, SJ, ed. *International Symposium on Chinese-Western Cultural Interchange in Commemoration of the 400th Anniversary of the Arrival of Matteo Ricci, SJ, in China*. Taibei: Fu Jen University Press, 1983.
Shahar, Meir, and Robert P. Weller, eds. *Unruly Gods: Divinity and Society in China*. Honolulu: University of Hawaii Press, 1996.
Shryock, John K. *The Origin and Development of the State Cult of Confucius*. New York: Century, 1932.
Sibau, Maria Franca. *Reading for the Moral: Exemplary and the Confucian Moral Imagination in Seventeenth-Century Chinese Short Fiction*. New York: State University of New York Press, 2018.

Singer, Irving. *The Nature of Love: Plato to Luther*. 3 vols. Chicago: University of Chicago Press, 1984.
Sivin, Nathan. "Copernicus in China." *Studia Copericana* 6 (1973): 63–122.
Smith, Huston. "Transcendence in Traditional China." *Religious Studies* 2, no. 2 (1967): 185–96.
Smith, Jonathan Z. *Imagining Religion: From Babylon to Jonestown*. Chicago: University of Chicago Press, 1982.
———. *On Teaching Religion: Essays by Jonathan Z. Smith*. Edited by Christopher I. Lehrich. New York: Oxford University Press, 2013.
———. *Relating Religion: Essays in the Study of Religion*. Chicago: University of Chicago Press, 2004.
Spalatin, Christopher A., SJ. *Matteo Ricci's Use of Epictetus*. Taegu, Korea: Waegwan, 1975.
Spence, Jonathan D. *The Memory Palace of Matteo Ricci*. New York: Penguin, 1983.
Standaert, Nicolas. *Chinese Voices in the Rites Controversy: Traveling Books, Community Networks, Intercultural Arguments*. Rome: Bibliotheca Instituti Historici SI, 2012.
———, ed. *Handbook of Christianity in China*. Vol. 1, *636–1800*. Leiden: Brill, 2001.
———. *The Interweaving of Rituals: Funerals in the Cultural Exchange between China and Europe*. Seattle: University of Washington Press, 2008.
———. *Yang Tingyun, Confucian and Christian in Late Ming China: His Life and Thought*. Leiden: Brill, 1988.
Stern-Gillet, Suzanne. *Aristotle's Philosophy of Friendship*. Albany: State University of New York Press, 1995.
Stuart, Jan, and Evelyn S. Rawski. *Worshiping the Ancestors: Chinese Commemorative Portraits*. Stanford, CA: Stanford University Press, 2001.
Sun, Anna. *Confucianism as a World Religion: Contested Histories and Contemporary Realities*. Princeton, NJ: Princeton University Press, 2013.
Taylor, Mark C. *Abiding Grace: Time, Modernity, Death*. Chicago: University of Chicago Press, 2018.
———. *About Religion: Economies of Faith in Virtual Culture*. Chicago: University of Chicago Press, 1999.
———. *After God*. Chicago: University of Chicago Press, 2007.
———, ed. *Critical Terms for Religious Studies*. Chicago: University of Chicago Press, 1998.
———. *Erring: A Postmodern A/theology*. Chicago: University of Chicago Press, 1984.
Tiedmann, R. G., ed. *Handbook of Christianity in China*. Vol. 2, *1800–Present*. Leiden: Brill, 2009.
Tillich, Paul. *Christianity and the Encounter of World Religions*. Minneapolis: Fortress, 1991.

———. *A History of Christian Thought: From Its Judaic and Hellenistic Origins to Existentialism*. Edited by Carl Braaten. New York: Harper and Row, 1968.

Tripole, Martin R., SJ, ed. *Jesuit Education 21: Conference Proceedings on the Future of Jesuit Higher Education*. Philadelphia: Saint Joseph's University Press, 1999.

———, ed. *Promise Renewed: Jesuit Higher Education for a New Millennium*. Chicago: Loyola, 1999.

Tu, Weiming, and Mary Evelyn Tucker, eds. *Confucian Spirituality*. 2 vols. New York: Crossroad, 2003–2004.

Twitchett, Denis, and Frederick Mote, eds. *The Cambridge History of China*. Vol. 8, *The Ming Dynasty, 1368–1644*, pt. 2. Cambridge: Cambridge University Press, 1998.

Van Kley, Edwin J., and Cyriac K. Pullapilly, eds. *Asia and the West: Encounters and Exchanges from the Age of Explorations: Essays in Honor of Donald F. Lach*. Notre Dame, IN: Cross Cultural, 1986.

Vries, Hent de. *Religion and Violence: Philosophical Perspectives from Kant to Derrida*. Baltimore: Johns Hopkins University Press, 2002.

———, ed. *Religion: Beyond a Concept*. New York: Fordham University Press, 2008.

Vries, Hent de, and Samuel Weber, eds. *Religion and Media*. Stanford, CA: Stanford University Press, 2001.

Wadell, Paul J., CP. *Friends of God: Virtues and Gifts in Aquinas*. New York: Peter Lang, 1991.

Wang, Richard G. *The Ming Prince and Daoism: Institutional Patronage of an Elite*. Oxford: Oxford University Press, 2012.

Wang, Xiaochao. *Christianity and Imperial Culture: Chinese Christian Apologetics in the Seventeenth Century and Their Late Patristic Equivalent*. Leiden: Brill, 1998.

Ward, Ann. *Contemplating Friendship in Aristotle's Ethics*. Albany: State University of New York Press, 2016.

Watters, Thomas. *A Guide to the Tablets in a Temple of Confucius*. Shanghai: American Presbyterian Mission, 1879.

White, Carolinne. *Christian Friendship in the Fourth Century*. Cambridge: Cambridge University Press, 1992.

Williams, Raymond. *Keywords: A Vocabulary of Culture and Society*. Rev. ed. New York: Oxford University Press, 1983.

Wills, John E., Jr., ed. *China and Maritime Europe, 1500–1800: Trade, Settlement, Diplomacy, and Missions*. Cambridge: Cambridge University Press, 2011.

Worcester, Thomas, ed. *The Cambridge Companion to the Jesuits*. Cambridge: Cambridge University Press, 2008.

Wu, David Chusing. "The Employment of Chinese Classical Thought in Matteo Ricci's Theological Contextualization in Sixteenth Century China (Inculturation, Accommodation, Faith/Culture)." PhD diss., Graduate Theological Union, 1984.

Xunzi. *Xunzi: The Complete Text*. Translated by Eric L. Hutton. Princeton, NJ: Princeton University Press, 2014.
Yang, Lien-sheng. "The Concept of 'Pao' as a Basis for Social Relations in China." In *Chinese Thought and Institutions*, edited by John K. Fairbank, 291–309. Chicago: University of Chicago Press, 1957.
Yao, Xinzhong. *Confucianism and Christianity: A Comparative Study of Jen and Agape*. Brighton, UK: Sussex Academic Press, 1996.
Yee, Cordell D. Y. "Cartography in China." In *The History of Cartography*, vol. 2, bk. 2, *Cartography in the Traditional East and Southeast Asian Societies*, edited by J. B. Harley and David Woodward, 35–231. Chicago: University of Chicago Press, 1994.
Yelle, Robert, Courtney Handman, and Christopher I. Lehrich, eds. *Language and Religion*. Berlin: De Gruyter Mouton, 2019.
Young, John D. *Confucianism and Christianity: The First Encounter*. Hong Kong: Hong Kong University Press, 1983.
———. *East-West Synthesis: Matteo Ricci and Confucianism*. Hong Kong: Centre of Asian Studies, University of Hong Kong, 1980.
Young, William, III. *The Politics of Praise: Naming God and Friendship in Aquinas and Derrida*. Burlington, VT: Ashgate, 2007.
Yu, Anthony C. "Readability: Religion and the Reception of Translation." *Chinese Literature: Essays, Articles, Reviews* 20 (1998): 89–100.
———. *State and Religion: Historical and Textual Perspective*. Chicago: Open Court, 2005.
Yu, Chun-fang. *The Renewal of Buddhism in China: Chu-hung and the Late Ming Synthesis*. New York: Columbia University Press, 1981.
Zetzeche, Jost Oliver. *The Bible in China: The History of the Union Version or the Culmination of Protestant Missionary Bible Translation in China*. Sankt Augustin, Ger.: Institut Monumenta Serica, 1999.
Zhang, Qiong. *Making the New World Their Own: Chinese Encounter with Jesuit Science in the Age of Discovery*. Leiden: Brill, 2015.
Zürcher, Erik. *The Buddhist Conquest of China: The Spread and Adaptation of Buddhism in Early Medieval China*. 2 vols. Rev. ed. Leiden: Brill, 2007.

Index

Abraham, 39, 187n17
accommodation, 11, 50, 51, 52, 53, 54, 76–77, 87, 114, 115, 155, 195n155, 204n93
Aelred of Rievaulx, Saint, 79
Aesop, 72
agapē, 4, 7, 28, 61 77, 79, 80, 182n9
Aleni, Giulio (Ai Rulue 艾儒略), 118, 121, 133, 162, 219n15, 223n51, 236n26. See also *Zhifang waiji*
Alexander the Great, 3, 62
alterity, 10, 26, 27, 40, 56, 58, 82, 83, 89, 143, 164, 177, 179, 213n35. See also other
Ames, Roger, 242n70
Ambrose, Saint, 77, 80
Ambrose, Saint, 23
Analects, The, 130, 182n12, 208n148
Anderson, Perry, 198n28
anti-Christian writings, Confucian, 159, 160, 164, 168, 235n10
aporia, 29, 38, 81
Arendt, Hannah, 79, 187n29
Aristophanes, 72
Aristotle, 3, 4, 5, 56, 57, 62, 63, 66–67, 72, 200n49, 201n53; *Eudemian Ethics*, 67; *Nicomachean Ethics*, 66
army of Christ, 18, 43

assimilation, 3, 5, 6, 11, 12, 21, 97, 128
astrology, 140, 229n32
astronomy, 13, 114, 126, 136, 137, 138–41, 142, 145, 220n24, 227n6, 227n15, 227n17, 230n46, 232n69
Augustine, Saint, 3, 17, 21, 23, 25, 33, 36, 62, 63, 66, 77, 78, 79, 80, 81, 93, 182n9, 182n10; *Confessions*, 33, 63, 78, 192n89, 200n40, 204n103, 205n114, 236n24; *On Christian Doctrine*, 182n9; *The Trinity*, 200n40; homilies, 200n40
axis mundi, 120. See also center of the earth; *dizhong*; *tuzhong*

Bailudong Academy (白鹿洞書院), 84
Ban Gu 班固, 121
barbarians, 58, 64, 97, 108, 109, 110, 112, 118, 119, 129, 131, 132, 133, 144, 148, 158, 160, 161, 165, 197n16, 216n58, 230n46, 236n27
Beijing 北京, 111, 184n30, 210n167, 217n73
being, 30, 39, 42
Being and Time, 34. See also Heidegger, Martin
Bell, Johann Adam Schall von (Tang Ruowang 湯若望). See Schall, Johann Adam

benevolence, 5, 207n139, 208n146
Benoist, Michel (Jiang Youren 蔣友仁), 147
Bible, 7, 8, 11, 21, 25, 28, 29, 32, 37, 39, 41, 43, 44, 45, 50, 51, 72, 73, 181n8, 182n9, 183n17, 185n7, 187n27, 190n66, 191n84, 191n85, 193n124, 195n151, 236n26
Blanchot, Maurice, 29, 56, 61, 190n70
Book of Changes (*Yi jing* 易經), 122, 150, 173, 243n79
Book of Documents (*Shang shu* 尚書), 119, 121, 138
Book of Songs (*Shi jing* 詩經), 123
brotherhood, 2, 18, 19, 49, 50, 58, 60, 161. *See also* fellowship
Buddhism, 92, 146, 147, 151, 152, 154, 164, 165, 166–67, 169, 170, 174, 222n43, 237n31, 237n34, 238n45, 238n47, 241n63

calendar, 13, 135, 136, 137, 138–40, 141, 142, 143, 149, 153, 156, 224n56, 226n3, 226n4, 227n6, 227n17, 228n30; Calendar, Chongzhen (崇禎曆書), 137, 227n10; calendar, authorized (正曆), 144; calendar, imperial (皇曆), 228n30; calendar, people's (民曆), 228n30; calendar, unwarranted (私曆), 144;
Calendar Office (曆局), 136
Calvin, John, 204n93; Calvinism, 187n28
Canary Islands. *See* Fortunate Islands
Caputo, John D., 29, 30, 41, 74, 190n73, 191n75, 224n52
caritas, 4, 7, 21, 61, 62, 71, 77, 79, 80. *See also* charity
Cassian, John, 23
Cassiodorus, 70, 71, 77, 202n68, 203n83

casuistry, 72, 76
Catholicism, 3, 5, 86, 87, 88, 162, 166, 222n43
center of the earth, the, 120–21, 219n15, 220n29, 221n30, 221n31, 221n37. *See also dizhong; tuzhong; axis mundi*
charity, 4, 7, 8, 24, 182n9, 183n19, 200n40. *See also caritas*
chastity, 22. *See also* vows
Chen Shouyi 陳受頤, 240n54
China, 1, 69, 89, 97, 105, 108, 114, 124, 174
Chinese base (*or* substance), Western function (中體西用), 149–50, 152, 154–55, 230n56
Chongzhen Calendar. See calendar
Christ, 19, 21, 25, 31, 37, 44, 45, 46, 48
Christianity, 1, 3, 6, 21, 27, 29, 34, 43–44, 49, 52, 61, 64, 74, 93, 136, 152–53, 164–65, 169–70, 186n20, 190n69, 223n49, 224n56, 235n9, 238n37, 242n70
Chunqiu fanlu 春秋繁露, 138, 228n23
Chunqiu gongyang zhuan 春秋公羊傳, 216n58
Church, Catholic, 21, 33, 49, 72, 187n28, 195n149, 220n23
Cicero, 3, 4, 55, 56, 57, 62, 68, 70, 71, 72, 73, 74, 75–78, 201n66, 203n86, 204n93, 204n103; *De amicitia*, 55, 56, 78, 80, 196n2, 201n66, 203n83; *De offciis*, 75; *De oratore*, 76; *De partitione oratoria*, 76; *Pro Sexto Roscio Amerino*, 71
Circular-Heaven theory, 120, 220n27
civilizations, 59–60, 110, 124
Clement, of Alexandria, 51
Cold War, the, 59, 60
communion, 7, 20, 45, 92
community, 19, 23, 50, 79, 100

compañiá de jesûs, 18
companion, 17, 18, 19, 24; companionship, 17, 18, 19, 32
Complete Map of All Ten Thousand Countries on Earth. *See* Kunyu wanguo quantu (坤輿萬國全圖), world map
Complete Rites of the Ming, 109, 110
Concept of the Political, The. *See* Schmitt, Carl
condition of possibility, 10, 21, 38, 56, 107, 178
Confucianism, 1, 2, 5, 10, 53, 54, 64, 87, 92, 131, 132, 157, 165, 168, 170, 173, 174, 175, 177, 178, 231n57
Confucius, 90, 91, 92, 93, 108, 126, 128, 130, 146, 159, 168, 169, 173, 174, 182n12, 196n8, 209n159, 210n164, 224n54, 243n80, 224n54
Constitutions, Jesuit, 17, 19, 26, 30, 43, 46, 73, 186n17, 188n37, 193n108
Copernicus, 220n23
cosmology, 116, 119, 121, 135
Counter-Reformation, 18, 43, 49, 187n28
Critchley, Simon, 88
cross-cultural relationship, 2, 4, 57, 146; cross-cultural communication, 180; cross-cultural encounter, 97; cross-cultural exchange, 2, 180
crusade, 19, 44
culture, 1, 2, 3, 4, 5, 9, 10, 19, 42, 51, 53, 56, 58–59, 63, 65, 68, 69, 88, 93, 95, 127, 129, 130, 154, 179, 212n18, 226n75
Cyprian, Saint, 77, 80

Da Ming lü 大明律 (*Ming Code*), 138, 227n16
Daoism, 8, 92, 146, 154, 165, 167, 170, 174

Daoist priest, 91, 210n164
Datong calendar (大統曆), 136, 137, 140, 141, 226n3
de 德 (virtue). *See* virtue
death, Christian, 32, 33, 34, 35, 36, 39
deconstruction, 11, 29–30, 95, 100
deity, 7, 28, 74, 90, 169, 173, 223n49, 242n68, 242n69; deity, absolute, 172; deity, Catholic *or* Christian, 131, 133; deity, ultimate, 172. *See also* God; Lord-on-High
d'Elia, Pasquale M., 71, 181n7, 202n82, 203n83
democracy, 60, 100, 198n28, 213n35
Derrida, Jacques, 10, 12, 17, 29, 33, 34, 38, 39, 40, 41, 42, 51, 53, 54, 55, 56, 57, 58, 61, 74, 82, 83, 98, 100–103, 104, 107, 125, 142, 174, 182n12, 190n69, 190n72, 193n121, 195n160, 196n164, 197n16, 212n18, 224n52, 237n30, 239n48, 243n77; *Archive Fever*, 179; *Adieu to Emmanuel Levinas*, 89, 100; *Gift of Death, The*, 34, 39, 192n87, 224n52; *On the Name*, 224n52; *Politics of Friendship*, 56, 89, 158, 175, 187n16; *Psyche: Invention of the Other*, 196n164; *Of Hospitality*, 113
Descartes, René, 21
Devotio Moderna, 45
Diaz, Emmanuel, Jr. (Yang Ma'nuo 陽瑪諾), 155, 233n76
difference, 2, 5, 10, 29, 30, 37, 40, 50, 52, 53, 56, 62, 63, 65, 77, 79, 127
Diogenes, 67
divination, 139, 140, 227n17
dizhong 地中, 120. *See also* center of the earth; *tuzhong*; *axis mundi*
Dominic, Saint, 188n41
Dominicans, 44, 76, 187n33

Dong Zhongshu 董仲舒, 138, 160
Dudon, Paul, 21

ecclesia militans, 19, 43, 185n12. *See also* army of Christ; *compañiá de jesûs*; soldiers of God
education, Jesuit, 72, 73, 75
Eliade, Mircea, 120, 210n163
Emperor, Chongzhen (崇禎皇帝), 137
endism, 61, 198n28. *See also* Francis Fukuyama
Engels, Frederick, 183n24
enmity, 58, 59, 80, 241n63
Erasmus, 72, 75, 78, 81, 202n76, 204n93
Europe, 3, 44, 49, 74–75, 117, 195n149, 209n159, 219n15
exemplum, 57, 63

Fang Yizhi 方以智, 145, 146, 149, 229n45, 232n69
father (common) (公父), 5
fellowship, 79; fellowship, Christian, 19
Feng Guifeng 馮桂芬, 231n56
Feng Yingjing 馮應京, 86
filial piety, 158–59, 162
"finding God in all things," 22, 42, 44, 47, 48, 49, 53, 54, 75
Five Relationships (五倫), 84, 85, 161
Formula Instituti (*Formula of the Institute*), Jesuit, 17, 22, 24, 37, 43
Fortunate Islands, 117
Foss. Theodore N., 209n158
Foucault, Michel, 147, 223n44, 230n51
Francis of Assisi, Saint, 188n41
Franciscans, 187n33, 188n41
fraternity, 27, 78, 79, 83, 99. *See also* brotherhood, fellowship
"friends in the lord," 11, 18, 22, 83, 185n14, 235n20

friendship, 1. 2, 5, 6, 10, 17, 18, 19, 20, 28, 29, 32, 33, 55, 56, 59, 67, 87, 90, 100, 180, 183n19, 197n16, 201n53, 235n20; perfect *or* ideal friendship, 56, 66–67, 78, 79, 81; friendship for utility, 66, 67; friendship for pleasure, 66, 67; friendship, ruler-minister, 235n19, 236n20. *See also* brotherhood, fellowship, fraternity
Fukuyama, Francis, 60–61, 198n27

Galileo, 220n23
Ganss, George E., 26, 32, 193n108
gift, 6, 33, 34, 35, 36, 37, 79, 80, 111, 130, 217n73; gift-giving, 217n71
globalization, 1
God, 2, 4, 5, 7, 11, 19, 21, 22, 23, 24, 25, 26, 27, 28, 29, 30, 31, 32, 33, 37, 38, 39, 40, 41, 42, 43, 45, 46, 47, 48, 49, 50, 51, 53, 61, 70, 71, 75, 86, 89, 114, 124, 160, 161, 170, 174, 193n121, 223n49, 236n25, 242n68. *See also* Catholic *or* Christian deity; Jesus Christ; Lord of Heaven
grace, 4, 7, 28, 30, 31, 32, 34, 82, 192n87
Gran Canaria. *See* Fortunate Islands
"greater glory of God," 19, 42, 46, 47, 48, 49, 75, 88, 186n17
Greeks, 3, 7, 51
Gregory the Great, 77. *See also* Pope Gregory I
guest, 7, 9, 83, 98, 101, 102–104, 105, 107, 114, 132, 170, 175, 197n16
Guo Moruo 郭沫若, 242n69
Guoyu 國語 (*Discourse of the States*), 138

Han Yu 韓愈, 133, 164, 165, 237n34

Hegel, Georg Wilhelm Friedrich, 57, 60, 198n28
Heidegger, Martin, 34, 123, 124, 190n72
Herodotus, 59
heterogeneity, 13, 29, 83, 114, 190n72; heterology, 39
Homer, 72
homogeneity, 9, 42, 61, 83, 104
Horace, 72
hospitality, 1, 2, 6, 8, 9. 10, 12, 98, 99–103, 107, 109, 110, 142, 143, 156, 180, 212n18; hospitality, absolute, 102, 103, 213n31, 239n48; hospitality, culture of, 95, 142, 148; hospitality, law of, 214n41; hospitality, rite of, 9, 12, 105, 106–107, 108, 214n47, 215n48, 215n49, 216n55, 217n66; hospitality, scrutinized, 213n31; hospitality, true, 213n34; hospitality, unconditional, 213n35, 214n36; hostipitality, 95, 216n54
host, 103, 105, 107, 123, 135, 142, 143, 157, 164
Huang Zongxi 黃宗羲, 145, 146, 161, 206n128, 230n46, 238n45
huihui li 回回曆 (Muslim calendar), 136
humanism, 72, 73, 75
Huang Zhen 黃貞, 236n26
Hung Ye 洪業 (William Hung), 218n6, 223n51
Huntington, Samuel, 59–60, 198n28

Idea of the Holy, The. See Otto, Rudolf
identity, 18, 41, 55, 56, 68, 74, 75, 81, 83, 90, 94, 172, 173. *See also* same, the
Ignatius of Loyola, 2, 20, 21, 22, 23, 24, 25, 26, 28, 29, 30, 31, 32, 33, 35, 36, 39, 42, 43, 45, 50, 51, 72, 185n12, 188n41, 189n52; theology of, 21; *Autobiography*, 24, 189n47, 194n136, 202n79; conversion of, 24; pilgrimage to the Holy Land, 24. *See also Formula Instituti*; *Spiritual Exercises*
imago dei, 41
Imitation of Christ. See Thomas à Kempis
immanence, of God, 20, 28, 190n68
Imperial Astronomical Bureau (欽天監), 136, 137, 138, 143
incarnation, 207n144
individuality, 21, 34, 85, 187n28, 187n33; individualism, 7, 21, 44, 187n28, 187n34. *See also* self
infallibility, papal, 44
infinity, 28; infinity, holy, 29; infinity, idea of, 99
Isocrates, 72

Jesuits, 1, 2, 6, 10, 17, 21, 22, 30, 31, 33, 35, 36, 38, 39, 42, 43, 44, 47, 48, 49, 51, 53, 65, 73, 76, 98, 110, 141, 143, 155, 156, 173, 178
Jesus Christ, 7, 8, 18, 19, 21, 24, 25, 29, 30, 31, 37, 32, 44, 45, 46, 48, 49, 88
Jiao Hong 焦竑, 207n146, 234n6, 239n49
jianhui 講會 (learning and discussing meetings), 84

Kant, Immanuel, 57, 60, 100–102
Kierkegaard, Søren, 40, 177
King Wen 文王, 85, 128, 236n26
Knowles, David, 44, 45, 188n41, 194n134, 194n135
Kunyu wanguo quantu 坤輿萬國全圖 (Complete Map of Ten Thousand Countries on Earth), 115–17, 220n22, 222n43, 223n49, 224n58. *See also* world map

Laozi, 92, 146, 147, 152, 159
Levinas, Emmanuel, 10, 12, 29, 39, 40, 61, 97, 98–100, 103, 104, 143, 156, 177, 237n30; *Otherwise than Being*, 98; *Totality and Infinity*, 98, 100, 158, 177, 238n36
li 理 (Principle). *See* Principle
Li ji 禮記 (*The Book of Rites*), 107, 108, 216n52, 228n31
Li Suiqiu 黎遂球, 122
Li Zhi 李贄, 64, 200n43, 200n44
Li Zhizao 李之藻, 126, 127, 128, 155, 227n9
Livy, 72
logos, 30
Longobardo, Niccolò (Long Huamin 龍華民), 136, 162
Lord of Heaven, 5, 6, 90, 159, 160, 161, 169, 170, 171, 172, 173, 236n25, 241n65, 241n66
love, 4, 5, 7, 8, 21, 25, 29, 39, 61, 63, 73, 78, 183n19
Lord-on-High, 70, 71, 74, 169, 170–174, 175, 202n82, 203n83, 236n25, 238n25, 241n65, 242n68, 242n69
Lu Jiuyuan 陸九淵, 127, 128–30, 131, 224n57, 225n63, 225n64, 225n65, 225n69, 225n70, 241n59
Lucian, 72
Luther, Martin, 43, 44, 186n26

Macao, 155, 158
Machus, 154, 231n60, 232n73
Mao Zedong, 183n25
Marx, Karl, 183n24
Martial, 62, 72
Maryks, Robert Aleksander, 76
Mazzolini, Sylvester, 44
McDermott, Joseph P., 206n134
McGinn, Bernard, 23
meditation, spiritual, 31, 32, 33, 36, 46

Mei Qianli 梅謙立 (Thierry Meynard, SJ), 234n6, 225n19
Mencius, 129, 144, 158
meridian origin, 117
Middle Kingdom, 13, 62, 110, 119, 123, 140, 143, 144, 148, 163
Ming dynasty, 13, 89, 132, 178
Ming jili 明集禮 (*Complete Rites of the Ming*)
mission, Jesuit, 1, 2, 3, 4, 22, 27, 43, 44, 47, 49, 50, 51
missionaries, 1, 50, 51, 53, 110, 130, 133, 157, 161, 232n69, 242n68
mobility. *See also* vows
monasticism, 23
Mongols, 150, 231n60
Montaigne, Michel de, 56, 57
Moretti, Franco, 124
Muslims, 60
mysterium tremendum, 27. 28, 29, 34, 190n69. *See also* wholly other

Nadal, Jerónimo, 17, 18, 33, 48, 202n76
Nanchang 南昌, 62, 64, 83, 86, 200n41
Nancy, Jean-Luc, 20, 124
Nanjing 南京, 64, 200n41, 207n146
Nanjing Persecution (南京教案), 154, 158, 233n76
Needham, Joseph, 138, 222n39
neighbors, 4, 7, 39, 40, 49, 65, 71, 110, 123, 182n9, 187n28
neo-Confucianism, 86, 240n55
New Learning of the Mind-and-Heart (心學), 84
Nietzsche, Friedrich, 56, 60
nómos, 57. *See also phúsis*
Nylan, Michael, 93

obedience, 37, 38, 39, 192n104. *See also* obedience, vow of

Oberman, Heiko, 187n33
Oedipus, 142
O'Malley, John W., 38, 39, 45, 75, 185n11, 184n137
omnia ad maiorem dei gloriam (everything for greater glory of God). *See* "greater glory of God"
omnia omnibus ([I become] all to all), 50, 54. *See also* Paul, Saint
On Friendship, 3, 5, 11, 55, 61, 62, 63, 65, 66, 69, 74, 77, 81, 86, 94, 199n36, 204n96, 208n148, 226n75
Opium War, 150
Origen, of Alexandria, 51
Ortelius, Abraham, 115, 117. *See also Theatrum orbis terrarum*
other, 2, 14, 34, 51, 53, 54, 56, 60, 61, 62, 63, 83, 89, 98, 99, 100–101, 103, 123, 124, 125, 143, 148, 152, 156, 160, 163, 164, 167, 173, 177; other, absolute, 39, 40, 89, 177; other, responsibility to *or* for, 99, 199, 164; otherness, 26, 27, 30, 33, 34, 42, 49, 51, 53, 54, 63, 77, 146; otherness, infinite, 81. *See also* alterity, wholly other
Otto, Rudolf, 27, 28, 29, 189n58, 190n69; *The Idea of the Holy*, 27
Ovid, 62

Patočka, Jan, 34, 190n69
Paul, Saint, 50–51, 52, 182n9, 195n151
pengdang 朋黨 (factionalism), 85
Persian Wars, The, 59
Peter, Saint, 25
philia, 4, 61, 80, 197n16
phúsis, 57, 58. *See also nómos*
Plato, 3, 4, 56, 57, 58, 59, 62, 197n16
Plautus, 72
Plutarch, 62, 70, 71–73, 74, 81, 203n83

pope, 3, 22, 38, 43, 44, 46, 49, 52, 179. *See also* supremacy, papal
Pope Gregory I, 77, 81
Pope Julius III, 188n40
Pope Paul III, 185n6
poverty, 22, 23, 26, 36
Poxie ji 破邪集 (*A Collection for Destroying Heterodoxy*), 165, 166, 211n3, 236n26, 234n4
Principle, 127, 128–30, 131, 132, 150, 151, 174, 225n69, 242n68
probabilism, 72, 76, 203n89
Protestantism, 23, 44, 179

Qian Zhongshu 錢鍾書, 231n58
Qingshu jingtan yiji 清署經談・一集 (*Discourse on the Canons in the Clear Studio, volume 1*), 158, 167, 168, 173. *See also* Wang Qiyuan
Qu Rukui 瞿汝夔, 89, 131, 208n155
Qu Shigu 瞿式穀, 131–32
Quintilian, 62

races, 58, 59, 60, 185n5, 197n16, 235n20
Rahner, Karl, 21, 191n78
Rapaport, Herman, 172
Rapport sans rapport. *See* relation without relation
redemption, 30, 207n144, 235n9
reform, calendar, 13, 135, 136–37, 141, 142, 143, 144, 226n3, 227n6, 227n7, 227n8
Reformation, 2, 19, 21, 43, 72, 177, 178, 185n5
relation without relation, 29, 39, 61; relation, relationless, 29
relation, host-guest, 103, 143. *See also* hospitality
religion, 8, 49, 53, 59, 72, 114, 172
ren 仁. *See* benevolence
Republic, 58. *See also* Plato

responsibility, 32, 34, 38–39, 50, 72, 82, 84, 89, 99, 100, 164, 214n41
Rho, Jacques (Luo Yagu 羅雅谷), 136, 227n8
Ricci, Matteo (Li Madou 利瑪竇), 3, 5, 6, 7, 11, 55, 61, 62, 69, 74, 90, 110, 114, 115, 116, 117, 124, 125, 173, 177, 181n5, 198n33, 199n35, 199n36, 202n82, 203n83, 209n158, 217n73, 222n43, 223n49, 223n51, 226n4
righteousness, 63, 69, 118, 128, 129
Rites, Ministry of, 9, 136, 234n3
royal agency of astronomy, 13
Ruan Yuan 阮元, 147–48
Ruggieri, Michel, 65, 81, 114, 195n157, 199n33, 200n46, 205n123
Rule, Paul, 89

same, the, 13, 53, 54, 56–57, 61, 74, 83, 101, 104, 157, 177, 178, 180; sameness, 4, 35; sameness, between China and the West, 128, 129, 130, 132
Satan, 7, 36
Schall, Johann Adam, 136, 142, 227n8
Schmitt, Carl, 8, 56, 58, 178, 182n12, 183n25, 196n13, 243n2; *The Concept of the Political*, 8
self, 21, 26, 28, 30, 32, 33, 34, 35, 36, 37, 38, 39, 45, 49, 51, 54, 60, 123, 124, 125, 142, 143, 146, 147, 148, 152, 156, 157, 163, 167; self, abnegation of, 45; 188n34; self-love, 45; self-will, 21, 26, 27, 31, 33, 37, 45, 49; self, irreducibility of, 39; selfhood, 26, 27, 31, 34
Seneca, 62, 81
Sengzhao 僧肇, 151
Shang dynasty, 173
Shangdi 上帝. *See* Lord-on-High
Shen Defu 沈德符, 200n43

Shen Que 沈㴶, 234n3
Shengchao zoubi 聖朝佐辟 (*Assisting the Holy Dynasty in the Refutation*), 158, 159
Shengyue guan 神樂觀 (Imperial Music Office), 91
Shun 舜, 85, 154
Sima Guang 司馬光, 237n34
Sima Qian 司馬遷, 228n26
singularity, 29, 30, 34, 35, 39, 40, 193n121
Sino-centrism 9, 12, 98, 105, 116, 121, 150, 157, 231n59
Smith, Richard J., 140, 228n31
Society of Jesus, 2, 8, 17, 18–19, 21, 23, 25, 36, 37, 38, 42, 43, 46, 52, 72, 87, 178, 185n6, 202n74, 208n150
soldiers, of God, 22, 185n7
Son of Heaven, 62, 93, 121, 138, 160
Song Yingxing 宋應星, 222n39
souls, to aid, 2, 3, 43
Sphere-Heaven theory, 120, 220n27
Spiritual Exercises, 17, 21, 22, 31–32, 33, 45, 86, 188n34, 189n52, 191n82, 192n101
Spiritual Friendship. *See* Aelred of Rievaulx, Saint
spirituality, Christian, 31, 34, 46, 88; spirituality, Ignatius's, 2, 3, 20, 21, 22, 31, 83, 88; spirituality, Jesuit, 3, 11, 19, 20, 21, 22, 25, 26, 27, 31, 36, 39, 42, 43, 44, 45, 46, 48, 49, 50, 54, 179, 186n19, 186n26; spirituality, crusade, 42, 185n3; spirituality, mission, 42; 179, 186n19; spirituality, interiorization of, 21, 22, 42, 45, 46, 48
Spring and Autumn Annals (春秋), 108, 110
stranger, 13, 133, 142, 146, 164
Studia humanitatis, 72, 73
subjectivity, 21, 34, 41, 99, 147, 163, 175, 214n41

Summa Theoloigca, 4. *See* Thomas Aquinas
Sun Lan 孫蘭, 149
Sun Yirang 孫詒讓, 220n29
Supremacy, cultural, 2, 13, 128; supremacy, papal, 21, 44; supremacy, of Lord-on-High, 171

Tang Xianzu 湯顯祖, 211n2
Tansu. *See* Tausu
Tausu 道士 (Daoist priests), 90, 91
Taylor, Mark C., 41, 186n19, 190n73, 198n28
Ten Chapters of a Strange Man (畸人十篇), 127
Terrenz, Jean (Deng Yuhan 鄧玉函), 136
Teresa of Avila, 25
Theatrum orbis terrarum, 115, 116. *See also* Ortelius, Abraham
theology, Christian, 3, 7, 52, 53, 56, 74, 81, 157, 171, 174, 199n33, 235n9; theology, Ignatius's, 20–21, 32, 42, 73; theology, Jesuit, 3, 27, 50, 88, 169, 187n33; theology, Luther's, 186n26; theology, Protestant, 204n93; theology, John Calvin's, 204n93
Thomas à Kempis, 20, 44, 45, 46; *Imitation of Christ*, 20, 45, 46, 194n136, 194n137
Thomas Aquinas, 4, 183n19
Three Dynasties (三代), 109, 154, 177, 237n34
ti 體 (base substance), 149, 151–52, 154, 155, 156
tianli 天理 (Way of Heaven), 128, 130
totality, 38, 49, 53, 54, 108, 121, 125, 131, 132, 216n58
tout autre est tout autre [every other (one) is every (bit) other], 17, 39, 40, 41, 61, 82

transcendence, of God, 20, 27, 28, 29, 30, 34, 190n68
Trent, Council of, 23
tributary system, 109, 118, 124, 148, 222n42, 229n31
Trigault, Nicolas, 209n158
Trinity, 207n142, 207n144, 234n9
True Meaning of the Lord of Heaven, The (天主實義), 5, 86, 92, 128, 158, 182n13, 202n82, 241n65
tuzhong 土中, 120. *See also* center of the earth; *dizhong*; *axis mundi*

undecidability, 38, 50, 104
union, divine, 17, 19, 20, 21, 22, 27, 30, 33, 49, 83

Valignano, Alessandro (Fan Li'an 范禮安), 51, 195n155
Valla, 72
virtue, 5, 62, 68, 69, 84
vows, Jesuit, 22, 23, 24, 43; vow, of chastity, 24, 25; vow, of poverty, 22, 23, 24, 188n41, 192n103; vow, of chastity, 22, 24; vow, of obedience, 22, 24, 37, 39, 43, 44, 188n41; special vow, of mobility *or* of instability, 22, 44, 45, 48. *See also* chastity; obedience; poverty

Wang Fuzhi 王夫之, 145
Wang Ji 王畿, 84
Wang Jiazhi 王家植, 127
Wang Pan 王泮, 115
Wang Qiyuan 王啟元, 158, 160, 167–68, 170, 171, 172, 173, 178, 241n63, 241n65, 241n66, 242n68, 242n71, 243n74, 243n80
Wang Yangming 王陽明, 84, 85, 86, 130, 131, 172, 225n71, 241n59
West, 1, 6, 13, 52, 60, 62, 64, 69, 74, 75, 97, 171

Westernization, the Movement of (洋務運動), 231n57
wholly other, 11, 20, 27, 28, 30, 35, 39, 40, 42, 49, 52, 53, 94, 189n58
world map, 12, 218n5, 218n6, 218n9, 219n12, 219n16, 222n43, 223n49. See also Complete Map of Ten Thousand Countries on Earth
Wuzazu 五雜俎, 168, 240n56, 241n57

xenoi, 4
xenophobia, 3, 65
Xie Gonghua 謝宮花, 144
Xie Zhaozhe 謝肇淛, 168, 222n42, 240n56
xijiao 西教 (Christianity or Western doctrine), 224n56
xin 心, 127
xixue 西學 (Western science and learning), 127, 224n56, 231n56
Xixue Zhongyuan 西學中源 (Chinese origin of Western learning), 145–46, 147–48, 150, 152
Xiyang xinfa liushu 西洋新法曆書 (The Book of the New Western Calendric System), 142
Xu Changzhi 徐昌治, 166
Xu Dashou 許大受, 124, 144, 158, 160, 161, 164, 166, 167, 168, 170, 241n65
Xu Fuyuan 許孚遠, 166, 167, 234n6, 238n44, 238n45
Xu Guangqi 徐光啟, 126, 136, 153–54, 155
Xunzi 荀子, 93, 94, 121, 215n50

Yang Guangxian 楊光先, 122–23, 144
Yang Tingyun 楊廷筠, 133
Yao 堯, 85, 154
Yao Lü 姚旅, 226n75
Ye Xianggao 葉向高, 118, 208n148, 211n2, 234n6, 238n44, 238n45, 239n49
Yee, Cordell D. K., 118, 219n17
yong 用 (practical application or function), 149, 150–51, 152, 155, 156
Yu Chunxi 虞淳熙, 211n3
Yuanwu 圓悟, 166, 211n3, 238n43
Yuanxian 元賢, 211n3

Zhang Huang 章潢, 84, 206n128
Zhang Zhidong 張之洞, 230n56
Zheng Guanying 鄭觀應, 231n56
Zheng Xuan 鄭玄, 215n50
Zhifang waiji 職方外紀, 118, 133, 218n1, 219n15, 220n21, 220n23, 221n36, 226n75, 226n78, 226n79. See also Aleni, Giulio
Zhou li 周禮 (Rites of Zhou), 105–106, 215n50, 220n29, 228n31
Zhou Xing 周星, 125–26
Zhuhong 袾宏, 211n3, 238n40
Zhu Xi 朱熹, 84, 151, 152, 241n59, 242n68
Zhu Yuanzhang 朱元璋, 109, 118, 138, 140–41 153
Ziesler, John, 47
Zisi 子思, 160
Zuozhuan 左傳 (Zuo's Commentary), 197n18

www.ingramcontent.com/pod-product-compliance
Lightning Source LLC
Chambersburg PA
CBHW030529230426
43665CB00010B/817